THE ORGANS
OF BRITAIN

An Appreciation and Gazetteer

JOHN NORMAN

DAVID & CHARLES
Newton Abbot   London   North Pomfret (Vt)

The quotation on page 13 is used by kind permission of Oxford University Press.

British Library Cataloguing in Publication Data

Norman, John
   The organs of Britain.
   1. Organs – Great Britain
   I. Title
   786.6′241   ML578

   ISBN 0-7153-8313-2

Typeset by Typesetters (Birmingham) Ltd,
Smethwick, West Midlands
and printed in Great Britain
by Redwood Burn Limited, Trowbridge, Wilts
for David & Charles (Publishers) Limited
Brunel House   Newton Abbot   Devon

Published in the United States of America
by David & Charles Inc
North Pomfret   Vermont 05053   USA

FOREWORD

Dr Lionel Dakers
Director, The Royal School of Church Music

I well remember watching with fascination while John Norman, complete with pocket tape-recorder, ruler and camera, carefully collected data inside the bowels of the organ of a north Devon church preparatory to drawing up a scheme for its restoration. That was all of twenty years ago, and now the same meticulous care and eye for detail is revealed in *The Organs of Britain*.

Here at last is a much-needed everyman's handbook to complement the more specialist volumes already available. This new book is not only written in language which is easily understood but is of gentle length, two qualities which make for comprehensiveness while rendering the subject matter eminently readable. For me, so much which has always been something of an enigma – and I suspect for others too – is here explained in simple and concise terms.

The chapter on the position and appearance of an organ, for example, contains so much good sense that it ought to be compulsory reading for anyone contemplating a new organ or a rebuild. Since the end of World War II, there has been an upsurge of informed new thinking on organ design. Many new influences, not least those coming to Britain from Europe, while exciting many, have infuriated others. The resulting breath of fresh air has been as good as the challenge, even the competition, that it has presented to English organ-builders.

This eminently practical guide allows no excuse now for the amateur, however well intentioned, to be uninformed; nor for the organist with little or scanty knowledge of organ construction to deviate from the right wavelength. I suspect, moreover, that many a professional will find much of value in these pages.

I am confident that John Norman's book will take its place, and rightly so, alongside those comprehensive guidebooks on every conceivable subject (from old silver and vintage cars to inexpensive pub lunches!) which delight and inform us. Today, there is no excuse for being at a disadvantage on any subject under the sun – least of all the organ. I greatly rejoice at commending this book and the expert who has written it.

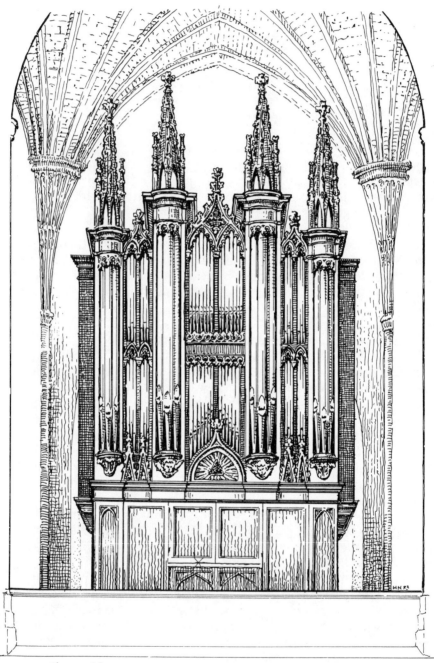

Wymondham Abbey

CONTENTS

To Jill
without whose patience and forbearance
this book would not have been possible

INTRODUCTION

They call it the King of Instruments. People have always found the organ a fascinating object for study. Indeed, critics have objected that enthusiasts are sometimes more interested in the instrument itself than in the music which is created with it. After all, is not a musical instrument merely a paint-box from which the composer and the performer draw the colours to paint their musical pictures? Evidence that the organ is more than this is provided by the high level of interest in the instrument, demonstrated by the number of societies for organists and for the study of the organ, and by the large volume of publications on the subject.

The fascination of the organ probably lies in its many-faceted nature. Firstly, there is the huge range and variety of its sounds. This book attempts a glossary of the voices within the organ yet, long as the list is, it would need a whole volume in itself to be complete. Secondly, there is the sheer variety of different instruments. Almost every organ is an individual creation, but even if this were not the case, the relationship of each organ to the acoustics of the building in which it stands guarantees an individual musical result. The mechanical complexity of the organ has its own fascination, especially since the mechanics have a vital influence on the ease of performance and even on the sound produced. This is akin, perhaps, to the interest which a keen motorist shows in the mechanics of his car since they have a vital influence on his enjoyment of driving. One can push this metaphor further: it is the power that the organist commands which is part of the thrill of 'driving' the instrument, a thrill which, if the history books are to be believed, found an early devotee in the Roman Emperor Nero.

The study of the organ also has aspects which are less directly related to musical performance. An organ is a very large piece of furniture and has thus been a focus for the decorative arts. This is perhaps less obvious in Britain than in some parts of the Continent, where rococo organ cases were designed as visual ornaments in their own right, often costing more than the instrument inside them. The organ also excites a strong historical interest, since it is so much more

9

long-lived than any portable instrument, with its design changing considerably over the centuries. The practice of rebuilding older organs may result in many periods of design being represented within one instrument.

The very complexity which accounts for the wide-ranging appeal of the organ can, however, be a deterrent to the novice. For this reason I have attempted, in the first three chapters, to explain the organ from first principles, without assuming any prior knowledge of the instrument. This approach may not be without interest for the experienced reader as well since, when exploring the many aspects of this fascinating instrument, it is all too easy to lose sight of the fundamental principles which guide its design and construction. To aid the novice reader further, glossaries have been provided, not only to many of the technical terms involved but also to the organ-builders with whose instruments he or she may come in contact.

The history of the organ is important and necessarily forms an integral part of each narrative chapter. However, a more detailed historical survey of the organ in Britain is included in chapter 3 along with the tonal structure of the instrument. This is because, ultimately, it is the interaction of changing musical requirements and the development of voicing skills which has been responsible for the majority of changes to the instrument down the centuries. The organ is almost unique among musical instruments in that the organ-builder normally deals directly with the player rather than any middleman or retailer. The close attention to individual requirements that results is a major reason not only for the wide diversity in design but also for the fact that, unlike that of the piano, organ design is still changing.

There are approximately 25,000 organs in the United Kingdom and it is impossible for one person to know them all. The instruments listed in the Gazetteer (over 290 organs) are drawn largely, though not exclusively, from my own experience. I am aware, of course, that in making any selection I may lose many friends either by omitting their favourite instruments or, worse, by making less kind comments than they would prefer. It is one of the joys of the study of the organ that there is room for many different and sincerely held opinions about a single instrument since judgements can only be relative, not absolute. I have, in general, not attempted to cover the surprisingly numerous late eighteenth-century and early nineteenth-century chamber organs which survive in country churches. These have been very adequately described elsewhere. In other respects, however, I have attempted to include at least sample instruments of all important styles, paying particular attention to the major instruments which survive to us. Over the past twenty years there has been a rapid and fundamental change in the design of the organ in Britain and the Gazetteer therefore includes many relatively new instruments in order that these changes may be examined.

It is in the nature of a book of this sort, containing so much factual information, that errors will creep in, a fact for which I apologise in advance. However, these will be fewer than they might have been thanks to the critical help that I have received from my friends. I am particularly grateful for the assistance given by Michael Gillingham, Donald Findlay, Nicholas Thistlethwaite, Bernard Edmonds and Nick Plumley. I am also greatly indebted to Ian Bell, Bruce Buchanan, Nigel Church, Frank Fowler, Christopher Gordon-Wells, Lady Jeans, Robert Pennells, Kenneth Prior, Christopher Rathbone, Alastair Rushworth, Justin Sillman, Gordon St John Clarke, Dennis Thurlow, Mark Venning, Henry Willis IV and Peter Wood for their assistance with stop-lists and other information. Most of all, I am grateful to the staff at Hill Norman & Beard who went to so much trouble to teach me the mysteries of organ-building, especially Walter Wolsey, the late Robert Lamb and the late Mark Fairhead. Finally, I must acknowledge my gratitude for all the organ lore passed on to me by my father, Herbert Norman, who has been responsible for most of the illustrations in this book.

JOHN NORMAN

NOTE

In describing the lower extent of the compass of the organ, the notation employed is that used over a long period in the Hill firm and which derives from the old G compass of the British organ. This is that double capitals describe a note in the range from the F♯ above present-day bottom C down to the G below bottom C, triple capitals a note in the octave below and quadruple capitals a note in the octave below that.

32ft	16ft	8ft
CCCC.....FFFF♯,GGG....CCC.....FFF♯,GG....CC.....FF♯		

1

WHAT IS AN ORGAN?

Of all musical instruments the organ is the loudest! Of course, the organ has many other characteristics, but before the invention of electronic amplification it was the only way to make a really loud musical noise. In the tenth century a monk called Wulstan wrote a poem about the organ in Winchester Cathedral:

> Like thunder, the strident voice assails the ear
> Shutting out all sounds other than its own
> Such are its reverberations, echoing here and there
> That each man lifts his hands to stop his ears
> Unable as he draws near to tolerate the roaring of so many different and
> noisy combinations.

Nowadays we tend to think of the organ principally as an aid to Christian worship, forgetting that for the first ten centuries of its life it led an entirely secular existence. Ktesibios, a Greek engineer who lived in Alexandria, invented the organ about 250BC. It is said that his wife learned to play it and became the first organist in history. The Emperor Nero brought an organ from Greece to Rome and was himself an organist. The organ was used to entertain audiences at theatrical events and even at gladiatorial contests in the amphitheatre. In its earliest form, before the invention of leather bellows, the compressed air was stored in a large jar inverted over water, the weight of displaced water providing the pressure. Such an instrument was called a *hydraulis*. By the standards of today, it was a very modest instrument with a single manual, perhaps four ranks of pipes and a very restricted key compass.

After the fall of the Roman Empire, knowledge of organ construction, like much of the Greco-Roman culture, died out in Western Europe and continued only in the Eastern Empire based on Byzantium (Istanbul). In Byzantium the organ became the symbol of imperial pomp, the personal property of the Emperor and an integral part of court ceremonial. Instruments were decorated with precious metals and inlaid with precious stones. Knowledge of organ construction even spread as far east as Baghdad, the Emperor of China being

13

sent one as a present from Baghdad in around AD1260. The organ in Byzantium continued to be used in this way for almost ten centuries until the fall of the Byzantine Empire in 1453. Strangely enough, its technical development had ceased and, if anything, the later instruments may have been cruder than their Roman ancestors.

Long before 1453, however, a strange and singular coincidence of events led to the knowledge of organ-building being re-imported to the West. In AD757 Emperor Constantine of Byzantium sent an organ as a present to Pepin, King of the Franks, as part of an exercise in diplomatic persuasion. The Greco-Roman organ having been forgotten, the arrival of this instrument created quite a stir. The organ was later destroyed in mysterious circumstances, but the court at Aix-la-Chapelle (Aachen) felt that it was a slur on their dignity not to have an organ like the Byzantine Emperor. Accordingly, when a monk called Georgius arrived at court in 826 claiming to have studied organ construction in Byzantium, he was immediately supplied with materials and men and told to make one.

Although the organ he constructed was, like its predecessor, a secular instrument, Georgius was a monk. He passed on his knowledge to his pupils, who like almost all educated men of the day were also monks. The first use of the organ in church worship is not recorded but, in the circumstances, it was hardly surprising that with rising ecclesiastical power and wealth the 'new invention' was used to add to the glory of the church. This trend may have been encouraged by the fact that Sylvester II, pope in the early eleventh century, had a reputation as an organ-builder in his younger days.

There was perhaps an additional practical reason. By the tenth century, romanesque architecture was replacing neo-Byzantine and churches of substantial size were being built. Religious vocal music had flourished in the monasteries from the sixth century onwards, especially those of the Benedictine order, and choirs of monks were becoming larger. It is much more difficult for a large choir to sing unaccompanied than for a small one. What better instrument was there than the organ to meet this need? Not only can the organ be played more loudly than any other single musical instrument, it can also produce a more sustained sound than a wind instrument, which is limited by its player's lungs, or than any stringed instrument. The organ is thus ideal for leading the singing of a large number of voices and this has remained the basis of its use in Christian worship for the past ten centuries.

The principle of replacing lung power by muscle power (and nowadays by an electrically driven fan) and of storing the air under pressure in a bellows to obtain a constant supply, not only allows the sound to be sustained but is also the source of its power. Many medieval accounts tell of the large numbers of people employed to pump early organs. The use of mechanical wind supply goes hand in hand with mechanical control of the notes, leading to the provision of a separate pipe for each note. The simple levers provided by the Romans were the precursors of the keyboard of today, the organ being the first keyboard instrument.

The principle of a separate pipe for each note has an important consequence. Most musical instruments have a relatively restricted compass, since there is a limit to the range of pitch which can be coaxed out of a single resonator. The lowest notes tend to be thin and soft and the high notes fat and characterless. With a separate pipe for each note, individually scaled and voiced to speak one note and one note only, the resonator of the organ pipe can be made to the optimum dimensions for that note. Freed of the limitations of a single resonator, the organ can go to both the upper and lower limits of the human ear. Indeed, at eight beats per second, the lowest note of the organ in Sydney Town Hall, Australia, goes over the threshold from sound into feeling.

This escape from the limitations of lung power has another consequence for the organ. The use of mechanical blowing does not allow the player to achieve musical expression by blowing the pipes gently or strongly at will. Much of the development of the instrument has been directed at providing other means of tonal variation. One form has been the provision of alternative ranks of pipes as voices which may be silenced or called upon to speak as required. Each different voice is called a 'stop' and normally consists of a complete and independent set of pipes. To those unfamiliar with the organ, the welter of stop-names in many different languages can be most confusing. Despite the presence of some stops named after orchestral instruments, the organ is not naturally a one-man orchestra. The basic sound of the organ is that of an open pipe, known on the stop-knob by the name Open Diapason or Principal. Air is blown through the foot of the pipe upwards across an opening called the mouth and vibrates either side of the upper lip. The vibration is amplified and controlled in pitch by the resonance of the air column in the body of the pipe. The recorder family of instruments works in much the same way. The length of the body of an organ pipe determines the resonant frequency of the air column within it and thus the pitch of the note produced. Since only the bass pipes are displayed in the cases of most organs, many people do not realise the relatively small size of the majority of organ pipes.

A variant of the Open Diapason pipe, which goes right back to

Roman times, is obtained simply by closing the top end of the pipe. This halves the resonant frequency of the air column in the pipe so that for a given note the body of the pipe need only be half as long. The important musical difference is that the stopped pipe resonates only to alternate harmonics of the fundamental, the first overtone being the third harmonic, one octave and a fifth above the fundamental. The other harmonics, including the octave, are suppressed. The sound produced is very characteristic of the organ, of a more or less flute-like quality, and unlike that of any other instrument. Stopped Diapason, Gedeckt (old German for Stopped), and Bourdon (French) are stops of this type as is the Quintaten stop, voiced to produce a particularly strong third harmonic.

More subtle changes to the shape of the pipe provide other gradations of tonal variation. A distinctive formant can be heard in the tone of an open pipe tapered to a smaller diameter at the top than at the mouth. Such pipes are often (inaccurately) called Gemshorn or have the German prefix 'Spitz' added to the stop-name. A small chimney added to a stopped pipe reintroduces a few of the even harmonics, hence the name Chimney Flute or Rohr Flute.

Whatever the shape of the pipe, the tone is influenced by its diameter relative to its length, known as the 'scale'. In a very wide pipe the resonances of the upper harmonics in the air column in the body of the pipe are suppressed, giving a 'flutey' tone. Conversely, in a very narrow pipe, where the upper resonances are not suppressed, the tone is said to be 'stringy'. Narrow-scale pipes are not easy to voice, but once the technical problems were overcome in the nineteenth century, the organ world saw a profusion of stops with such names as Viola da Gamba and Viole d'Orchestre. Having a narrower mouth, narrow-scale pipes are naturally softer, and this characteristic has also been exploited to give tonal variety by the provision of softer stops. The oldest of these stops, the Dulciana, goes back to the eighteenth century; the Salicional and the Vox Angelica are nineteenth-century developments.

All the different stops so far discussed have been produced by variations of the basic Diapason pipe. Generically, these are known as 'flue-pipes' after the flue from which wind is blown across the pipe-mouth. Most organs have some pipes which are constructed on a completely different principle, one which is also believed to go back to the organ's invention in classical antiquity. Known as 'reed-pipes' or just 'the reeds', they work on similar principles to the woodwind in a modern orchestra and clearly evolved from similar roots. The reed itself is a single reed as in a modern clarinet or saxophone. The acoustic principle is not unlike the flue-pipe in that the vibrating reed

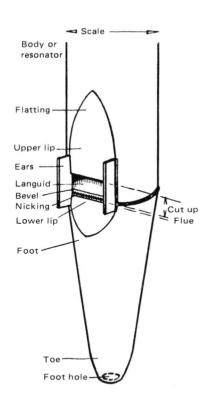

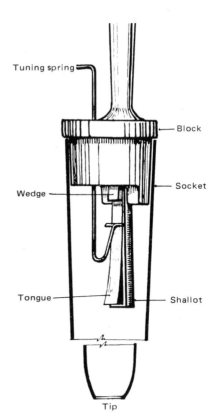

Fig 1 The parts of the flue pipe   *Fig 2* The parts of the reed pipe

is the fundamental source of sound which is amplified and modified by the resonance of the air column in the pipe above it. At this point the similarity ceases, since the pipe is generally tuned not by varying the length of the pipe but by varying the vibrating length of the brass reed. This difference does cause some practical problems, since the result is that reed-pipes react to changes in temperature in a rather different way from flue-pipes and need more frequent tuning.

The tone of the organ reed is essentially more powerful than that of a flue-pipe and has a higher harmonic content as well. Within that generalisation there are enormous variations, much wider variations than would be thought possible from the basically woodwind construction of the reed pipes. The most common organ reed-stop is called Trumpet and bears more than a passing resemblance to the brass instrument of the same name. It has simple conical resonators of approximately the same length as Open Diapason pipes of the same pitch. The musical use of the Trumpet, like almost all reed-stops, is twofold. It can provide a distinctive sound when used on its own yet it also adds the final climax when added to a chorus of flue-

17

stops. Another reed-stop with full-length resonators is the Oboe and its variants. It is softer than the Trumpet and has pipes of narrower scale with a two-part construction of the resonator, a narrow conical 'shank' surmounted by a more sharply flared 'bell' partially covered over. This construction introduces characteristic formants to the sound, though the tone is only distantly related to its counterpart in the modern orchestra.

A more drastic change of tone is achieved by making the resonator basically cylindrical. The effect is similar to that of putting a stopper in an Open Diapason pipe; the length of the pipe is halved for a given pitch and the tone consists only of the odd-numbered harmonics. This is the characteristic tone of the Clarinet family of stops, strongly coloured but generally softer than stops of the Trumpet family because the half-length pipe provides less amplification of the sound of the reed.

As the pitch is mainly determined by the reed rather than by the air column in the pipe, it is also possible to make reed-pipes of less than half-length; this is not possible with flue-pipes. Fractional-length reeds, as they are generically known, are relatively soft but tend to have a very bright sound as the small resonator has so little influence on the buzz of the vibrating reed. In order to give the sound a characteristic colour in spite of this lack of influence, the resonators are often of complicated or even bizarre shapes. The most common such stop is the grossly misnamed Vox Humana.

It is natural with climax stops such as Trumpets that artists should try to enlarge the bounds of dynamic range by seeking out new ways of making them still more powerful. In seventeenth-century Spain horizontal reed-pipes were developed, projecting from the organ case just below the feet of the display pipes. All else being equal, this just about doubles the power of the pipes and gives a marvellously fresh and commanding sound as well. Horizontal reeds are now occasionally found in Britain and in other parts of Europe also.

Mechanical developments in the nineteenth century permitted the exploitation of another way of increasing the power of reed-stops, the use of increased wind pressure. Increasing the wind pressure has only a limited effect on the power of flue-pipes, but on reed-pipes it not only increases the power but makes them more stable in tuning. Unfortunately, heavy pressure can also take away the brilliance, and for this reason its use for reed-stops has fallen somewhat into disrepute. Both heavy-pressure reeds and horizontal reeds are essentially solo stops, their power making them less suitable for blending with a chorus of flue-stops.

The most important way in which the power and tone of an organ may be varied has been left until last: the use of stops of different pitch. This is fundamental to the tonal structure of the organ and dates back to its Greek and Roman origins. Where volume of sound is concerned the human ear works in a way which requires explanation. The range of sound energy between the softest audible sound and the threshold of pain is about one to a million. In order that we may comprehend such a vast range, a sound which appears to us as being twice as loud actually contains ten times as much sound energy. This being so, it would take ten pipes of the same pitch, sounding together, to double the power of the organ. Such an arrangement would be hopelessly uneconomic in wind consumption, in effort required to operate the keys and in space and cost. Fortunately, if a second set of pipes, one octave higher than the first, is added to the fundamental, the ear accepts them as single tones at the fundamental pitch but with added brilliance. This phenomenon appears entirely natural because most other instruments become brighter in tone as they are played more loudly. The second set of pipes can be made apparently to double the power, yet with a wind consumption not ten times as much as before but less than double.

This principle has been developed to produce the Diapason Chorus, made up of stops of varying pitches from the sub-fundamental upwards and including almost every conceivable audible harmonic multiple of the basic pitch. It is customary for the pitch to be expressed in terms of the length of the body of an open pipe sounding the bottom C on the organ keyboard. This is two octaves below middle C and for a fundamental stop is 8ft. The sub-fundamental is 16ft and the octave 4ft. One octave and a fifth up is the third harmonic which is thus $\frac{8}{3}$ or $2\frac{2}{3}$ft, occasionally abbreviated to 3ft. The fourth harmonic is $\frac{8}{4}$ or 2ft, the fifteenth note in the scale above the fundamental. The fifth harmonic, two octaves and a third up, is similarly the seventeenth or Tierce and is $\frac{8}{5}$ or $1\frac{3}{5}$ft.

Although they should all blend together to produce a single brilliant tone, the constituents of the chorus have different effects. The Unison pitches 4ft, 2ft, 1ft etc add power and brilliance, but leave the basic tone colour unaltered. The Quint pitches $2\frac{2}{3}$ft, $1\frac{1}{3}$ft etc also add some brilliance, but colour the sound as well. By another quirk of the human ear, the resulting 'difference tones' also result in an apparent strengthening of the fundamental. The Tierce pitches produce still more colour, giving a 'reedy' effect, but need care in use for reasons which will be explained below. Other possible pitches are the seventh harmonic $1\frac{1}{7}$ft or 'flat twenty-first' and the ninth harmonic $\frac{8}{9}$ft or 'None'. These produce even more strongly coloured effects, so strong as to be almost unusable. The reason for this is that,

19

like all keyboard instruments, the organ is capable of playing polyphonic music and the parts would become hopelessly confused.

It is because of its polyphonic nature that the organ is self-sufficient as a solo instrument or instrument of accompaniment. One cannot conceive of an orchestra of organs nor is one necessary. The sheer economy in musical manpower which is achieved by one person playing a relatively powerful polyphonic instrument is one reason why cinema owners in the 1920s preferred theatre organs to orchestras for the purpose of accompanying silent films. Indeed, apart from the pedal harpsichord, the possibilities of polyphony are greater on the organ than on any other solo instrument. How else could one person perform a six-part fugue?

Polyphony is also an important factor in the sheer power which an organ is capable of, since the principle of pitch difference by which the chorus achieves its power applies also to chords, which are correspondingly more powerful than single notes. After all, sounding two notes an octave apart on a single stop produces the same effect as holding one note on two similar stops an octave apart in pitch. In this lies the problem of combining polyphony with the 'remote' harmonics in the chorus structure. On a keyboard instrument with necessarily 'tempered' tuning (more about this in chapter 3), the intervals held in a chord will not necessarily be the same as the true intervals to which the members of the chorus are tuned. This can lead to unacceptable dissonances. The most obvious case of this is the seventh harmonic, whose C pipes will sound a note somewhere in the crack between A and B♭. These dissonances do not arise if a stop is played one note at a time – as a solo. Thus the Cornet stop, in which five pipes sound together to make up the complete harmonic series to the fifth harmonic, is mainly intended as a solo stop. Another, the Sesquialtera, sounding the third and fifth harmonics, is also used sparingly in chordal music.

The concept of stops which have more than one pipe per note, generally called mixtures, is common to most British organs since 1680. It is usual for most members of the Diapason Chorus above 2ft pitch to be grouped together in this way. There are a number of reasons, both musical and mechanical, for this grouping. Separate stops would introduce greater mechanical complexity. More importantly, if each rank were separately controlled, the addition of each succeeding pitch to those already drawn would add less and less as each stop was added. Furthermore, the higher pitches of chorus mixtures would become inaudible in the upper part of the keyboard unless the pitch of each rank 'breaks back' to a lower one for the treble notes. In a single stop this would be very disconcerting, but in a

20

mixture with several ranks breaking at different points the break should be much less noticeable.

Although the human ear is unhappy with dissonance, especially in the sustained sounds which an organ produces, it is also unsatisfied by perfect consonance. Just as ten first violins sound very different from a single violin amplified, so the Diapason Chorus sounds very different from a single stop of the same harmonic structure. The reason is that no matter how accurately the organ is tuned, it is impossible to eliminate slight variations of phase between the various harmonics; the resulting undercurrent of movement in the steady sound gives it life. This 'chorus effect' is why the ear does not tire quickly of such a sound. One of the problems with electronic imitations of the pipe organ is that many of them have little or no true chorus effect, with the result that the ear tires of the sound relatively quickly.

This problem also affects the pipe organ when single stops are in use. Loud climax reed-stops are not really affected; they are used for such short periods that the ear does not have time to tire of them. Softer solo voices, however, are affected and for many centuries organ-builders have provided an artificial means of adding movement to their sound by introducing a regular pulse into the wind supply, a device known as the Tremulant. This is used particularly with the softer reeds such as the Clarinet and stops of the Vox Humana type. In the case of the softer flue-stops, the ear can also be satisfied in a more sophisticated way by introducing a second soft stop tuned very slightly sharp to the first. The Voix Celeste is the most common such stop and has a continuous mild undulation.

One of the most impressive features of an organ to the inexperienced observer is the fact that it is generally provided with multiple rows of keys, a characteristic shared only with some harpsichords. The early Roman and medieval instruments had but one 'manual', as a set of keys is called. The provision of multiple manuals did not come about until the fifteenth century in Germany and the Low Countries and not until the early seventeenth century in Britain.

The route by which this development took place is quite curious. Very soon after the organ's invention by Ktesibios, the Romans developed a simple stop control to enable various ranks of pipes to be brought into use to vary the tone. After the fall of the Roman Empire and at some stage in the translation of the technology of organ-building from Rome to Byzantium and back to Western Europe, a number of features of the instrument were quite literally forgotten. The Roman organ had been provided with simple keys operating slide-valves which had springs to return them. The early medieval organs had only the bare slides which had to be pulled out for the note to sound and then pushed in when the note was finished with! No wonder it became usual for two organists to be employed, playing a ponderous duet. More manageable key-actions were soon re-invented but the omission of any stop-action lasted for several centuries and had a major effect on the development of the instrument. The use of multiple pipes per key continued and organs became larger to support the singing of large choirs of monks. Without any stop-action, these instruments were inflexible and could not be played softly. It became general to supplement the powerful fixed organs with rather smaller instruments called 'Positives' which, with some effort, were movable, and still tinier instruments called 'Portatives' which could be carried by one person and used in procession.

In due course it became customary to provide the organist of the 'Great organ' with a Positive organ close by so that loud and soft sounds could be alternated. Where the main organ was on a gallery, it was a convenient arrangement to stand the Positive behind the player, the pipes facing out over the gallery rail. Organists soon tired of having to turn round to play the smaller instrument, and when the great technical development of the organ began in the fifteenth century builders brought the action of the smaller instrument under the player to a second keyboard placed below that of the main organ. The Portative was similarly translated to a position behind the music desk to make a third manual, the German *Brustwerk*. It is perhaps ironic that soon after this development took place the stop-action was re-invented. The survival of the second and third manuals, together with the separate departments of the organ with which they are associated, was assured by the flexibility which they give the player not only for quick alterations of tone or dynamic level but also for using a different registration (combination of stops) for each hand. Chapter 3 will examine the characteristics of the various departments of the organ; it is perhaps sufficient here to say that to fulfil their role of enlarging the dynamic flexibility of the instrument it is essential that each manual has its own separate tonal character.

Organs in Britain were only generally constructed with pedal keyboards after about 1800, but the idea of pedal keys is much older, probably being first used in Germany in the late fourteenth century, although its origins are obscure. If we go back to the period when two organists had to be employed, pushing the key-slides in as well as pulling them out, separate bass and treble keyboards were sometimes provided. One could suppose, therefore, that when the key-action was re-invented, it might have seemed logical to provide a bass keyboard operated by the feet to augment a treble keyboard for the hands. Later, perhaps, the compass of the two keyboards overlapped. Then a coupler provided to connect the manual keys to the pedal keys would enable them to be used as an alternative for the lower notes which were heavy to play with the fingers.

It is hoped that this chapter has given the reader a general view of the organ, not only what it is but also the logic behind its structure and how it came to be that way. The organ is a fascinating instrument, essentially mechanical and, to its critics, inflexible; yet, because of its mechanical nature, the organ is capable of an astonishing intricacy of musical texture and of a wider variety of pitch, dynamic level and harmonic variety than any other single instrument. This is why it is called the King of Instruments.

2

HOW TO LOOK AT ORGANS

Position, appearance and construction

Organists often indulge in an activity known as the 'organ crawl'. Though considerably more sober than the 'pub crawl', after which it is named, this activity is nevertheless eminently enjoyable. Why is this so? After all, no one goes on Saturday afternoon tours of grand pianos!

Organ-builders are generally individualists so that differences between makers go far deeper than mere nameplates on consoles. Nevertheless, by itself, this cannot account for the variety which makes the exploration and comparison of organs an absorbing pastime. Paradoxically, it is the relative inflexibility of the organ which has led to its variety, since the musical design of the instrument has varied at different times in response to varying repertoire and musical priorities. Indeed, the practised eye can often date an organ to within fifteen or twenty years merely from an examination of the stop-list. As the organ is a very long-lived instrument, many instruments remain in use whose design dates back to an earlier period. Large organs are often 'rebuilt' and now contain work of many different periods.

There is one factor outside the instrument which makes a considerable difference to the sound of an organ. The acoustics of the building in which it is situated are sometimes said to be the most important 'stop' on the organ. A long reverberation assists an instrument which does not have the pianoforte's sustaining pedal and, since a long reverberation goes hand in hand with low acoustic absorption, the organ will not have to work so hard for its living. Obviously an organ in a large cathedral needs to be capable of a far greater range and power than an instrument in a small chapel, so organs vary enormously in size not only with the dimensions of the building but also with the depth of the pockets of those who paid for them. This is particularly true of organ cases and their decoration, though it will also be affected very much by the date of construction.

Given that it is their variety that makes organs so interesting to explore and to compare, what should one look for when visiting an instrument for the first time? First, where is the organ placed? From the time of the Reformation up to about 1850, the great majority of organs were placed at the back of churches in the 'west-end' position, often on a gallery. An organ in this position, in the open and on the main axis of the building, will speak out clearly and directly to the congregation. The tone is fresh and direct and the reverberation of the building can add warmth without leading to a rhythmic jumble. Some will argue whether listening to the sound of an instrument coming from behind is natural, and the non-conformist chapels, without an all-important sanctuary to worry about, evolved an almost standard layout with the organ in front of the congregation and immediately behind the pulpit.

In the seventeenth and eighteenth centuries, the amateur choirs in parish churches were considered relatively unimportant and were normally accommodated on the west gallery in front of the organ, out of sight of the congregation but conveniently close to the organist. In cathedrals, the professional choral tradition has always been strong and the singers occupied the stalls in the choir originally provided, before the Reformation, for monks. It therefore became natural in cathedrals to place the organ on the screen which divided the choir from the nave. Being west of the choir, it occupied the same relative position as in a parish church so far as the daily choral services were concerned. Organs in this position have a two-sided case with a back 'front' facing down the nave.

In the twenty years following 1845 a substantial change took place in the layout of Anglican churches, a change which had major effects on organ position and design. At this time the Church of England felt that it had to go back to its medieval roots, one of the symptoms of which was the abandonment of 'secular' Georgian architecture for the revival of 'sacred' Gothic. Parish churches were urged to copy the cathedral pattern, to dress their choirs up in surplices and to place them in choir stalls between the altar and the people. Congregational hymn singing became an established part of the service, screens between choir and people were considered undesirable and were removed from a number of cathedrals, perhaps the best known being Wren's screen in St Paul's Cathedral, London.

The consequence of these changes was that between 1845 and 1865 nearly every west-end organ in a parish church was moved. Very few retained a west-end organ combined with an east-end choir. Wymondham Abbey in Norfolk was an exception, but the problems of accompanying a choir from a distance of over 100ft (30m) are not inconsiderable! Oxford and Cambridge college chapels are mostly small enough and their choirs good enough for the west position to be retained but the only other exceptions were some of the smallish city churches built in London in the classical style after the Great Fire.

Where then was the organ to go? Some of the larger churches, such as Bath Abbey and Sherborne Abbey, had sizeable transepts near the choir which could conveniently accommodate an organ. Others were by no means so fortunate and organs were placed in side aisles, side chapels and specially constructed organ-chambers on one side of the chancel. Some country churches without side aisles had the organ divided either side of the chancel with long action trackers passing under the floor. One organ, in an apsidal side chapel, had to be fitted with a five-sided bellows to get it in! It became general to place organ-chambers on the north side of the chancel, where the organ received less heat in the summer and the tuning was more stable. (Curiously, this position was often copied in Australia, where, of course, the climatic position is reversed.)

The result of moving a west-end organ to an aisle or chamber in the east was usually a disaster. Hemmed in by masonry and no longer on the main axis of the building, the instruments sounded weak and inadequate. Within a few years they were mostly replaced by new and larger organs which could make more sound, though they could never replace the clarity and even spread of sound which the west-end organs had. The story in the great cathedrals was much less uniform. Gloucester, Exeter, Wells, Norwich, Southwell and York retained the old arrangements with the organ on the screen. St Paul's in London took the screen down, found the organ inadequate in a side aisle, tried a separate transept organ and eventually settled for an instrument apparently divided either side where the screen had been. Westminster Abbey ended up with similar arrangements but retaining the screen. Peterborough and Canterbury hid their organs up in the triforium, whilst Winchester and Chichester put them in the north transept. Bristol divided its organ between two bays of the north choir aisle. Ingenuity truly reigned supreme, though it was inventiveness in hiding the bulk of an increasingly large instrument rather than ingenuity in acoustic layout! Not surprisingly, the results were variable; many cathedral instruments are superb for accompanying the choir but their remoteness and indirect sound to the congregation make them less than perfect for recitals and for leading congregational singing. For the latter purpose a number of cathedrals have now acquired separate nave organs or nave divisions controlled from the main organ.

A few parish churches have recently moved back to the west-end for leading the congregation, combined with a small chancel organ

Fig 3 Organ-case cut away to show key-action with rollerboard

for the choir. Nevertheless, it has become increasingly clear that there is no single correct position, ideal for all churches. The combination of liturgical, architectural and musical requirements is individual to each building. However, the idea of shutting the organ away in a tone-killing organ-chamber is now thankfully dead and the organ accepted as a free-standing piece of furniture.

As probably the largest piece of furniture in a building, the appearance of the organ is not unimportant. Indeed, the study of organ casework is a major section of the study of the instrument. The appearance of the Roman organ was purely functional, with simple panelling to cover the mechanism and a stay to hold the pipes in position. Medieval Portatives and Positives retained this form into the fifteenth century, albeit with some added decoration. Nevertheless, by the end of the fourteenth century large organs had formal cases, and by the early seventeenth century the organ built by Compenius for the King of Prussia to dance to (now in Frederiksborg Castle, Denmark) had a highly carved and decorated case with wooden pipes covered with plates of ivory.

The organ case appears to have developed as a result of both practical requirements and mechanical invention. Portatives and Positives could be locked away in a safe place when not in use, but the main organ was too heavy to be moved and needed protection against dust, vermin and vandals. This protection could be achieved by building a wooden box around the pipes with doors on the front which could be opened when the organ was in use. Such a box would look much more elegant if it were symmetrical, but early organs necessarily had their pipes arranged from bass to treble in the same order as the keys. The invention of the roller allowed the key-to-soundboard connections to be transferred sideways if required, liberating the pipe layout from exact correspondence with the keys so that alternate notes could be moved to the other end of the soundboard and a symmetrical layout achieved. The earliest surviving playable organ, in the church of Notre Dame de Valère, Sion, Switzerland, dates from about 1400 and has a case of this form. The bass pipes are in 'towers' at the ends and the treble pipes in a separate symmetrical compartment in the middle. The result is an organ whose case has a distinctive silhouette and which can provide the background for considerable architectural decoration.

The development of the symmetrical organ case came at a time when gothic architecture was already retreating in the face of the new ideas of the Renaissance, based on a revival of Greek and Roman forms. The result is that truly gothic organ cases (as opposed to nineteenth-century Gothic Revival cases) are indeed rare. The case

Fig 4 The organ in Old Radnor Church, Wales

of the Sion organ, with its crockets, pierced decoration and castellated towers, is pure gothic, as is that of the oldest organ case in Britain which dates from the early 1500s. This is the very curious case at Old Radnor on the Welsh border, the decoration of which has been described as having been borrowed from a series of Tudor chairbacks. Nevertheless, it has many characteristics which have continued to be fundamental to organ-case design. First, one notices that the case, like that of the Sion organ, is 'waisted in' at the bottom. This follows the mechanical construction in that the invention of the rollerboard allowed the pipes to be spread over a greater distance than the width of the keyboard. Even so this was not sufficient to permit all the bass pipes to stand in a single line and the longest stand in a 'V' formation alternating with panels of smaller pipes. This alternation of 'towers' with 'flats' is the foundation of the architectural form and decoration of the organ case. The three-towered case is probably the most common of all traditional forms, either with the tallest tower in the centre, or with two prominent side towers and a smaller tower in the centre. A rather extreme example of the latter form is the well-known main organ case in King's College Chapel, Cambridge. Some nineteenth-century Gothic Revival cases, however, have the outer towers suppressed, leaving only a central tower with two flats. Smaller organs can also have a simple two-towered design with a single central flat. Four-towered cases are not uncommon on the larger instruments of the eighteenth and late seventeenth centuries and the Milton organ in Tewkesbury Abbey has a five-towered case. Not all the towers are of V-shaped form on plan, indeed a semi-circular plan is more usual, often with the supports delicately carved. The towers can also be flat on plan, merely the length of the pipes differentiating them from the flats between. Sometimes different plans can be combined in one case as, for example, at Trinity College, Cambridge, where the two centre towers are semi-circular, supported on cherub's heads, whilst the smaller outer towers do not project at all. Some instruments built in the eighteenth century, however, have cases where the flats are not flat at all but of V-shape or ogee-form on plan!

One of the basic complications of organ-case design is that all the pipes are of different lengths, as determined by the pitch of the note required. There are a number of devices to get round this problem. The crudest is to make the smaller pipes over-length, cutting away the back so that the upper false-length does not form part of the resonator. However, if the false-length is more than trivial it destroys the proportions of the pipes, giving them an etiolated look as well as spoiling their speech. Another device is to fill the case with large pipes

Fig 5 The organ of the Church of Notre Dame de Valère, Switzerland

only, using additional non-speaking 'dummy' pipes to fill up the space. Such cases are often coarse and lacking in variety of texture. The more extreme examples from the early twentieth century can be downright dull.

If we look again at the organ case at Sion, we can see two more ways of coping with varying pipe-lengths. In the first place the case does not have a level top, the central portion being sloped more or less to follow the line of the pipe-tops. Secondly, the blank spaces at the tops of the towers are partially filled with some delicate gothic tracery. Turning to the Old Radnor case, we can see a development of this principle with the tracery following down the line of the pipe-tops and concealing their precise lengths with what we call a 'pipe-shade'. The variation in the height of the pipe-tops is also minimised by varying the length of the feet, with the longest pipes having the shortest feet, thus creating an attractive sloping mouth-line and exaggerating the natural change of proportion between bass and treble pipes.

In the late nineteenth and early twentieth centuries some architects reversed this arrangement, giving the largest pipes the longest feet to retain a more constant ratio between body and foot lengths. This arrangement can be effective if the top silhouette of the case is exaggerated to play up the difference in pipe-lengths. If this is not done, the designer is forced to use too much false-length, spoiling the length-to-width proportions of the pipes.

The Dallam case at King's College, Cambridge illustrates another way of achieving a sloping mouth-line. Instead of giving the treble pipes longer feet, they are elevated by standing on a sloping toe-board. These were sometimes made curved, and Renatus Harris, among others, extended this to provide oval compartments of flats such as can be seen at All Hallows, Twickenham and those by Samuel Green at Greenwich Naval College.

In Holland and Germany organs acquired, at an early date, additional soundboards and pipes at a level above the main organ so it was natural that this should be reflected in the case by showing upper levels of front pipes. This could also be used as a device for making up the height of the case, as can be seen by looking again at the Old Radnor case, where there are two-storey flats of small pipes to make the top of the case up to a level line. However at Old Radnor, as indeed in many later British cases, there was no upper soundboard and the upper pipes do not speak. Occasionally an organ-designer finds that he has not enough long pipes even for all the towers in which case these too can be made of two storeys. The 1790 Geib case at St Mary's, Stafford has a central tower like this as has Dr Arthur Hill's 1916 case at Beverley Minster, while the W. D. Caröe case at Winchester College Chapel has a three-decker tower!

The average parish church or chapel organ, however, built in the second half of the nineteenth century, does not have a case following any of these models. The reasons for this are bound up in the history of ecclesiastical architecture. The fundamental principles of organ-case design, going back to the fifteenth century, transferred from gothic to Renaissance architecture with alterations only in decoration, not in fundamental form. The British organ case varied little in essentials from 1600 to after 1800, nor did the 'Gothick' style make much change except for the addition of spirelets and finials. From about 1840 architects tired of 'secular' Georgian and of the 'unscholarly' Gothick and searched for the 'real' medieval gothic. Some of the more scholarly organ cases of this period derived directly from the few medieval gothic examples surviving on the Continent, adapted to the generally larger size of late nineteenth-century organs. A. W. N. Pugin designed two brilliant small organ cases (Jesus College, Cambridge and South Pickenham Church) and others in this field were J. L. Pearson (Westminster Abbey), G. F. Bodley and, later, Dr A. G. Hill. In this century S. E. Dykes Bower has designed many scholarly cases, mainly in Renaissance style. One can often tell an architect's case from that of an organ-builder – it nearly always has more wood in it. One can see this by looking at the 'woodiness' of Sir Christopher Wren's only surviving organ case, in St Paul's Cathedral, London. Organ-builders, by contrast, want the sound to get out and put in as many speaking pipes and as little wood as possible. That may well be the reason why so many nineteenth-century organ-builders followed the lead of Sir George Gilbert Scott and others who felt that the true medieval simplicity was best expressed in an organ case which consisted only of bass pipes plus any necessary supports.

In a sense, they were right. The organ case had long lost some of the functional reasons for its existence. No longer was it an ornamental box needed to keep out dust and vandals; few British organ cases had been made with a roof for some time, and doors disappeared, other than for some chamber organs, before 1600. In the second half of the nineteenth century the majority of new organs were no longer free-standing pieces of furniture but had been tailored into organ-chambers or other recesses in the building structure. Thus the case was reduced to a fence of bass pipes hiding the interior. With the organ tucked into a low aisle or organ-chamber, any structure above the pipe-tops would obstruct the egress of sound, and woodwork other than a simple post-and-rail pipe support was eschewed. The naked pipe-tops, without pipe-caps, were very occasionally finished off with little crowns (as at Exeter College, Oxford). A later modification was to hide the post and stay-rail behind the pipes, and cases of this sort have regrettably continued to be made almost up to the present day, including such major instruments as those in Guildford Cathedral and Birmingham University.

The reaction to these dull fences of bass pipes, many of them dummies, came first from America, where Walter Holtkamp, who hated organ-chambers, gave the opinion: 'I don't want my tone mixed, predigested and rendered into an impersonal mass. I prefer to sit in the same room with the pipes and do my own mixing'. Holtkamp developed a style of organ layout in which every pipe was seen, the small treble pipes at the front and the bass pipes at the back. The

33

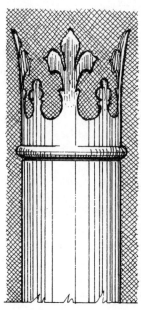

Fig 6 A pipe-top on the organ
of Exeter College, Oxford

layout of the soundboard was varied, using electric action, to produce
the best massing of large numbers of small pipes. Holtkamp built
relatively few organs, none for Britain, but he influenced many other
builders and a number of instruments were built following his ideas in
the period 1950–70, including the organ in the Mormon Hyde Park
Chapel, Kensington and both organs in the Royal College of
Organists. When the organ is new, the style is visually attractive,
especially in plain modern buildings, but it looks less happy when the
pipes have dulled with time.

The organ has been considered so far as a single 'box of whistles',
as one piece of furniture. This is not always so in practice. In chapter 1
the process whereby the organ acquired multiple sets of keys by
incorporating smaller organs within one instrument was described.
When our seventeenth-century forebears wrote of a 'double organ'
they meant an organ standing on a gallery with a second and smaller
case projecting out from the gallery edge behind the player. They
called this smaller case and its contents the 'Chair' organ to distinguish it from the larger 'Great' organ. Such a layout was at one time
very common and although in later years the 'Choir' organ, as it
became, was more often incorporated within the main case, many
examples of such a layout remain, especially in our cathedrals and
college chapels. The contrast between two organ cases of different
size can often be very attractive to look at. This difference is sometimes heightened where the two cases are of different date, which is
less uncommon than might be supposed.

Fig 7 The Holtkamp organ in St. Charles Roman Catholic Church, Parma, Ohio, USA

On the Continent the concept of the 'double organ' was carried much further, especially in the magnificent instruments built in Holland and in Hanseatic north Germany in the early eighteenth century. These instruments not only had the double organ arrangement with a smaller Chair organ (German *Ruckpositiv*) but also had separate casework for the Pedal organ. The British organ had no Pedal organ then, or for another century, but the Hanseatic organ often had two Pedal cases either side of the *Hauptwerk* (Great organ), sometimes adjoining it and sometimes separate. Larger instruments had a third manual department clearly visible, either an *Oberwerk* above the *Hauptwerk* or a *Brustwerk* below it. These

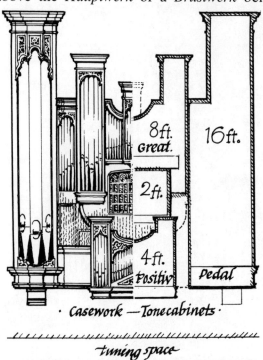

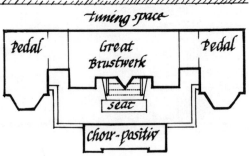

Fig 8 Hanseatic werkprinzip organ layout

instruments also had roofs to the various cases, an important point to which we will return.

In Britain the double organ layout fell into disuse after 1700 and was almost killed off in our parish churches by the movement of organs away from the west end in the nineteenth century. In their new positions in aisles and organ-chambers height was often in very short supply. As a result, the Victorian organ was mostly laid out on a single level to save height, the manual departments being one behind the other. The Pedal stops, each on a separate soundboard, were either right at the back or on one or both sides. This type of layout combined with the complex acoustic reflections resulting from the typical north aisle organ-chamber to give many instruments a diffuse sound, ideal for a variety of soft romantic tone colours but which degenerated into a distant roar when leading congregational singing.

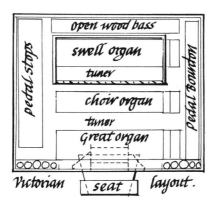

Fig 9 Victorian British organ layout, plan view

More recently, as the music of the composers of the baroque period has become more widely performed, especially the works of Bach, musicians have become dissatisfied with the sound of the British organ. Since 1950 ease of travel and the wide distribution of gramophone records have opened the public ear to the sound of the surviving Hanseatic organs of Bach's time. The result has been that organ-building has taken a new direction, paralleling the increasing interest in early music generally. The effect on the tonal design of the organ will be covered in chapter 3 but the effect on organ layout and appearance has been profound. The instrument has again become a free-standing piece of furniture with a vertical rather than a horizontal layout. One division does not stand in front of another so the tone is not diffused and the organ is very shallow. Following the *werkprinzip* of the Hanseatic organ, each division normally occupies a separate case or obvious division of the main case, each with its own roof.

It is now realised that, whatever the original function may have been, a roof to the organ case does more than just keep out the dust; it also has important effects on the tone of the instrument, adding a remarkable warmth and resonance, the latter being especially noticeable in a dry acoustic. How does this come about? A light timber 'tone-cabinet' is formed by the casework with sides, back and roof constructed as tightly round the pipes as reasonable access for tuning will allow. Even the open space above the front pipes is kept to a minimum or filled with perforated pipe-shades. One result is to throw all the sound energy forward so that less sound is wasted in the rafters and the pipes need be blown less hard, giving a warmer sound. The resonance comes from the air resonances characteristic of enclosed spaces. These are complex, not harmonic, and ascend in pitch as the space is made smaller, thereby pushing the resonance further into the audible range. Many people think that the structural resonances of thin panelling also contribute.

The *werkprinzip* discipline strongly dictates the case outline, often giving the instrument a distinctively shaped silhouette. Following the functional trend in modern architecture, many case designers have relied on these silhouettes to provide the main visual interest of the instrument, keeping timber sections and mouldings as simple as possible. This has been particularly true of organs by Scandinavian builders, though visual interest has been added by unusual grouping of the display pipes, as in the Danish-built organ in Robinson College, Cambridge, for example. Only in the pipe-shades have designers sometimes allowed themselves a relatively free hand with decoration, occasionally using copper or other metals as an alternative to pierced wood.

The use of a relatively wide range of timbers and of pipe materials is another characteristic of present-day case design, in line with current trends in furniture. Indeed, organ cases have always been made of the normal furniture materials of the time. Thus, up to the eighteenth century, oak was the usual material, sometimes now so aged that it appears almost black. All is not always what it seems, however. For example, although the pre-Commonwealth Choir organ case at Gloucester Cathedral is oak, the 1666 main case is partly of pine, grained to look like oak. Pine became very much cheaper in the nineteenth century and its use became general for all but the grandest work, taking over from the Spanish mahogany which had become popular after the middle of the eighteenth century.

The material from which the pipes are made is not always obvious. The Romans used bronze, but since medieval times organ pipes have generally been made of alloys of tin and lead. The metal can be cast in sheets ready for making up into pipes and can be readily worked with hand tools and manipulated by the voicer. The tonal implications of pipe materials will be discussed later, but where large display pipes are concerned the main criteria are stability, appearance and cost. The more tin there is in the alloy, up to a maximum of about seventy per cent, the stronger the metal and the more attractive and long-lasting its appearance. On the other hand, tin being many times the price of lead, there are economic incentives for minimising its use. In practice, organ-builders in Spain, Holland and Germany have lavished more money on organ cases than British builders, combining polished 'tin metal' display pipes with the generous use of gold-leaf on the woodwork. In Britain, seventeenth- and eighteenth-century practice was mostly to use only about twenty per cent tin and then to cover the front pipes in gold-leaf, leaving the woodwork ungilded. Not all gilded pipes are metal; dummy pipes are sometimes carved pine, gilded over.

Sometimes in the early seventeenth century the front pipes were covered in hand-painted decoration, with just the mouths gilded. Original examples of such decoration may be seen at Gloucester Cathedral and at Framlingham Parish Church, Suffolk. In the nineteenth century stencilled and painted decoration became common. This process was known as 'diapering' and some organs so treated have been described as looking like 'rolls of linoleum'. Striking examples of this type of ornamentation can be found in the J. L. Pearson case at Eton College Chapel and in the R.C. Carpenter case at Sherborne Abbey as well as at Durham Cathedral. Very occasionally one sees pipes with patterns embossed on the surface of the metal. This practice seems to have originated in Holland in the sixteenth century; a brightly polished tin-metal pipe embossed in facets will catch the light in a very jewel-like way. Noel Mander's organ at Corpus Christi College, Cambridge has some pipes of this form and there is one in his nave organ case at Canterbury Cathedral.

The shape of the mouths of the pipes can also be used for decorative effect. Although the lower lip is nearly always semi-circular, there is considerable scope for variety in the shape of the top lip which has to join the cylindrical upper part of the pipe to a flat surface. The lip can be pointed, in a shape known as the 'bay-leaf', or round-topped, sometimes called a 'French mouth'. The use of a boss above the point of a bay-leaf mouth is generally attributed to Father Smith. In the largest pipes the lips are made from a separate piece of metal

39

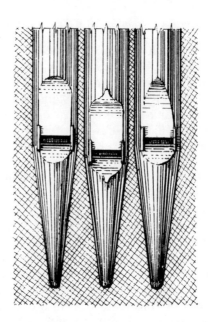

Fig 10 Decorative pipe-mouths

and the upper and lower extremities may be raised away from the pipe body to emphasise the outline. Most organ cases use only one shape of pipe-mouth, but a mixture of mouth types can be seen in seventeenth-century organ cases by Thomas and Renatus Harris.

Tin-lead alloy, whilst relatively easy to work, is not the most rigid of materials especially if the tin content is fairly low. This can be a problem with very large pipes because their weight, concentrated on the tip of the pipe-foot, causes the tips to bend into a shape resembling an elephant's foot. Some nineteenth-century builders put more tin in the metal, the resulting 'spotted metal' having not only greater strength but also an attractive mottled effect on the surface. Other builders experimented with wrought iron, but from about 1870 onwards most display pipes have been made of zinc with 'pipe metal' reserved for the lips and other parts that the voicer has to manipulate. Zinc is relatively cheap and relatively strong; it can be made thin so that the pipe is not too heavy, though this can mean that the note itself is also lacking in weight. However, naked zinc is not particularly nice to look at. It oxidises relatively quickly to a powdery matt grey and most zinc pipes are ultimately painted; it is almost impossible to gild zinc satisfactorily. For these reasons zinc is now less popular, and either polished tin metal or polished or oxidised copper is commonly used in new organs.

Having considered the position of the organ within the building and looked at its casework and appearance, we can now approach the instrument itself and the console from which it is played. Apart from its functional capabilities, the console is often a fine piece of furniture in its own right. Consoles richly decorated with inlay are a Continental phenomenon rather than a British one but certainly this is where an organ-builder puts his best cabinet-maker to work. Even if the case is pine, the console is usually oak because pine will not take the wear and tear of constant use. Other timbers sometimes used are mahogany (in conjunction with a mahogany case), walnut and afrormosia. Sometimes more exotic woods are used for contrasting effect, and ivory has for long been a favourite material not only for keys but for other accessories.

The most usual position for the console is also the obvious one, on the front of the organ in the middle, set into the case sufficiently far to allow it to be closed off by sliding or folding doors. This layout is sometimes referred to as 'en fenêtre'. The advantage of such an arrangement is that it makes the action connections short and simple. The disadvantage is that the player depends on a large mirror over the music desk to see what is going on around him – hence the famous Hoffnung cartoon of the organist with the speed-cop visible in his rear-view mirror!

In some countries the console was reversed, with the player facing away from the instrument and the action passing under his feet. It allowed the player to see directly about him. This arrangement is not often seen in Britain, but the late nineteenth-century development of tubular pneumatic action allowed the console to be tied far less rigidly to the organ, leading to the evolution of the free-standing detached console. The invention of electropneumatic action reduced the delays inherent in long tubular actions and also cut down the size of the connection to a few electric cables giving still greater freedom of layout. Robert Hope-Jones, who developed the first widely used electropneumatic action, actually had a photograph taken of himself playing the organ in Birkenhead parish church from a console outside the church door!

The detached console became almost universal in the theatre organ, where the consoles were often housed in highly exotic enclosures and placed on an electrically powered lift so that the player could emerge from the depths and rise, playing, into the spotlight. In cathedrals and large churches, where the position of the organ often made communication between choir and player something of a problem, the provision of detached consoles also became common. In those cathedrals where the organ is on a screen and is used for services both in the chancel and in the nave, two consoles are sometimes found.

Like all new inventions, the detached console was pushed to its artistic limits and beyond. The speed of sound is finite and, however good the action, its response will seem slow to a player over 40ft (12m) away from the pipes, purely through acoustic lag. There are problems of balance too; an organ at the west-end played from a console in the chancel will be nearer to the congregation than to the organist who may be quite unaware of the vigour with which he is attacking their ears! For these reasons, and because of the trend back to mechanical key-action, the detached console has fallen almost completely out of favour.

The manual keys are the heart of the console and have really changed surprisingly little in the past five hundred years. Early keys were relatively short, with ebony sharps and natural keys of some light-coloured timber such as boxwood. Quite often the front faces of the natural keys, below the playing surface, were decorated, either with a horizontal moulding or with a semi-circular pattern. The width of the keys has remained almost standard, being governed by the need to span an octave but yet be able to insert the middle fingers between the sharp keys. By the eighteenth century it had become customary for all keyboard instruments to have the key coverings reversed, with black naturals and light-coloured or ivory sharps. The near universal use of ivory for the natural keys dates from about 1780 and, again, is characteristic of all keyboard instruments. Only relatively recently have organ and harpsichord keyboards diverged from the custom in piano-making, where the use of ivory-coloured plastics has now entirely replaced the real thing. The better organ-builders have resisted this trend and where ivory cannot be afforded prefer to use wood- or bone-surfaced keys.

The popularity of romantic music in the nineteenth century meant that players alternated between manuals more frequently and also developed the practice of 'thumbing-down', picking out a solo on a lower manual with the thumb whilst the other fingers remained on the manual above. This required the playing surfaces of the manuals to be as close together as possible and led to the development of over-hanging manuals in which the wooden slip which supports the key guide pins is set back from the front face of the keys. In order to provide clearance for the back of the fingers playing the manual below, the front face of the key is either angled or, in the best work, of ogee form. For similar basic reasons, on organs with three or more manuals, it is common to incline the upper manuals a few degrees towards the player.

The pedal keyboard, or 'pedalboard' for short, was of very limited compass when first introduced to this country and had very short keys designed to be played with the tip of the shoe. As the compass expanded, it was found useful to make the keys longer to allow the feet to be passed one in front of the other. The longer compass led to problems in the other direction though, since the keys could not be too close together or a wide shoe would play two notes at once. Conversely, if the pedalboard were too wide, the top and bottom notes would be out of reach. The inventive German organ-builder, Edmund Schulze, showed an instrument at the 1851 Great Exhibition with a concave pedalboard, the notes at either end being higher than those in the middle. It is reputed that this attracted the attention of S. S. Wesley who persuaded Henry Willis to copy the idea for his magnum opus in St George's Hall, Liverpool and, in addition, to make the keys radiate from a point behind the organ stool. The radiating keys, placed further under the manuals than a straight pedalboard, permit a different pedalling technique, making use of the heels as well as the toes. The radiating and concave pedalboard was gradually to become standard in Britain and the USA, though it remains uncommon in France, Germany, Holland and Scandinavia. This has led, since about 1960, to attempts to re-introduce the straight pedalboard, partly on grounds of economy and partly by players trained in Continental playing styles. Pedal keys suffer much more wear than manual keys, of course, so they must be robust. Appearance is less important, since one should play by feel, but where rosewood is used for the sharps it gives a clear differentiation from natural keys which may be of white birch, sometimes with a top surface of rock maple.

The stop-action, unlike the key-action, usually requires a fair amount of force to operate it. This is most easily accommodated by providing a knob, something like a small drawer knob, which is pulled out to bring the stop 'on'. This is the origin of the everyday expression 'He pulled out all the stops', signifying maximum energy. At first the stops were differentiated by paper labels with manuscript inscriptions, fixed to the 'jamb' through which the stops protruded. This method continued to be used in France to the end of the eighteenth century. In Britain, however, it became customary to inlay an ivory plate in the surface of the knob and to engrave the stop-name on the plate. In the eighteenth and early nineteenth centuries this engraving was in manuscript, but Victorian organs mostly have excellent hand-engraved upper case lettering filled with black wax. Early in the present century this was replaced for a while by photo-chemical 'endolithic' engraving, but this had a relatively short vogue as it fades to an unattractive brown after a few years.

At an early date it became usual to place the stop-knobs in vertical columns on two jambs either side of the keys and music desk, parallel to the line of the keys but, for convenience, set back a few inches from the line of the key fronts. This was simple in construction, made it easy to see which stops were drawn, and allowed simple mechanical connection to the soundboard mechanism. With the nineteenth-century trend to music with more changes of tone and power, more frequent operation of the stops was called for and different arrangements were tried. In France, Cavaillé-Coll developed a console, easy to see over, with the stops arranged in horizontal terraces on either side of the keys. Some Hill organs of the 1870s had a version of this style, but the arrangement which became standard was to retain the vertical columns but with the jambs angled toward the player.

When the development of tubular pneumatic key-action divorced the organ console from the fairly rigid relationship which had formerly tied it to the layout of the organ, it was necessary to devise pneumatic means of moving the stop-action also. This meant that the pneumatics did the work and that the stop-knob, being now merely a control, could be made relatively light in operation. The knobs could be made smaller and closer together, facilitating operation in groups. In order to retain a sufficiently large area for engraving the name, the knob-heads were now made of solid ivory, in the same way that the tiny knobs of chamber organs had been made a century earlier. Solid ivory knobs have remained the standard in the best work ever since.

A free-standing stop-knob console is a fairly bulky piece of furniture and Robert Hope-Jones, who so strongly advocated detached consoles in the 1890s in conjunction with his then new electropneumatic action, devised a completely new and much more compact form of console, one example of which still partly survives in St George's Church, Hanover Square, Mayfair, London. Here the stops were controlled by small 'tilting tablets' of ivory, horizontally pivoted and engraved with the stop-name on the face; one pressed the bottom for 'on' and the top for 'off'. The tablets were arranged almost touching in a horizontal arc. This arc form was to become the basis of the 'horseshoe' shaped consoles which were standard for the theatre organ of the 1920s.

Theatre-organ consoles use 'stop-keys', plastic or ivory tablets sloping down towards the player and hinged at the back. The organ writer G. A. Audsley (who disliked them) described stop-keys as 'a row of gigantic teeth'. The stop-key is pressed down for 'on' and flipped up with the finger for 'off'. If 'double-touch cancelling' is provided an extra firm push, or a push at the back of the key, will cause all other stops to be put 'off' giving an instant solo. The use of the stop-key is not confined to theatre organs, restrained versions of the horseshoe console being commonly used on three-manual instruments in the period 1930–50 and, in a simplified version with the stop-keys in a single straight line under the music desk, was virtually standard for two-manual organs up to about 1970. Indeed, stop-keys are still in use for small extension organs and for electronic imitations, though all other instruments are now made with conventional stop-knobs.

The problem with the stop-key console is that it ignores the fundamental ergonomic fact that when playing the organ one has no time actually to read the stop-names: this has been done beforehand and the position remembered. It is much easier to memorise the position of a well-spaced knob than one of a row of closely spaced and identically shaped stop-keys. American builders have attempted to get the best of both worlds by combining conventional stop-knobs on jambs with a single row of rocking-tablets or stop-keys under the music desk to control the numerous couplers with which their organs are provided. This arrangement reduces the height of the console and has been used in Britain by Willis and others.

In the 1930s a further form of stop-control was developed for what became known as the luminous console. Those made by Rutt have 'tilting tablets' sprung to a midway position with a small coloured indicator light which comes on with the stop, the whole effect being reminiscent of a railway signal cabin of the period. Those made by Compton are more conventional, looking very like a stop-knob console but with engraved ivory-coloured studs in place of the knobs. When the studs are pushed, they glow 'on' from an internal light, a second push putting them off. The Compton type is very quiet and convenient to use; the cost of the 'on–off' reversible mechanism plus the problems of miniature bulb replacement prevented its perpetuation.

Organists have always wished to be able to change the stops rapidly at critical points in the music. In the eighteenth century a pedal was sometimes provided, coupled to a hidden duplicate stop-action which could quickly cut out certain predetermined stops and as quickly reinstate them when released. This 'shifting movement' was introduced by Abraham Jordan in 1730 but was costly to make, inflexible (the stops affected could not be altered except by major reconstruction) and operated 'blind', misleadingly leaving the stops in their original positions. In the 1840s J. C. Bishop invented 'composition pedals', a series of iron pedals, projecting through the kneeboard above the pedal keys, which drew or withdrew preselected groups of stops. Commonly three each were provided for the Swell and Great manuals with an additional 'reversible' pedal which drew the Great-to-Pedal coupler if it were off or cancelled it if it were on.

Mechanical composition pedals are often noisy in operation, so when pneumatic action was invented it was an obvious step to make the pedal merely a control, allowing pneumatic mechanism to move the stop-knobs. It was but a short extra step for Henry Willis, in his organ for the Great Exhibition of 1851, to provide a very convenient additional control in the shape of a 'thumb piston' located between the manuals. Although it was another fifty years before they became common, pistons have made rapid stop changes very much easier, largely eliminating the assistants formerly required at recitals to help draw the stops on large instruments.

Normally a visit from the organ-builder was needed to change the selected combination of stops, but towards the end of the nineteenth century pneumatic mechanisms were developed which enabled the current stop-setting to be recorded on a particular piston or composition pedal by means of a setter knob and then reproduced at will. One local newspaper, reporting this feature on a newly completed organ, is alleged to have recorded that 'the instrument is fitted with a mechanism which enables the organist to change his combinations without leaving his seat'! The mechanism by which this was achieved was not unlike the adjustable mechanical tuning buttons on present-day car radios but it was the development of electric action which made the 'piston action' so much cheaper to make and allowed the lavish provision of pistons characteristic of the theatre organ. By the 1930s pistons were provided not only for each department, but sometimes general pistons too, affecting the whole organ. The general piston most commonly provided is the (non-adjustable) General Cancel, or 'Good Night' piston as it is sometimes affectionately called. This most useful of devices, pressed at the end of a piece, ensures that no stop is left out by accident to trap the unwary player.

Electric-action pistons were fairly easily and inexpensively adjusted by banks of switches, concealed on the console, either in pull-out drawers or behind a hinged music desk. Nevertheless, the use of the setter system persisted in the most important organs, despite the cost, because of its convenience to the player. Since about 1970 the setter system has become more general, the advent of solid-state technology having cut the cost dramatically compared with previous electromechanical 'memories'. Indeed, today it is quite practicable to provide multiple sets of memories so that different performers can have their own private piston settings.

Not everyone is happy with all these technological wonders, the very complexity of which can affect their reliability. With small organs they are unnecessary, hand registration being sufficient, with stop-knobs mechanically connected to the action. Larger instruments, with more stop-knobs to control, are, however, very much easier to play if pistons are provided. This has led to the continued use of electric stop-action on instruments whose action is otherwise totally mechanical. If it can be afforded, some builders now use mechanical stop-action for reliability, supplemented by an electro-pneumatic or solenoid-driven piston action – truly a 'belt and braces' approach.

With the development of all these aids to the player, plus the obvious wear and tear to which the console is subjected, it is not surprising that the average life of the console of a large organ is much shorter than that of the rest of the instrument. Pedalboards and manual keys wear, music desks are attacked by the 'drawing-pin worm' and the player of our larger instruments can be genuinely assisted by the latest in piston controls. The result is that often the console is much younger than the rest of the instrument. In fact, except on chamber organs, consoles made before 1850 are now very rare indeed and should be zealously preserved.

There may be one more control on the organ console which has not yet been mentioned: either a pedal at the treble end with a stick to latch it down or, above and behind the pedal keys, in the centre of the kneeboard, an outsize version of the accelerator of an up-market motor car. This is known as the swell-pedal, and we will investigate its function and use further when we come to consider the tonal structure of the instrument (see chapter 3).

Finally, quite a number of organ consoles have a curious device in the form of a cylindrical brass or ivory weight hanging from a string which disappears into the face of the stop-jamb over a small pulley. This is the 'tell-tale', an indicator of how much wind there is in the bellows and a most necessary device when the wind was raised by a man pumping a bellows-handle. Stories of these men are still legion and Oliver Wendell Holmes even published a poem about them. The tell-tale is these days something of an ornament: organists and railway enthusiasts being sometimes one and the same person, it is perhaps not surprising that at one time the organ in the chapel of Bedford School had a scale model of a Stanier steam locomotive which progressed across the top of the music desk in response to varying demands on the organ wind supply!

The Roman *hydraulis* had a pair of simple piston pumps to compress the air but this was replaced at an early date by bellows, similar to a blacksmith's bellows today, plus a second set to replace the hydraulic cistern and store the air between strokes. This principle of two bellows – one, called the 'feeder', being the pump and the other larger one providing the storage – is quite fundamental, yet, like the stop-action, was forgotten at some stage in the transfer of organ-building knowledge to Byzantium and back again to Europe. Instead, medieval organs had multiple feeder bellows which were operated in turn to maintain a continuous supply. Modern copies of medieval Positives have been made with two feeders, lifted alternately and allowed to drop back under their own weight. These work perfectly satisfactorily.

The detailed design of the bellows is interesting for the methods used to maintain a constant pressure irrespective of the extent to which they are inflated, a most necessary objective because quite small variations in wind pressure will adversely affect the tuning of the organ. By the fifteenth century the simple bag of the blacksmith's bellows was replaced by a series of ribs and folds which allowed a much greater movement of the top board, hence a much greater capacity, with the result that the very large numbers of bellows needed for the bigger early medieval organs were no longer required. Nevertheless, the problem remained that, with a hinge at one end, a large angle of movement will obviously reduce the pressure when the weighted top is well above the horizontal. This effect was minimised later by having the bellows drop to an angle below the horizontal when closed so that its average position was more nearly level. There was, however, another difficulty; the ribs and folds exert a force on the top of the bellows which increases the pressure when nearly empty and reduces it when full. With multiple tiny ribs the effect was small but these were expensive to make and later instruments used fewer ribs. Even when the bellows had resumed its role as a pure storage reservoir, with one or more separate feeder bellows, this pressure variation was still important. From about the 1780s the hinged 'diagonal bellows' was replaced in Britain by the horizontal bellows, though it took almost another eighty years to become general in Germany; the organ that Schulze built in 1862 for Doncaster parish church still had diagonal feeders only, without a storage reservoir.

The horizontal double-rise bellows is the standard form of bellows to be found inside many Victorian parish church organs up and down the country. Built without a hinge, it has double the capacity of a diagonal bellows of the same size. The wind pressure is kept constant by providing a double set of ribs, one set folding in and the other folding outwards, neatly cancelling out their effect on the pressure. The floating frame between the two sets of ribs is held in position by a set of iron levers known (inaccurately) as a 'counterbalance'. The normal method of hand-blowing, often still in position though seldom

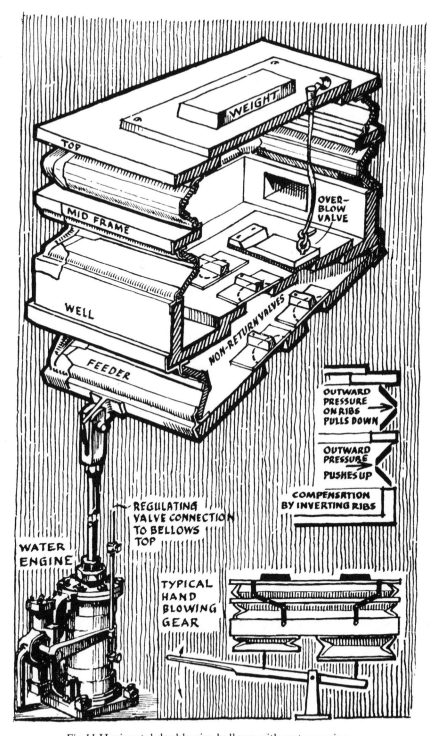

Within the figure:

WEIGHT

TOP

MID FRAME

OVER-BLOW VALVE

WELL

NON-RETURN VALVES

FEEDER

REGULATING VALVE CONNECTION TO BELLOWS TOP

WATER ENGINE

OUTWARD PRESSURE ON RIBS PULLS DOWN

OUTWARD PRESSURE PUSHES UP

COMPENSATION BY INVERTING RIBS

TYPICAL HAND BLOWING GEAR

Fig 11 Horizontal double-rise bellows with water engine

usable, is with a pine handle projecting about 4ft (1.25m) and connected to two feeders to make it double-acting. Eighteenth-century chamber organs were frequently fitted with a long single-acting iron pedal so that the player himself could blow, though an alternative handle at the side was sometimes provided. Larger organs could have more than one handle, and towards the end of the nineteenth century a wheel operating multiple feeders with cranks was sometimes provided. The German system of treadles, connected to the feeders by rope, is seldom, if ever, found in Britain.

The wind pressure of the organ is determined by the weight of the top of the bellows. Normally the framed and panelled top is insufficiently heavy and additional weights are required. Sometimes old flagstones were used, but most instruments have iron weights. Frequently these have the initials of the organ-builder cast into them; this can be a useful means of identifying the original builder of an instrument which has subsequently been altered. The pressure can be measured by a water manometer, a U-shaped glass tube half filled with water. One end is open to the air and the other connected to the organ wind supply. The difference in height between the two columns of water is the pressure and is measured either in inches or millimetres. In the early nineteenth century this was normally in the range 2¼–3¼in (55–80mm) but as the century progressed, and ever larger organs were more and more confined to organ-chambers, wind pressures began to rise. The really large organs were blown by steam-operated feeders at vast expense – the first being by Hill in 1854 – and later in the century Hill installed gas engines at Westminster Abbey. None of these machines now survives in use, nor probably any examples of their rival, the water engine. The water engine also dates from the 1850s. David Joy (the inventor of the Joy valve gear for steam railway locomotives) supplied five 'hydraulic engines' for the 1859 Gray & Davison organ in Leeds Town Hall. The water engine derived its power from the pressure of the public water supply and was much more widely used than steam or gas engines since power was instantly available and could be controlled from the organ console without additional assistance. The pressure of the water supply was variable, however; it was not unknown for the vicar to delay the last hymn until after the street-watering cart had been refilled from the main. The controlling stop-cock may still be seen in position on the consoles of late nineteenth-century instruments and the name of one of the more successful makers, Watkins & Watson, survives as a maker of rotary fan blowers.

As soon as electricity became available, it was natural to make use of the electric motor to drive the bellows feeders. A slow-speed

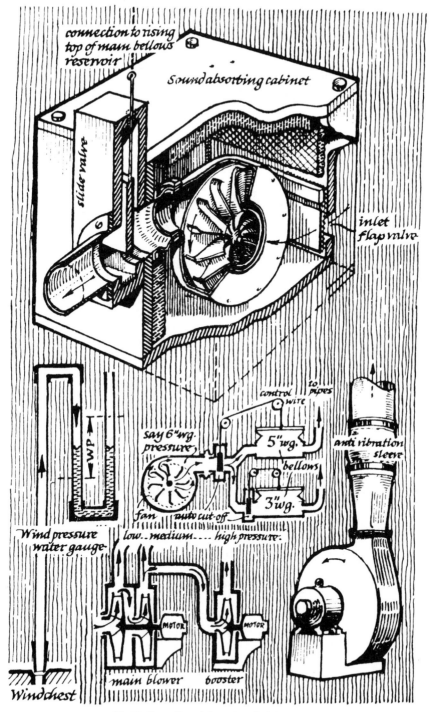

The following labels appear in the figure:

connection to rising
top of main bellows
reservoir

Sound absorbing cabinet

slide valve

inlet
flap valve

control
wire

to
pipes

say 6"wg.
pressure

5" wg.

bellows

3" wg.

anti vibration
sleeve

WP

fan

auto cut-off

low. medium.... high pressure.

Wind pressure
water gauge

MOTOR

MOTOR

main blower

booster

Windchest

Fig 12 Centrifugal-fan electric blowing

51

direct-current motor was geared down with worm, belt or chain gear to drive a crankshaft operating three feeders. The motor speed was controlled by inserting resistances when the main bellows was full. The equipment installed by Hill in 1913 in the City church of St Mary Woolnoth, was still in use until recently, and operated beautifully smoothly. It was so massively constructed that it outlasted the direct-current electricity supply that made it possible. Almost at the same time, however, a much more efficient and convenient method of using electric power was devised, one that is now virtually universal. Organ wind pressures are not very high in engineering terms and a centrifugal fan of suitable diameter, driven at about 1,000 or 1,500 rpm, can easily sustain a pressure of 6in (150mm) water gauge. If higher pressures are required, two fans can be used in series. The apparatus is compact, the flow of wind steady rather than in pulses and a constant-speed motor can be used since blocking the outlet when the bellows is full automatically reduces the load on the motor. Even though today most blowers run at 2,950 rpm they are quiet enough in a sound-resistant cabinet to be placed within the organ.

The advent of the fan blower completely changed organ wind supply. Feeders are not required and a large bellows is no longer needed to store wind. All that is necessary is a valve to regulate the steady flow of wind from the fan down to the required pressure, and this can be controlled by a relatively small bellows. If the valve is reasonably quick-acting, the bellows only moves through a small distance, so the double-rise construction is an unjustified complication, the pressure variation due to a single large rib being approximately cancelled out by the opposite variation achieved by replacing some of the weights with springs. Nevertheless, small single-rise bellows have their problems; any organ wind supply has a resonant frequency which shows itself as a variation in pressure when a heavy chord is released. The inertia of the air rushing along the wind-trunk causes this effect, which can be ameliorated by the provision of 'concussion bellows' at the soundboard to absorb momentarily some of the excess pressure. The large volume of a double-rise bellows keeps the resonant frequency low (around two or three times per second) and this is less offensive to the ear than the faster 'dither' resulting from the smaller volume of single-rise bellows.

One way of avoiding the problems of unsteady wind is to make the wind-trunk from the bellows as short as possible. In the first decade of this century some organs were built with a 'universal air chest' where the soundboard and bellows were combined in a box large enough to provide internal access to the mechanism, eliminating the wind-trunk altogether. More recently, the use of a low friction butterfly or simple

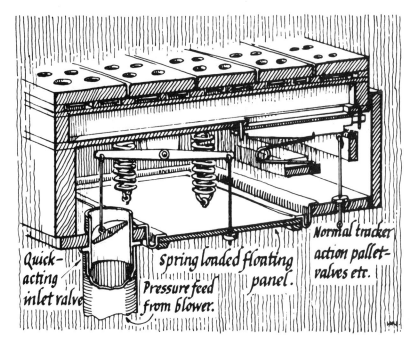

Fig 13 Schwimmer bellows built into a slider sound board

disk-valve has allowed the bellows to be made smaller still, to the point where it can be just a spring-tensioned diaphragm fitted to the bottom of the soundboard, again eliminating the wind-trunk. This device is known by its German name, the *schwimmer*. Both the universal air chest and the *schwimmer* can provide a wind supply that is totally steady, to the point that the conventional tremulant is ineffective. Players complain that the result is lifeless and there is now a move back to traditional separate bellows and even, in the search for inspiration from history, back to diagonal bellows, though the practice varies from builder to builder.

Details of the key-action will not be immediately obvious to anyone looking at an organ for the first time, but they will certainly be relevant the moment he or she touches the keys. We have already referred to the invention of the roller which allowed the key-to-soundboard motion to be transferred sideways, but we have not mentioned the backfall, which is used to transfer motion generally in the same plane as the keys, or the use of squares which turn the action through a right angle. These components are connected by long thin strips of wood, called 'trackers', which convey the motion of the key. Their ends are fitted with wires to connect to the rollers, backfalls or squares. The wire often has a thread on it carrying a self-locking adjustable leather nut, called a 'button'. This is used for setting up

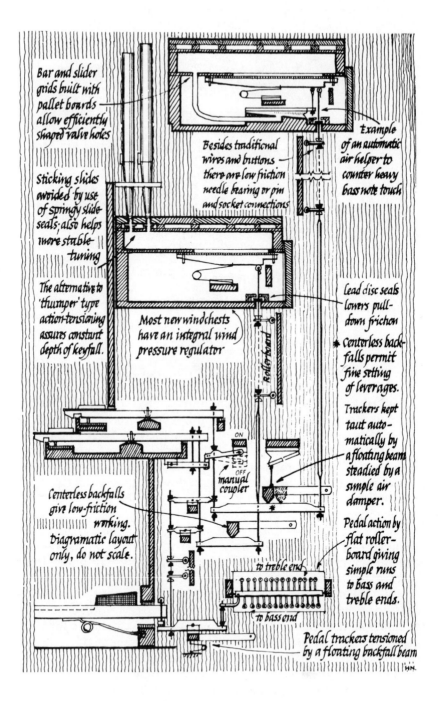

Fig 14 Present-day backfall-type tracker action

and regulating the action. Some actions use round or rectangular wooden connections which push instead of pull. These are called 'stickers'. They can only be of limited length, otherwise they would bend sideways when pushed, but can be found in chamber organs and for short connections in larger instruments.

If the key-touch is to feel crisp and positive there must be no lost motion in the connections, so the organ is best designed with action going up and down rather than with trackers running horizontally, when they tend to sag under their own weight. It also helps if the action is kept taut, so most actions have a weighted 'thumper' on top of the keys, out of sight behind the desk, which exerts a gentle pressure all the time and takes up any variation in the relationship between keys and soundboard resulting from differences of temperature or humidity. For this to work, it is essential that the action is accurately adjusted; if the keys are uneven, the thumper will press harder on some notes than on others. Many modern organs have more sophisticated systems of action tensioning than the thumper, whereby the tension is applied to a 'floating backfall' and the depth of touch is fixed. Such a system normally needs a damping device to prevent sudden movement of the backfall when a very heavy chord is held.

One of the lessons that has been learned in recent years is that it is important to reduce the inertia of the moving parts to a minimum if the action is to be responsive and to follow the player's fingers precisely. This has meant cutting away any non-functional timber, using thinner trackers than before and designing the organ to keep the action as simple and direct as possible. In pursuit of this ideal some builders have copied the old French 'suspended action' in which backfalls are eliminated and the trackers are connected to the tops of the keys, forward of the pivot, thus obtaining a direct vertical pull. This arrangement works well in small organs but is difficult to combine with the couplers and tensioning devices needed in larger instruments.

In the past, the main problem with mechanical tracker key-action has been the sheer effort required to depress the keys, particularly with the manuals coupled. This became a real problem in the middle of the nineteenth century when organs became larger and wind pressures were increased. The problems of designing a light action increase as the square of the size of the organ and were not helped by Victorian ignorance of the engineering mathematics involved. The pallet valves or 'pallets' in the soundboard need considerable force to overcome the pressure of the wind which normally helps to hold them closed. If these valves are wrongly proportioned or the leverage of

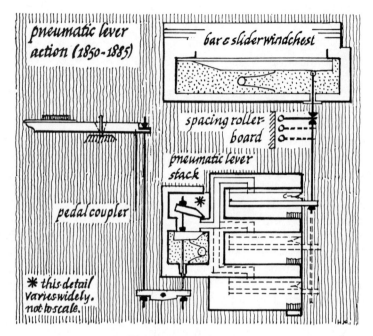

Fig 15 Pneumatic lever action

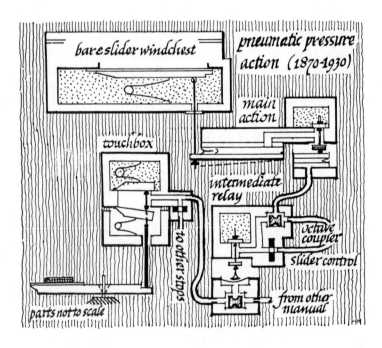

Fig 16 Tubular-pneumatic action

the action is wrong, then the 'touch' is unnecessarily heavy. Today, quite large organs can be built with an excellent touch and tracker action, but in the middle of the nineteenth century this was a real problem and organ-builders turned to pneumatic power to help them out.

Pneumatic lever action was the first form of pneumatic action and was used purely as a means of lightening the touch. Although a British invention, it was much more widely used in France than in this country. Since the action was expensive to make, it was quite common to fit it only to the Great organ where the couplers could be arranged to work through it, thus lightening the coupled touch. The principle of operation is that depression of the key operates a pallet valve which is smaller than the one in the soundboard. Air from this valve is taken to a small bellows, known as a pneumatic 'motor'. This motor is connected by trackers to the pallet in the soundboard and, when inflated, opens it. Lever actions generally date from 1850 to about 1885. They were apt to be noisy and relatively few now remain.

The next development was to separate the valve operated by the key from the motors working the soundboard pallets and to connect the two by lead tubing. The first major use of tubular pneumatic action was by Willis in the organ of St Paul's Cathedral, London in 1872. Willis divided the organ in two (the arrangement we see today) and used a tubular action to connect the console on the north side to the Swell and Choir organs on the south side. We have already noted that tracker-action organs are best with a fairly vertical layout, and it is perhaps self-evident that the layout must also be simple if complication of the action and consequent expense is to be avoided. Tubular-pneumatic action released organ-builders from these constraints since departments could be placed wherever the tubes would reach, without worrying about rollerboards, backfalls and squares. Organ-builders rapidly discovered that by using a chain of valves and motors – small motor working small valve controlling larger motor etc – the action could be made sufficiently sensitive for quite tiny tubes to be used. Furthermore, with some extra relays and tubing, the manual coupling could be incorporated in the action so that the key-touch is quite unaffected by the number of couplers drawn. Mechanical action was usually retained for the pedal couplers. Numerous examples of organs with this type of action can still be found, though dust and pollution eventually rots the leather motors which then require recovering with fresh split-sheepskin.

A later development of tubular-pneumatic action was the 'exhaust' action. As its name implies, the principle is that the air is 'exhausted' from the tube to make the note come 'on' instead of the other way

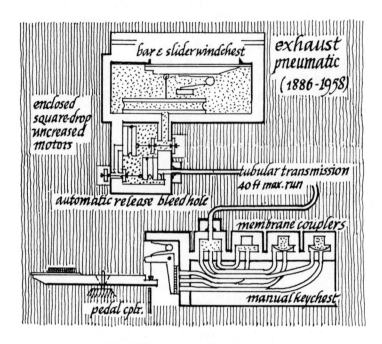

Fig 17 Exhaust-pneumatic action

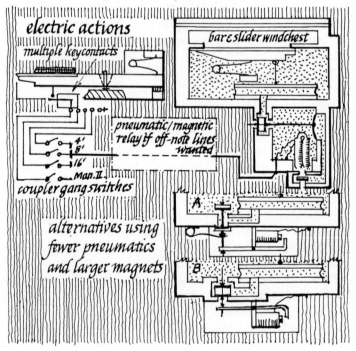

Fig 18 Electropneumatic actions

58

round. In theory, such an action ought to be unreliable because any leakage can produce a 'cipher' (a note stuck 'on'). In practice, it proved to be the most long-lasting and reliable of the pneumatic actions, since all the leather action motors are inside the soundboard, under air pressure, and are thus protected from atmospheric pollution. The coupling action, a series of membranes, has few moving parts and is very compact. Exhaust action was made only by certain builders and 'charge action' versus 'exhaust action' was a hot topic of debate in the first twenty-five years of this century. Exhaust action continued to be made up to about 1960.

The weak link of all tubular actions is the lead tubing. Poorly supported tubes will sag in time and may become choked as they flatten themselves on bends. A more fundamental difficulty is that the puff of air which triggers the mechanism will travel along the tube no faster than the speed of sound, 55ft (16.5m) in a twentieth of a second. If the console is far from the pipes one has a double delay: the puff of air going one way and the sound itself coming back. This has given pneumatic actions a general reputation for unresponsiveness which, if the console is detached, may well be deserved.

The problems of heavy touch in the mid-nineteenth century led people to think of using large magnets to open the soundboard pallets. The influential Dr H. J. Gauntlett proposed that the organs in the Great Exhibition of 1851 should be connected with electric action so that they could all be played together. He later took out a patent for electric action, which was quite unworkable at the time. Willis built a successful action for Canterbury Cathedral in 1886 but it was Robert Hope-Jones who startled the organ world in the 1890s with several major instruments fitted with his electropneumatic action and with consoles so far detached that tubular action would have been too sluggish to be playable. Problems with the tungsten key-contacts made the Hope-Jones action unreliable and few, if any, remain in their original condition today. The early electric actions were expensive to make and Hope-Jones went bankrupt. He fled to America, where his ideas were taken up, developed and made to work reliably by the Rudolph Wurlitzer Co, who then shipped them back to Europe in the form of the Wurlitzer Unit organ to accompany the silent films in the new motion picture theatres of the 1920s. Daily use in the cinema soon refined the design, and from about 1930 most new instruments were made with electropneumatic action.

An electropneumatic action is similar to an exhaust pneumatic action but with the smallest pneumatic movement replaced by an electromagnetically operated valve. The tubing is replaced by a multicore cable; multi-contact switches constitute the coupling mechanism. When the number of couplers or borrowings exceeds the number of fine silver contacts that can be accommodated under the keys, relays are required. These relays may themselves be electro-pneumatic and are sometimes, as in the Compton organ, combined with the coupling switches in one mechanism. Hope-Jones ran his organs from batteries but later instruments derived the power for their electric action from a rotary generator driven by a belt from the blower. A voltmeter is fitted at the console so that belt-slip can be detected.

Since about 1960 most electric actions have been powered by a static transformer-rectifier set and the voltmeter omitted. People are sometimes concerned by the potential risk of fire from a fault in electric action. In fact, this is most unlikely as the power available from the normal 15 volt supply is so small. Not all organs fitted with electropneumatic action were originally built as such; probably the majority are rebuilds of organs originally fitted with other actions. It is quite common to find instruments with basically a pneumatic action which has been adapted to electric transmission, perhaps in conjunction with a new console.

The development of the unit extension organ involved the use of a completely new design of soundboard, so it is appropriate at this point to explain the principles of organ soundboard construction. Although invisible to the player, the soundboards can have an important influence on the working of the instrument.

First of all, the term 'soundboard' is completely misleading; nor is the alternative 'windchest' much better. The soundboard of a harpsichord or piano is an essential acoustic link between the vibrating string and its surroundings. The soundboard of an organ fills no such function. Basically, it is a box on which the pipes stand, fed with wind from the bellows and containing mechanism to let the air into the feet of the appropriate pipes. In the Roman organ this control was obtained by a set of bronze slides with holes communicating with similar holes in the fixed metal sheets above and below them and which formed the top of the soundboard. These slides were directly connected to levers on the keys and were returned by springs. The slider soundboard most commonly found in organs today works on very similar principles, save that it is made of wood and that the whole construction is turned through a right angle, so that the slides form the stop-action instead of the key-action. The key-action is connected to a series of pallet valves, long narrow pieces of pine, hinged at one end, with their surfaces covered in soft leather or felt and leather. In the classic construction of the slider soundboard these pallets sit on a pine grid, the spaces between the bars of the grid forming windways which conduct the air to all the pipes sounded by a given key. The top of the grid is sealed by a mahogany 'table' with holes drilled to admit air to each pipe. Above the table are the upperboards with matching holes countersunk on the top surface to accept the tips of the pipes. Between the upperboard and the table are thin sliders, connected to the stop-action and also with matching holes coinciding with the others when the stop is 'on'.

The slider soundboard depends for its satisfactory working on being properly airtight between the parts and especially on the accurate fitting of the slides themselves. Too little clearance and the slide will be stiff, causing the stop-action to stick; too much clearance and the wind will 'run' along the slide causing unwanted pipes to half sound. When churches began to be heated in the nineteenth century, this construction gave trouble. The relative humidity of the atmosphere drops from its normal seventy per cent to under fifty per cent in a heated building in winter, causing timber to lose moisture and to shrink at right angles to the grain. As the pine grid was necessarily at right angles to the grain of the table, slides and upperboards, this construction ensured that when the humidity dropped much below fifty per cent the mahogany table would split, allowing wind to run between one bar channel and another. The splits destroyed the glue joint between grid and table so that the table was no longer held flat, causing the slides to stick.

In Germany and in America the winter climate is drier than in Britain, and in those countries the slider soundboard was abandoned in favour of sliderless soundboards, in which there is a separate pallet for each pipe, and the note-grid and slides are eliminated. The stop-action is a large valve, called a 'ventil', which admits air to a chamber containing only those pallets governing a particular stop. The note-action, connecting all the pallets in the various stop-chambers governing one note, is relatively complex and requires a separate pneumatic motor for each pallet. However, the motors have a relatively short life as they are either external or the leather has wind pressure on it all the time the organ is on but both note and stop are 'off'. An improved sliderless soundboard, developed in America, is the 'pitman' soundboard in which the ventils are eliminated, the soundboard being full of wind all the time. Both ventil and pitman soundboards were used by some British builders in the period 1930–65.

The unit organ developed by Wurlitzer also has a one-pallet-per-pipe action, with the soundboards continuously full of wind. Instead of being pneumatic, as in the pitman soundboard, the stop-action is by electric switching, each pipe-action having its own magnet. This system was widely copied, not only for theatre organs but also for church organs constructed on the unit system. A disadvantage of all these sliderless soundboards is their large number of pneumatic motors. Although they have a long life in the pitman and unit chest systems, when they do fail, the cost of repair is correspondingly high. A more fundamental criticism of the sliderless soundboard is that the action is not guaranteed to be simultaneous for all the stops drawn, though this is normally only a practical problem if the soundboard is badly designed or in bad order. More modern sliderless soundboards may use electromagnetic action (sometimes called 'direct electric' action). Here a more powerful magnet is used, capable of directly opening a pallet big enough to feed a single pipe. This eliminates the maintenance liability of the leather pneumatic motors, and in this form the action is measurably faster than electropneumatic action so that lack of simultaneous action is not then a practical problem.

The most serious weakness of some sliderless soundboard designs is the placing of the pallet immediately under the foot of the pipe. The faster the action the more problems this causes. The sudden movement of the pallet generates a momentary vacuum in the foot of the pipe, which then has to have its languid set lower to get quick speech, spoiling the tone of the pipe. A proper expansion chamber between the pallet and the pipe-foot will overcome this problem completely, as it does in slider soundboards, but its absence will seriously affect the speech and tone of the flue-stops.

The use of larger magnets (known as lever magnets) only became practical when builders learned how to suppress the spark which jumps across the key or relay contacts when the magnet circuit is broken, and which erodes the fine silver wire of which the contacts are made. The development of the solid state relay first used in 1963 virtually eliminated key-contact wear and, in conjunction with diode rectifiers used as one-way valves, replaced the use of mechanical key-action relays with their associated action delay. Solid-state coupling became available in about 1969 and is now widely used.

Multiplexer actions are now on the market which take solid-state switching one stage further. Instead of hundreds of wires connecting the keys to the organ, there is a single coaxial cable, used in conjunction with a circuit which scans the key-contacts many times per second to see which notes are 'on'. A second scanning circuit in the organ, in phase with the first, decodes which notes are which. This mechanism is exceptionally compact and easy to install but its real importance lies in the attachment of a solid-state 'memory' which can remember what the organ has played and reproduce it again at will. The artistic possibilities of this device have yet to be fully explored, both in terms of a teaching aid and the possibility of using it as a contemporary 'player' mechanism, an unattended organ performing music which has been distributed not on paper rolls but in the form of magnetic tape or floppy disc.

Some organ-builders advocate the application of electromagnetic/direct electric action to slider soundboards. Such an action is usually quiet (having no pneumatic valves to exhaust) and promises longevity (no leather motors to wear out). It also uses more current, although this is not a problem if the solid-state coupling action has been properly engineered. Unfortunately, direct action can also be slow, because of the inertia, both mechanical and electrical, of the large magnets which are needed. The most sophisticated builders have overcome this weakness by the use of multiple small magnets or by using a single smaller magnet combined with a pneumatic 'helper'.

Despite all these developments and inventions, the majority of new organs are being made not with the latest in electric actions, but with mechanical tracker actions and slider soundboards. This is mostly due to the *Orgelbewegung* (Organ Reform Movement) whose full influence will be discussed in chapter 3. England is probably the only country in the world where construction of the slider soundboard never ceased, despite its problems in conditions of varying humidity. Organ humidifiers have been developed which can help protect old soundboards, but for new construction the slider soundboard has been re-engineered. The problem of splitting is eliminated by changing the material of the table to either plywood or chipboard, the pallets being seated on a separate pallet-board instead of directly on the soundboard grid. The provision of a resilient seating around each pipe-hole takes up inaccuracies in the slide fitting and reduces the risk of leakage.

As already mentioned, tracker action has also been re-engineered and today quite large organs can be built which have an excellent touch. Nevertheless, one cannot attribute the revival of tracker action to mere dogmatism, so what are the advantages to be set against detached consoles and the other seductive features of electric action? Certainly, a good tracker action will probably last longer but such a mundane matter is not really all-important to musicians. More important is the fact that the player can control the attack of a classically-voiced stop by the way in which the keys are put down. This sounds a rather esoteric point, even though one can prove that the difference of attack is audible to the audience as well as to the player. Research in another field may provide the answer. Scientists have found that typists make fewer mistakes on their (electric action) computer terminal keyboards if the touch weight decreases at the moment the contact is made. They call this 'tactile feedback', the ability to feel with one's fingers when the key has done its work. Such a touch is characteristic of good tracker action and may well be the reason why players prefer it. If, by this means, organists feel that they have better control, they will play more accurately, just as the typist does. It is this better performance and the self-confidence that goes with it that is an asset to the music. Even if the audience cannot directly hear the difference in attack, it will still be worth while if the performance as a whole is enhanced.

3

HOW TO LOOK AT ORGANS

History and tonal structure

The majority of musical instruments have evolved over the years into something approaching a static form. Today's concert grand piano is the same in all essentials as one made eighty years ago. The design of the violin has hardly changed since Antonio Stradivari. Yet the organ, much older than either of these, continues to change, like the Vicar of Bray, to reflect the priorities of the day.

It was inevitable that, with poor communications, the organ would develop in separate directions in different countries. By the end of the eighteenth century, the organ had developed distinct national characteristics. However, one cannot study the British organ in isolation since organ-builders did travel, even three hundred and fifty years ago, and ideas gradually migrated from one country to another. In this century these migrations have accelerated as communications have become easier and the gramophone record and the tape cassette have facilitated the transfer of knowledge. Thus national characteristics seem now to be diminishing and organ design moving towards a more international character.

It is arguable whether this record of continuous change in artistic design will be continued further in response to new musical stimuli. It has to be admitted that contemporary music is probably played less frequently today than in any previous period; nor does contemporary music appear to be leading the organ in any particular direction. There are those who maintain that the organ of early eighteenth-century Hanseatic north Germany was the high point of the design of the instrument, that all subsequent development has been decadent and that on this basis organ design should now remain static, copying historic models as accurately as possible. On balance, this seems unlikely to happen, but enough has been said to underline the importance of history in the tonal structure of the organ and it will be used as a framework for the following description.

As a result of the destruction of organs by the Protestant zealots in the mid-sixteenth century, we have almost no records of the British organ before 1600, and only scanty evidence of its development before 1660. Although a few organ cases survive – Old Radnor (Powys), Stanford-on-Avon (Northamptonshire), King's College, Cambridge, Tewkesbury Abbey (Gloucestershire) (built for Magdalen College, Oxford) and Framlingham Church (Suffolk) (built for Pembroke College, Cambridge) – the earliest complete instrument is the tiny 1602 chamber organ of three stops now in Carisbrooke Castle, Isle of Wight. Even this instrument is now thought to have been imported. What we do know is that the organs were mostly quite small, almost invariably with but a single manual, and on nothing like the grand scale of the three-manual and pedal instruments built in the sixteenth century for major churches in Holland and Germany.

It is open to conjecture that the British organ was perhaps influenced by Italian artists brought over by Henry VIII during the Renaissance. Certainly the Italian organ, with its single manual and its stop-list composed almost entirely of a chorus of Diapason-tone pipes, was very similar to the little that we know of the design of British organs of the period. Compare the stop-list of the 1508 organ in Milan Cathedral with that of the Great organ of Robert Dallam's 1639 instrument for Lichfield Cathedral.

	Milan	*Lichfield*	
Tenore	(Open Diapason 8ft)	Open Diapason	8ft
Octava	(Octave 4ft)	Open Diapason	8ft
Duodecima	(Twelfth 2⅔ft)	Principal	4ft
Quintadecima	(Fifteenth 2ft)	Principal	4ft
Decima nona	(Nineteenth 1⅓)	Twelfth	2⅔ft
Vigesima seconda	(Twenty-second 1ft)	Small Principal	2ft
Vigesima sesta	(Twenty-sixth ⅔ft)	Twenty-second	1ft
Vigesima nona	(Twenty-ninth ½ft)		

These stop-lists illustrate the importance of the chorus of Diapason-toned pipes in the tonal structure of the organ. It is the bass pipes of these stops which we see on display in organ cases, and the pitches above the unison are named according to their relation to it, the tone quality being assumed. The scale (diameter) of a typical pipe is in the range 1–1¼in (25–31mm) at treble C 8ft pitch. In the Roman organ all the pipes seem to have been made the same diameter, but as the compass of the instrument was probably little more than an octave this would cause no great problems. This constant scale was retained by the early medieval builders, but as the compass increased to over two octaves so a pronounced change in tone quality between treble and bass became unavoidable. Medieval theorists argued that to retain a constant tone quality the proportions of the pipes should remain constant. Thus, just as a pipe an octave higher is but half the length so it should also be half the diameter. In practice this does not work very well either; the upper notes become too thin. Organ-builders tempered theory with practical experience, one way being to work to the theoretical scale, halving the diameter every octave, but adding a 'secret' constant to the width of every pipe, effectively slowing up the reduction in the diameters of the treble pipes.

Once a practical scaling method had been established which could retain a consistent tone quality over a range of four octaves or more, organ-builders learned to use scale as a means of varying tone quality. Italian organs, for example, were equipped with wide-scale Flauto stops. Returning again to Robert Dallam's Lichfield Cathedral instrument, we find that the second manual had a flute stop too, in this case made of wood. We also find that there was a Stopped Diapason. Here we have a pipe which obtains its tonal difference in another way: by making it stopped, the even-numbered harmonics are suppressed. The scale is no larger than the Open Diapason, often a little smaller, but the stoppering normally puts the voice at least theoretically into the flute category. The suppression of harmonics is aided by making the pipes of wood and this leads us to the whole question of the influence of pipe materials on tone.

In general, it is the shape and scale of a pipe which determines the tone. This is only to be expected since, except for reed-pipes, the primary vibration is purely a movement of air. Nevertheless, unless made of a totally inert material, the pipe structure cannot help but vibrate also and this must influence the tone to some extent. In practice, this effect seems to be more important in the bass than in the treble: the difference between a wooden Stopped Diapason and a metal one is almost undetectable in the top octave, but very apparent in the bass. Although there are considerable differences between builders, the general practice is to use different materials in a way which complements differences in pipe scale and shape. Thus it is usual to use wood for bass pipes of essentially flute tone, usually a straight-grained pine. English builders have also commonly used wood for stopped pipes because of the mechanical difficulties of fitting stoppers satisfactorily into pipes of tin–lead alloy.

A more subtle difference is obtained by varying the proportions of lead and tin in metal pipes. Again, in the best work, different materials are used to complement differences in basic tone colour. Thick metal containing under twenty per cent tin is used for Flutes but 'richer' metal, cast thin but of adequate strength by using fifty per cent tin (spotted metal) or seventy per cent tin (tin-metal) is used for

Principals and string-toned stops. The use of high tin content pipes to aid brilliance in a large building is very common in northern Europe. Nevertheless, many highly regarded British organs contain few pipes, if any, with over twenty-five per cent tin.

Returning once more to Robert Dallam's organ for Lichfield Cathedral, we find that it was what was then called a 'double organ'. In other words it had two manuals, Great and 'Chayre', the latter projecting from the gallery edge behind the player. This was not a characteristic of the Italian organ but seems to have originated first in Holland around 1450, finding its way to England only in 1613 (at Worcester Cathedral, by Thomas Dallam, father of Robert). One suspects that the double organ became fashionable fairly rapidly. Certainly the organs of York Minster (1632) and Magdalen College, Oxford (1637) were so constructed and some instruments with only one manual had false screens erected behind the player designed to look like a Chair organ. These may be seen today at Stanford-on-Avon and at Framlingham.

Then came disaster. War broke out between King Charles I and Parliament, and in 1644 the Puritan-dominated Parliament issued an ordinance 'for the speedy demolishing of all organs' in churches. As and where they took control this was implemented. A few organs were taken down and stored; the Magdalen College, Oxford organ was moved to Hampton Court to entertain Cromwell, but the majority of church instruments were smashed. The Puritans almost entirely destroyed our heritage of pre-Commonwealth organs.

Organ-building came to a halt, of course; Robert Dallam, a Roman Catholic, had fled to Brittany in 1642. He seems to have adapted very quickly, soon becoming the leading builder in the area. The cases of his organs in Quimper Cathedral and St Pol de Léon Cathedral survive in their original homes to this day. He adopted French tonal designs which included reed-stops and mixture stops, not previously a part of the British organ. On the Restoration of the monarchy in 1660 Robert Dallam returned to England, leaving one son in Brittany to carry on the business there. Dallam was immediately in demand, but his 'French' scheme for New College, Oxford was rejected and Robert died whilst working on the more conventional organ on which the college had insisted.

British organ-building began again where it had left off. Such was the haste to make good the destruction of the Commonwealth troops that major instruments were built by makers of whom little had been heard previously, some of whom soon disappeared again from the record. The two-manual organ built by Thomas Harris for Worcester Cathedral in 1666 had a stop-list very similar to its 1613 predecessor:

Great organ		Chaire organ	
Open Diapason	8ft	Open Diapason	8ft
Open Diapason	8ft	Stopped Diapason	8ft
Principal	4ft	Principal	4ft
Principal	4ft	Fifteenth	2ft
Recorder	4ft	Twenty-second	1ft
Twelfth	2⅔ft		
Fifteenth	2ft		
Fifteenth	2ft		
'One place for another stop'			

Thomas Harris was Robert Dallam's son-in-law. Like him, he had built organs in Brittany and it is intriguing to guess whether the 'place for another stop' was intended for a mixture stop. The previous year Harris had built the organ in Gloucester Cathedral. The contract stop-list is lost but we know that the 'ffurniture' stop was a gift of the Bishop of Oxford! The cases and a substantial number of pipes survive in the current instrument, including some mixture pipes which would seem to be the remains of the first mixture stop in a British organ, just ahead of the 'Furniture' stop in Thomas Thamar's organ for Winchester Cathedral the following year. Gradually the new ideas crept in, sometimes experimentally as in John Loosemore's 1665 organ for Exeter Cathedral which had 20ft long bass pipes in separate cases, perhaps in emulation of earlier experiments in Holland. John Loosemore also included a Trumpet stop in a house organ at Nettlecombe Court, Somerset. Mixture-stops reappear in a single-manual organ built in 1671 for the Sheldonian Theatre, Oxford by Bernard Smith. The probable stop-list of this organ was:

Open Diapason	8ft	
Stopped Diapason	8ft	
Principal	4ft	
Twelfth	2⅔ft	
Fifteenth	2ft	
Sesquialtera	III	Bass
Cornet	III	Treble
Trumpet	8ft	Treble

Smith's origins are obscure; he trained in Bremen, north Germany, but spent some ten years in Holland before coming to London in 1667. He may have been the son of the Christianus Smith who made a chamber organ in 1643 which still exists. Perhaps he was sent, as a teenager, to Germany to learn his trade away from the Civil War. An English girl bearing the same name as his wife arrived in the same parish in Holland the year that he moved from Germany. On the other hand, he may have been German (in Holland he used the name of Smitt) and the end of the trade wars would have permitted his move to England in 1667. Smith had built a two-manual organ, which still exists in the Grote Kerk in Edam, with mixtures and a reed-stop, so he was clearly aware of the latest practice in northern Europe. His British instruments, from the start, were very different from those which went before, with mixtures and reed-stops in place of the wasteful duplication of chorus stops which had been so usual in the pre-Commonwealth organ. Nevertheless, Smith was clearly an adaptable man, since one of his speciialities was the voicing of very sweet-sounding Stopped Diapasons made of wood, a talent he would hardly have learned in Holland or Germany where the use of wooden pipes was much less usual. One important feature of the organ he built for the Sheldonian Theatre was the design of the divided mixture stop. The treble part was a Cornet, a solo stop containing a Tierce rank. The bass part was a Sesquialtera, which in Germany and Holland is a part-chorus part-solo stop. Later, Smith was to go on to make the Sesquialtera a full-compass chorus stop and to set a trend in mixture design which was to last for a couple of centuries, and which was unique to the British organ.

This is perhaps the point in our narrative where it will be helpful to consider mixture stops. They come under many names, accompanied by mysterious numbers, and require some explanation. First, though, it is necessary to take a step back and look at the origin of the 'mixture'. It will be remembered that the medieval organ had no stops, all ranks of pipes sounding whenever the keys were played. The re-invention of stop-controls in the fifteenth century allowed individual ranks to be separated, as in the Italian organ. However, in northern Europe, whilst other departments acquired stop-action, the Great organ – the *Blockwerk* – remained without stops for up to another century. Eventually the graver pitches were drawn as separate stops, the remainder of the *Blockwerk* becoming one or more mixtures. Take, for example, the *Hauptwerk* (Great organ) at Breda, Holland, built in 1534:

Prestant	8ft
Prestant	4ft
Mixtuur	
Scherp	

In other words, the upper part of the Diapason Chorus is not controlled as separate stops, as in the Italian organ, but as one or more mixture stops. It is conventional to describe the number of pipes per note – the number of ranks – in Roman numerals, eg Furniture IV. The logical way of describing the pitch is to use the nominal length of the bottom C of each pipe, just as one does for individual stops, eg 1⅗ft, 1⅓ft, 1ft. The fractions look to have more to do with mathematics than with music but need not be too frightening when it is remembered that the smaller the fraction the higher the pitch of the mixture. Indeed, with this notation, it is very easy to see what actual notes are involved. For example, 2ft, 1ft, ½ft and ¼ft are all unison ranks. The paradox is that ranks with a three in the fraction are quints (1⅓ft, ⅔ft, ⅓ft) but that ranks with a five in the fraction are thirds (1⅗ft, ⅘ft, ⅖ft).

An alternative method of specifying mixtures, which does at least involve whole numbers, is to use the names of the pitches in numeral form. Thus, a 2ft rank is 15 notes of the scale above the unison, is known as a Fifteenth and is written 15. Similarly a 1ft will be written 22. The higher the number the sharper the mixture. The problem comes with determining the notes; one just has to remember that 15, 22, 29, 36 are unisons, 12, 19, 26, 33 are quints and 17, 24, 31 are Tierces. The system also becomes a little confusing on the Pedal since a Pedal Fifteenth is a 4ft stop, not 2ft.

The mixture is normally the summit of the Diapason Chorus, and the pitches used will follow on from the separate stops lower down. A mixture capping a Great organ chorus with Principal, Twelfth, Fifteenth might well be 'Furniture IV 19.22.26.29' or 'Furniture IV 1⅓ft' (the pitches of the other ranks being inferred). As so described, however, the composition of a mixture only tells part of the story. It states the notes that speak at bottom C, but not the notes, or even the relative pitches, at any other part of the compass. In practice, nearly all mixture stops that are part of the Diapason Chorus 'break back' to graver pitches on their way up the keyboard. The sensitivity of the human ear to sounds above the top note of a Fifteenth falls away after the age of forty years and, without breaks, the top notes of a chorus mixture which is reasonably sharp in the bass would degenerate into inaudible squeaks in the upper register.

One might expect that the breaks in a mixture would distort the melody, and indeed this can happen with mixtures that break back a complete octave, eg:

Notes	Composition		
1–24	15	19	22
25–56	8	12	15

In theory this might lead to a descending fourth becoming an ascending fifth, though the jump will be partially concealed by the graver stops of the chorus that will be drawn with the mixture. However, if the breaks are only a fourth or fifth at a time they become, in practice, almost undetectable.

Notes	Composition		
1–19	15	19	22
20–31	12	15	19
32–56	8	12	15

The 'break' principle can be taken further; since the musical function of the mixture is to add brightness and definition to the bass registers and to add power to the upper register, it is scarcely necessary for the pitch of the mixture to progress from bass to treble at all. One is reminded of Professor Charles Taylor's maddening 'everlasting scale' which tricks the ear by gradually varying the proportions of the harmonics in each electrically generated note as the scale ascends. This is done in such a way that by the time the octave is reached it is identical to the first note. Thus the scale appears to ascend everlastingly without actually going up in pitch at all. Some of the higher-pitched mixture stops approach this situation. One of the modern mixtures at Gloucester Cathedral breaks eleven times – a change in composition every five notes – and the pitch rises only a major sixth in four and a half octaves. High mixtures such as this are necessary in large buildings, where at high frequencies the acoustic absorption of the air itself would otherwise dull the sound of the instrument.

The names of mixture stops designed for use with the Diapason Chorus are not always very specific, many mixtures just being labelled 'Mixture'. Sharp Mixture means what it says, and Cymbal means a higher pitch still. Harris' Furniture (anglicised from the French *Fourniture*) is a Great organ mixture which is fairly full and not too sharp. However, there is another class of mixtures where the names are precise and tell the player all he needs to know about their sound and musical use. The most distinctive is the Cornet, to which we have already referred in connection with Smith's instrument for the Sheldonian Theatre, Oxford. This stop was known to the Dallams; they had put Cornets in their organs in Brittany twenty years earlier, but it was left to Smith to introduce it to England. The Cornet is unique among mixtures in that in its V rank form it needs no other stop drawn with it, a stopped 8ft rank being included to provide the fundamental, or, as Renatus Harris was later to put it in his abortive bid for a contract at Durham Cathedral, 'speaking intierly of itselfe without being mix'd with any other stops to healp it out in number'. There are no breaks but the Cornet is normally a short-compass stop and in Britain usually runs from middle C up only. The pipes are wider in scale than the Diapasons (especially the Cornets in French organs) and the composition of 1.8.12.15.17 gives a dark reedy sound, the reediness coming from the seventeenth, a Tierce rank. The Cornet is not usually drawn with the Diapason Chorus but is used as a prominent solo stop. In France it was also used with the reed-stops to add power to the relatively weak treble notes of the reeds.

Another mixture with a Tierce in its make-up is the Tertian (17.19), but the Sesquialtera (12.17) is more common. These have pipes of Diapason scale and, unlike the Cornet, need stops of fundamental pitch to be drawn with them. Their effect is thinner and, though reedy, not at all imitative of reed-pipes. In addition to its solo function, the Sesquialtera can also be drawn with the Diapason Chorus to give it a reedy flavour. In Britain, rather confusingly, Sesquialtera is also used as the name for a purely chorus mixture and this practice seems to have been started by Smith. In this form the Sesquialtera has III ranks, usually with the composition 17.19.22. Most chorus mixtures consist only of quints and unisons; this use of a Tierce gives a permanent reedy tang to the full chorus which is peculiar to the British organ.

The typical Bernard Smith organ, with reeds and mixtures, was a considerable break with the organ of the pre-Commonwealth and immediate post-Commonwealth periods. It was to set a style which, with variations, was to last about 150 years. Smith's first two-manual organ was for Christchurch Cathedral, Oxford, built in 1680:

Great organ		*Chair organ*	
Open Diapason	8	Stopped Diapason	8
Stopped Diapason	8	Principal	4
Principal	4	Flute	4
Twelfth	2⅔	Fifteenth	2
Fifteenth	2		
Tierce	1⅗		
Sesquialtera	III		
Cornet	IV		
Trumpet	8		

Smith was obviously a considerable inventor; he soon went on to try other ideas. One of the these was to provide additional keys and pipes, beyond the normal twelve in the octave, to try to overcome one of the fundamental limitations of keyboard instruments, that of temperament. On any keyboard it would appear that three successive intervals of a third make up an octave. In fact, three successive perfectly-tuned thirds are slightly flat to the octave. The reason lies in the basic mathematics of music: an octave is double the frequency of vibration and a perfect third is 5/4 times the frequency. Three thirds are $5/4 \times 5/4 \times 5/4 = {}^{125}/_{64}$, which is slightly less than two. Similar problems also arise with other intervals. Early organs probably had such an erratic wind supply that these matters were academic. Nevertheless, builders eventually evolved a system whereby for the six most commonly used keys the thirds were tuned true. This meant, in effect that the black notes were C♯, E♭, F♯, G♯ and B♭. Any attempt to use, say, G♯ as A♭ would result in a very badly tuned 'wolf' note.

By the late seventeenth century composers were becoming restless at the restriction in usable key signatures. In Germany, the response was to try new methods of tuning in which some of the intervals were 'tempered' (ie deliberately tuned not quite true), but in Britain Smith's response was to provide additional black keys for A♭ and E♭ raised behind the normal keys for G♯ and D♯, together with the necessary additional pipes and action. He provided these for his new organ for Durham Cathedral in 1683 and for the Temple Church in London in the following year. Neither has survived however, though similar instruments have been built in America recently.

The Temple Church instrument had, in addition, a more significant novelty, a third manual, the boxed-in Echo organ. Large organs in Holland and Germany had been constructed with three manuals perhaps two hundred years before but their design had never been copied in Britain. In any event Smith's third manual was not a copy of a German *Brustwerk* or even a Dutch *Bovenwerk*, though it could perhaps trace descent from a French idea. We know that one Paris organ had an Echo division as early as the 1580s, though it had only one stop, a Cornet. Like the French prototype, Smith's Echo was normally a half-compass department, though the Temple organ did, unusually, have two stops of full range. The idea was a success and another Echo followed in Smith's organ for St Paul's in 1697:

Great organ		*Chayre organ*		*Echo organ*	
Open Diapason	8	Quinta Dena Diapason	8	Diapason	8
Open Diapason	8	Stopped Diapason	8	Principal	4
Stopped Diapason	8	Principal	4	Nason	4
Principal	4	Hohl Flute	4	Fifteenth	2
Hohl Flute	4	Great Twelfth	2⅔	Cornet	
Great Twelfth	2⅔	Fifteenth	2	Trumpet	8
Fifteenth	2	Cimball			
Small Twelfth	1⅓	Voice Humaine	8		
Cornet		Crum Horne	8		
Mixture					
Sesquialtera					
Trumpet	8				

74

One can see that the Echo department was, in tonal structure, an Echo Great organ. This is quite unlike any Continental model known to the author. Conjecturally, it may have been Smith's replacement for the duplicated Great organ chorus of Dallam's pre-Commonwealth organs, in which one of each pair of stops may have been softer than the other. Be that as it may, the third manual department continued in this sort of design for the next hundred and fifty years.

What did a Smith organ sound like? Chamber organs apart, we have no complete Smith instruments remaining to us. However, most of Smith's pipes in the University organ of the University Church of St Mary the Great, Cambridge remain in the present instrument. The wooden stopped pipes, by their nature, can have been little altered, and these have a pleasant, "sweet" sound with a prominent third harmonic. It is more difficult to judge the extent of alterations to the metal pipes. As they stand, they give a slightly mild sound, less strident than old north German organs but less 'flutey' than old Italian instruments. Smith's pipes were also, if the surviving Harris pipes in the Gloucester Cathedral organ are a reliable guide, slightly bolder in scale and in sound than those of a generation before.

Smith's organs had remarkably fine Renaissance cases, arguably better proportioned than those of both his predecessors and his successors. These cases were often highly decorated with pierced work and carving, though only the St Paul's Cathedral case, designed not by Smith but by Sir Christopher Wren, steps over the boundary into the baroque.

Smith had two nephews in the business, who later built organs on their own. To distinguish him from them, he was commonly referred to as 'Father Smith'. He was organ-builder to the King, and from 1670 until his death in 1708 built many of the important instruments of his day. Smith's only real rival was Renatus Harris, son of the Thomas Harris we have already mentioned, who in his turn had been son-in-law to the younger Dallam.

Renatus Harris attracted attention when he challenged Smith over the contract for the Temple Church in London, leading to the famous 'Battle of the Organs'. Father Smith thought that he had the contract but Harris persuaded the Benchers to let him install a rival instrument in another part of the church. There is a story to the effect that Harris arranged for the bellows of Smith's organ to be cut just before a public trial of the instruments. If so, this was to no avail as a decision was made in Smith's favour by the infamous 'hanging' Judge Jefferies. Harris had to remove his organ; he is said to have used parts in his later instrument for Christ Church Cathedral, Dublin, now in St John's, Wolverhampton. Renatus Harris was undoubtedly a worthy rival for Father Smith; his actions were reputed to have been better and he was a celebrated voicer of reed-stops. However, like all good reed voicers, Harris had a reputation for being awkward and this may be the reason why he received slightly fewer important commissions than Smith. Nevertheless, he furnished six cathedrals with organs and over a dozen of the cases of his instruments survive. Like Smith, Renatus Harris' cases had a standard of elegance which his successors seldom equalled. He copied his father's taste for varied pipe-mouth shapes and tended to go in for a slightly more flamboyant and 'architectural' style than Smith.

Harris' stop-lists were in many respects very similar to Smith's, save for the provision of chorus mixtures without tierces (some even called Sesquialtera!) and the provision of separate Tierce stops. He copied Smith's Echo organ idea and went further, building the first four-manual organ in Britain for Salisbury Cathedral in 1710. This made use of Harris' invention by which two departments shared a common soundboard and stops were borrowed 'by communication', as he described it, from one manual to the other. His system involved a complex series of one-way 'fly-pallets' to stop the air flowing back to where it was not wanted. Although complicated, the system continued to be used by his successors and, with mechanical variations, has been used intermittently by various builders up to the present day. In the eighteenth century its general use was to share stops between Great and Choir organs, the Choir organ being incorporated in the main case instead of in a chair case. Even without the borrowing mechanism, chair cases gradually fell from favour.

Harris also attempted to introduce the Pedal organ to Britain. Father Smith's organ in St Paul's Cathedral served well for the daily services in the choir but must have sounded remote in the distant nave, west of the dome. In 1712 Harris published a proposal for a grand west-end organ for the cathedral on the Continental model, with six manuals and a Pedal organ, so that, as he said, 'the Organist can carry on three Fugues at once'. The proposal came to nothing but only eight years later Christopher Shrider, Father Smith's son-in-law and successor, did add a set of pedals to Smith's organ, though whether they had any pipes of their own is uncertain. Renatus Harris himself never actually provided any pedals though, only two years after his death in 1724, his son John Harris did when he built an organ for St Mary Redcliffe Church, Bristol in partnership with John Byfield, who was Renatus' son-in-law.

The real development of the Pedal organ in Britain had to wait a further century, but another invention had a more immediate effect. Abraham Jordan was an organ-builder with a sideline. He imported sherry from Portugal, where Faustinho Carvalho had been building organs with pipes enclosed in a box with an adjustable opening, connected to a lever on the console. In particular, Carvalho added a department so constructed to the organ in Seville Cathedral, Spain in 1703. Jordan admitted no connection and when he built an organ for the church of St Magnus the Martyr, London Bridge in 1712 with one department 'adapted to the art of emitting sounds by swelling the notes', he claimed the idea for his own. Although the mechanism was crude, with a simple sliding panel on the front face of a very thin box, the idea caught on quickly and all the Echo organs of the previous generation were speedily converted.

As the eighteenth century progressed, there was a gradual loss of interest in the Choir organ matched by a corresponding increase in the use of the Swell organ. In other respects stop-lists remained almost unaltered from the Smith organs of the previous century. One can see this in the stop-list of the organ built for St Mary's Church, Rotherhithe, London in 1765 by John Byfield (son of the John Byfield mentioned above):

Great organ		Choir organ		Swell organ	
Open Diapason	8	Stop'd Diapason	8	Open Diapason	8
Stop'd Diapason	8	Principal	4	Stop'd Diapason	8
Principal	4	Flute	4	Principal	4
Nason	4	Fifteenth	2	Cornet	III
Twelfth	2⅔	Vox Humana	8	Trumpet	8
Fifteenth	2			Hautboy	8
Sesquialtera	IV				
Cornet	V				
Trumpet	8				
Clarion	4				

The Swell organ compass was now from 'Fiddle G', down a fourth from middle C. Note too the Hautboy (Oboe) stop which was to become a fixture in the British Swell organ. Much of this instrument still remains.

We also have the case and pipes, at least, of instruments by a number of other mid-eighteenth-century builders, in particular Richard Bridge and Thomas Schwarbrick, both of whom were pupils of Renatus Harris. Not only their stop-lists but also their organ cases kept basically to the pattern of the previous century, disregarding the excesses of the rococo which flowered in Germany and in Spain. The only changes of any substance were the absence of separate chair cases and also the provision of full-width lower cases, so that the sides of the organ were straight and without the overhang characteristic of the seventeenth century.

We have now reached a period when a more romantic approach to music was beginning to affect the design of the organ. In addition to the popularity of the new Swell departments, organ-builders explored the use of stops which are at a completely different dynamic level to the normal Diapason Chorus. This was achieved by using a much smaller pipe-scale. The idea was introduced by John Snetzler, a Swiss who is reputed to have been trained in Passau in south Germany, and who emigrated to London in the 1740s. The south Germans had developed the use of narrow-scaled pipes to produce a tone with more harmonic development, one which they rashly claimed imitated the sound of the Viola. Narrow-scaled pipes are not easy to voice, as they tend either to speak slowly or to overblow to the octave, a problem which troubled Loosemore with his relatively narrow 20ft long pipes at Exeter, back in 1665. Snetzler knew the south German trick of making the so-called 'box mouth' which has a single strip of metal, horizontal in front of the bottom lip, bent up at the ends to form the two ears. This steadies the speech of the pipe and is still used on Quintadena pipes. The soft stop which Snetzler introduced, with approximately the same harmonic development as the Diapason but only a fraction of the power, he called the Dulciana. It remained a frequent component of the British organ stop-list until relatively recently, only falling from favour in the past twenty-five years or so.

Snetzler made a great many chamber organs, a popular fitment at that time in the houses of the wealthy. A fair number of these have survived, including some which were shipped to colonial America. From about 1760 Snetzler was organ-builder to the King but none of his larger instruments remains intact. However, many of Snetzler's pipes are still in use in the organ of Beverley Minster, enough to get some idea of the pipe-scales which he used. Like Father Smith before him, once he had determined the pipe-scale for a given building it was used for all similar stops. At Beverley, the Stopped Diapason pipes (metal pipes with fixed tops and chimneys, tuned by the ears) are all the same scale on each of the three manuals. Even the 4ft Flute is the same, only the 'cut-up' (height of the mouth aperture) is different. Snetzler's organs had a reputation for brilliance of tone as his Diapason scales were slightly smaller than those of his predecessors and he was more ready to use a high proportion of tin in the metal.

Smith had used approximately the same scale for all the pipes of the chorus but, once the idea of small-scale pipes had become accepted, it became another tool in the voicer's armoury. It is written of George England, pupil and son-in-law of Richard Bridge, that he scaled successive ranks of the chorus one note smaller, so that by the time he had reached the top rank of the mixture it had become almost a Dulciana.

Another voicing trick introduced at this time had a most curious ancestry. We have already referred to the spread of a more romantic approach to music at this time. Britain was largely spared the antics of the 'Abbé' Vogler who, in his recital tours round Europe proposed the most extraordinary stop-lists, full of mutation stops, but without mixtures. His idea was to generate a multitude of solo sounds and to reinforce the fundamental, justifying his schemes by quoting the newly discovered scientific theory of difference tones. For example, suppose the ear hears two pure tones whose pitch is two and three times the fundamental, then it is deceived into believing that there is a third tone present, whose frequency is the difference between the first two. The difference between two and three is one so the ear hears a soft fundamental in addition to the other two. This principle was used by John Snetzler and by Samuel Green (his successor as organ-builder to the King) to provide a suitable bass to an Open Diapason in a chamber organ or other instrument with insufficient height. Stopped Diapason pipes were provided to generate some fundamental plus a prominent third harmonic and a second set of pipes, of 4ft pitch and relatively pure tone, sounded with them to give the second harmonic. The pitches appear to coalesce into a single tone, the difference tones strengthen the fundamental, and the complete harmonic series characteristic of the open pipe is provided. A similar device, but with only the difference tone for the fundamental, was developed in Victorian times to obtain apparent 32ft tone from 16ft and $10\frac{2}{3}$ft pipes sounding together.

Samuel Green's position as court organ-builder was probably undeserved. Judging from his surviving instruments, they were not all that well made, but certainly they were different. Instead of the relatively brilliant tone of Snetzler's organs, Green provided a softer, sweeter sound, with pipes that were blown relatively gently. This was very successful in chamber organs heard in intimate surroundings, and can be listened to for long periods without tiring. However, it lacks impact in larger buildings, and none of his English cathedral organs has survived in its original building, though two are now in use in much smaller churches. Nor were his organ cases always popular. As Sir John Sutton put it, writing with the hindsight of 1847: 'Green . . . began to engraft innumerable pinnacles and incorrect details upon his tasteless boxes. The ornamental parts resemble barley sugar ornaments . . .'. This is a little harsh, but then early Gothick organ cases are something of a joke.

Green adopted Snetzler's Dulciana stop and tried the effect of a

Dulciana chorus of 8ft, 4ft and Mixture in the Swell organ of the instrument he built for the Chapel of the Royal Naval College, Greenwich. In this instrument Green extended the compass of the Swell down to FF in the bottom octave, thus taking the department out of the realm of being purely for the right hand. Indeed, it was his work with the Swell which was Green's most important contribution to the development of the organ. Snetzler had made some chamber instruments with all the pipes enclosed in a swell-box, but in 1790 Green enclosed the whole of his new organ for St George's Chapel, Windsor in a large swell-box. The instrument was not a success, the organ being made far too soft. In addition, Green's swell-boxes were too lightly made to give much range of expression. In order to even attempt such an instrument, Green realised that he needed a better mechanism for opening the box than the sliding shutters used hitherto. A few years earlier the harpsichord-maker, Tschudi, had used tilting louvres to make an expressive harpsichord. One such instrument is in the collection at Fenton House, Hampstead, complete with the 'Venetian' louvres which Green copied and which rapidly superseded the earlier form.

With all this attention on the Swell organ, it is not surprising that the Swell now began to supersede the Choir organ as the second manual of a two-manual instrument. A typical example is the organ built for the chapel of Ashridge College, Hertfordshire by Thomas Elliot in 1818:

Great organ		*Swell organ*	
Compass: GG to f, 58 notes (no GG♯)		Compass: Tenor F to f, 37 notes	
Open Diapason	8	Open Diapason	8
Open Diapason (from Gamut G)	8	Stopped Diapason	8
		Principal	4
Stopped Diapason	8	Hautboy	8
Principal	4		
Flute	4	*Pedal organ*	
Twelfth	2⅔	Compass: GG to C, 17 notes	
Fifteenth	2	(no GG♯)	
Sesquialtera	II	Pedal Diapason	8
Mixture	II		
Trumpet	8		

This organ survives in an almost unaltered condition and is a fascinating bridge between the eighteenth-century tradition and what was to come. In some ways it looks back to Snetzler and Green with its sweet-toned Stopped Diapasons and elegant console. The internal construction, however, is considerably more robust than anything which came out of the eighteenth century, and the swell-box has the pitched roof which was later to be characteristic of the work of William Hill, who at that time had just joined Elliot, and who was later to marry Elliot's daughter. (The bright pupil who marries the master's daughter and succeeds to the business was an essential part of tradition in many of the longer-lasting organ-building dynasties!)

To our eyes, the most curious feature of the Ashridge organ, like virtually all British church organs for the previous two centuries, was the compass. Although chamber organs almost always had a compass down to CC, two octaves below middle C, there seems to have been, early on, an idea that the larger the church the deeper should be the compass. Thus the 1536 Antegnati organ in Brescia Cathedral, Italy, went down to CCC (three octaves below middle C) and Father Smith did likewise at St Paul's Cathedral, despite the problems imposed by Wren's case. In practice, however, GG (two octaves and a fourth below middle C) became the working standard for church instruments. This is the reason why virtually all seventeenth- and eighteenth-century church organ cases are about 14ft high above the impost, since the largest pipe, the bottom note, is about 11ft long in the body.

In countries where the Pedal organ has become established by the end of the sixteenth century, there had been no musical need to retain the long compass and the bottom note had become stabilised at CC. It was for instruments with separate Pedal organs and CC compass that Bach had written all his music. Against this background, the Ashridge organ is incredibly archaic, combining a long compass Great with a short compass Swell and a very odd compass Pedal. There really is remarkably little music that one can play on those pedals. The pedals themselves were still something of an innovation though they had, by this time, acquired some pipes of their own, pipes of the same pitch as the Open Diapason, but of large scale and made of wood to give weight and depth. Quite a number of old instruments had wide-scale wooden 'Pedal pipes' added in the first part of the nineteenth century.

William Hill appears to have been dissatisfied with the restful but unmajestic tone of the British organ. In 1827 Elliot and Hill rebuilt the organ in Christ Church, Newgate Street, City of London, with Pedal pipes one octave in pitch below the manuals, so that the lowest note was GGG (21⅓ft nominal length). The following year they replaced the unison Pedal pipes at Westminster Abbey with GGG pipes. In 1829 Elliott and Hill tried another tack. Possibly taking their cue from Father Smith and St Paul's Cathedral, they built the organ for the Hall of Christ's Hospital School, London with a manual compass down to CCC, so that the bottom note of the Open Diapason was 16ft. The same idea was repeated in the very large instruments built for York Minster in 1829 and for Birmingham Town Hall in 1834. The pedalboard was carried down an extra seven notes to match the manual compass, so that it now had a compass of two octaves. At Christ's Hospital the 'Wood Diapason' was in unison with the manuals (ie 16ft), but the York and Birmingham instruments had both 16ft and 32ft stops, York having the first 32ft reed in Britain (called Sackbut) and Birmingham the first 32ft front pipe (made of iron). In the days before railways, the transport of such large pipes was a problem. Tradition in the Hill firm has it that the giant 32ft front pipes were sent to Birmingham by water, in specially chartered canal boats. This would have been quite possible as the Town Hall is close to Cambrian Wharf in Birmingham and the Hill factory was equally near the then Cumberland Market Basin in London.

In the 1830s, William Hill (on his own now) met the redoubtable Dr Henry Gauntlett, and the British organ world was to be changed by their relationship. Gauntlett had travelled in Holland and Germany and been impressed by the big Dutch organs leading Lutheran congregations in powerful singing of the chorales. He was a great protagonist of hymn singing as a part of Christian worship and a prolific composer of hymn tunes himself. He realised that the British organ, as it then was, was inadequate to support powerful unison singing; this coincided with Hill's search for power and grandeur in his instruments. Gauntlett persuaded Hill to adopt the 'German compass' from CC, two octaves below middle C, for all manuals, including the Swell organ. At first sight, this might seem to reduce rather than enhance the grandeur of the organ, by eliminating the lowest octave. In practice, it meant that Hill could introduce 16ft stops on the manuals. This made far more difference than an extra octave of pipes which could really only be used by transposing the music downwards, thereby destroying its brilliance. As Hill himself claimed, the shorter compass enabled a wider range of pitches to be provided for each individual note.

These theories were first put to the test in a further rebuild of the Christ Church, Newgate Street instrument in 1838, when the Great organ acquired a Double Open Diapason 16ft and a Double Trumpet 16ft. In 1840 Hill carried out a reconstruction, amounting almost to a new organ, of the Father Smith instrument in St Peter's Church, Cornhill in the City of London. This was on a similar basis but also introducing a French stop, the Bourdon, which, being stopped and therefore only half-length, allowed him to provide 16ft manual tone where there was no height for taller pipes.

Gauntlett, in his turn, was influenced by Mendelssohn, who visited London on recital tours seven times between 1829 and 1846. Mendelssohn was a great protagonist of Bach's music, hitherto almost unheard in Britain. It was a matter of considerable embarrassment on his early visits that there was no organ in London on which Bach could be played as written. Gauntlett persuaded Hill to provide pedalboards of 27 notes, CCC to D, to cover these requirements and, in addition, to provide a proper Pedal department. The Newgate Street instrument had no less than 10 stops on the Pedal:

Great Wood Diapason	16
Wood Open Diapason	16
Metal Open Diapason	16
Principal	8
Twelfth	5⅓
Fifteenth	4
Sesquialtera	VI
Mixture	V
Posaune	16
Clarion	8

Unfortunately, perhaps through lack of space, all this magnificence was limited to the bottom octave, the remainder of the pedalboard having to depend on manual-to-Pedal couplers only. However, in 1841, in the new organ for Great George Street Chapel, Liverpool, Hill provided, for the first time, a Pedal organ of complete twenty-seven note compass.

This organ must have been a success because not only did Hill build at least a further nine instruments with the CC compass and Pedal organs before 1850, but the idea was swiftly copied by his rivals: J. C. Bishop at St Giles', Camberwell, London in 1844 (at the instigation of S. S. Wesley) and by Robson at St Michael's, Chester Square in 1847. The latter was the first organ where the Pedal compass was increased upwards to F, giving a total of 30 notes. The introduction of the Pedal organ was not without its opponents, especially amongst the older players. Nevertheless, the 1855 Willis organ in St George's Hall, Liverpool was probably the last significant instrument to be built with the long compass; after this the present-day CC compass became the rule.

It would be impossible to overstate the effect of the change of compass. Virtually all the old long-compass organs were rebuilt or replaced in the course of the next forty years, a process which was helped on its way by the movement of organs from nave to chancel described in chapter 2. A new console had to be provided, of course, to match the new compass and even where the old case was retained, the layout of the organ had to be changed drastically. At the very least a new Swell organ soundboard and supporting frame was required and, with a full 8ft compass, substantially more space and height was needed. Space also had to be found for the new Pedal organs. These changes led to the ungainly sight of swell-boxes peeping over old cases and Pedal pipes standing outside the case, sometimes laid down horizontally in efforts to hide them. The result of all this was that, chamber organs apart, there are very few instruments indeed which survive from the pre-1840 period in an unaltered form. The remaining early 'German compass' organs from the 1840s and 1850s are some of the oldest instruments we have that have not been drastically rebuilt.

The change in compass was not the only innovation resulting from the collaboration of William Hill and Dr Gauntlett. With a full compass the Swell could take its place as the main alternative to the Great organ, leaving the Choir organ as a collection of mildly voiced accompanimental stops. The stop-list of the 1841 Great George Street Chapel organ, already mentioned, shows this:

Great organ		*Swell organ*		*Choir organ*	
Bourdon &		Bourdon &		Open Diapason	8
Tenoroon	16	Tenoroon	16	Dulciana	8
Open Diapason	8	Open Diapason	8	Stopped Diapason	8
Open Diapason	8	Dulciana	8	Clarabella	8
Stopped Diapason	8	Corno Flute	8	Principal	4
Quint	5⅓	Stopped Diapason	8	Stopped Flute	4
Principal	4	Quint	5⅓	Wald Flute	4
Flute	4	Principal	4	Oboe Flute	4
Tenth	3⅕	Suabe Flute	4	Cremona	8
Twelfth	2⅔	Twelfth	2⅔		
Fifteenth	2	Fifteenth	2	*Solo organ*	
Doublette II	2	Flageolet	2	Tuba Mirabilis	8
Sesquialtera III	1⅗	Sesquialtera III	1⅗		
Mixture III	⅔	Mixture II	⅔	*Pedal organ*	
Posaune	8	Echo Cornet V		Open Diapason	16
Clarion	4	Contra Fagotto	16	Bourdon	16
		Cornopean	8	Principal	8
		Trumpet	8	Fifteenth	4
		Oboe	8	Sesquialtera V	3⅕
		Clarion	4	Trombone	16

As can be seen, the Swell organ is larger than the Great and the fluework is not dissimilar in general design and in scale. The presence of the swell-box would make the tone more distant so that it could be used antiphonally with the Great, but the loss in power was made up and the tonal character set apart by the presence of five reed-stops as against two on the Great. This equality of power between Swell and Great and the dependence on reed-stops to distinguish the departments was the fundamental principle of the British Swell organ, one which is only now under threat even though it was largely peculiar to the British Isles.

There are those who will say that, in terms of tonal design, William Hill's organs of the period 1840–60 are the summit of British organ-building and that we would do well to learn what we can from them. What then are their salient characteristics, as evidenced by those instruments of the period which have not been greatly altered? The first thing that is apparent is the presence of relatively generous pipe-scales, combined with low-cut mouths. Even with Hill's quest for power and grandeur, he retained something of the sweetness and the restful quality so characteristic of Green's work. Hill's organs are essentially moderate, devoid of extremes, and have an absence of harshness which is perhaps their ultimate hallmark. The robustness of construction which also characterised Hill's work influenced other builders in the second half of the nineteenth century and set a standard not always attained today. Hill's larger organs suffered from a heavy key-touch but many of his smaller instruments remain in use with remarkably few changes. Equally remarkable is the way in which the characteristics of Hill's work were preserved over a very long period by his son Thomas and grandson Dr Arthur Hill.

There is yet one more innovation of Hill's still to be discussed. The Great George Street organ was a four-manual with a 'Solo organ' consisting of one stop, the Tuba Mirabilis. He had added a similar stop in the previous year to the Birmingham Town Hall organ. Organ transcriptions of orchestral music were becoming popular and a dominant reed gave an additional tone colour for solo use. Increasing the scale of a reed-pipe only adds a modest amount of power, but Hill discovered that increasing the wind pressure produces additional power more or less in proportion to the pressure, all else being equal. Hill found that with a thick brass tongue and a shallot faced with leather he could make the pipes respond to the high pressure, which, at a reputed 12in (300mm) water gauge, was about four times that of the rest of the instrument.

Hill's greatest rival at this time was the firm of Gray & Davison, run by Frederic Davison who had briefly been Hill's partner in 1838 before leaving to join John Gray (and John Gray's daughter!). Gray had earlier been Elliot's main rival. Gray & Davison were somewhat more conservative than Hill and when they did get round to dominant reed-stops they set about it in a different way. Gray & Davison's 1859 colossus in Leeds Town Hall (with a 26 stop Great organ!) had an Ophicleide stop which, though not visible, was arranged horizontally in the Spanish manner using a more moderate, if still elevated, wind pressure. At about the same time they fitted a visible horizontal Grand Tuba to the organ in Ludlow parish church but the idea failed to catch on, nor did the harmonium-reed half-length Pedal 32ft which was part of the Leeds organ. Another rival, already mentioned, was J. C. Bishop who invented the open wood flute called the Clarabella, fitted on the Great organ instead of the Stopped Diapason, or, in old organs, used to replace the Cornet, by now out of fashion.

An important event in the history of British organ-building was the Great Exhibition of 1851, held in the Crystal Palace in Hyde Park, London. All the major organ-builders exhibited, including Edmund Schulze from Germany. We shall return to Schulze later but the most successful exhibit was a large 70 stop three-manual by Henry Willis, who was only thirty years old at the time. Financed as a speculation by Sir James Tyler, it brought Willis' name to the fore. There were a number of mechanical novelties; Henry Willis was a prolific inventor and this was one of the first large organs in Britain to use the pneumatic lever action. Although the exhibition organ was an immature work, it was good enough to secure the contract for a very large instrument of four manuals and 108 stops in St George's Hall, Liverpool, which Willis completed in 1855. This organ established him as an organ-builder of the first rank and for the rest of the nineteenth century Willis competed with Hill for the leading instruments. Willis' organs were even more massively constructed than Hill's earlier instruments, though his pneumatic actions have not, in general, stood the test of time. The country was prosperous and Hill's and Willis' output was many times greater than that of the builders of the first half of the century. New firms sprang up in great numbers, many of which are listed in chapter 4.

Although Willis' stop-lists were not very different from Hill's, there were very distinct tonal differences. Like Hill before him, Willis took some ideas from abroad. He adopted Schulze's narrow-scaled stopped pipes, the so-called 'Lieblich' Gedeckts, for his stopped flutes and Cavaillé-Coll's double-length Harmonic Flutes (with which Hill had also experimented) for many of his open ones. However, Willis' most distinctive innovation was the way in which he made use of heavy pressure for his reed-stops. As we have seen, Hill had used heavy pressure purely to obtain power, but Willis, although power was also his objective, used heavy pressure to obtain a different and more refined tone colour.

In order to understand how Willis used heavy pressure, it is necessary to elaborate a little on the description of the reed-pipe given in chapter 1. In the bottom of the reed-pipe (known as the 'boot') is a brass tongue, the 'reed', which beats against the open side of a brass tube known as the 'shallot'. The tongue and shallot are wedged into a lead casting called the 'block'. The vibrating length of the tongue can be varied by means of a specially shaped wire which holds the tongue against the shallot, the other end projecting up through a hole in the block. This is the tuning spring. Like the flue-pipe, the reed is a coupled system, the vibrations of the reed tongue on the shallot admitting pulses of air which are modified by the resonator to the required tone quality. The vibrating mass of the reed is much greater than that of the air in the mouth of a flue-pipe so the reed is less controlled by the pitch of the resonator. This means that the pipe can be tuned by both altering the reed, via the tuning spring, and by altering the length of the resonator.

However, the two methods of tuning a reed-pipe are not fully interchangeable. If the note is tuned sharp at the tongue and then brought back to pitch by effectively lengthening the resonator, the resulting note will be softer and smoother than before. The converse operation yields a loud and rasping note. When wind pressures of the order of 2½–3½in (60–90mm) of water are used, the reeds cannot be regulated too smooth or they will be of insufficient power to balance the fluework. Willis realised that by using higher wind pressures he could regulate to a smooth tone yet retain more than sufficient power. Of course, it was not quite as easy as that. For one thing, it is difficult to regulate the bass notes to a smooth tone for the note tends to 'fly off' to the octave. At first, Willis used differential wind pressures between treble and bass, another idea imported from Cavaillé-Coll, as was the use of harmonic (double-length) pipes to enhance the power of the treble. Later, Willis developed the use of brass weights, screwed to the tongues of the bass pipes. These allowed the note to be regulated much 'closer' without flying off and overcame the long-standing problem of over-loud reed basses, a phenomenon which Willis abhorred. Another tactic was to change the shape of the shallot. Hitherto this had had a parallel-sided opening, with a square end. A bevelled end, known as a 'beak' shallot, gave added rasp to Trumpet stops. Both Hill and Willis used what is now called a 'closed' shallot. This is made tapering, the smaller end being inserted into the block. The opening is restricted to the larger end of the shallot and shaped as an elongated triangle. The shorter the 'V' of the triangle, the softer and smoother the tone becomes.

What were the advantages of all this? First, Willis achieved a degree of regularity and tuning stability hitherto unknown with reed-stops. Reeds not only appear to go out of tune, since they react differently than flues to temperature change, but also actually do go out of tune because dust particles become lodged between the tongue and the shallot, altering the vibrating length of the reed. Willis put mitred 'hoods' on reed-pipes to discourage dirt from dropping down the pipes. Higher pressures not only blow away more of the dust but also the thicker tongues, curving away more sharply, are less likely to be affected. Curving the reed tongue is the most demandingly accurate manual operation involved in organ-building; any slight kink or 'flat' in the curvature will cause the tongue to strike the shallot instead of rolling down over the opening, generating a metallic rattle. The greater curve resulting from higher wind pressure makes such problems easier to avoid. In addition, by slotting the resonators to provide a tongue of metal for easy adjustment of the tuning length, the voicer can adjust individual pipes to get the regulation from note to note almost as even as is possible with flue-pipes.

What were the disadvantages? The principal evil, more apparent in the works of his imitators than in Willis' own instruments, was that the smoother reed tone did not blend so well with the flue chorus. Indeed, if the high pressure was overdone the chorus could be obliterated. A problem with the heavier tongues was that the pipes did not speak so quickly; Willis tried to counteract this in the treble by fitting short boots standing in specially lowered rackboards, thereby reducing the amount of air required to fill the boot. The loaded bass tongues have another effect, less easily described, reducing the definition of the note and taking away the rasp which parallels that of the orchestral brass when played loudly. However, in an age when music was becoming steadily more romantic, evenness of regulation and 'pureness of tone' was the more esteemed and Willis' instruments were bold enough that an organ placed in the chancel could, if necessary, blast away sufficiently to lead a distant congregation in the nave. He collected much business as a result, including orders from no less than seventeen cathedrals, and his reed-voicing methods were soon copied by other builders and, indeed, remained the norm until the 1960s.

The tonal difference between the Hill and Willis organs was accentuated by a scaling practice which, like the CC compass, came from Germany, but about which surprisingly little has been written. It will be remembered that organ-builders had modified the theoretical halving of the diameter each octave by adding a 'secret' constant to the width of every pipe. The effect of the constant was considerable in the treble but negligible in the bass where the constant became very small in relation to the pipe diameter. The result of the old scaling method was that when William Hill started making 32ft pipes for the first time he ended up with absolutely enormous scales for the bottom notes, the CCCC pipe in the centre of the case at Birmingham being 22in (560mm) in diameter. It is fairly easy to calculate that this is exactly the scale which could result from extending the normal treble scales by this method. The year after the Birmingham organ was built, in 1835, J. G. Töpfer published his theories on pipe-scales which advocated the use of geometric progressions in their calculation. Using pseudo-scientific arguments, he postulated that the pipe diameter ought to halve every sixteen notes. Töpfer's theories were widely adopted, and Willis came to use them extensively. Their practical effect was not only to avoid the enormous basses characteristic of Hill's early work (and also that of Samuel Green) but also for the treble pipes to be smaller than before. As Willis also made his unison stops louder as they ascended the scale, the resulting brilliance helped to mask the fact that, with the increasing interest in solo tone colours, a decreasing emphasis on the Diapason chorus led to the upperwork being scaled smaller still.

Willis continued Hill's trend to differentiate the tone of the Swell organ from that of the Great. Higher pressure allowed him to emphasise further the role of the reeds, and he reduced the scale of the flue-stops, making them narrower than on the Great. It might be thought that, with all these smaller scales, the Willis organ would have been anaemic. In fact, if anything the reverse was the case because Willis adjusted the 'cut-up' of the pipe-mouths to compensate. The cut-up is the height of the top lip of the mouth above the bottom lip. It governs the natural frequency of the edge-tone vibrations which energise the air column in the pipe body, though they are largely controlled in pitch by the resonance of that air column. Increasing the cut-up allows the pipe to be blown harder. To some extent cut-up and pipe-scale are interchangeable, a wide pipe with a low cut-up producing a tone which is broadly similar in harmonic content to that of a narrower pipe with a higher cut-up. However, there are significant differences. Samuel Green achieved his 'sweet' tone with wide scales and a low cut-up; Hill's earlier work also tended this way. Willis' higher cut-ups and narrower scales produce a 'hard' sound, useful for energising large buildings in which the acoustical absorption of the air acts as a filter for over-brilliant pipes but tiring to listen to at close range. In the bass this harder sound was encouraged by the use of a tuning slot some distance down from the top of the pipe, a device which Willis copied from Cavaillé-Coll. It was this difference in voicing philosophy which led to Willis' contempt for old pipes and to all the fuss when he discarded Green's pipework at Wells Cathedral in 1857. This can be contrasted with Hill's sympathetic treatment of Father Smith's pipes at Great St Mary's, Cambridge in 1870.

Curiously for such an innovator, Willis retained the English tierce-based chorus mixtures, even in the face of the change to equal temperament. It will be recalled that Father Smith's quarter-tones had no commercial success as an attempt to solve the problem of temperament, after which the whole matter was rather forgotten, though a modified tuning was evolved to ease the restrictions on usable keys. In Germany the 'tempered' tunings of Werckmeister, Kirnberger and others led eventually to the use of 'equal temperament' where the errors of tuning, both in the thirds and in the fifths, are spread equally amongst all keys. Equal temperament began to be used in France in the early part of the nineteenth century and spread to England in the 1850s, becoming the norm for the piano. Its universal adoption for organs, where the sustained tones show up some of the weaknesses of equal temperament, took longer, almost to the end of the century. Equal temperament produces distinctly sharp thirds and when chords containing them are played they will clash with the true thirds in mixtures containing tierces, producing a distinctly acidic effect. One way around this problem is to use only unison and quint-sounding ranks in chorus mixtures. Interestingly, it was William Hill's practice to use the tierce only in the two lowest octaves. Whether this was due to a recognition of the problem of temperament is debatable since, as early as 1818, the Ashridge organ had a Sesquialtera where the tierce drops out at middle C.

To conclude the description of 'Father' Willis (as he is commonly called to distinguish him from his son and grandson, also called Henry), the following stop-list of the organ in Union Chapel, Islington, London, built in 1873, gives an example of his mature style:

Great Organ		Swell Organ	
Double Open Diapason	16	Contra Gamba	16
Open Diapason	8	Open Diapason	8
Flauto Dolce	8	Lieblich Gedackt	8
Stopped Diapason	8	Salicional	8
Claribel Flute	8	Vox Angelica	8
Principal	4	Gemshorn	4
Harmonic Flute	4	Lieblich Flöte	4
Twelfth	2⅔	Mixture	III
Fifteenth	2	Vox Humana	8
Mixture	III	Oboe	8
Trumpet	8	Trumpet	8
Clarion	4	Clarion	4

Choir Organ		*Pedal Organ*	
Viol d'Amore	8	Open Diapason (wood)	16
Lieblich Gedackt	8	Open Diapason (metal)	16
Claribel Flute	8	Bourdon	16
Dulciana	8	Principal	8
Concert Flute	4	Ophicleide	16
Lieblich Flute	4		
Piccolo	2		
Corno di Bassetto	8		

Notice the retreat from William Hill's complete Pedal department. The early 'Pedal pipes' had added a bass to the manual notes played through the manual-to-pedal couplers. This may have been the origin of the general habit of always playing with a manual-to-pedal coupler drawn, which made the Pedal chorus less than essential for general hymn accompaniment. Interestingly enough, on their largest instruments, where players could be expected to perform the works of Bach, both Willis and Hill continued to provide a full Pedal organ chorus. However, for the average parish church the Pedal organ was often abbreviated to 'Little Boom and Big Boom' – a stopped Bourdon, as imported by Hill in 1840, and a so-called Open Diapason. Invariably made of wood and of large scale, the tone of this stop is that of an open Flute, not a Diapason at all. As a clear descendant of the pre-1840 Pedal pipes, originally overscaled to provide weight when the first examples were of unison pitch, the fashion for its use long outlasted its origins.

Edmund Schulze, of Paulinzelle, Germany, had an impact on British organ design out of all proportion to the number of instruments installed here. His philosophy of Diapason Chorus design was the complete opposite of Willis'. Not only were Schulze's mixtures as large in scale as the rest of the chorus but also he obtained power on moderate wind pressure with wide scales and wide-mouthed pipes. The big scales were prevented from making the tone flutey by being combined with wide mouths. The mouth width is generally defined as a proportion of the pipe circumference. Diapasons normally have a 'fourth mouth' or a 'four and a half mouth' (²⁄₉ths), or something in between. This width was virtually standard for all pipes before the nineteenth century. Narrower 'fifth mouths' are used for open Flutes and for Dulcianas, where an aggressive sound is not required. Schulze energised his Diapasons with a 'three and a half mouth' (²⁄₇ths), at the expense of a rather explosive transient when the pipe began to speak. Schulze's work was sufficiently admired for several firms, including J. J. Binns of Leeds and T. C. Lewis of London, to go to some trouble to copy his ideas and Schulze's voicer was hired by

Forster & Andrews of Hull after Schulze's death.

Another voice which Schulze brought over from Germany was the 'Lieblich Gedact'. This is a stopped pipe some ten notes smaller than the long-established Stopped Diapason. Such a modest scale is made flutey by giving it a very high cut-up indeed and arching the top lip as well. The top lip is not 'flatted' but follows the cylindrical curve of the body. Schulze's Lieblich was so widely copied that his scale of 2in (50mm) at 4ft C was virtually standard for stops of this type for all sizes and makes of organ long after his death. Bass pipes, made of wood, are of a different construction to the traditional stopped pipe, the block having a sloping front. Such pipes made a cheap and space-saving Swell 16ft stop, but the bass notes 'cough' if one attempts to get any real power out of them. 'Lieblich' tone makes a clear solo but does not blend with Diapasons like a Stopped Diapason does.

In the long term, Schulze's influence was greatest in another direction. A practical voicing problem is that it is difficult to blow a narrow-scale pipe hard without the note flying up to the octave. This problem has been mentioned before in connection with the Dulciana and is one reason why the Salicional stop, which became a regular feature of the Swell organ from the 1860s, at first ran only down to tenor C in full-length pipes. It was just not possible to make the narrow-scaled pipes speak reasonably promptly in the bass. Schulze either knew or invented a device originally called the 'harmonic bridge', a horizontal bar in front of the pipe-mouth, which, applied to narrow-scaled wood pipes, enabled him to obtain a prompt speech without overblowing. Thus he was able to carry a violoncello-like tone down into the bass. It remained to William Thynne and his colleague, John Whiteley, working together to voice what is now the Grove Organ at Tewkesbury Abbey, to apply the same principle to narrow-scaled metal pipes using what is now known simply as the 'bar' to stabilise the speech not only in the bass, but through a substantial part of the compass.

It is in the nature of man to explore the limits of any new technique, and the invention of the bar enabled narrower and narrower-scaled pipes to be voiced. The limit was reached in the organs of Robert Hope-Jones, in which some of the Viole d'Orchestre stops, as they were called, are twenty or more notes smaller than an average Diapason. Hope-Jones' organs were extraordinary inside, the pipes being either of very narrow scale (known to tuners as 'stair-rods') or, alternatively, of very wide scale. The fat pipes were very pure, loud flutes, which he called by the name of Tibia. Hope-Jones wrote: 'I confess myself in agreement with those who consider that the 8ft instrument, commonly called an orchestra, possesses sufficient brilliancy, and in disagreement with those who would fain add "chorus work" in the form of a few hundred piccolos playing consecutive fifths, thirds, and octaves with each and all of the individual instruments comprising it'. He viewed the organ as an orchestra of solo voices. This was perhaps a natural outcome of the romantic outlook on music current in the last decade of the nineteenth century, made possible by voicing techniques which enabled a wider range of power and tone quality between stops than ever before. Of course, without a chorus, there would normally have been a problem in making the instrument loud enough, but mechanical blowing and electropneumatic action allowed him to use high pressures. In his own words: 'It is easy to voice an organ consisting entirely of 8ft stops in such a manner that it shall sound as bright or even brighter than an orchestra'. A Hope-Jones' 'Diapason Phonon', with a large scale, thick pipe walls and a high cut-up with the top lip covered in leather, was capable of immense power on 10in (250mm) wind. On large organs he used up to 20in (500mm) for loud, smooth reed-stops. Such an organ would naturally consist almost entirely of 8ft stops and the term 'octopod' has often been used irreverently to describe instruments of this type. The 8ft emphasis did not preclude 16ft stops on the Pedal. Indeed, Hope-Jones correlated weight with grandeur and always included a massive wooden Tibia Profunda. He was critical of the thin tone (by his standards) of bass pipes of Diapason tone and invented a pipe called a Diaphone. To give an idea of the power possible, it should be mentioned that Diaphones have been used as marine foghorns! They are really a sort of reed, with a felt and leather pad on the end of a stiff leaf-spring covering a circular hole. The pipes are only used in the bass (where they may be half-length) and are massively heavy in tone, though also remarkably prompt in speech. Only a few firms copied the technique, although the John Compton company made them into the 1950s.

Hope-Jones went bankrupt before building many instruments, but he was another builder whose influence greatly exceeded his output. No one else went to such extremes but his ideas influenced a whole generation of organ-builders, most noticeably in the development of the theatre organ.

In the early 1900s the new entertainment of the cinema began to attract the public. The silent films needed some accompaniment, if only to cover the sound of the projector, so it became usual to hire a pianist to extemporise an appropriate musical atmosphere. As the cinema became more popular, the size of the theatres began to outstrip the decibels available from a piano. Orchestras were expensive and, as early as 1908, John Compton added electric contacts to a pianola in the Tamworth Picture Palace and connected it up to some pipes. In 1910 Norman & Beard built two perfectly conventional organs for cinemas in Islington and Peckham Rye, London, one of which was designed by Sir George Martin, the organist of St Paul's Cathedral! By 1920 Henry Willis III had built a very substantial 48 stop four-manual for the Elite Cinema, Nottingham. A steady stream followed from Jardine, Hill Norman & Beard and others, all basically conventional organs, albeit with percussions and a heavy romantic bias.

Despite all this activity, the conventional organ, however romanticised, was not the direction which the theatre organ was to take. After his bankruptcy Hope-Jones had set up in business again, this time in America, where he began to develop his 'unit orchestra' principle. To understand the unit principle, it is necessary to look back a little. William Hill had fitted the organ in York Minster with a Swell Super Octave-to-Great coupler. In other words, as well as the notes played, the notes an octave higher are sounded with the coupler drawn, boosting the power of the Swell in full organ. Such couplers were expensive and added to the weight of touch of a tracker instrument but became relatively simple with tubular pneumatic action. In the Royal Albert Hall organ, London, Willis fitted a Super Octave coupler on itself, ie without coupling to another manual, and this became the usual form. Octave couplers were normally confined to the Swell organ (and the Solo organ if there was one) but Hope-Jones had commonly provided a Great Super Octave as well, and the provision of Sub-octave couplers also became common.

Octave couplers could be provided easily and cheaply with electric action and, using sliderless soundboards, it was relatively simple to fit a separate action to each stop, each with its own octave couplers. Hope-Jones carried this further and built organs based on unison stops, but with individual couplers to provide a range of stops in 16ft,8ft,4ft,2⅔ft and 2ft pitches, all derived from one 'unit' or set of pipes. He even contemplated the provision of a separate swell-box for each unit but this was too cumbersome to control easily and Hope-Jones compromised by enclosing the whole organ in two swell-boxes, the Solo and the Accompaniment. In 1910 Hope-Jones ran into financial trouble once again and he sold his factory and patents (and himself) to the Rudolph Wurlitzer company of North Tonawanda, near Buffalo. Wurlitzer's were makers of mechanical nickelodeons and player-pianos and foresaw the possibilities of the unit organ in the picture theatres, continuing its sale and development after Hope-Jones' death in 1914.

John Compton was the first British builder to take up the unit organ system. In 1923 he built a four-manual instrument on the unit system for the Pavilion Theatre, Shepherds Bush, London, complete with a copy of the Hope-Jones/Wurlitzer 'horseshoe' console. This brought the unit system to the fore and in 1925 a 'Mighty WurliTzer' was imported from America for the New Gallery Cinema, Regent Street. Through the medium of broadcasts on the then new 'wireless', this instrument achieved a huge audience and the real explosion of the theatre organ had begun. The Compton organs were basically similar to the Wurlitzers and within a year Hill Norman & Beard had announced the Christie Unit Organ along similar lines. The unit organ had taken over.

The unit system made it possible to build an instrument of apparently 100 stops from a dozen ranks of pipes, an electrically operated piano and a 'toy counter' of percussion instruments. One can see Hope-Jones' influence from a list of the basic ranks of the Wurlitzer which was installed in the Regal Cinema, Kingston upon Thames in 1931.

Main chamber	Diaphonic Diapason
	Concert Flute
	Violin
	Violin Celeste
	Vox Humana
	Oboe Horn
Solo chamber	Tibia Clausa
	Saxophone
	Kinura
	French Trumpet
	English Horn

Many instruments were smaller than this, with perhaps only five or six ranks, but they derived their power from a preponderance of reed-stops. The overall impression of these instruments is of reediness and a great weight of sound with prompt-speaking diaphonic basses. The all-pervading Tibia was used not only as a solo stop but also to thicken the tone of the other ranks, and it has been said that the Tibia is as fundamental to the theatre organ as the Diapason to the conventional instrument. With so few pipes, the 'chorus effect' was almost absent and the instrument is normally played with the tremulant running continuously.

The 1920s boom in cinema building created an enormous demand for these instruments. It was, however, very short-lived. In 1929 the first 'talkies' arrived, removing the *raison d'être* of the theatre organ at a stroke. Relatively few were made after the early 1930s and all production ceased in 1939. Many instruments continued in occasional use up to the 1950s but most of the surviving organs are now in specially adapted private houses. As a developing art form, the theatre organ came to a halt in 1930, but its influence lives on in electronic organs for home entertainment whose tonal design is still largely based on Robert Hope-Jones' one-man orchestra.

The unit organ principle spread from the theatre into the conventional organ, driven largely by the enthusiasm of John Compton who built a number of quite substantial instruments on this basis, especially in the 1920s and 1930s. Given a large enough organ, say a dozen ranks or more, the effect can be to give increased flexibility to a medium-sized instrument. Unfortunately, the principle generally came to be used to allow an apparently adequate instrument to be based on only three or four ranks of pipes. Such organs promise a reasonable variety of tone but, in practice, become monotonous on anything more than a brief acquaintance. For these reasons most of the leading builders stood out against the unit organ, though they were not averse to making use of octave borrowing on the Pedal organ, where the provision of separate soundboards for the main Pedal stops had made this a common and economical practice since the turn of the century. Another related practice was the provision of soft Pedal stops which were 'borrowed' from 16ft manual stops. Arthur Harrison was an influential exponent of this device; by the 1920s he had become the pre-eminent builder of the conventional organ, taking the place of Norman & Beard who had flourished particularly in the first decade of the century.

Both Harrison & Harrison and Norman & Beard were influenced by Hope-Jones; indeed, Norman & Beard had supplied many of the parts of the Hope-Jones organs under sub-contract. Both used heavy Diapasons, voiced with leathered lips on high pressure, and also provided smooth-toned reed-stops, voiced on heavy pressure. Neither, however, espoused the abandonment of the Diapason Chorus which characterised Hope-Jones' work, and Arthur Harrison, influenced by his friend Lt.-Col. George Dixon, developed a style which, in a way, was a natural follow-on from Father Willis. Harrison further differentiated the structure of the Swell organ from that of the Great by providing it with relatively bright reeds surmounting and dominating a mild Diapason Chorus. The Great organ was characterised by a large number of unison Diapasons, graded in power, with rather small-scaled upperwork culminating in a 'Harmonics' mixture which contained not only the tierce but also the seventh harmonic, the 'flat twenty-first'. The Great reeds were massive and smooth, generally with a transfer coupler so that they could be played from the Choir manual and used as a solo with accompaniment on the Great flues. The overall effect of a big Harrison is one of smooth refinement dominated by big, smooth reeds.

The Choir organ had been dying for years and Arthur Harrison almost killed it off. In a three-manual instrument he gave the Choir the character of one of his Solo organs. These, in themselves, were quite distinctive, being basically several abbreviated choruses of very diverse families of stops. Apart from the Tuba, the pipes were normally enclosed in a swell-box. The Solo which Harrison added to the Gloucester Cathedral organ in 1920 is typical:

Quintaton	16	Viole d'Orchestre	8	Orchestral Bassoon	16
Harmonic Flute	8	Viole Celeste	8	Clarinet	8
Concert Flute	4			Tuba	8

Octave, sub-octave and unison off couplers

(Earlier, at Ely Cathedral, Harrison had provided a Viole chorus which included a 'Cornet de Violes' mixture.)

The man who was perhaps least affected by Hope-Jones was Henry Willis III. Grandson of Father Willis, he had taken over the firm at the early age of twenty-one years, soon gaining the contract for Liverpool Cathedral, the largest organ in Britain, and pursuing his own independent line. Willis III organs reflected the taste of the time with big Diapasons and smooth reeds, but the instruments are not as heavy as Norman & Beard or Harrison's work and they have a colourful virility which sets them apart. Willis had close contacts with organ-building in America, for example his detached consoles were made to a design by Ernest Skinner. Several of his senior staff joined American firms and had a definite influence on the course of organ design in that country. Willis also travelled to Europe where he observed the first effects of the *Orgelbewegung* (the Organ Reform Movement) which was to transform organ-building.

In 1906 Albert Schweitzer, who was later to earn fame as a medical missionary, had published a pamphlet in which he argued that the organ of the time, in Britain and France as well as in Germany, was quite unsuitable for Bach. This was most certainly true, but as long as the general view of organ music was symphonic and romantic his words fell on deaf ears. The pendulum began to swing back, however, after 1920 when Schnitger's 1688 organ in the Jacobikirche, Hamburg, which must have been known to Bach, came to public notice, virtually unaltered. Musical trends were turning away from romanticism and towards a renewed interest in the music of the early eighteenth century, the so-called baroque period, a name derived from the architectural style of the time. From 1926 the *Orgel-*

bewegung, led by Christhard Mahrenholz, began to affect builders in Germany and Denmark, causing organ-building in those countries to change completely over the next twenty-five years. Surviving instruments of the baroque period were intensively studied and great efforts put into understanding their make-up so that the music of Bach and his contemporaries could be reproduced in a manner as close as possible to the original interpretation.

The effect on British organ-building of this change of direction has been gradual, very gradual at first, but remarkably persistent. In 1926 Henry Willis III introduced the first flute mutation stops on the Choir organ – a Nazard and a Tierce – in his rebuild of the organ in the Jesuit Church, Farm Street, Mayfair, London. They were scaled and voiced in a nineteenth-century manner but, nevertheless, the idea was gradually copied and by 1940, when the new Norwich Cathedral organ was built by Hill Norman & Beard, the Diapason Chorus had begun to resume some of its former importance. For a while, the organ world of the 1930s was distracted by the emergence of the electronic organ which, because of its economy in space and cost, threatened to take over from pipes. In practice, the electronic organ has proved something of a damp squib, using its technology merely to produce a cut-price imitation of the pipe organ, often twenty years out of date in tonal design. If their makers had had the imagination to exploit the possibilities of electronics to offer new facilities and widen musical horizons, as has happened more recently in the world of 'pop' music, our story might well have been different.

After the hiatus of World War II, gramophone records began to circulate of Bach performances on restored Schnitger organs in north Germany. Their style was so different to that which had evolved to play the same music on a Harrison organ that it caused immediate debate. Most of the argument was about one feature of these instruments: the explosive, if uneven, attack of the pipes when starting their note. This was in total contrast to the smooth and almost hesitant speech of Arthur Harrison's work. The debate opened up a detail of voicing technique which had never previously come to public notice: the practice of 'nicking', a series of light cuts inserted by the voicer in the edge of the languid and lower lip. No one knows when nicking was invented. Certainly, from surviving wooden pipes, which are difficult to alter, it must go back at least to the seventeenth century. The effect of the nicks is to reduce the amplitude of the 'edge-tone' generated by the air vibrating either side of the upper lip and to make it more susceptible to control by the air column in the pipe body (a principle also used to quieten the exhaust of jet aircraft engines). A pipe without nicks will speak quickly and explosively

98

with a pronounced 'spit' before it settles down to the correct note which, in itself, has a considerable 'fuzz' of non-harmonic overtones. Light nicking reduces these overtones and controls the spit. Heavier nicking slows up the speech and considerably curtails the upper harmonics but is essential for pipes blown hard on heavy pressure. Over the centuries voicers had gradually increased the depth and number of the nicks, leading finally to the smoothness of the Arthur Harrison style.

Initially there was an over-reaction. From about 1950 J. W. Walker and Hill Norman & Beard both started to voice some Choir organ pipes completely without nicks, controlling the explosive speech with a very narrow flue opening. Instead of being regulated in power by closing up the tip of the foot to control the wind supply, the foot is left wide open and the regulation obtained by varying the flue. Later, Grant Degens and Bradbeer applied this principle to whole instruments which became well known for their aggressive sound. Today, voicers have learned other techniques for controlling pipe-speech, and excessive 'spit' should no longer be a problem.

Organ-builders of the 1950s generally located their 'baroque' voicing on the Choir organ, which had almost completely lost its purpose in the romantic era. They introduced small choruses and copious mutation stops in attempting, with varying degrees of success, to turn the Choir organ into an anglicised version of the north German Positive. For the rest of the instrument the changes were more gradual, with bolder choruses than would have been provided twenty years earlier but often still with reed-stops on heavy pressure. John Compton's joke in naming the stops on the three near-identical manuals of his temporary electronic instrument for the Royal Festival Hall, London in 1951 – with the Great organ stops in English, the Swell organ stops in French and the Positive in German – was symptomatic of the eclectic approach.

The eclectic philosophy was particularly common when Victorian or Edwardian instruments were rebuilt. A typical rebuilding scheme of 1957 is shown on page 100. Note the complete mixture of languages in the stop-names and the reappearance of the Spanish horizontal Trumpet as well as a Choir organ consisting largely of a Cornet Separé.

A major turning point came with the organ in the Royal Festival Hall, London, opened in 1954. This was the first large British organ with a stop-list designed in accordance with the north German *werk* principle with clearly differentiated Principal (Diapason) and Flute choruses on each manual. In the Royal Festival Hall this German-style fluework was combined with French light-pressure reed-stops

Great organ			*Swell organ*	
Contra Geigen	16		Lieblich Bourdon	16
Open Diapason I	8		Violin Diapason	8
Open Diapason II	8		Wald Flute	8
Stopped Diapason	8		Salicional	8
Octave	4		Voix Celeste	8
Spitz Flute	4		Geigen Principal	4
Twelfth	2⅔		Rohr Flute	4
Fifteenth	2		Fifteenth	2
Quartane	II		Quint Mixture	III
Harmonic Trumpet	8		Contra Fagotto	16
			Oboe	8
Pedal organ			Trompette	8
Resultant Bass	32	(derived)	Octave	
Open Wood Bass	16		Sub-Octave	
Geigen Bass	16	(Great)	Unison Off	
Sub Bass	16			
Lieblich Bourdon	16	(Swell)	*Choir organ*	
Octave Wood	8	(derived)	Chimney Flute	8
Geigen Principal	8	(derived)	Octav	4
Bass Flute	8	(derived)	Gemshorn	4
Choral Flute	4	(derived)	Nasat	2⅔
Twenty-second	2		Blockflöte	2
Trombone	16		Tierce	1⅗
Fagotto	16	(Swell)	Larigot	1⅓
Trumpet	8	(derived)	Sifflöte	1
Clarion	4	(derived)	Krummhorn	8
			State Trumpet	
			(horizontal)	8

and the result, built with a very wide but also fairly deep layout, can only be described as individual. The organ was designed by Ralph Downes, who combined his musicianship with an interest in voicing and a meticulous approach which enabled him to direct its construction by craftsmen trained in a different idiom. Its success in attracting the general musical public to the sound of the organ helped to make the baroque organ respectable.

The basic tenet of the *werk* principle is that each department of the organ should occupy a clearly defined separate location and that the fundamental pitches of the departments should also be varied. Thus an organ might have a 16ft-based Pedal, an 8ft-based Great and a 4ft-based Positive. This scheme needs to be followed consistently through the whole stop-list. Thus the flutes at corresponding pitches should be of broadly similar type and the mixture compositions should ascend in the same way, though not to the extent of being an octave apart. The reeds should also follow a similar pattern with, say, a full-length 16ft reed on the Pedal, an 8ft Trumpet on the Great and a half-length reed, such as a Krummhorn, on the Positive. If there is a third manual division it may be a *Brustwerk*, located above the console, based on 2ft and with a fractional-length reed such as a Regal or Vox Humana.

In the romantic development of the organ which culminated in the Hope-Jones 'one-man orchestra', individual stops varied widely in their dynamic levels from the fff Tuba Mirabilis to the ppp Vox Angelica. The result was a very wide dynamic range but a relatively limited ability to blend the colours of different stops. By contrast, pure *werk* principle instruments have no loud or soft stops, the common dynamic level making it possible to blend almost any pair or group of voices. Whilst this does restrict the dynamic range, the result is a wealth of combinational possibilities which give the instrument great life, variety and colour.

After the Royal Festival Hall organ, some musicians became not only dissatisfied with the eclectic organ but also felt that we should go further and follow the Continent in copying precisely the construction of the instruments of eighteenth-century Hanseatic Germany. As early as 1936 Hill Norman & Beard had built, for Susi Jeans, an organ with mechanical tracker action and pipes imported from Germany, and in 1965 Queen's College, Oxford imported an instrument from Frobenius of Denmark which followed eighteenth-century practice very closely. In particular, there are separate tone-cabinets for each department and the action is totally mechanical. The stop-list is:

Great organ		*Brustpositive*		*Pedal organ*	
Gedeckt	16	Gedeckt	8	Subbass	16
Principal	8	Principal	4	Principal	8
Rohrflute	8	Rohrflute	4	Gedeckt	8
Octave	4	Gemshorn	2	Octave	4
Octave	2	Quint	1⅓	Mixture	III
Sesquialtera	II	Scharff	III	Fagot	16
Mixture	IV	Cromorne	8	Schalmei	4
Trumpet	8				

For lack of height a Pedal 16ft Principal is omitted, but this does not destroy the balance of the scheme. The one concession to the romantic organ is that the *Brustpositive* is fitted with Swell-shutters to the front of the tone-cabinet. Therein lies a problem, since such a department is an expressive Positive, not a Swell organ as we have come to know it.

Following the Queen's College instrument, adoption of the principles of the Hanseatic organ has gradually spread, including not only the tonal design and voicing but also the use of tone-cabinets and, from about 1970, mechanical action. Until recently, however, a more fundamental aspect of the organ remained unreformed: its tuning. A number of builders have now abandoned equal temperament and adopted one or other of the compromise temperaments of the eighteenth century. These compromise temperaments are more flexible than mean-tone, which confines one virtually to six key-signatures, but do involve some tempering of the thirds so that whilst some keys are preferable to others, few, if any, are totally unusable. It follows from this that each key-signature has its own character instead of merely moving the pitch up or down, as in equal temperament.

Another break with Victorian practice is a further change in pipe-scaling methods. The whole history of pipe-scaling is a succession of mathematical 'laws' which have helped craftsmen to control and record what they are doing, but which have had to be modified so that the finished result appeals not to the rule-book but to the ear. As early as 1900 the first Herbert Norman, of Norman & Beard, had become dissatisfied with Töpfer's rigid geometric progressions and had varied the 'halving ratio' from stop to stop and from octave to octave. More recently, Ralph Downes' historical research has shown that older Continental builders varied their scales considerably from stop to stop. Builders now still use Töpfer's scales as a basis for calculation but vary the scales between the different constituents of the chorus to emphasise particular characteristics in different parts of the compass.

The difficulty with a precise copy of the Hanseatic eighteenth-century organ is that whilst the eclectic organ did not hold together as a single artistic whole – in particular, the Choir/Positive frequently stood away from the rest of the instrument – musicians still want to be eclectic in their choice of music. Whilst the works of Bach and his contemporaries form the backbone of the repertoire, the argument for the Hanseatic organ assumes that all music written since 1800 is unworthy, which is patently not the case. The problem lies in the lack of dynamic flexibility of the Hanseatic organ. The 'terrace dynamics' of the Bach organ (the steps by which the power can be augmented) are insufficiently flexible for Liszt, Reger and César Franck, or indeed for more recent composers. One can add to the dynamic range with dominant stops, such as light-pressure horizontal reeds, without seriously compromising the basic design and, in larger instruments, soft stops, such as Salicionals and Celestes, can also be accommodated, but the swell-box is another matter. In fact, the swell-box appears to be easily the most enduring feature of the post-Bach organ, though organ-builders are now anything but unanimous on the design of the Swell organ.

The fundamental difficulty lies in fitting the Swell into the *werk* principle concept of a different pitch for the main fundamental Diapason-tone stop of each manual. As we have seen, the Swell organ evolved as an 'Echo Great', only taking on a role as a true secondary chorus in the nineteenth century, and, even then, relying on reed-stops for power. This is a very different concept to that of a 2ft-based *Brustwerk*, even if swell shutters are fitted to the front of the tone-cabinet. The problem is that a 2ft-based division fits neatly into the shallow *werk* principle layout, whereas an 8ft-based Swell is very often impossible to accommodate in the same vertical plane as the other manuals. Some have compromised by setting the pitch of the Principal/Diapason at 4ft whilst retaining the *Brustwerk* position under the Great organ. This does have the disadvantage that, with mechanical action, the Great organ is pushed very high, as for example in the 1979 Rieger organ at Christchurch Cathedral, Oxford. There is now more variety in the design of the Swell organ than ever before; we await the next stage in its evolution with impatience!

The other theme which runs through much recent work is one of conservation. Organ pipes do not wear out, though the metal does soften a little with time, mostly in the first ten or fifteen years. Over an extended period reed-tongues lose their 'set' and flue-pipe languids drop a little, spoiling the 'freshness' of the tone. These can be re-set, but with changes in taste it was taken as natural in times past that Samuel Green should throw out John Snetzler's pipes, that Father Willis should dispense with Green's and that Arthur Harrison should discard those of Willis. The same applies to organ actions. A break from this custom, carried out under the guidance of Cecil Clutton, was the careful restoration of the organ by Renatus Harris in All Hallows, Twickenham in 1940. The restoration of the Wymondham Abbey organ in 1954 by Hill Norman & Beard was another landmark, yet, as recently as 1963 an eminent organist seriously proposed the 'Harrisonisation' of the Father Smith organ in Great St Mary's, Cambridge. Our respect for the best of what remains to us has increased in recent years and springs from a growing interest in the British organ as our heritage, as distinct from the Hanseatic German prototype of the *Orgelbewegung*. Flue voicing with a very pronounced 'spit' in the initial speech is now less common than it was, and a few light nicks on the languid are accepted as a means of control, not a violation of dogma. Certainly some of the instruments of the 1960s now sound somewhat 'rough' to current ears, though, however critical we are, we should resist the impulse to tinker with them, just in case tomorrow brings a different view of their virtues.

It has been shown how the techniques of voicing, the stop-list and the general historical development of the British organ are all bound up with one another. It is to be hoped that, with this background, the reader will be able to see and hear some of the instruments described in the Gazetteer with a more informed understanding.

4

ORGAN-BUILDERS

Some of the organ-builders whose names you may encounter when exploring organs in Britain.

Abbott & Smith Isaac Abbott was a Hill man who set up for himself in Leeds in 1869. In spite of considerable Schulze influence, his instruments retained some Hill flavour. On his retirement, the firm became Abbott & Smith and their work became more run-of-the-mill. They nevertheless got their hands on some quite large organs, including Leeds Town Hall, which they spoiled.

Henry Ainscough Built in Preston in the second half of the nineteenth century and mostly found in Lancashire, his instruments have a certain rough vigour.

Cedric Arnold His converted sweet factory in Thaxted, Essex was the source, from about 1930 to 1970, of some simple and well-cased organs.

John Avery Worked on some quite major organs in the last quarter of the eighteenth century though none now remains in the condition in which he left it. He is said to have been a good builder when sober!

Bates Bates of Ludgate Hill, London built many small organs in the first half of the nineteenth century, often with quaint Gothick cases. A number still survive and are increasingly treasured. He also built organs with barrel player mechanisms.

von Beckerath Rudolph von Beckerath was a major German builder of the post-war period. He claimed to have invented the *schwimmer* bellows. His organ at Clare College, Cambridge does not really do his work full justice.

Bedwell Oxford and Cambridge supported several firms of 'hack' organ-builders in the nineteenth century, supplying the lesser

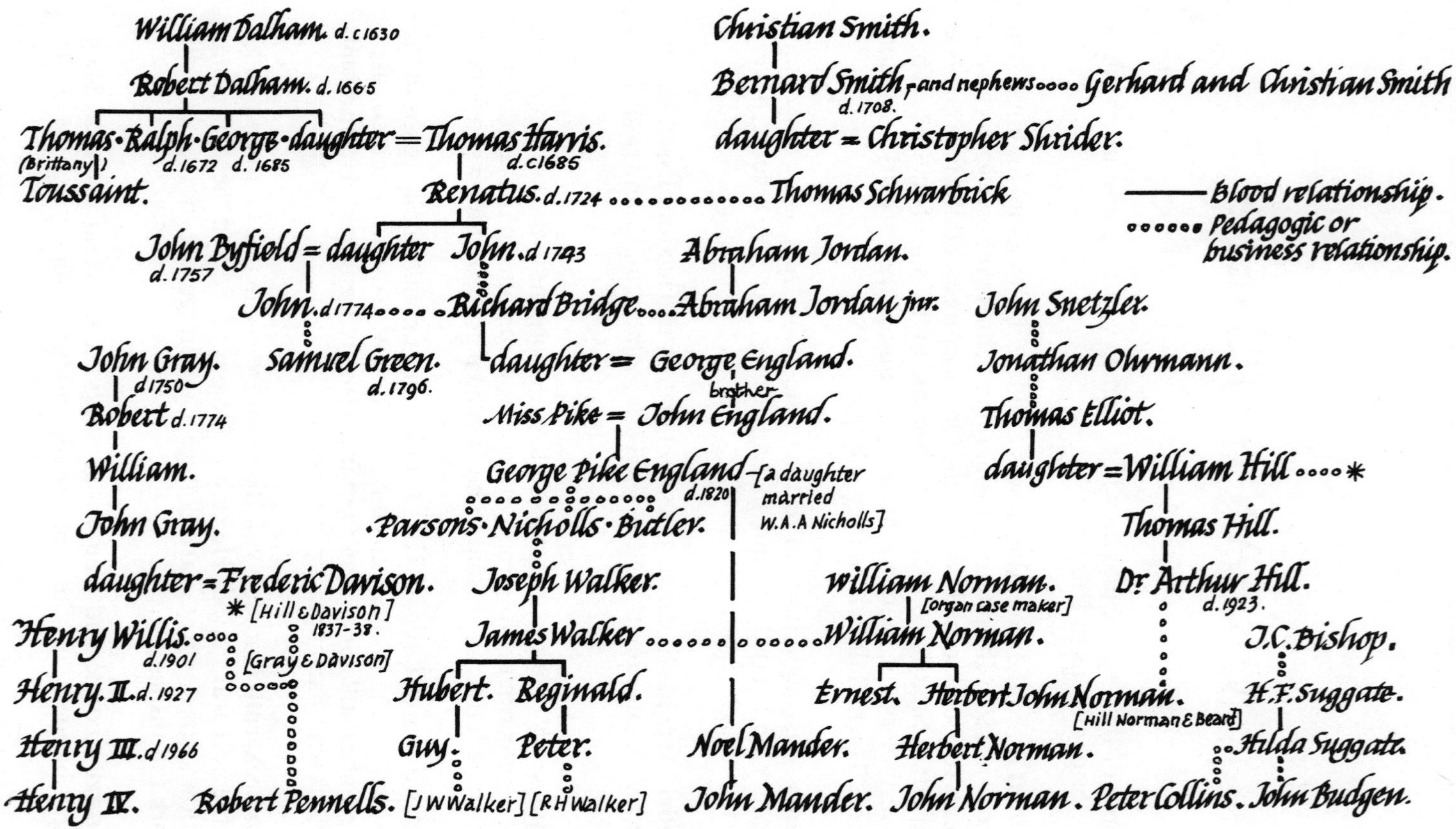

Fig 19 'Family' tree of prominent organbuilders

churches, whilst the big names built the major college organs. Bedwell was such a firm, based in Cambridge.

Bevington Although the firm lasted through several generations from 1795 to the 1940s, and although they built some large organs, Bevington's were best known for the numbers of small organs they made for country churches in the 1860s and 1870s. Many are only single manual, generally with simple post-and-rail cases. A surprisingly high proportion are still in use, if often neglected. They are worth hanging on to, even if they do not rank as great art.

J. J. Binns The largest and sometimes the best of the turn-of-the-century Leeds organ-builders, his major works could be very good and he fitted a most handsome console to the Schulze organ at St Bartholomew's, Armley, Leeds. The lesser organs were not always to the same standard.

Bishop & Son A firm of very long lineage. J. C. Bishop was a pioneer of the C compass organ in the 1840s. He was a prolific inventor; the composition pedal, the concussion bellows and the Clarabella stop are all due to him. The firm survived, despite indifferent work at the end of the nineteenth century, and since 1950 they have established a name for conservative restoration work.

Booth Joseph Booth, of Wakefield, was an early nineteenth century pioneer of the Pedal organ and also experimented with the pneumatic lever. His *magnum opus* in the Brunswick Chapel, Leeds is unfortunately no longer extant.

Richard Bridge A mid-eighteenth-century London builder who built organs for several large Hawksmoor churches, of which that in Christ Church, Spitalfields, London is the grandest. His cases were very fine, with 'flats' of ogee form. For a time he worked in consortium with Byfield and Jordan.

Brindley & Foster A product of the late nineteenth-century organ boom, Brindley & Foster was based in Sheffield but had a national clientele. Early Brindleys with tracker action are good sound organs. Later instruments used a crude pneumatic action and a unique sliderless soundboard design which may have been cheap to make but is certainly expensive to repair. As a consequence most have now disappeared.

Bryceson Bros They started with barrel organs, like Bates, but went on to build more substantial instruments. The second generation Bryceson was the first builder in Britain to experiment with electro-pneumatic action, in 1868.

John Byfield There were three generations of John Byfields. The first was son-in-law to Renatus Harris. Like Richard Bridge, the Byfields provided their organs with excellent three-tower classical cases. The 1765 instrument by the younger Byfield at St Mary, Rotherhithe, London has survived with only modest alteration.

Christie The Christie Unit Organ was the trade name under which the theatre organs made by Hill Norman & Beard were marketed in large numbers between 1926 and 1932. They were so named after John Christie, then chairman of the firm, who later became famous as the founder of the Glyndebourne Opera.

Church & Company Nigel Church has been building organs in Stamfordham, just outside Newcastle, since 1971. He concentrates on new mechanical action organs.

P. D. Collins Peter Collins trained with Bishop and with Rieger in Austria. His work ranges from chamber organs, of which he is a leading maker, to some of Britain's largest new instruments. Collins organs are often notably compact in relation to their contents.

John Compton John Compton was an early practitioner of electric action and an inventive genius who flourished in the first half of this century. His developments included the 32ft Polyphone and the luminous console. He was by far the most whole-hearted exponent of the 'unit organ' concept which he used in some quite large instruments as well as in large numbers of theatre organs. John Compton was responsible for the commercial introduction, in the 1930s, of the Compton 'Electrone', an electrostatic instrument invented by Leslie Bourn.

Peter Conacher & Co Conacher's made numbers of sturdy and reliable parish church instruments at their Huddersfield works and sent them all over the world in the late nineteenth century. They were never great art but their simple reliability has won them many friends. To distinguish their instruments from those made by other branches of the same family their nameplates at one time bore the legend 'Peter Conacher & Co, The Old Firm'!

Cousans, Sons & Co This Lincoln-based firm was closely associated at the beginning of this century with the early development of the rotary electric blower, in addition to being organ-builders in their own right.

Crang & Hancock Eighteenth-century improvers of other people's organs, parts of their instrument in Barnstaple parish church survive. After Crang's death, James Hancock made chamber organs, including one which survives at Pertenhall dated 1783.

Thomas and Robert Dallam Father and son and, in many ways, the founders of British organ-building. Thomas kept a fascinating diary of his journey to install an organ-clock which was a present from Queen Elizabeth I to the Sultan of Turkey. His organ case in King's College Chapel, Cambridge will ensure that he is not forgotten. Robert Dallam built all the important organs in the Laudian revival period of the 1630s and, from the scanty survivals, his work seems to have been of high quality, especially the casework. A Roman Catholic, Robert fled to Brittany during the Commonwealth, returning at the Restoration but dying in 1665. Renatus Harris was his grandson.

Percy Daniel A present-day westcountry firm. Under the direction of Walter Gulvin until recently, they have specialised in fitting new action to older instruments.

James Davis Born in Preston and came to London about 1790. This was not a prosperous time for organ-builders but contemporary sources said that he had built more organs than anyone else since Green. Very few survive, though there are two in Wymondham Abbey, Norfolk.

Thomas Elliot He was the not inconsiderable link between two famous builders. He took over the remains of the Snetzler firm at the beginning of the nineteenth century and, in his turn, was succeeded by his son-in-law, William Hill. At least two of his smaller organs survive unaltered and show both a Snetzler-like voicing style and the beginnings of Hill features of construction.

England There were three Englands: George ('Old England'), his brother John and John's son, George Pike. The son carried on the traditions of eighteenth-century organ-building through into the early nineteenth century. Quite a number of their instruments remain, though not unaltered.

Flentrop Dirk Flentrop, of Zaandam, Holland, has built his baroque-revival instruments for churches and universities all over the world. There is one in the Concert Hall at Eton College and another in the Queen Elizabeth Hall, London.

Flight & Robson Less successful together than Robson was after they parted company in 1832, Robson, like Hill, was strongly influenced by Dr Gauntlett. Chamber organs apart, his work survives only as part of later instruments.

Forster & Andrews A successful partnership between a salesman (Forster) and a technician (Andrews). Based on Hull, they constructed large numbers of solidly built instruments in the second half of the nineteenth century. Despite the use of very little tin in their pipes, their voicing style, which was influenced by Edmund Schulze, could be quite energetic.

Th. Frobenius & Son This Danish builder was responsible for the first sizeable modern mechanical action organ in Britain, at Queen's College, Oxford. It is still arguably his best.

John Geib We know little of Geib, save that the case of his 1790 organ at St Mary, Stafford still survives. He also made square pianos and later emigrated to New York.

Grant, Degens & Bradbeer This firm (formerly Grant, Degens & Rippin or just Degens & Rippin) made a dramatic entry upon the British organ scene in the 1960s, led by Maurice Forsyth-Grant. They were major exponents of the neo-classical organ, allied to imaginative case design. In retrospect, their style now seems brash, though never uninteresting.

Gray & Davison Frederic Davison joined John Gray, who had been Elliot's chief rival, in 1838 when he left his partnership with Hill to marry Gray's daughter! In the 1840s and 1850s they were probably the most important builders after Hill. Later they rebuilt earlier instruments to the C compass and added Pedal organs. The firm declined after 1880 (their later instruments are best avoided), but the firm continued a separate existence until 1970.

Samuel Green Green replaced John Snetzler as organ-builder to the King and built many important instruments from about 1780 up to his death in 1796. His success was largely due to royal patronage as some of his larger organs were not wholly satisfactory, many being moved or rebuilt within a few years of his death. The quality of internal construction was somewhat rough, but his instruments have elegant mahogany cases and a very distinctive 'sweet' tone. Though lacking forcefulness in a large building, a Green organ is remarkably restful to listen to, an effect achieved with wide-scaled pipes gently voiced. He was one of the first organ-builders to increase the usefulness of the Swell organ by providing efficient shutters (copied from Tschudi's harpsichords) and by extending the compass below middle C which had previously been the norm. Some instruments completed shortly after his death bear the name of his widow, Sarah Green.

Thomas Harris and Renatus Harris Thomas Harris, son-in-law of Robert Dallam, lived in France during the Commonwealth. At the Restoration of the monarchy in 1660 he returned to England where he received important commissions for Gloucester and Worcester cathedrals. His son Renatus built six cathedral organs in England (Chichester, Winchester, Bristol, Ely, Norwich and Salisbury) as well as one in Ireland (Dublin). Renatus Harris' rivalry with Bernard Smith became very public yet the style which, between them, they established was to last with only minor variations for around a hundred and fifty years.

Harrison & Harrison Originally based in Rochdale, Harrisons moved to Durham in 1872 and came to prominence when the second generation took over and Arthur Harrison successfully rebuilt the Hill organ in Ely Cathedral in 1908. Arthur Harrison continued to rebuild Hill's and Willis' cathedral organs over the course of the next thirty years – thirteen cathedral organs in all. His style, influenced by Lt-Col George Dixon, was very romantic, yet the organ chorus was not forgotten, with very strong differences of character between the manuals. Harrison instruments acquired a reputation for finish and mechanical reliability. After the war, under Cuthbert Harrison, grandson of the founder, they built the organ in the Royal Festival Hall, London, in collaboration with Ralph Downes.

Hele & Co A Plymouth-based firm which carried out work throughout England in the late nineteenth century, their later work was undistinguished, though the company is now under new direction.

Wm Hill & Son William Hill was the finest British organ-builder of the nineteenth century and possibly of all time. He started with Birmingham Town Hall in 1834, and later became the leading advocate of the now standard C compass and the provision of adequate Pedal organs. He built many important instruments, a few of which remain unaltered to this day. Thomas Hill took over from his father in 1871; his *magnum opus* is in Sydney Town Hall, Australia. The work of the firm was concluded by Dr Arthur Hill, author of a standard work on organ cases, who designed the distinguished cases at Peterborough and Chichester cathedrals and Beverley Minster. The tonal structure of the Hill organ of the 1850–60 period is often taken to be that of the ideal British organ, sufficiently influenced by Continental practice to be complete yet not over-romantic nor in any way forced in tone.

Hill Norman & Beard This was an amalgamation (more fully, Wm Hill and Son & Norman and Beard Ltd) of the two firms which merged in 1916. In 1923 the company came under the chairmanship of John Christie of Glyndebourne who provided eccentric leadership, pushing the company into the unit theatre organ business. After the war, Hill Norman & Beard combined an early movement toward classical voicing with an eclectic outlook which, for example, included the reintroduction of horizontal Spanish Trumpets. Although they revived the use of tracker action for small organs as early as the late 1950s, they were also pioneers of electric action, introducing solid-state relays in 1963, moving on more recently to actions with memory and playback facilities.

G. M. Holdich Built a few large instruments, including one for Lichfield Cathedral in 1861, but is now best known for his organs for village churches which are particularly common in East Anglia.

Robert Hope-Jones The Hope-Jones Organ Co only survived a few years (1889–1903) and did not build many organs, but its influence was great. Firstly, Robert Hope-Jones was trained as a telephone engineer and he was the first organ-builder to provide electric action as standard. Although his electric mechanism became a byword for unreliability, the basic design principles were almost universally followed until relatively recently. Secondly, his instruments were of extraordinary tonal design – true 'octopods' – all 8ft stops and the pipes either grossly fat (Tibias) or unbelievably etiolated (Violes d'Orchestre). Hope-Jones' avowed intention was to turn the organ into a one-man orchestra and, after his death, the Wurlitzer firm in America built on his ideas to create the unit theatre organ, using tonal principles which govern the design of light entertainment organs, electronic as well as pipe, to this day.

Hradetzky Gregor Hradetzky comes from the beautiful town of Krems on the Danube in Austria. His organs are not quite as inventive as those of Rieger, his Austrian rival. The four-manual at the University of St Andrews, Scotland features a very striking console with terraced stop-jambs.

Hunter Built solid and reliable though musically unadventurous organs in Clapham, London in the late nineteenth and early twentieth centuries.

Ingram Eustace Ingram was a Willis man who took over Holdich's business. One of his sons, another Eustace, was for a time Hope-Jones' partner; the other, Arthur, built up a large business in Edinburgh.

Jardine This firm was originally known as Kirtland & Jardine. Kirtland was Samuel Renn's nephew and inherited his business. Starting in 1848, they were the leading builders in the Manchester area and continued in operation until relatively recently. A cousin went to America and built excellent organs in New York.

E. J. Johnson Successors to Miller in Cambridge, this firm has recently produced a number of interesting small chamber organs as well as the organ in St Catharine's College, Cambridge.

Henry Jones Henry Jones of Fulham, London built a large number of mechanically sound but tonally rather ordinary organs in the mid to late nineteenth century.

Jordan Abraham Jordan and his son were London builders of the early eighteenth century. As well as being an organ-builder, Jordan had a sideline as a wine importer. This may have been the reason why he was the first man in England to provide a controllable swell-box, a device which had been invented in Portugal a few years before.

E. H. Lawton Built organs in Aberdeen, Scotland. Although his standards were rough and his main business local, he was remarkable for also exporting organs to New Zealand and to Africa.

Laycock & Bannister Previously an unremarkable firm based on Keighley, Yorkshire, this company is now under the same direction as Nicholson.

T. C. Lewis One of the better builders of the turn of the century, Lewis was very much influenced by the work of Edmund Schulze. He provided ringing and powerful Diapason Choruses at a time when the growth of the romantic tradition made them unfashionable. In a reverberant building the result can be thrilling, but in a less reverberant one it can be tiring.

H. C. Lincoln Was a rival to Gray and to Elliot in the 1820s and 1830s. Some of his chamber organs survive, as does a three-manual now at Thaxted, Essex.

John Loosemore Was clerk of the Works to Exeter Cathedral in the seventeenth century and organ-building appears to have been something of a sideline for him. The case of his Exeter Cathedral organ survives, altered and without the splendid embossed tin bass pipes for which it was originally famous.

N. P. Mander Noel Mander came to the fore in the immediate post-war period and first established a reputation for scholarly restoration, especially of chamber organs. His scrupulous restoration of eighteenth-century organ cases has led to a very high standard of cabinet-work and finish throughout his instruments. Today his firm is one of our major builders.

Marcussen & Son A very fine Danish builder, notable for solid construction and good finish, his few instruments in Britain barely do him justice.

Martin & Coate Martin built some substantial if undistinguished organs in the Oxford area. When he died at the end of the nineteenth century, the business was continued by Coate, who was his son-in-law.

Metzler The organ in the Smith case at Trinity College, Cambridge is by Metzler, a present-day builder from Zurich, Switzerland.

Miller Arguably the better of the two 'hack' organ-builders in Cambridge in the late nineteenth century.

Michell & Thynne Also Beale & Thynne – two short-lived firms of the 1880s and 1890s, notable for clever and well-executed romantic voicing which others were to copy but seldom to equal.

Alfred Monk An old Monk of the 1880s is a good sound instrument with a solid chorus. Later instruments, under the name of Monk & Gunther, never achieved the same standard.

Nicholson In the nineteenth century there was a whole family of Nicholsons building organs in various parts of the country. Of these, the Worcester firm became the best known. In the twentieth century Nicholsons were for a time a subsidiary of Compton, then later under the direction of Stanley Lambert. Now in Malvern, the firm has enjoyed a renaissance under its current management.

Norman & Beard Originally E. W. Norman, then Norman Bros & Beard, they at first built fairly plain but solid organs in Norwich, Norfolk. In the late 1890s the firm expanded greatly, becoming Norman & Beard Ltd in the process. In their heyday they built an organ a week and employed over two hundred craftsmen in Norwich and London. The organs are romantic in style and are very solidly built. The Norman & Beard exhaust-pneumatic action has a spongy key-touch but is very reliable and a considerable number survive in their original condition. The company amalgamated with Hill in 1916.

Geo. Osmond This Taunton company has built up a considerable connection west of Bristol. It is now under common management with Hill Norman & Beard.

Phelps & Associates Lawrence Phelps is one of the most brilliant organ designers alive. After training with Aeolian-Skinner in the USA, he revitalised the tonal side of Casavant Frères in Canada. His career as an independent organ-builder has had its ups and downs and his only British instrument is at Hexham Abbey, Northumberland.

Phipps Phipps was the nineteenth-century Oxford counterpart to Bedwell of Cambridge; he did the lesser work (badly) whilst the big names supplied the colleges.

The Positive Organ Co This firm flourished in the early years of this century as suppliers of small organs, mostly of one manual, to country and mission churches. The instruments were built to standard designs and purchased from a catalogue. Many featured intricate pneumatic mechanism to provide a Melodic Bass which catered for players who could not manage the pedals by playing the 16ft Bourdon on the lowest note only of a manual chord. Similarly, in the absence of a

115

second manual, a Melodic Diapason could be made to solo the treble note of a right-hand chord. The firm was directed by Thomas Casson, a retired banker, whose son became the distinguished actor, Sir Lewis Casson.

Samuel Renn Was apprenticed to James Davis, his uncle. When Davis retired, Renn transferred the business to Stockport, becoming the main organ-builder in the Manchester area in the years 1823–44. He was relatively prolific but only a few of his instruments remain in their original condition, though a fair number of his early Gothic Revival cases survive.

Rieger Under the direction of Joseph von Glatter-Götz, Rieger of Schwarzach, Austria, have exported a number of instruments to Britain in recent years. Rieger organs have particularly responsive tracker key-actions though their tonal characteristics and case designs are often controversial.

Rothwell The brothers Rothwell established their reputation in the 1910–40 period. Their claim to fame was their unusual consoles in which the stops were operated by small stop-keys located between the manuals so the registration could be changed without lifting the hands from the manuals.

Rushworth & Dreaper Came to prominence after 1920 and became one of the largest firms of organ-builders in Britain. They are associated with the well-known Liverpool music-house.

Timothy Russell Russell was for a time in partnership with John England in the early nineteenth century. Some of his work survives in the organ now in Chiswick Parish Church, London.

R. Spurden Rutt An east London builder of the early twentieth century, he specialised in small and economical two-manual organs.

Edmund Schulze Schulze of Paulinzelle, Germany, exhibited an instrument at the Great Exhibition of 1851 in an attempt to gain business in Britain. The actual number of instruments built was not very great, but his influence was profound. He introduced the small-scale Lieblich Gedeckt stop to Britain, most builders even copying his pipe-scale exactly; his string-tone stops were the starting point for the development of really narrow-scale strings. He also provided powerful Diapason Choruses voiced on relatively light wind pressure and with generously scaled mixtures. The firms of Lewis, Forster & Andrews and Binns all copied his ideas in varying degrees.

Thomas Schwarbrick (or Schwarbrook) Presumably of German origin, he trained with Renatus Harris and, based on Warwick, built a number of important instruments in the first half of the eighteenth century, including one for Birmingham parish church, now the Cathedral. His cases, copied from one of Harris' designs had graceful gabled flats. Happily, some of them still survive.

Christopher Shrider (or Schreider) He was son-in-law to the famous Father Smith and carried on his business for a time, building organs in much the same style. His epitaph is a remarkable example of eighteenth-century humour.

> Here rests the musical Kit Schrider
> Who Organs built when he did bide here;
> With nicest Ear he tun'd 'em up:
> But Death has put the cruel Stop;
> Though breath to others he conveyed
> Breathless alas! himself is lay'd.
> May he who us such Keys has giv'n,
> Meet with St Peter's Keys of Heav'n!
> His Cornet, Twelfth and Diapason,
> Could not with Air supply his Weasand.
> Bass, Tenor, Treble, Unison,
> The loss of tuneful *Kit* bemoan.
> (T. Webb: *A Select Collection of Epitaphs*, 1775)

Bernard Smith One of the most famous names in organ-building history, he is commonly referred to as Father Smith, to distinguish him from his nephews who worked with him. Smith trained in Bremen, Germany and was established as an organ-builder in Holland before setting up in London in about 1667. He changed the English organ from its Italianate pre-Commonwealth form, introducing mixtures and cornets as well as reed-stops. Smith became the leading builder of the prosperous late seventeenth century. Although none of his church instruments survives unaltered, many fine cases remain, most with at least a few original pipes inside.

John Snetzler Snetzler was born in Schaffhausen, Switzerland and trained in Passau, Germany. He started building organs in London in the 1740s, eventually occupying premises on the site of the present-day Foyle's bookshop. Snetzler brought to England the south

German knowledge of voicing small-scale stops and was the inventor of the Dulciana. Like Smith eighty years earlier, Snetzler was very much the leading builder of the day. As well as major instruments, he also built a considerable number of chamber organs, many of which are still in existence.

Henry Speechly The firm of Speechly of Dalston, in east London, was founded in the late nineteenth century. Some of Speechly's early work was good, reminiscent of Willis, with whom he had trained.

Thomas Thamar An organ-builder who flourished in the busy period immediately after the Restoration of the monarchy in 1660, though he was later eclipsed by Smith. One of his organs, built for Pembroke College, Cambridge, still exists in Framlingham Church, Suffolk.

Vowles There was an organ-builder in Bristol throughout the eighteenth and nineteenth centuries, and Vowles had a hand in almost every West country organ in the period 1860–90.

Ernest Wadsworth Wadsworth had been Jardine's foreman and set up with his brother in the second half of the nineteenth century. Their main reputation was local to the Manchester area, although Wadsworth also built a number of instruments for Scotland.

J. W. Walker & Sons The firm of Walker claims to be the organ-builders with the oldest roots. Founded in 1827, they trace their origins back to the Dallams via Harris, Bridge, the Englands and England's successor, Nicholls. Walkers' remaining early work is now highly regarded, distinguished by generous scales for the bass and Pedal pipes. Walkers were early users of pneumatic lever action. Their turn-of-the-century instruments were musically dull but exceedingly solidly constructed. In the 1950s and 1960s they built large numbers of small extension organs but, under new management, they are now Britain's most prolific builder of organs with tracker action.

R. H. Walker & Son This was a post-war breakaway from the main Walker firm, run by Peter Walker. They built a number of mostly small mechanical action organs.

Wells–Kennedy Partnership Based on Lisburn, Christopher Gordon-Wells has become a leading builder in Northern Ireland since 1966.

Williamson & Hyatt A partnership of an able designer and a competent voicer which produced surprisingly good organs in the 1950s and early 1960s. They later joined up with Cedric Arnold.

Henry Willis Willis burst upon the organ scene with a large instrument for the Great Exhibition of 1851. He and Hill were the two major organ-builders of the nineteenth century, his best instruments dating from 1860 to 1890. Henry Willis was a considerable inventor, developing the radiating and concave pedalboard as well as tubular pneumatic action. His attitude to earlier organ-builders whose work he rebuilt was even more cavalier than most, but it was the excellence of his reed-voicing which really set him apart. Henry Willis is generally known as Father Willis to distinguish him from later members of the family. The firm enjoyed a considerable renaissance in the 1920s under Henry Willis III who retained a clear tonal structure to the instrument when everyone else was building 'octopods' with little other than unison stops.

Wurlitzer The Rudolph Wurlitzer Company of North Tonawanda, NY, USA developed the electric action 'unit' organ, based on the tonal ideas of Robert Hope-Jones. They marketed it very successfully to the then new 'motion picture theatres'. Very large numbers were imported from 1925 to the early 1930s, few of which now remain in their original venues.

5

TECHNICAL TERMS AND STOP-NAMES

There are so many technical terms used in organ-building that complete coverage is impossible. However, a selected glossary may at least help you to dazzle your friends with erudite remarks.

CONSOLE

Compass The range of the keyboards. The organ has never had as long a compass as other keyboard instruments since its range is extended by stops of different pitch. The lower extent of the compass is now universal at C two octaves below middle C, but many large instruments were built in the period 1660–1850 with a compass extending down an additional fourth to G, even sometimes to F or the C below. It was replaced by the C compass when Pedal organs became universal. A very few 'long compass' organs still remain.

Composition pedals Invented by J. C. Bishop in 1844. Pressing down the pedal with the toe automatically draws a preselected combination of stops.

Crescendo pedal Uncommon in Britain except on concert organs, it looks like a balanced Swell pedal but actually brings on all the stops of the organ, one by one, as the pedal is moved toward the horizontal. The stop-knobs are not moved so a prominent light is necessary to remind the player when it is in use.

General piston Most pistons affect only the department under whose keys they are placed, but General pistons affect the whole organ, couplers included. A General Cancel piston puts off all the stops and couplers and is usually placed safely out of the way under the treble end of the lowest keyboard.

Key-touch The feel of the keys – most important to a player. A badly designed mechanical action may give a very heavy touch which is tiring to play. Equally, a poor pneumatic or electric action may have too light a touch. Tracker action has a natural initial resistance as the pallet is opened which gives the player confidence. Some electric

120

actions have tried to imitate this with special springs to give a so-called 'toggle-touch'.

Manual Keys played by the hands, as opposed to keys played by the feet. Most organs have one row of keys or manual per department of the organ, apart from the Pedal organ. Thus, a two-manual organ may have a Great organ and a Swell organ, and a three-manual, Choir, Great and Swell. The more manuals provided, the greater the flexibility in playing the instrument. In general, the maximum is four manuals; it is difficult to make a five-manual console comfortable for anyone without gorilla arms.

Pedalboard The pedal keys and their frame. Although manual keyboards are almost standard in design, pedalboards vary considerably. They may be square and flat, or square and concave so that the highest and lowest notes are easier to reach, or they may be radiating and concave to facilitate the use of the heel. The radiating pedalboard was invented by Willis in 1854 and is now much the most common in Britain and the USA, though relatively unusual in Continental Europe.

Pistons Once referred to by a small boy as the 'press-buttons', the pistons are so named after a brass instrument's pitch-changing pistons, which have a similar shaped head. The function is the same as that of a composition pedal, that of drawing a preselected combination of stops. Thumb pistons are located in the key-slips under the manuals. As the thumb can exert less power than a composition pedal operated by the foot, the provision of thumb pistons implies an electric or pneumatic stop-action. Toe pistons are then often provided in place of composition pedals.

Reversible pistons Provided to operate couplers, they are reversible in operation in that the position of the stop is always reversed. Thus, if the coupler is already out the piston will cancel it, or if in it will draw it.

Setter piston The master piston which allows a combination of stops to be drawn by hand and then 'captured' on a piston, which will then always draw that combination until reset. The mechanism required for this facility was formerly very expensive but has become much less so since the invention of solid-state action.

Stop-keys A form of stop control adopted for the well-known 'horse-shoe' theatre organ console since a large number of stops could be accommodated in a compact console. Stop-keys found more general favour for a while but their use is now largely restricted to electronic organs.

Stop-knob The traditional form of stop control. The substantial knob allows the player to exert sufficient force to move the slider directly.

Even if electric or pneumatic stop-action is provided, the use of stop-knobs is preferred since the player can locate them more easily by position without having to read the inscription each time.

Swell pedal Controls the opening of a swell-box in which the pipes of one division are placed to allow continuous control of the volume of sound. The pedal may be of the balanced type which is hinged at its centre so that the ball of the foot is pressed to open the swell-box and the heel of the foot to close it. For convenience, a balanced pedal needs to be in the centre of the pedalboard. Before 1900 a 'trigger' Swell pedal was generally provided. Located at the treble end of the pedals, it is pressed down to open the swell-box, closing by itself unless held with a ratchet. A romantic slow crescendo is difficult with a trigger swell, though a sudden sforzando may be easier.

CASEWORK

Bay-leaf The shape of the lips most commonly used for organ pipes in the case. The lower lip is semi-circular, the upper lip arched and pointed.

Chair case (German *Rückpositiv*) Small organ case placed behind the player, projecting over the edge of the gallery or screen and normally containing the Positive or Choir organ. The origin of the name, originally spelled 'chayre', is still a subject for debate.

Corbel A bracket which appears to support any overhanging part of the case, commonly an opportunity for a display of carving and nearly always fitted where the lower part of a case is narrower than the upper.

Cornice The upper edges of the flats and towers that make up an organ case. In seventeenth and eighteenth century work the cornices are often elaborately moulded.

Cove A length of concave panelling. It is not common in the sides of British organs but is often found below a projecting front as in the Scott case in the Lady Chapel at Liverpool Cathedral.

Double case An organ normally situated on a gallery or screen, which has a main case on the body of the screen and a smaller case, the chair case, on the edge of the gallery, is said to have a double case.

Dummy When architects, instead of organ-builders, began to design cases they discarded the discipline of working to the sizes of bass pipes available. Consequently special non-speaking case pipes are provided, known as dummies and made without languids. Sir Ninian Comper was a well-known offender; his cases are almost all dummies as the pipes are too small to be useful.

Flat The front pipes between the towers; generally arranged in a straight line on plan. Seventeenth and eighteenth century cases

122

obtained much variety with different arrangements of flats and towers.

French mouth A pipe mouth with a semi-circular lower lip and with the upper lip semi-circular at the top. This form was particularly favoured by Hill. Some 16ft and 32ft front pipes have raised lips in which the upper and lower extremities of the lips curl forward away from the pipe-body, emphasising the lip shape.

Front pipe It is economic and attractive to stand the bass pipes in the case of the organ. The Royal Albert Hall organ, London has 32ft front pipes of polished tin metal and Leeds Town Hall organ's pipes are of iron. Most front pipes before 1850 were made of 'plain metal' containing twenty per cent tin and finished with gold leaf. In Victorian times stencilled decoration became popular, as in the 'rolls of linoleum' at Eton College Chapel. Bare zinc pipes (post-1870) look horribly dull and are often spray-painted. Recent organs have included polished or oxidised copper front pipes as well as polished tin metal.

Impost The main horizontal rail of the case which runs across the width of the instrument just below the feet of the front pipes.

Moulding A length of shaped wood which has a curved pattern in section, often derived from classical Greek designs. Mouldings are frequently used to decorate the join between a panel and its frame and to emphasise the edge of a horizontal rail.

Over-length There is a fundamental problem in the design of an organ case, in that a proper sequence of pipes rapidly becomes too short to fill the full height available, especially in the 'flats' between the towers. This is overcome by fitting longer feet to the smaller pipes or by covering the gap with pipe-shades. In the nineteenth and early twentieth centuries it became common instead merely to make the pipe longer than necessary to sound the proper pitch. The excess length is called the over-length. If overdone, over-length ruins the pipe-speech as well as the visual proportions.

Pipe-cap The best organ cases have woodwork above the tops of the front pipes, often with carved pipe-shades to fill the space between the shorter pipes and the case itself. That part of the case which joins the upright posts above a tower of front pipes is called a pipe-cap.

Pipe-shade The ornament which fills the gap over the top of the shorter front pipes. In old organs this was an opportunity for good wood-carving. In modern organ cases, pipe-shades have also been made of tin or copper.

PIPE-CAP

Return The side of an organ case, including the sides of the towers. If returns are omitted, the case lacks solidity.

Speaker A front pipe which does speak, as opposed to a dummy.

123

Tone-cabinets Normally formed from casework which fits closely round all sides of the soundboards, including roofs. A practice imported from the Continent in recent years, it not only helps direct the sound of an organ in the required direction, but, more importantly, adds a warmth and sense of reverberation. This comes from the resonances of the air volume in the cabinet and perhaps resonances of the thin timber walls also.

TONE-CABINET

Tower The part of an organ case where a few of the largest pipes are grouped together, often arranged in a projecting semi-circle or a 'V' shape on plan. Towers add interest to an organ case and seventeenth- and eighteenth-century cases are often categorised into two-, three- and four-tower cases.

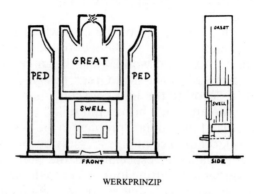

WERKPRINZIP

Werkprinzip An untranslatable German term. It describes the principle whereby an organ is arranged in a very shallow layout only one soundboard deep, the various departments being arranged either vertically or horizontally directly behind the front casework. This layout can give the organ a very distinctive shape in silhouette. The layout suits mechanical tracker action very well, and by minimising floor space may enable an organ to be placed in a more favourable position than in the conventional organ-chamber. Being generally free standing, such an organ is more easily saleable and adapted to another building than one built into a chamber. More important is the fact that a *werkprinzip* organ, with tone-cabinets, gives a freshness and clarity of sound which is quite distinctive and can enable a relatively small instrument to succeed where a larger organ was previously needed.

124

MECHANISM

Backfall Long centrally pivoted lever used in mechanical key-actions to transfer the movement horizontally away from the console (also used in the coupling action).

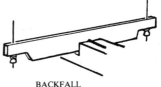

BACKFALL

Balancer A pneumatic device which reduces the 'pluck' of the bass notes of large organs with tracker action. Used by Hill in the 1880s, it was reinvented in the 1960s.

Barker lever A mechanism, named after its inventor, which uses pneumatic power to reduce the effort required to operate a mechanical key-action. Expensive and inherently noisy, it was often fitted to the Great organ only, as in the old Walker at Romsey Abbey. Much used by Cavaillé-Coll in France, it is now rare in this country, where it was superseded by tubular pneumatic action.

Bellows The general term used for any wind-storage device, otherwise known as a reservoir or wind regulator. Formerly used to store wind between strokes of the hand blowing, its function today is limited to controlling the flow from an electric blower and to absorbing sudden changes in wind demand. Bellows with two sets of ribs to give extra capacity are known as double-rise. Cast-iron bellows weights often show the initials of the organ-builder.

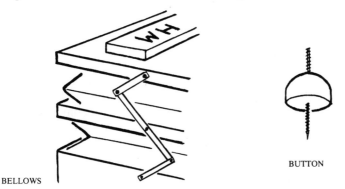

BELLOWS

BUTTON

Button A complete misnomer. Americans call it a 'leather nut', which is more accurate. They are made of hard leather (or plastic) and are screwed along a threaded wire to regulate a mechanical key-action.

Chest magnet Developed from Robert Hope-Jones' original design and also known as a 'hair-pin' magnet from the shape of the iron core, these magnets have an armature which is itself a tiny pneumatic valve. The magnet uses little current, but on the other hand needs a chain of pneumatic relays if a substantial or rapid effort is required.

Concussion A small auxiliary bellows, not connected to a wind-control valve, attached to a soundboard or wind-trunk to reduce 'unsteady wind' resulting from excessively long wind-trunks.

Conveyance Not a legal document but a duct which conveys wind to a bass pipe standing away from the soundboard, perhaps in the case. It is often made as a lead pipe, mitred at the turns, not bent.

Coupling action Enables the pipes of more than one department to be sounded together by connecting their key-actions. The connection is one way; Great-to-Pedal enables the Pedal keys to sound the Great organ but does not enable the Great to sound the Pedal. The coupling action is the least reliable mechanism in the organ. Whether the action is mechanical tracker, pneumatic or electric, it is nearly always the coupling action which wears first.

Direct electric action Also known as electromagnetic action, uses magnets to open the pallet valves under the pipes directly, without intermediate pneumatic mechanism. The action is more rapid than electropneumatic mechanism but has mostly been used only on sliderless soundboards. The design of satisfactory direct electric actions for slider soundboards is difficult, though the organ at Gloucester Cathedral is so fitted.

Double-touch Usually found on theatre organs. One can solo out a treble reed or accentuate a pedal note with a drum roll by pressing the key harder beyond its normal movement. It was also fitted in the 1930s to more sober instruments (including King's College Chapel) to cancel other stops by double-touch stop-keys or stop-knobs.

Electropneumatic action Electric action using electricity for coupling and control but using pneumatic mechanism actually to operate the soundboard pallet valves. Developed by Hope-Jones in the 1890s, it is still used when electric action is fitted to slider soundboards.

Expansion chamber In a slider soundboard the wind channels which distribute the wind to the slides act as an expansion chamber, reducing the initial suction as the pallets open. The best sliderless soundboards have substantial added expansion chambers between the pallet and the pipe-foot. Without this feature, flue-pipes speak more sluggishly than on a slider soundboard.

Feeder An auxiliary bellows, generally fitted under the main bellows, which is an essential part of hand (or foot) blowing. It is connected to the bellows handle and alternately sucks in air and expels it through valves into the main reservoir. A 'cuckoo' feeder is an arrangement of twin diagonal feeders resembling those fitted in cuckoo clocks.

Humidifier A device fitted to the wind system of an old organ to protect the slider soundboards and other parts from splits and warping caused by the low winter humidity resulting from modern central heating systems. The humidifier blows a gentle stream of moist air through the wind system of the organ when it is not in use – much more effective than a bucket of water under the bellows!

Lever magnet Invented in the 1930s, the magnet has a hinged lever which is attracted to the magnet core. Using more current than a chest magnet, the greater power developed enables electro-pneumatic mechanism to be simplified.

Pallet The valve which opens to let air into the foot of the pipe. A flat valve, covering a windway from the inside, with a soft surface of leather on felt. Slider soundboards have very long narrow pallets, other soundboards round ones.

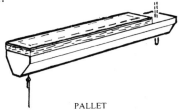

PALLET

Pitman You can indulge in a little one-upmanship if you know what this is – unless you meet someone who asks you to explain how it works! The pitman is a very tiny two-position three-way pneumatic valve which is crucial to the stop-action of the pitman sliderless soundboard – virtually the standard soundboard in America for many years and used here by Willis and by Hill up to about 1960.

Pneumatic action More accurately, tubular-pneumatic action. A key-action which works by sending puffs of wind down a bank of lead tubes connecting the console to the soundboards. The puff of wind triggers a sensitive valve that controls the main pneumatic action which opens the soundboard pallet. Pneumatic action allows more latitude in the layout of the organ than tracker action and reduces the playing effort to that required to open a small valve. The response, however, tends to be sluggish. A later variant was exhaust-pneumatic action, in which the air is let out of the tube to sound the note. This is less sluggish and lasts longer as the moving parts are more effectively sealed against dust and dirt.

Pneumatic motor A small bellows which converts pneumatic power into mechanical force. A pneumatic action may have a chain of motors, the smaller one operating a valve which controls a larger one and so on. The 'motor' may be external and visible, in which case it is inflated with wind to make it work, or internal and enclosed in the action, in which case it will be exhausted so that the surrounding wind pressure will cause it to collapse when required. A motor may be 'square-drop' or a 'book-motor' hinged at one end.

Rackboard Placed about 4½in (12cm) above the upperboard or top surface of the soundboard, the rackboard has a hole for each pipe accurately fitted to hold the pipe vertical.

Roller A bar of wood or metal which transmits the motion of a mechanical key-action sideways. The height taken by the roller-

127

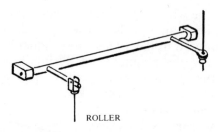

ROLLER

boards is often a critical factor in the layout of tracker organs.

Roller valve A common type of wind control valve in which a flat piece of leather is unwound from a roller to restrict the air flow as the bellows fills. Less prone to stick than a slide valve, its inertia nevertheless makes it unsuitable for small reservoirs and *schwimmers*.

Roosevelt A particular design of detachable pneumatic motor and pallet used in sliderless soundboards invented by Hilborne Roosevelt, a relative of the American presidential family.

Schwimmer This German word, for which there is no accepted English equivalent, describes a small wind reservoir and wind control built into the organ soundboard. A relatively modern invention, it replaces most of the bellows and wind-trunking in the bottom of an organ, making access to the action mechanism much easier. The wind supply is also much steadier than with conventional bellows and wind-trunks; so much so that a conventional tremulant is useless. Some musicians find this very steady wind supply too mechanical and prefer the slight variations inseparable from conventional bellows and wind-trunks.

Slider soundboard Virtually the standard form of organ soundboard, in which the notes are controlled by long pallet valves and the stops by perforated slides which engage or not with holes in the soundboard table beneath them. In its original form it is very liable to split or warp under conditions of varying humidity, leading to its abandonment outside Britain after about 1870. The use of modern materials has enabled a comeback in the past twenty years. Virtually the only soundboard which can be used with tracker action, however, it cannot be used with extension or in unit organs. The term soundboard is really a misnomer; even the alternative 'windchest' is not much better. It is really a large box containing the pallet valves and stop-action, and on which the pipes are stood.

Solid state The use of transistor systems in electric key-actions to replace mechanical relays and coupling switches, and also in adjustable piston mechanisms. First used by the author in 1963, the merits of solid state are the subject of much argument among organbuilders. Wear of key contacts is reduced, delay from mechanical relays is eliminated and reliability is generally better than mechanical coupling switches. Unfortunately, in some systems, faults need special expertise to repair, and early problems with adjustable piston mechanisms received bad publicity.

Swell-box A heavily constructed timber box covering all the pipes of a department. It has adjustable louvres to release the sound to the extent required. Most organs have one or more departments enclosed in a swell-box in order to provide the stepless crescendo needed in romantic music. Theatre organs are totally enclosed in swell-boxes for that reason.

Thumper The wooden rail, often weighted with lead, which rests on the keys of a mechanical action organ just behind the music desk. Free to float up and down if humidity changes affect the action, it serves to tension the action, keeping lost movement to a minimum (providing the keys are evenly regulated so that they all touch the thumper). Some new tracker organs have a fixed thumper and use more sophisticated tensioning devices which keep a fixed depth of key-touch.

Tracker The thin strip of pine used to transmit a pulling movement in a mechanical key-action is not to be confused with a sticker, which pushes instead. The name has come to be applied to the whole action (tracker action) and even to the whole organ (a tracker organ). Tracker action has the reputation of lasting longer than pneumatic or electropneumatic mechanisms, but also, deserved on some old organs, of being heavy to play. It imposes a discipline on the organ layout and virtually rules out a detached console. However, a good tracker action gives an immediacy and precision of control which no other action can attain.

Whiffle-tree The most usual type of electropneumatic remote control for swell-shutters. The curious name comes from the series of linkages which connect the pneumatic motors to the output lever. Derived from the harness required to divide the load of a waggon equally among many horses, the mechanism, drawn out diagrammatically, could be said to resemble a tree.

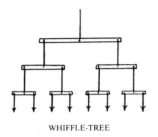

WHIFFLE-TREE

PIPES AND VOICING

Body The main part of a flue-pipe, from the mouth upwards. It is the resonance of the air column in the body which governs the pitch and much of the tone quality. The body is normally parallel but can be tapered to make a Gemshorn stop, or flared out at the top with a conical section called a bell.

Boot The lower part of a reed-pipe, containing the block into which is fitted the shallot and the reed-tongue. Boots are normally all the same length in the treble like the feet of flue-pipes, though Father Willis made his treble boots much shorter.

Classical voicing The style of voicing in which the foot of the pipe is left fully open, the languid is not nicked and the pipe is regulated by adjusting the width of the flue. The resulting speech is very rapid and may be preceded by an audible transient tone or 'chip'.

BOOT

CONE-TUNING

EARS

Cone-tuning The flue-pipe is cut to just under correct length and the top coned in lightly until the pipe is in tune. Subsequent tuning with a tuning-cone flattens the pipe by coning it in further or sharpens it by coning it out. Pipes so tuned have very stable tuning, but can be damaged by repeated coning, especially if the pipe metal contains much lead. Cone-tuning was superseded in this country by tuning slides about ninety years ago, but has returned to favour.

Cut-up The height of the mouth of a flue-pipe, between bottom lip and top lip. After the scale, this is the most important factor governing the tone. A low cut-up gives a bright but gentle sound. A high cut-up and more wind gives a harder and bolder tone. New pipes are made with a very low cut-up which is increased by the voicer until it is right. Woe betide he who accidentally goes too far!

Ears Two projecting pieces of metal either side of the mouth of the pipe. Their precise shape and size can often help determine the origins and age of a pipe. Ears are usually omitted from treble pipes, but large ears of soft metal which can be bent to shade the mouth are an excellent method of tuning small chimney flutes and other stopped pipes.

Foot The bottom part of a pipe, generally tapered, below the mouth. The foot has no effect on the tone, merely holding up the rest of the pipe! Classically voiced pipes have open feet; in romantic voicing they are closed up at the tip to regulate the wind supply.

Flue The slit-like gap between the languid and the bottom lip of the mouth. Air escapes from the foot through the flue, blows across the mouth and vibrates either side of the top lip to initiate the sound.

Half-length Reed-pipes need not be their full theoretical length! If a light bass is required, half-length pipes take less space and are quicker speaking. Many Fagotto stops have half-length bass pipes, as have many modern 32ft stops (Bath Abbey and Wymondham Abbey, for example).

Harmonic A harmonic pipe is double-length (though a harmonic stopped pipe is treble-length). Harmonic flutes have a hollow, pure sound, but blend poorly with other stops. Harmonic treble pipes are often fitted to reed-stops on heavy pressure as they stay in tune better. The big Willis reeds at Liverpool Cathedral have double harmonics – quadruple length!

Languid The metal plate which divides the body of a pipe from the foot. The front edge is not soldered to the foot but is bevelled and forms the rear edge of the flue.

Nicks Small cuts made in the bevelled face of the languid and on the inside of the bottom lip. These irregularities in the edges of the flue reduce inharmonic noises from the mouth of the pipe and reduce or eliminate 'chip' when the pipe first speaks. Nicking also makes the tone duller and smoother and can slow down the speech. Although eschewed in classical voicing, light nicking has been in use for at least two hundred and fifty years. A similar technique is used to quieten the exhaust of aircraft jet engines!

NICKS

Polyphone Reinvented by John Compton and used by him to produce a soft 32ft stop. A single stopped pipe has chambers attached to its side which when opened deepen its pitch. This takes the compass down to low E, the bottom four notes all playing EEEE! The principle is very old, there being a three hundred year old polyphone in the Emperor's organ in Toledo Cathedral, Spain.

Reverberation Not strictly part of the pipes or voicing, but is often said to be the most important stop on the organ. It is a measure of the time taken for the sound to die away at the end of a chord. Organ and choral music sound better in a building of high reverberation. Reverberation is enhanced by high ceilings and hard surfaces, but is

131

reduced by soft furnishings, carpets and large congregations.

Scale The measure of a pipe's diameter for a given length. A wide scale gives a flutier tone, as in a Blockflöte; a narrow scale encourages harmonics, as in string-toned stops. The scale of a pipe is the most important factor in determining its tone and may be characteristic of the builder; Schulze tended to use wide scales, Willis to use narrow ones. Carefully worked out scales, not only between different stops but between treble and bass, are the hallmark of a good organ-builder.

SCALE   SHALLOT

Shallot The short tube which is effectively the bottom end of the resonator of a reed-pipe. One side has a flat face with an opening in it against which the reed vibrates. The shape of the shallot can make a substantial difference to the tone; a parallel shallot with a wide, long opening gives a brighter sound than a tapered shallot with a short, narrow opening. French shallots have domed ends and are an important ingredient in the French reed sound at the Royal Festival Hall, London.

Spotted metal Contains 55–60 per cent tin, 40–45 per cent lead and nothing else. The spotted effect is quite natural, not applied, and happens automatically when metal of the right composition is cast. Samuel Green was one of the first to use spotted metal (for his reed-stops), but the high cost of tin prevented its wide use until popularised by Lewis in the late nineteenth century. Sometimes used for front pipes, its appearance became an accepted guarantee of quality, since the costly tin content could not be faked. The tin makes the sound a little brighter and the pipe somewhat stronger than the softer and more usual 'plain metal'.

Tin metal Contains 70 per cent tin, not 100 per cent. At this composition the spotted effect disappears, but the metal is hard and dulls very slowly, making an ideal, if costly, front pipe. The sound is harder and brighter as well which helps clarity in reverberant acoustics. Until recently tin metal was rarely used in Britain, despite its popularity in Continental Europe, though Snetzler used it for his Dulciana stops.

Tongue Curving the tongue is the core of the reed voicer's art. Too much and the pipe will be slow, too little and there will be no power. The tongue is the vibrating reed, and alternatively covers and

132

uncovers the opening in the shallot, the puffs of air being amplified by the resonator to give the required tone. The tongue, like the shallot, is normally made of brass. Father Willis developed a technique of putting a 'load' on the tongue of a bass pipe which gives a 'smooth' bass sound.

Tuning slide A band of thin tinned steel which is slipped over the top of a flue-pipe to form a telescopic sleeve. The springiness of the steel holds the slide in position, though it may be tapped up or down to tune the pipe. Tuning slides displaced cone-tuning in Britain and the USA because of the damage cone-tuning does to soft 'plain metal' pipes. However, slides eventually corrode and the tuning is less stable, so that the fitting of slides to old cone-tuned pipes should be avoided where possible.

Tuning spring A piece of wire projecting from the block of a reed-pipe, the other end of which presses on the reed-tongue. By varying the vibrating length of the reed-tongue, the pitch of the pipe is adjusted. The tuner will tap the spring up to flatten the note or down to sharpen it with a 'reed knife', a long shaped metal bar which is quite incapable of cutting anything!

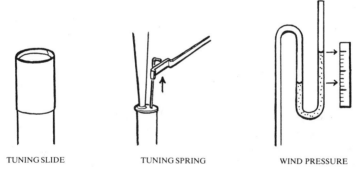

TUNING SLIDE   TUNING SPRING   WIND PRESSURE

Wind pressure Measured with a U-shaped water gauge and is expressed as so many inches (or millimetres) of water. Robert Hope-Jones said that all the mystique of wind pressures was bunk and decreed that his organs should be voiced on 5in (125mm) and 10in (250mm) throughout (though I think the Double-tongued Tuba at Worcester was on 20in/500mm). Wind pressure is nevertheless important, especially for reed-stops, but depends on the style of voicing as well as the size of the building and its acoustics. Classically voiced organs are happiest on 2½–3¼in (65–85mm) though the famous eighteenth-century Cliquot at Poitiers Cathedral is on 5in (125mm). Higher pressures are needed for romantic voicing and in really large buildings. Willis used 30in (750mm) for the Trompette

Militaire at St Paul's Cathedral, London and 50in (1250mm) for the Liverpool Cathedral Tuba Magna, but such pressures are exceptional.

STOP-NAMES

Owing to the native inventiveness of organ-builders a full list would take up the entire book. This is a mere introduction.

Acoustic Bass The most common 32ft stop there is, perhaps because it is a bit of a cheat. The low octave is obtained by sounding pipes of 16ft and 10⅔ft together, generating a difference tone at 32ft pitch. The ear is only deceived in this way at very low pitches.

Acuta A mixture stop. Despite the name, it was often used by Compton for a mixture of 1⅓ft and 1ft pitch, which is not particularly sharp.

Aeoline A string tone, one of the quietest stops on the organ and more edgy than the more usual Salicional. Only found on romantic organs of the early twentieth century.

Bärpfeife Found in organs of Continental origin or inspiration. A short-length soft reed-stop, like a Vox Humana but fatter in scale and in sound.

Basset Horn Not a horn but a clarinet. In the orchestra it is a bass clarinet but in the organ it is usually at normal pitch.

Bass Flute Generally an extension, not a real stop, it consists of the Pedal Bourdon 16ft played one octave up at 8ft.

Bassoon Derived from the woodwind and made of narrow-scale conical reed-pipes. Samuel Green used it as a full-compass 8ft stop, but it is more common as a 16ft stop or as the bass pipes of an Oboe stop and sometimes labelled 'Oboe and Bassoon' on the knob.

Bell Gamba A mild string-tone stop of the 1850–75 period. Made like a Gemshorn with a tapered body to add edge to the tone plus a flared top (or 'bell') to make a more 'horny' tone. Not made once the technique of voicing small-scale string stops had been developed. It is now rare.

Blockflute Anglicised from *Blockflöte*. Used in the seventeenth century by Father Smith but also common in organs constructed after 1960. An open bright-toned flute generally at 2ft pitch or 4ft on the pedal. The flutiness comes from a wide scale, not from a high cut-up as in the Piccolo.

Bombarde A powerful reed-stop at 16ft pitch on the manuals and 32ft (Contra Bombarde) on the pedal. The name implies something fatter and louder than a Trumpet and it may even be of Tuba intonation. Sometimes a whole family of powerful reed-stops is brought together as a Bombarde division.

134

Bourdon The universal accompanimental 16ft bass tone of the smaller British organ. A stopped flute pipe, generally of wood, which gets its flutiness from a high cut-up rather than a wide scale. Easy to voice, and if not too small, prompt in speech, blending surprisingly well with Diapasons of higher pitch. It is less successful as an 8ft manual stop.

Chimney Flute The name may sound odd until you see the pipes, which have a narrow metal 'chimney' sticking up from an otherwise stopped metal pipe. It gives a hint of the even harmonics otherwise missing from a stopped pipe.

Choral Bass A 4ft pedal stop of half-flute half-Diapason tone. The pipes are generally wide scale and often tapered.

Clarabella A smooth solo flute. Made of open wood pipes and invented by Bishop in the mid-nineteenth century to replace the Mounted Cornets then going out of fashion. Does not blend well with Diapason tone.

Claribel Flute Early twentieth century. Even smoother than the Clarabella.

Clarinet The organ reed-stop which most nearly resembles its orchestral counterpart. The half-length parallel bore pipes emphasise alternate harmonics to give a distinctive colour.

Clarion A trumpet played at 4ft pitch. 'Clairon' is not a printer's error, but the French name for the same stop.

Clear Flute A 4ft Clarabella. May be wood or metal pipes.

Concert Flute A solo Harmonic Flute, voiced very smoothly.

Contra Bass A rather vague name for a 16ft stop of mildly stringy tone. 'Contra' anything normally means a 16ft stop or 32ft on the Pedal.

Cor Anglais An oboe stop with a 'double bell', in other words the pipe first widens then narrows at its end. This elaborate construction gives a characteristic colour to the sound.

Cornet Sounds almost like a reed-stop, but is made of several ranks of flue-pipes. Unlike other compound stops, the pipes are voiced more as flutes than Principals. The Cornet includes 2⅔ft, 2ft and 1⅗ft pitches and, if of 5 ranks, 8ft and 4ft as well. These combine to produce a single tone colour. In the bass the ear is not deceived so the stop is from tenor G or middle C up only.

Corno di Bassetto Italian for Basset Horn. Father Willis often called his clarinets by this name.

Cornopean Similar to a Trumpet but, like its obsolete orchestral namesake, rather broader in scale and tone. An almost standard stop in nineteenth-century British Swell organs.

Cremona Nothing to do with the city where the violins came from, it is an anglicisation of the German *Krummhorn*, a narrow-scale bright-toned clarinet.

Cymbal A lightly voiced mixture stop which is almost as sharp as a mixture can be, with many breaks of pitch. Widely favoured as the mixture stop of a classical Positive division.

Cymbalstern Not organ pipes at all but a set of small high-pitched bells which sound in sequence continuously when the stop is drawn. Often a star on the case revolves as well. For high days and feast days only!

Diaphone Neither a flue-stop nor a reed but a circular padded valve on the end of a steel spring. Developed by Hope-Jones as a quick-speaking powerful 16ft bass. An important component of theatre organ sound.

Dolce A soft, slightly stringy stop made of pipes larger at the top than at the mouth. A curiosity.

Doppelflute Another curiosity. A stopped flute with two mouths per pipe, one at the front and another at the back!

Double A prefix to denote a stop one octave lower than unison, eg Double Trumpet 16ft on a manual or Double Open Diapason 32ft on the pedal.

Dulciana Similar in tone to an Open Diapason, but much softer and much narrower in scale. An almost exclusively British stop invented by Snetzler in the eighteenth century.

Dulzian A soft reed-stop with half-length parallel pipes like a Clarinet but wider scale leading to a 'buzzy' non-imitative sound.

Fagotto Italian for Bassoon, but has come to mean a slightly more powerful stop midway between Trumpet and Bassoon. Often found in Swell organs of the 1950s (Contra Fagotto 16ft) or as a light 16ft pedal reed-stop sometimes called Fagot. The lowest notes often have half-length resonators.

Fifteenth Fifteen notes up the scale from the unison makes this a 2ft stop (Pedal 4ft). An important component of the Diapason or Principal Chorus.

Flageolet A small-scale open metal flute at 2ft pitch. The high cut-up makes this a romantically voiced stop.

Flauto Traverso A solo stop – 8ft or 4ft – in direct imitation of the orchestral flute. Treble pipes are double-length ('harmonic'). Normally metal, but occasionally made with turned wood pipes.

French Horn The smoothest-toned reed it is possible to make. Little louder than a flue-stop, though normally on about 6in (150mm) wind pressure. Only found on large romantic organs.

Fugara A small-scale 4ft stop of south German origin. Almost string tone.

136

Furniture Sometimes spelled Fourniture. A chorus mixture stop of three or more ranks to top the Great organ Diapason/Principal chorus. It should be bold without being shrill.

Gamba Italian for leg, this is an unfortunate shortening of Viola da Gamba.

Gedeckt (or **Gedackt/Gedact**) Variations on a German word meaning covered. A rank of stopped pipes.

Gedecktpommer A fairly wide-scaled *Gedeckt* with a low cut-up giving a prominent third harmonic (twelfth from the fundamental).

Geigen German for violin, but has come to be a prefix indicating a somewhat stringy version of a Diapason stop. Geigen Diapasons and Geigen Principals are commonly found in Swell organs of the period 1920–60.

Gemshorn The original Goatshorn was an instrument of the Renaissance period with a soft flute tone. The organ stop is a bright Principal. The pipes have tapered bodies giving the tone a distinctive formant.

Grand Open Diapason, Grand Bourdon A prefix used in the 1850s to distinguish a Pedal organ stop. (Rather in the spirit of the *Great Western Railway*.)

Grave Mixture A mixture stop of relatively low pitch, generally 2⅔ft and 2ft pitches.

Gross One octave lower pitch than usual. Gross Tierce 3⅕ft is an example.

Harmonic Flute An open flute with treble pipes of double-length overblown to speak the octave. The stop is smooth and can be beautiful but blends badly with Principals. Copied by British builders from nineteenth-century French organs. Also as Harmonic Piccolo, Harmonic Claribel etc.

Harmonics A mixture stop, usually found on the Great organ, including a Tierce rank (fifth harmonic) and a flat twenty-first rank (seventh harmonic). The sound is reedy and rather acid. Invented by Arthur Harrison and characteristic of the 1900–40 period.

Harmonic Trumpet High-pressure reed-stops need treble pipes with double-length resonators in order to make them loud enough. Harmonic Trumpets use high pressure to gain enhanced power.

Hautboy An anglicisation of Hautbois. An almost essential component of the English Swell organ right back to the early eighteenth century. An oboe.

Hohl Flute (or **Hohlflöte**) An open wood flute introduced to this country by Edmund Schulze in the mid-nineteenth century. Smoother and more powerful than the Clarabella. It has an inverted mouth and the pipe is often wider than it is deep. Sometimes the pipes are triangular. Father Smith also used the name in the seventeenth century for a metal flute.

Horn Not the same as a French Horn, more a hunting horn. Generally made like a Trumpet but with wider-scale pipes. The result is often fat without being smooth.

Horn Diapason An Open Diapason with a slot in the side of the pipe just below the top which emphasises certain harmonics, giving a somewhat hard tone. A stop of the early twentieth century.

Keraulophon An English stop with a Greek name. A mild string with a round hole in the side of the pipe near the top, having a similar effect to the slot of a Horn Diapason.

Kinura Greek for Harp, but the stop is a very thin-sounding Oboe. Invented by Hope-Jones and mostly used in theatre organs.

Koppel Flute (or **Koppelflöte**) Introduced to this country with the neo-classical revival, and a popular stop in 4ft pitch. The pipes are part cylindrical with an open tapered upper portion. Expensive to make, their quasi-stopped tone is very versatile and a good blender.

Krummhorn See **Cremona**.

Larigot Originally French, this is another stop which has become popular in neo-classical organs because of its versatility. The name specifies a stop of 1⅓ft pitch, two octaves and a fifth above the fundamental. The pipes are nominally flutes but are often voiced brightly so that they will add to a small chorus in the absence of a mixture.

Lieblich Gedackt (or **Lieblich Flute** or **Lieblich Bourdon**) Introduced to this country by Edmund Schulze in his organ for the 1851 Great Exhibition, this stop was widely copied for the next hundred years, even to Schulze's exact scale. It is a narrow-scale stopped flute, the flutiness arising, despite the narrow scale, from the very high arched mouth. Unsuitable for neo-classical organs.

Melodia A very pure-toned open wood flute. Almost exclusively American.

Mixture A stop with multiple high-pitched ranks, designed to cap and to reinforce the full chorus. The number of ranks is often shown on the knob in roman numerals. The composition of a mixture is specified as the pitches sounding at bottom C, though in practice these 'break back' to lower pitches as the compass is ascended.

Mounted Cornet A Cornet stop which is placed on a separate block above the other pipes, fed by long conveyances from the soundboard. The height helps the tone to speak out more directly and the space saved on the soundboard keeps the depth of the organ to a minimum.

Musette A very narrow-scale Clarinet, mostly used in theatre organs.

Nachthorn An open metal flute of very wide scale indeed. A relatively narrow mouth gives an almost 'cooing' sound. Found in neo-classical organs where the pedal is big enough to have separate 4ft or 2ft flutes.

Nason Flute A 4ft stopped flute with a low mouth, giving a prominent third harmonic, almost a quintaten. Seventeenth-century stops were of wood, but it can also be made of metal pipes.

Nazard Has its origins in the classical French organ in which it plays an important part. Almost unknown in England until fifty years ago. A flute-toned stop of 2⅔ft pitch which can combine with flutes and other 'mutation' stops to make distinctive solo voices. A component of the Cornet Séparé.

None The ninth harmonic or three octaves and a semitone above the fundamental. A rare high-pitched mutation stop.

Oboe Not actually an imitation of the orchestral instrument, more a soft trumpet with Oboe flavouring. A favourite English Swell organ stop.

Octave The Diapason/Principal stop sounding one octave higher than the Principal for that division. An Octave can be, for example, an 8ft stop on the Pedal, 4ft on the Great and 2ft on the Positive. Also used as a prefix (eg Octave Quint 2⅔ft).

Octavin A 1ft stop of half-flute half-Principal tone.

Open Diapason The fundamental non-imitative sound of the organ; the sound made by an open pipe whose scale is neither wide nor narrow. Manual pipes are normally of metal. The case pipes of an organ are normally the bass pipes of the Open Diapason. Although the name is restricted to the fundamental pitch, the tone occurs in more pitches than any other, forming the Diapason Chorus. Just to confuse the unwary, an Open Diapason on the Pedal organ is not a Diapason in tone but a powerful open flute made of wood.

Ophicleide In the orchestra, a keyed brass instrument; in the organ, a reed-stop of considerable power, generally on high wind pressure. Normally a Pedal stop.

Orchestral Oboe Thinner and more acid in sound than the plain Oboe, this is a deliberate attempt to recreate the sound of the orchestral instrument. Found on the Solo organs of large romantic instruments. Difficult to voice and as difficult to tune!

Piccolo An open 2ft flute vaguely imitative of the orchestral instrument and found in romantic organs. Sometimes made of harmonic (double-length) pipes.

Plein Jeu A chorus mixture stop of at least three ranks. The main chorus mixture in the Swell organ is sometimes so named if the reed-stops, with which it should blend, are voiced in the French manner.

Pommer Short for **Gedecktpommer.**

Posaune Similar to the Trumpet but with rather wider scale reson-

139

ators. A nineteenth-century stop, popular with Hill and with Willis on the Great and on the Pedal.

Prestant French for **Principal.**

Principal The name has two meanings. In the traditional English organ, of all periods, it is an Open Diapason-toned stop of 4ft pitch (or 8ft on the Pedal). In the Continental tradition, it is the fundamental Diapason tone, often referred to as Principal tone, on each manual. As such, the bass pipes are normally in the case and the pitch will vary with the division, eg Great Principal 8ft, Positive Principal 4ft. The Continental usage has become fairly common in British organs since about 1960.

Quarte de Nazard A fourth up from the Nazard. A convoluted way of describing a 2ft Flute. With the Nazard and Tierce, part of the French Cornet Séparé and now frequently incorporated into British organs. Also used in the seventeenth century when Harris anglicised the name to 'Cart'!

Quint A stop which speaks a fifth above the Principal. Thus it could be 10⅔ft on the Pedal, 5⅓ft on the Great and 2⅔ft on the Positive. Normally Diapason/Principal tone.

Quintaten (or **Quintadena**) Stopped pipes of moderate scale voiced with a low mouth to give a slightly acid tone with a strong twelfth. Used by Father Smith in St Paul's Cathedral, London and occasionally by Hill, but rare before 1950. The harmonic development allows it to blend with a chorus of Principals when used as a manual 16ft stop.

Rauschquint A rather gravely pitched two-rank mixture of 2⅔ft and 2ft ranks, generally without breaks. In other words, a Twelfth and a Fifteenth sounding together.

Recorder A 2ft Flute stop, generally tapered somewhat.

Regal A whole family of soft-toned reed-stops in which the resonator is so short as to have little control of the reed. Some have resonators of complex construction to colour the tone. A German stop almost unknown in Britain until relatively recently.

Rohr Flute (or **Rohrgedeckt**) Rohr is German for chimney. See **Chimney Flute.**

Rohrquinte A Quint stop made of Chimney Flute pipes.

Rohr Shalmey A reed-stop of odd-looking half-length pipes, looking rather like a set of cocoa tins perched on gas pipes. The pipes stand well in tune and have a distinctive colourful sound. Good as a pedal 4ft solo stop but of limited power.

Sackbut A Renaissance trombone. When William Hill made the first 32ft reed in Britain, for York Minster, he called it Sackbut.

Salicional An extremely common stop in English organs from 1865 to

1955. Normally found in the Swell organ, it is made and voiced much like a Dulciana but is less gentle and has a long slot at the top of the pipe giving it a hardness which counteracts emasculation of the tone by the swell-box.

Scharf Just means 'sharp' in English. A high-pitched mixture, generally only a little less sharp than a Cymbal.

Septième (or **flat Twenty-first**) The seventh harmonic of the fundamental. Fairly rare as a stop on its own, it can be an ingredient of useful solo sounds but is a disaster in chords.

Sesquialtera In the classical German organ and most modern British ones this is a two-rank mixture of Twelfth and Seventeenth (perhaps Nineteenth and Twenty-fourth in the bass octave). It gives a reedy tone to the chorus and can be an ingredient of a bright solo. Father Smith used the name for a three-rank chorus mixture with a Seventeenth speaking rank and this usage continued in British organs to the end of the nineteenth century.

Shalmey (or **Schalmei**) A bright-toned oboe, just as its orchestral counterpart was.

Sharp Mixture A high-pitched mixture.

Sifflöte A high-pitched open flute, generally at 1ft.

Sordun Sounds like a very low-pitched and muffled goat. This soft 16ft pedal reed has very short-length resonators constructed rather like car silencers. It needs less space than almost any other 16ft stop.

Spindleflute A narrow scale Koppel Flute with a rather high cut-up to the mouth. Very characteristic of the work of Henry Willis IV.

Spitz Flute (or **Spitzflöte** – sometimes anglicised to **Spire Flute**) Open pipes, tapered like a Gemshorn, but wider scale to give a flute, yet with harmonic overtones which derive from the taper. The stopped version, Spitzgedeckt, is virtually unknown in Britain but is sometimes met elsewhere.

Spitzquint A quint-sounding stop made up of Spitz Flute pipes.

Stopped Diapason A particularly English stop characteristic of organs from 1660 to 1900 and again since 1950. The fairly wide scale is approximately an Open Diapason cut in half and stopped, with a low enough mouth to give a definite third harmonic. Many are wooden, indeed Father Smith used oak pipes. Blends very well with Diapason/Principal tone and can be used, like chips, with everything.

Suabe Flute The name given by Hill to his 4ft open flutes. A soft Clarabella.

Subbass This stop has now taken over from the Bourdon as the universal mezzopiano Pedal 16ft flue-stop. The mouth is lower than a Bourdon, giving more third harmonic yet not so much as a Pommer or Quintaten.

Sub Bourdon A 32ft Pedal stop. The lower notes are usually so pure and soft as to be felt rather than heard.

Super Octave A Diapason/Principal-toned stop one octave higher than the octave. In other words, a Fifteenth.

Teint A two-rank mixture sounding the seventh harmonic and the sub-octave of the nineteenth harmonic. A peculiar stop developed by Maurice Forsyth-Grant for the organ of New College, Oxford.

Tenoroon A name used by William Hill in the 1840s for a 16ft manual stop extending down only to tenor C.

Tertian A two-rank mixture consisting of the seventeenth (fifth harmonic) and the nineteenth (sixth harmonic). Similar in use to the Sesquialtera, it tends to growl because of the lower difference tone between the two ranks.

Tibia Clausa A very wide-scale rank of stopped wood pipes, voiced for power and smoothness. Invented by Robert Hope-Jones. A much-used rank in every theatre organ.

Tibia Plena As above, but open wood pipes.

Tierce A flute-toned mutation stop two octaves and a third from the fundamental, making it the fifth harmonic. Gives a reedy flavour to flute combinations and forms part of the Cornet.

Tremulant Not a rank of pipes, but a device to affect those already drawn. The regular variation of the wind supply causes distinctive modulation of a solo stop, generally a flute or a reed. An essential component of the theatre organ, which has little chorus work, it is also useful on conventional instruments of all periods.

Tromba A Trumpet stop voiced on heavy pressure, generally 5–7in (125–175mm), in order that it can be regulated to a smooth tone without loss of power. Smooth and well-regulated tone was prized in romantic organs for solo purposes but is achieved at the expense of brilliance and blend.

Trombone A pedal 16ft stop bearing the same relationship to the Pedal organ as a Trumpet does to the Great organ. Similar in construction to the Trumpet though larger in scale; the bass pipes may have wooden resonators.

Trompeta Real Spanish for State Trumpet. Pipes projecting horizontally from the organ case were developed in Spain in the seventeenth century as a way of making very loud music on low wind pressure. At their best, when not too loud, horizontal trumpets can create a very special sound in a large building.

Trompette A trumpet stop, voiced more or less in the French manner, to give additional brightness. This should be achieved by the use of domed open shallots for the reed to beat on.

Trompette-en-chamade A horizontal trumpet voiced with French shallots. See **Trompeta Real.**

Trumpet The most widely used reed-stop in the organ. Not really imitative of the orchestral instrument but the basic organ reed sound from full-length conical pipes. As well as its solo capabilities, the Trumpet also blends well with the Diapason/Principal Chorus. With a Double Trumpet and a Clarion it can form a reed chorus of its own.

Tuba In the organ the Tuba is not a bass instrument but a very powerful reed-stop with a relatively smooth tone almost like a Tromba. The combination of high power and smooth tone needs exceptionally heavy wind pressure, at 12–20in (300–500mm) the highest in the organ and often needing a separate electric blower.

Tuba Magna The Tuba at Liverpool Cathedral is so named. On 50in (1250mm) wind pressure!

Tuba Mirabilis The name William Hill used for his first high-pressure reed, at Birmingham Town Hall. Truly a miracle!

Twelfth Twelve notes up from the unison, or an octave and a fifth, gives this member of the Diapason/Principal Chorus a nominal length of 2⅔ft. Occasionally this is rounded to 3ft. Although a member of the upperwork, the difference tone generated in combination with 4ft and 2ft stops helps to reinforce the fundamental.

Unda Maris Literally a wave of the sea. A Flute Celeste (see *Voix Celestes*).

Viola de Gamba (or just **Viola**) Softer than a Diapason and narrower in scale to give more harmonic development, the nearest orchestral sound is that of a bowed string, hence the name. Unlike its use in the orchestra, this tone is not the foundation of the chorus and choruses of Violas are rare in the organ.

Viole d'Orchestre Much narrower in scale than a Viola and hence much thinner in sound. Developed by Thynne as a deliberate copy of orchestral string tone and exploited by Robert Hope-Jones. Its use is confined to organs of the late romantic era and to theatre organs. A Viole Celeste is a Celeste stop made of Viole d'Orchestre pipes.

Violin Diapason A cross between a Diapason and a Viola.

Violoncello Generally an 8ft stop on the Pedal. Although a mild string-tone, non-imitative, surprisingly, the pipes are sometimes made of wood. Adds definition to a Pedal line without adding much power. Characteristic of the late nineteenth-century British organ.

Violone Similar to the Violoncello but a 16ft stop. Normally the third or fourth 16ft stop on the Pedal of a large turn-of-the-century instrument.

Voix Celestes Derived from the old Italian Fiffaro stop, Celeste stops became common in the Swell organs of romantic instruments from about 1865. Characteristically they are of Salicional or soft Viola da

143

Gamba tone and tuned very slightly sharp of the unison rank with which they are always drawn. The beats which result give a lush ethereal sound which helps to compensate for the lack of chorus effect when playing softly on a single stop. An essential component of the romantic organ.

Vox Angelica Similar to the Voix Celestes but less stringy; almost a Dulciana in tone. Commonly the softest stop on the organ and very occasionally tuned flat instead of sharp to the unison.

Vox Humana Literally the human voice. This is the cause of more humour than any other organ stop. It is the only reed-stop with short resonators which made the transition from the classical to the romantic organ. Its characteristically nasal sound can be used with a Tremulant as a distinctive solo voice; in the classical organ it can also blend with a bright chorus. Like all short-length reeds it sounds out of tune when the temperature varies.

Wald Flute In the classical organ the Wald Flute is a bright 4ft or 2ft stop, wider in scale than a Principal, but with perhaps a slight taper and voiced with sufficient harmonics to double as part of the chorus. In the romantic organ it is an open wood flute, rather like a 4ft version of a Clarabella.

Zauberflöte Literally magic flute. The origin of the name is obscure. It is a stopped flute, made treble-length and voiced to speak its third harmonic. Has been used as a component of a Flute Celeste or Unda Maris.

Zink A pedal 2ft reed of Continental origin using large scale Clarinet-type pipes voiced suitably boldly.

GAZETTEER

The Gazetteer has been arranged alphabetically by county. The stop-lists are given as they appear at the console, except that prepared-for stops are omitted. Since information on borrowed stops has not always been available, they are not separately distinguished in the interests of consistency. However, the reader should anticipate that most Pedal organs made or rebuilt between 1900 and 1970 may have a fair proportion of borrowed stops. The provision of manual-to-pedal and intermanual couplers is virtually standard and can be assumed. The key-action of any unrebuilt organ constructed before 1870 can be assumed to be tracker unless otherwise noted. If more recent instruments have tracker action, it is noted; they can otherwise be assumed to have electric or electropneumatic action.

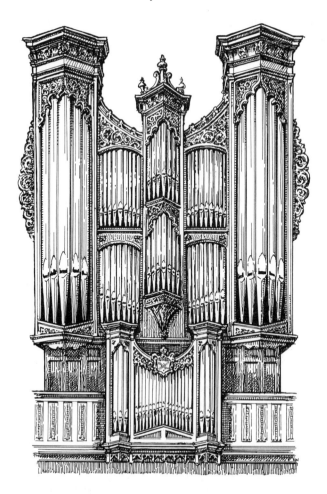

BATH ABBEY
(SEE P146)

ENGLAND

AVON

BATH The Abbey
Hill 1868; Norman & Beard 1895; Hill Norman & Beard 1972

GREAT		SWELL		SOLO (enclosed)		PEDAL	
Double Open Diapason	16	Open Diapason	8	Concert Flute	8	Double Open Wood	32
Open Diapason	8	Lieblich Gedeckt	8	Viole d'Orchestre	8	Open Wood	16
Gemshorn	8	Violoncello	8	Viole Celeste	8	Principal	16
Stopped Diapason	8	Voix Celeste	8	Harmonic Flute	4	Violone	16
Octave	4	Principal	4	Vox Humana	8	Sub Bass	16
Principal	4	Lieblich Flute	4	Orchestral Oboe	8	Echo Bourdon	16
Block Flute	4	Super Octave	2	Clarinet	8	Octave	8
Twelfth	2⅔	Larigot	1⅓	(unenclosed)		Bass Flute	8
Fifteenth	2	Quint Mixture		Tuba Mirabilis	8	Choral Bass	4
Furniture 19.22.26	III	15.19.22.26	IV			Hohl Flute	2
Sharp Mixture 29.33	II	Sharp Mixture 26.29.33	III	CHOIR (enclosed)		Mixture 12.15	II
Double Trumpet	16	Fagotto	16	Bourdon	8	Sharp Mixture	
Posaune	8	Trumpet	8	Flûte Ouverte	4	19.22.26.29	IV
Clarion	4	Oboe	8	Nazard	2⅔	Double Trumpet	32
		Clarion	4	Quarte	2	Trombone	16
POSITIV				Tierce	1⅗	Trumpet	16
Gedeckt	8			Plein Jeu 22.26.29	III	Tromba	8
Prestant	4			Chromorne	16	Rohr Shalmey	4
Rohrflöte	4			Trompette	8		
Oktave	2						
Sesquialtera	II						
Scharf 29.33.36	III						

James Vertue's famous print of Bath Abbey, dated 1750, shows the organ on a choir screen. This was Abraham Jordan's instrument of 1708. When the Abbey was 'restored' by Sir George Gilbert Scott in 1868 the screen was taken down and Hill built a new four-manual (with just one stop, the Tuba, on the Solo) which stood on the floor of the north transept. In 1895 the organ was divided into several sections with the aid of tubular pneumatic action, only to be reunited when the present north transept gallery was erected in 1914 and the case, designed by Sir Thomas Jackson, was added. With vestigial carved 'wings', it is less flamboyant than some of his cases but nevertheless looks very handsome, despite some slightly odd foot-lengths to the front pipes.

The projecting chair case dates only from 1972 and was designed by Alan Rome, after an idea by Herbert Norman. It contains the 6 stop Positiv which was added at that time. At the same time, alterations of the romantic period to the Swell and Great organs were undone and these departments largely restored to their Hill origins. However, the romantic Norman & Beard Solo organ was preserved without change. The Pedal upperwork and Double Trumpet 32ft date from 1972, as does the remodelling of the Choir organ to provide for the music of the classical French instrument. Despite these diverse influences, this organ is one of my favourite instruments, a liking increased by the elegant console with its arched compartments for the stop-jambs retained from the Norman & Beard console.

The statue of King David now standing under the organ was originally on top of one of the towers of Jordan's organ. The other two are in Yatton church together with Stopped Diapason pipes from that organ.

BRISTOL The Cathedral
Harris 1685; Walker 1907

GREAT		SWELL		SOLO (enclosed)		PEDAL	
Double Open Diapason	16	Bourdon	16	Harmonic Flute		Double Open Diapason	32
Open Diapason (large)	8	Horn Diapason	8	(unenclosed)	8	Open Diapason	16
Open Diapason (medium)	8	Open Diapason	8	Gamba	8	Open Diapason	16
Open Diapason (small)	8	Stopped Diapason	8	Voix Céleste	8	Violone	16
Stopped Diapason	8	Dulciana	8	Harmonic Flute	4	Contra Gamba	16
Wald Flöte	8	Vox Angelica	8	Clarinet	8	Bourdon	16
Principal (large)	4	Principal	4	Cor Anglais	16	Dulciana	16
Principal (small)	4	Harmonic Flute	4	Orchestral Oboe	8	Quint	10⅔
Flute	4	Twelfth	2⅔	Tromba (unenclosed)	8	Principal	8
Twelfth	2⅔	Fifteenth	2			Stopped Diapason	8
Fifteenth	2	Mixture (15.19.22)	III	CHOIR		Dulciana	8
Mixture 15.19.22	III	Contra Fagotto	16	Double Dulciana	16	Trombone	16
Double Trumpet	16	Horn	8	Open Diapason	8	Trumpet	8
Trumpet	8	Oboe	8	Stopped Diapason	8		
Clarion	4	Vox Humana	8	Viol di Gamba	8	LADY CHAPEL ORGAN	
		Clarion	4	Dulciana	8	(*Harrison 1956*)	
				Flute	4	Stopped Diapason	8
				Gemshorn	4	Principal	4
				Fifteenth	2	Flute	4
				Cornet Mixture		Fifteenth	2
				(12.17.21 flat)	III	Mixture (15) 22.26	III

Renatus Harris must have learned quickly from his defeat at Bernard Smith's hands in the 'Battle of the Organs' in the Temple Church, London. Smith had provided a third manual, the Echo organ, and Harris quickly copied the idea for Bristol Cathedral. Apart from the cases and their tin-metal front pipes, nothing of this instrument probably now remains. Harris had provided a Choir organ borrowed 'by communication' from the Great organ. The borrowing mechanism must eventually have given trouble for in 1786 Seede of Bristol added a separate 5 stop Choir organ in a chair case. A few pipes from this remain in the present organ and the case (sold in 1860 and converted into a book-case) returned to the cathedral in 1956 and was reconverted to house a new Harrison & Harrison tracker one-manual instrument for the Lady Chapel. This was one of the first modern British tracker organs.

Harris' organ was taken off the screen in 1860 and the back and front cases placed side-by-side between the columns of the north aisle. They still stand there, minus the crown and mitres which stood on the towers and with altered lower panelling. The east case is of Harris' 'round-shouldered' form with single-storey flats set in rich carving. The west case is still more elaborate, with segmental pediments on supporting columns. Of all Harris' cases, this most nearly approaches the rococo.

The 1860 instrument, by Vowles, was largely a new organ but did not last long, being replaced by the present J. W. Walker instrument, with tubular pneumatic action, which still survives to this day. It is typical of its date and period, even though a fair proportion of the flue-pipes have their origins in the earlier instruments.

Clifton Cathedral (Roman Catholic)
Rieger 1973

HAUPTWERK		RUCKPOSITIVE		BRUSTWERK (enclosed)		PEDAL	
Principal	8	Metallgedackt	8	Holzgedackt	8	Principal	16
Rohrflöte	8	Principal	4	Rohrflöte	4	Octav	8
Octav	4	Koppelflöte	4	Nassat	2⅔	Subbass	8
Superoctav	2	Gemshorn	2	Principal	2	Fagott	16
Sesquialter	II	Quintlein	1⅓	Terz	1⅗	Schalmei	4
Mixture 19.22.26.29	IV-VI	Scharff 26.29.33.36	IV	Cimbel 29.33	II		
Trompete	8	Krummhorn	8	Regal	16		

Clifton Cathedral is one of our most successful examples of modern ecclesiastical architecture. Although not large, it achieves a sense of space and mystery which is rare in new churches. The Rieger organ, however, is short on mystery and long on straightforwardness – not that it

147

fails to match the building. In fact, Joseph von Glatter-Götz's theatrical case, with its combination of triangles and rectangles, is an excellent fit with the triangular and hexagonal architecture. The oak-faced panels of the three-compartment *Hauptwerk* case even mimic the massiveness of the concrete.

The straightforwardness of the instrument arises from the economy of the design. A Cathedral organ has to have three manuals (or does it?) and, with only 26 stops, there is no room for subtleties. The Pedal organ, in particular, is a model of achievement in only 5 stops, one of them a 16ft Principal. The other side of this coin is that the organ has to work hard for its size. The jumps in the dynamic level as one draws the chorus culminate in the six-rank mixture on the *Hauptwerk*, a stop which almost doubles the power of the organ. The lack of mystery, which even the enclosure of the *Brustwerk* with glass shutters cannot remedy, arises because there simply is no room in the design for alternative 8ft stops. Perhaps we should not cavil at this, or at the lack of aids to registration. After all, it is its lack of compromise that gives the instrument such a strong personality.

BERKSHIRE

READING All Saints' Church
Willis c1865, 1900

This three-manual is a much more ordinary Willis than that in the Town Hall, with a simple post-and-rail case. Despite later modifications, the unique tubular-pneumatic action remains intact. Possibly designed by Vincent Willis, the action has cleverly designed relays which allow the player an element of control over the speed at which the pallets open, like tracker action. Incidentally, even Willis made mistakes. The Swell soundboard of this organ has the C pipes at the opposite end to the other manuals. As a result, all the pneumatic tubes have to run from one end of the soundboard to the other, crossing over in a glorious tangle.

Holy Trinity Church
? England; Gray & Davison 1876; Shepherd 1981

GREAT		SWELL		PEDAL	
Bourdon	16	Stopped Diapason	8	Grand Open Diapason	16
Open Diapason	8	Keraulophon	8	Grand Bourdon	16
Stopped Diapason	8	Principal	4	Principal	8
Dulciana	8	Flute	4	Flute	8
Principal	4	Fifteenth	2	Fifteenth	4
Twelfth	2⅔	Sesquialtera	II	Full Mixture 19.22	II
Fifteenth	2	Sharp Mixture 26.29.33	III	Sackbut	16
Furniture 19.22.26.29	IV	Hautboy	8	Regal	4
Trumpet	8	Clarion	4		

This is a collision of two organs. Most of the Swell and about half the Pedal is from the former Gray & Davison instrument. The main case and most of the Great organ is from the organ formerly in All Saint's Church, Oxford (now the library of Lincoln College). The builder is not known but the case bears a strong resemblance to the work of G. P. England, which would date it before 1820. The two detached Pedal towers are in pastiche of G. P. England style. The organ has tracker action, except for the Grand Open Diapason on the Pedal, and the shallow layout has the Swell organ over the Great. The instrument looks very pretty on the west gallery, the Pedal towers being nicely proportioned in relation to the main case. The cases were painted and marbled by Nicholas Krasno.

The Town Hall (illustrated on the jacket)
Willis 1864, 1882

GREAT		SWELL		CHOIR		PEDAL	
Double Diapason	16	Double Diapason	16	Lieblich Gedact	8	Open Diapason	16
Open Diapason I	8	Open Diapason	8	Viol d'Amore	8	Violone	16
Open Diapason II	8	Stopped Diapason	8	Salcional	8	Bourdon	16
Claribel Flute	8	Principal	4	Flûte Harmonique	4	Principal	8
Principal	4	Piccolo	2	Piccolo Harmonique	2	Ophicleide	16
Flûte Harmonique	4	Sesquialtera	III	Corno di Bassetto	8		
Twelfth	2⅔	Cornopean	8	Oboe	8		
Fifteenth	2	Hautboy	8				
Mixture	III	Vox Humana	8	SOLO			
Posaune	8	Clarion	4	Hohl Flute	8		
Clarion	4			Concert Flute	4		
				Orchestral Oboe	8		
				Tuba	8		

Although far from being the largest of the nineteenth-century Town Hall organs, the instrument at Reading is one of the most successful. This is partly a testimonial to the importance of the acoustics of the building, since the Town Hall has the reputation of being an extraordinarily good music room. Built for a much smaller hall, in which it had the reputation of being somewhat aggressive, the instrument was enlarged when the present hall was built by adding the unenclosed Solo organ, the 4ft reeds, additional 16ft flues and the Pedal Trombone. The wind pressure of the reed-stops was also increased. It all sounds a bit *ad hoc*, yet the result is an unqualified success. The organ has the bolder mixtures and Swell fluework characteristic of Willis' earlier instruments and the reeds, though firm, still show signs of the French influence which inspired Willis' formative years.

The other glory of the Reading Town Hall organ is the exuberant case. Designed by Thomas Lainson, architect of the Hall, it was, as far as we know, his only organ case. This is surprising as the flamboyance of his Victorian baroque style, with its unconventional curved towers and massive caryatids either side of the console, indicates a designer familiar enough with his subject to take liberties with conventional forms and get away with it.

Despite the 1882 reconstruction, this instrument is historically important as changes since then have been trivial and it is the only four-manual by Father Willis to have survived with its original action. The weight of the key-touch confirms one's suspicions about mid-Victorian tracker actions, despite the pneumatic lever action on the Great and a now-unique early tubular action to the Pedal Open Diapason.

BUCKINGHAMSHIRE

ETON Eton College Chapel (see Plate 5)
Hill 1882, 1902

GREAT		SWELL		CHOIR		PEDAL	
Double Open Diapason	16	Open Diapason	8	Rohr Flute	8	Double Open Diapason	
Open Diapason I		Stopped Diapason	8	Dulciana	8	(metal)	32
(heavy wind-8″)	8	Salicional	8	Unda Maris	8	Open Diapason (metal)	16
Open Diapason II	8	Voix Celeste	8	Suabe Flute	4	Open Diapason (wood)	16
Open Diapason III	8	Principal	4	Salicet	4	Violone	16
Stopped Diapason	8	Stopped Flute	8	Nazard	2⅔	Bourdon	16
Principal	4	Fifteenth	2	Gemshorn Tierce	1⅗	Bass Flute	8
Octave	4	Mixture 19.22.26.29	IV			Fifteenth	4
Flute	4	Contra Fagotto	16			Octave Flute	4
Twelfth	2⅔	Double Trumpet	16	SOLO		Bass Cornet 12.17	II
Fifteenth	2	Hautbois	8	Harmonic Flute	8	Bass Quartane 19.22	II
Mixture 19.22.26	III	Horn	8	Viole d'Orchestre	8	Trombone	32
Posaune (heavy wind)	8	Clarion	4	Viole Celestes	8	Trombone	16
Clarion (heavy wind)	4			Harmonic Flute	4	Trumpet	8
(The 3 stops on heavy		POSITIF (playable from		Piccolo	2	Clarion	4
wind are also playable on		Choir manual)		Orchestral Oboe	8		
the Choir manual).		Echo Diapason	8	Orchestral Clarinet	8		
		Gedeckt	8	Tuba (heavy wind-14″)	8		
		Spitzflote	4				

This magnificent organ seems to grow out of the Gothic Revival screen which divides the chapel from the ante-chapel. The double-sided case is by J. L. Pearson and the east face is unusual in that it contains no flats at all: it is all towers. A group of three 8ft towers in the centre is flanked by two 16ft towers, flanked in their turn by two 32ft towers. The mouths of the 32ft pipes are at console level and one can almost feel the draught as they speak! The painted decoration on these pipes is of superb quality, some of the best of its type.

The organ is quite shallow from front to back, following the classical tradition of being only one department deep, although subsequent additions and the bulky 1902 tubular pneumatic action have left the interior very cramped. So much so that when, in the 1920s, an additional wind-trunk was needed to provide 14in (350mm) wind pressure for the Tuba, the only space that could be found for it was inside one of the lower pressure wind-trunks!

The diminutive chair case became empty after 1902 but was brought into use again in 1955 when the small 3 stop unenclosed Positif was built for it by Hill Norman & Beard around some wooden Stopped Diapason pipes from the organ which Father Smith had built for the college around 1700. The four-tower case of this organ is now in Hawkesyard Priory, Rugeley, Staffordshire. The Positif was the first modern example in a projecting chair case. Modest tonal alterations were made to the organ in 1960 and in 1985 it is to be restored by Mander. Essentially, however, this instrument remains a fine example of a late Hill, combining a wide range of romantic tone colours with the singing chorus work which is characteristic of Hill's organs.

It was the success of this organ which led John Christie to the Hill firm and, eventually, to the Christie Unit organ. But that is another story!

Eton College Memorial Hall
Mittenreiter 1773; Flentrop 1973

HOOFDWERK		RUGWERK		PEDAL	
Bourdon	16	Gedekt	8	Bourdon	16
Prestant	8	Prestant	4	Prestant	8
Holpijp	8	Fluit	4	Gedekt	8
Octaaf	4	Gemshoorn	2	Octaaf	4
Fluit	4	Larigot	1⅓	Fagot	16
Quint	2⅔	Dulciaan	8		
Octaaf	2				
Cornet	III				
Mixtuur	IV				
Trompet	8				

It comes as something of a surprise to find an eighteenth-century Dutch double organ case in a British public school. In fact it came from the English church in Rotterdam. This case is at least as rich and elaborate as British cases of the same period, with the same use of carved swags as pipe-shades. It is smaller than British cases of the eighteenth century, since it was made to house a CC compass organ, not the extended British long compass to GG.

Henry Willis III built a three-manual organ for the hall in 1924, using the Mittenreiter case to house the Great organ, which included some of the original pipes. This instrument was notable chiefly for an outrageous misprint on the console. The Great organ retained the Dutch stop-names from the Mittenreiter organ. However, the engraver misread the script on the original Holpijp knob and the Willis console sported a draw-stop boldly labelled 'Holpup'!

In 1973 Flentrop, of Zaandam in Holland, built a new tracker-action two-manual organ within the restored case, again retaining the surviving Mittenreiter pipes. It is a typical good modern Dutch instrument, the second manual being the unenclosed Rugwerk in the chair case. It was one of the first modern instruments to be tuned to unequal temperament.

CAMBRIDGESHIRE

CAMBRIDGE Christ's College Chapel
? Smith 1705; Bishop 1983

GREAT		CHOIR		PEDAL	
Open Diapason	8	Stopped Diapason	8	Bourdon	16
Stopped Diapason	8	Principal	4	Principal	8
Principal	4	Flute	4	Gedackt	8
Flute	4	Gemshorn	2	Octave	4
Twelfth	2⅔	Quint	1⅓	Mixture	III
Fifteenth	2	Mixture	III	Posaune	16
Tierce	1⅗	Crumhorn	8	Trumpet	4
Mixture	III-IV				
Trumpet	8				

This is a new organ which looks like an old one. The case, in fact, is old and dates back to 1705, as do some of the pipes of the Great organ chorus. The remainder is new, built under the direction of John Budgen, but in the old spirit with two unenclosed manual divisions. Both Great and Choir are in the same case, as they were when the case was new, a relatively early example of such a layout.

The case was always ascribed to Father Smith but, in fact, the college contracted to Charles Quarles, the organist at Trinity College. The same arrangement was made at Pembroke College in 1708 and the main case there is very similar indeed. It is thought that Smith made most of the instrument for Quarles, but that the case may have been made by a local cabinet-maker after Smith's style.

Clare College Chapel
von Beckerath 1971

GREAT		SWELL		PEDAL	
Principal	8	Gedackt	8	Unterbass	16
Rohrflöte	8	Principal	4	Principal	8
Octave	4	Rohrflöte	4	Choralflöte	4
Blockflöte	4	Octave	2	Rauschpfeife	IV
Nasat	2⅔	Larigot	1⅓	Fagott	16
Flachflöte	2	Sesquialtera	II	Schalmei	4
Mixtur	V	Scharff	IV		
Trumpet	8	Bärpfeife	8		

This was the first of the imported tracker organs in Cambridge and is von Beckerath's only instrument in Britain. Rudolph von Beckerath was a pioneer of the organ-building revival in Germany after the war, and it is a pity that this instrument does not do him better justice. This is an intimate chapel and the bold pipe-scales lead to a 'full organ' that needs to be used with care. The case makes no attempt to echo the architecture of the chapel but is a typically well-finished but neo-brutalist expression of the structure of the instrument.

Corpus Christi College Chapel
Mander 1968

GREAT		SWELL		CHOIR		PEDAL	
Quintaton	16	Bourdon	8	Chimney Flute	8	Open Diapason	16
Open Diapason	8	Dulciana	8	Principal	4	Subbass	16
Stopped Diapason	8	Vox Angelica	8	Clear Flute	4	Echo Bass	16
Principal	4	Spitz Flöte	4	Nazard	2⅔	Principal	8
Nason Flute	4	Fifteenth	2	Block Flute	2	Flute	8
Twelfth	2⅔	Nineteenth	1⅓	Tierce	1⅗	Gemshorn	4
Fifteenth	2	Sharp Mixture	III	Mixture	III	Mixture	IV
Full Mixture	III	Bassoon	16	Cremona	8	Fagott	16
Mounted Cornet	V	Trumpet	8	Trumpet	8	Shawm	4
Trumpet	8			Clarion	4		
Clarion	4						

2 Cymbelsterns

The Corpus Christi organ was the last large new college instrument in Cambridge to have electric action and it replaced a much-altered tracker organ by Flight. The glory of this instrument has to be its sumptuous double case designed by Stephen Dykes Bower. If the main case towers are, perhaps, rather shallow, the richly gilded pipe-shades and the finely chased tin-metal front pipes with their varied mouth-shapes more than compensate.

The tonal design of the organ is basically English, with a *werk* principle Diapason pitch relationship added. The Choir organ gains by its projection in a chair case, the Swell and Great being side-by-side behind the arch. The Swell is unusual in combining a 2ft-based chorus and Sharp Mixture with a combination of half-length and full-length reeds. The console, a very handsome piece of cabinetwork, takes advantage of electric action to provide alternative radiating and straight pedalboards.

Emmanuel College Chapel
? Smith 1686; Norman & Beard 1907; Hill Norman & Beard 1963

GREAT		SWELL		POSITIF (in chair case)		PEDAL	
Contra Viola	16	Quintaten	16	Rohrflöte	8	Subbass	16
Open Diapason	8	Open Diapason	8	Prinzipal	4	Contra Viola (Great)	16
Gedeckt	8	Stopped Diapason	8	Waldflöte	2	Quintaten (Swell)	16
Octave	4	Echo Gamba	8	Spitz Quinte	1⅓	Principal	8
Harmonic Flute	4	Voix Celeste	8			Bass Flute	8
Twelfth	2⅔	Principal	4	CHOIR (enclosed)		Octave	4
Fifteenth	2	Super Octave	2	Hohlflöte	8	Open Flute	4
Sifflöte	1	Mixture 15.19.22	III	Dulciana	8	Super Octave	2
Mixture 19.22.26	III	Contra Fagotto	16	Lieblich Flöte	4	Trombone	16
Trumpet	8	Cornopean	8	Nazard	2⅔	Trumpet	8
Clarion	4			Flageolet	2	Clarion	4
				Tierce	1⅗		
				Krummhorn	8		
				Trumpet	8		

This is another Cambridge instrument with an allegedly Father Smith case, though this attribution is now questioned. College records indicate that it probably dates from 1686 but are silent on the builder's name. The chair case has similarities to the east face of the King's College case, and to the reputed Renatus Harris case now in Little Bardfield Church, Essex. The main case looks more likely to have been Smith's work.

The present organ dates from 1907 with some earlier pipes. The Swell, Choir and Pedal departments are located in the pavilions at the back of the gallery. The chair case was empty for many years but gained a new four-stop Positif when the organ was reconstructed with a new three-manual console and action in 1963. This was one of the first modern projecting Positives.

Gonville and Caius College Chapel
Klais 1981

GREAT		SWELL		RÜCKPOSITIV		PEDAL	
Bourdon	16	Gedacktflöte	8	Rohrgedackt	8	Offenbass	16
Principal	8	Salicional	8	Venezianerflöte	4	Subbass	16
Gemshorn	8	Vox Coelestis	8	Nasard	2⅔	Octave	8
Quintade	8	Principal	4	Principal	2	Spitzflöte	8
Octave	4	Rohrflöte	4	Terz	1⅗	Tenoroctave	4
Flute Octaviante	4	Blockflöte	2	Sifflet	1	Hintersatz 12.15.22	III
Superoctave	2	Sesquialter 12.17	II	Cremona	8	Lieblich Posaune	16
Larigot	1⅓	Mixtur 26.29.33.36	IV			Trompete	8
Cornet	V	Basson Hautbois	16				
Mixtur 19.22.26.29	IV	Trompette Harmonique	8			Tracker key-action.	
Trompete	8	Vox Humana	8				

Hans Gerd Klais, of Bonn, West Germany, has gained a name in recent years for departing from the neo-brutalist style of casework which originated in Scandinavia in favour of a more decorated appearance. The new double case has taken its colour and general architectural texture from the gallery front and from the roof panelling, but not everyone will approve of its obvious solidity or of the strong horizontal lines which result from the omission of pipe-shades.

Despite the intimate surroundings, the organ is not over-powerful, although one notices that the tone-cabinet of the relatively flutey *Rückpositiv* gives this department a much more 'forward' tone than that of the rest of the instrument, which is not provided with tone-cabinets. A similar effect can be heard at Emmanuel College, where the layout is the same. There being a considerable distance between the main and chair cases, the console is semi-detached. It has angle jambs and elegant, if impractical, flush-fitting rosewood pistons. The Swell organ is relatively soft but surprisingly English in sound, perhaps because of the full-length reeds, contributing to an overall atmosphere of being slightly more English than the English.

The Guildhall
Hill 1882; Hill Norman & Beard 1925

This three-manual instrument was built with a Solo department instead of a Choir organ and received its not unscholarly case in the 1890s at the hands of Dr Arthur Hill. Unfortunately, the horizontal fan Tuba was removed in 1925, at which time the instrument gained its detached towers of small-scale 32ft pipes.

Jesus College Chapel

There are two organs in Jesus College Chapel, standing side-by-side in the gallery on the north side.

The Sutton Organ
Bishop 1849

CHOIR		ECHO		PEDAL	
Open Diapason	8	Open Diapason	8	Bourdon	16
Stop Diapason	8	Stop Diapason	8		
Principal	4	Open Flute	4		
Chimney Flute	4	Fifteenth			
Twelfth	2⅔	(originally Principal 4)	2		
Fifteenth	2				
Tierce	1⅗				
Mixture 19.22	II				

This organ is one of the very few instruments with a case which is known to have been designed by Augustus Welby Northmore Pugin, the noted architect and Victorian specialist in Gothic Revival decoration. It has a typically Pugin angularity, and the richly decorated shutters were a conscious archaism, as indeed was the whole instrument, which incorporates a Stopped Diapason and a Chimney Flute of Father Smith pipes. The original console survives, but the organ is now played from a new two-manual and pedal console provided by Noel Mander when he restored the organ in 1967.

The Main Organ
Mander 1971

GREAT		SWELL		CHOIR		PEDAL	
Open Diapason	8	Gedact	8	Stopt Diapason	8	Subbass	16
Chimney Flute	8	Salicional	8	Principal	4	Principal	8
Principal	4	Celeste	8	Nason Flute	4	Spitz Flute	4
Nazard	2⅔	Principal	4	Fifteenth	2	Mixture 22.26.29	III
Fifteenth	2	Gemshorn	2	Cimbel 29.33	II	Posaune	16
Tierce	1⅗	Sharp Mixture 22.26.29	III	Regal (*en chamade*)	8		
Fourniture 19.22.26.29	IV	Bassoon	16	Trumpet (*en chamade*)	8	Tracker key-action	
		Trumpet	8				

The main organ replaced an Arthur Harrison of 1927 which had incorporated the Sutton Organ as two of its four manuals. Despite the incorporation of a non-speaking eighteenth-century chamber organ front, the case inevitably suffers by comparison with the splendour of Pugin's masterpiece in the next bay. The unique feature of this organ is that not only does it have a horizontal Trumpet but also the only British example of a horizontal Regal.

King's College Chapel
Dallam 1606; Hill 1859; Harrison 1934, 1968

GREAT		SWELL		CHOIR (enclosed)		PEDAL	
Double Open Diapason	16	Quintatön	16	Double Salicional	16	Double Open Wood	32
Open Diapason I	8	Open Diapason	8	Open Diapason	8	Open Wood	16
Open Diapason II	8	Violin Diapason	8	Claribel Flute	8	Open Diapason	16
Stopped Diapason	8	Lieblich Gedeckt	8	Salicional	8	Geigen	16
Octave	4	Echo Gamba	8	Dulciana	8	Bourdon	16
Principal	4	Echo Salicional	8	Gemshorn	4	Salicional	16
Wald Flute	4	Vox Angelica	8	Suabe Flute	4	Echo Violone	16
Octave Quint	2⅔	Principal	4	Nazard	2⅔	Violoncello	8
Super Octave	2	Lieblich Flute	4	Dulcet	2	Flute	8
Open Flute	2	Fifteenth	2	Tierce	1⅗	Rohr Flute	4
Sesquialtera	III	Mixture	IV	Larigot	1⅓	Principal	4
Mixture	IV	Oboe	8	Twenty-second	1	Open Flute	2
Contra Tromba	16	Double Trumpet	16	Dulzian	8	Mixture	V
Tromba	8	Trumpet	8	Contra Tromba	16	Double Ophicleide	32
Octave Tromba	4	Clarion	4	Tromba } from Great	8	Ophicleide	16
				Octave Tromba	4	Trombone	16
						Cor Anglais	8
				SOLO (enclosed)		Posaune	8
				Contra Viola	16	Tromba	8
				Viole d'Orchestre	8	Schalmei	4
				Viole Octaviante	4		
				Cornet de Violes			
				10.12.15	III		
				Harmonic Flute	8		
				Concert Flute	4		
				Cor Anglais	16		
				Clarinet	8		
				Orchestral Hautboy	8		
				French Horn	8		
				Tuba (unenclosed)	8		

With such a perfect setting, architecturally and acoustically, this is an organ which cannot fail! The instrument justifies its place on the screen by the fine carving and distinctive silhouette of the organ case. The west face of the case is certainly by Thomas Dallam and gives the appearance of a receding perspective, a favourite trick of the Dallam family. It is the oldest large organ case to which we can give a definite date and one which is exceptionally rich in figure carving. Originally the front pipes were embossed to complete the rich effect. The chair case, by Lancelot Pease in 1661, is equally richly decorated.

In 1688 Renatus Harris put a new organ in the cases; this instrument was rebuilt or replaced by Avery in 1804. William Hill carried out a major rebuilding in 1859, when the main case was made much deeper and the console moved to the north side. A new console with tubular pneumatic action was provided in 1888, when the Solo organ was added. The instrument was again rebuilt, this time by Harrison & Harrison, in 1934 and the same firm made tonal changes to the Great, Choir and Pedal organs in 1968.

The instrument as it now stands is a fascinating example of repeated enlargements during the romantic era of organ design. Despite the deepening of the main case, its capacity is limited by the low centre. Consequently, much of the organ is within the screen rather than in the case itself, the 32ft Double Open Diapason being laid horizontally. Nevertheless, one should not decry Arthur Harrison's work; the Solo organ is one of his finest examples of voicing in the romantic style, even if the Tuba is almost French Horn-like in its smoothness. Finally, one must not forget the most important stop on this organ: the incomparable acoustic!

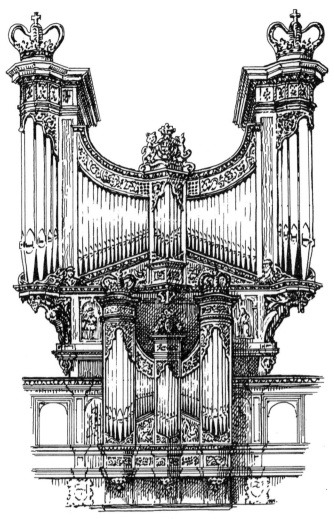

KING'S COLLEGE CHAPEL, CAMBRIDGE

Little St Mary's Church
Bishop 1978

GREAT		SWELL		PEDAL	
Open Diapason	8	Cone Gamba	8	Bourdon	16
Stopped Diapason	8	Stopped Diapason	8	Principal	8
Principal	4	Principal	4	Bassoon	16
Twelfth	2⅔	Flute	4		
Fifteenth	2	Gemshorn	2		
Tierce	1⅗	Mixture	II		
Mixture	II	Hautboy	8		

This new tracker organ is built round pipes from the 1850 James Corps organ formerly in Necton Church, Norfolk. The case and the tribune gallery were designed by Lawrence Bond. The Swell is above the Great and the case design manages to incorporate the upper part of the swell-box without destroying the shapely three-tower form.

155

Pembroke College Chapel
? Smith 1708; Mander 1980

GREAT		CHAIRE		PEDAL	
*Open Diapason	8	*Stopped Diapason	8	Bourdon	16
*Stopped Diapason	8	*Principal	4	Principal	8
Principal	4	*Nason	4	Fifteenth	4
Twelfth	2⅔	Fifteenth	2	Mixture	IV
Recorder	2	Cymbal	III	Bass Shawm	16
Tierce	1⅗	Vox Humana	8	Trumpet	8
Furniture	IV				
Cornet	V	*Pipes apparently by Smith.			
Trumpet	8				

Father Smith has always been considered to have been the original builder of the Pembroke College organ, largely on the strength of the undoubted Smith pipes which it contains. The college, however, contracted to Charles Quarles, the organist of Trinity College, for a new organ. This was duly supplied in 1708, the previous organ being moved to Framlingham Church (where it still remains). It seems probable that either Quarles subcontracted the making of much of the instrument to Smith, or that he used parts of the earlier Smith organ at Trinity College. This was then being displaced by Smith's new and grander instrument, the case and some pipes of which still remain at Trinity.

Looking at the double case of the Pembroke College organ, it becomes obvious that the two parts do not belong together. The main case is very similar to the one supplied by Quarles to Christ's College in 1705, but the detail of the carving of the pipe-shades and of the brackets adjoining the central tower is different to that of fully authenticated Smith cases; the sharp-pointed side towers are more reminiscent of some of Robert Dallam's work. The chair case is more likely to have been made by Smith, but is equally puzzling since it has a unique double flat between two fairly bold semi-circular towers. Perhaps Quarles had it adapted from a wider case with a third tower in the centre?

Like so many other Cambridge college instruments, the Pembroke organ was rebuilt by Hill in the nineteenth century, when Swell and Pedal organs were added, and a further rebuild by Norman & Beard in 1902 provided exhaust-pneumatic action. The present instrument was designed from the standpoint that the organ should be scaled down to match the original case. For this reason a Swell is omitted and the Pedal organ stands behind the rest of the instrument in a separate case, enabling the main case to be restored to its original shallow depth. The compass extends to an additional low AA, a token of the original long compass. Musically, the remaining Smith pipes have been used as the inspiration for the new instrument, although the stop-list departs from Smith's original by having a flute for the Great organ 2ft and by adding a Cymbal and fractional-length reed to the Chaire organ. These give the Chaire a north European sound in keeping with the Hamburg training of John Mander, who voiced the instrument.

Peterhouse College Chapel
Snetzler 1765; Mander 1963

GREAT		SWELL		CHOIR		PEDAL	
*Open Diapason	8	Salicional	8	*Echo Dulciana	8	Open Diapason	16
Stopt Diapason	8	*Stopt Diapason	8	*Stopt Diapason	8	Bourdon	16
*Principal	4	*Principal	4	*Flute	4	Octave	8
Nason Flute	4	Fifteenth	2	*Principal	4	Flute	8
*Twelfth	2⅔	Mixture	III	Gemshorn	4	Fifteenth	4
*Fifteenth	2	Oboe	8	Nazard	2⅔	Flute	4
Mixture	II			Gemshorn	2	Trombone	16
Trumpet	8	*Wholly or partly by		Tierce	1⅗	Trumpet	8
		Snetzler.		Larigot	1⅓	Clarion	4
				Trumpet	8		

Peterhouse College Chapel has one of the most complete large Snetzler organs which remain to us. The case is of typical British seventeenth/eighteenth century form with three towers.

The two-storey flats have characteristic Snetzler curved tip-boards for the lower storey, and the instrument remains in its original gallery position. The gilding is modern.

Snetzler's organ had 9 stops on the Great (4 of which remain) and 4 each on the Swell and Choir, sharing a single row of keys and common action. Dr Arthur Hill rebuilt the organ in 1895 in a consciously conservationist spirit, retaining black natural keys in a new three-manual C compass console. The Mander rebuild retained tracker action to most of the instrument, but used electric action to provide Pedal and Choir organ upperwork.

Queen's College Chapel
Binns 1892

This is a typical example of a late Victorian organ by the best of the Leeds organ-builders. It is, however, the dramatic Gothic Revival case by Bodley, free-standing on the screen, which attracts attention. The coved overhang, at the front as well as the sides, makes the organ appear to soar up to the ceiling, an effect which justifies the vertical emphasis of its otherwise rather narrow-scale display pipes.

Ridley Hall Chapel
Norman & Beard 1903

GREAT		SWELL		PEDAL	
Open Diapason	8	Violin Diapason	8	Bourdon	16
Wald Flute	8	Lieblich Gedeckt	8		
Echo Dulciana	8	Principal	4	Exhaust-pneumatic action.	
Flute d'Amour	4	Hautbois	8		

If you want to know what a turn-of-the-century 'octopod' was like, this is an unaltered example.

Robinson College Chapel
Frobenius 1981

GREAT		SWELL		PEDAL	
Principal	8	Gedakt	8	Subbass	16
Fløjte	8	Gamba	8	Oktav	8
Oktav	4	Principal	4	Gedakt	8
Fløjte	4	Fløjte	4	Superoktav	4
Quint	2⅔	Nasard	2⅔	Mixtur 22.26.29	III
Oktav	2	Oktav	2	Fagot	16
Blokfløjte	2	Larigot	1⅓	Skalmej	4
Terts	1⅗	Scharf 22.26.29	III		
Mixtur 19.22.26.29	IV	Krumhorn	8	Tracker key-action.	
Trompet	8				

It is instructive to compare this instrument with the Queen's College, Oxford organ, built sixteen years earlier by the same maker, especially as the stop-lists are remarkably similar. Acoustically, the Cambridge organ is in a much drier environment and this emphasises the almost clinical precision of this unashamedly Scandinavian instrument. The most successful department is the Swell which, unusually, is placed forward in a chair case. The relatively deep tone-cabinet adds warmth to the sound and the Krumhorn has a roundness not present in the Oxford example. The crescendo is provided by edge-pivoted glass shutters. The arrangement of the Pedal organ is somewhat odd, with the upperwork and mixture conveyed to a position below the soundboard and speaking out through slots in the lower panelling.

In its appearance the organ expresses its three tone-cabinets most clearly and their simple sloping roofs reflect the shape of the chapel ceiling. The division of the pipes of each department into six sections is a common feature of Frobenius' work.

157

Church of St Andrew the Less
? 1854

The one-manual organ in this church is believed to date from 1854. The case has a rich central tower with an embossed pipe, side flats and doors. Sometimes attributed to Pugin, it was certainly influenced by Sir John Sutton.

St Catharine's College Chapel
Johnson 1979

GREAT		SWELL		CHOIR		PEDAL	
Open Diapason	8	Stopped Diapason	8	Gedeckt	8	Principal	16
Stopped Diapason	8	Salicional	8	Principal	4	Dulciana	16
Principal	4	Voix Celeste	8	Coppel Flute	4	Octave	8
Open Flute	4	Principal	4	Nasat	2⅔	Stopped Flute	8
Nazard	2⅔	Fifteenth	2	Octave	2	Fifteenth	4
Fifteenth	2	Mixture	II-III	Spitz Flute	2	Nason Flute	4
Nachthorn	2	Fagot	16	Terz	1⅗	Mixture	III
Tierce	1⅗	Trumpet	8	Quint	1⅓	Bombarde	16
Mixture	II	Clarion	4	Cymbel	III		
Scharf	II	Krummhorn	8				
Trumpet	8						

This splendid double case was a rare archaism in 1894 when it was designed by Thomas Garner (Bodley's partner) to house the then new Norman & Beard organ. This instrument was replaced in 1979 by the current organ, to date William Johnson's major work, advised by Peter Le Huray. It is a tracker-action instrument, with the new Choir organ designed as a classical Positive and located in the previously empty chair case. The Swell organ, however, and about two-thirds of the Great organ are based on the pipes of a Bishop organ of the late 1850s. The overall result is more of a modern eclectic organ than most of the other new instruments in Cambridge.

St John's College Chapel
Hill 1838, 1867; Hill Norman & Beard 1955

GREAT		SWELL		CHOIR (unenclosed)		PEDAL	
Double Open Diapason	16	Lieblich Bourdon	16	Prinzipal	8	Sub Bass	32
Open Diapason	8	Open Diapason	8	Quintade	8	Open Wood	16
Geigen Diapason	8	Rohr Gedeckt	8	Glockengamba	8	Violone	16
Spitz Principal	8	Echo Salicional	8	Oktav	4	Bourdon	16
Stopped Diapason	8	Vox Angelica	8	Gemshorn	4	Dulciana	16
Octave	4	Principal	4	Nasat	2⅔	Lieblich Bourdon	16
Spitz Principal	4	Lieblich Flute	4	Blockflöte	2	Principal	8
Harmonic Flute	4	Fifteenth	2	Sifflöte	1	Bass Flute	8
Octave Quint	2⅔	Larigot	1⅓	Zimbel 29.33.36	III	Fifteenth	4
Super Octave	2	Mixture 22.26.29.33	IV			Nachthorn	4
Mixture 19.22.26	III	Oboe	8	SOLO (enclosed)		Mixture 19.22.26.29	IV
Flute Cornet 12.15.17	III	Double Trumpet	16	Quintatön	16	Contra Posaune	32
Trumpet	8	Cornopean	8	Hohl Flute	8	Ophicleide	16
Clarion	4	Clarion	4	Viola da Gamba	8	Posaune	8
				Viole Céleste	8	Schalmei	4
				Lieblich Flute	4		
				Harmonic Twelfth	2⅔	Cymbelstern	
				Piccolo	2		
				Harmonic Tierce	1⅗		
				Clarinet	8		
				Trompeta Real	8		
				(unenclosed, with 37 pipes			
				en chamade)			

Robert Dallam made a double organ for St John's College in 1636 and the two cases still exist, though not in Cambridge. Apart from a very few older pipes, the present instrument has its origins in the three-manual which William Hill built in 1838 and later enlarged for the new Scott chapel. Sundry alterations and additions were made by Norman & Beard and by Arthur

Harrison, but the organ assumed its present form in 1955.

The Royal Festival Hall apart, this instrument was the first major organ to break away from the mould of the Arthur Harrison school of tonal design. It is the epitome of the eclectic organ, with an independent and largely unextended Pedal, a Germanic Choir organ (a Positive in all but name), plentiful mutations and mixtures, and a Spanish-inspired horizontal Trompeta Real. The name means State Trumpet, though this stop was more of an original creation than an historical copy. The belled and flared ends of the tin-metal pipes were designed to catch the light as they project over the false chair front of one of J. Oldrid Scott's twin cases of 1889. In 1955 there was no contemporary experience of the voicing of horizontal reeds and a trial chord of pipes was tested on 15in (375mm) wind pressure – audible out in Trinity Street! – before a more moderate pressure was selected.

The design of the instrument was evolved by George Guest, director of the famous St John's College Choir, and Mark Fairhead, Head Voicer of Hill Norman & Beard, who always considered it his finest work.

St Luke's Church
? Harris 1715; Hill 1854

GREAT		SWELL		CHOIR		PEDAL	
Open Diapason	8	Double Diapason	16	Stopt Diapason	8	Open Wood	16
Stopt Diapason	8	Open Diapason	8	Dulciana	8		
Octave	4	Stopt Diapason	8	Octave	4		
Open Flute	4	Octave	4	Flute	4		
Octave Quint	2⅔	Super Octave	2				
Super Octave	2	Horn	8				
Sesquialtera 17.19.22	III	Oboe	8				
Trumpet	8						
		Stopped Bass	8				
		(permanently on)					

Some of the pipes of this instrument are over 250 years old, the organ having been built for St Mary's Church, Whitechapel, London in 1715. It is reputed to be the work of Renatus Harris and the last instrument that he built in London before retiring to Bristol. Hill rebuilt the organ to CC compass in 1854 and provided a tenor C Swell; the original case was replaced about this time. Many of the Swell stops still terminate at tenor C, the organ having come to St Luke's in 1877 and having undergone little change since.

Sidney Sussex College Chapel
Harrison 1963

GREAT		SWELL		PEDAL	
Open Diapason	8	Violin Diapason	8	Sub Bass	16
Stopped Diapason	8	Gedackt	8	Principal	8
Octave	4	Principal	4	Flute	8
Open Flute	4	Nazard	2⅔	Choral Bass	4
Super Octave	2	Gemshorn	2	Wald Flute	2
Mixture	IV	Mixture	III	Fagotto (Swell)	16
		Contra Fagotto	16		
		Trumpet	8		

A competent but unexciting organ, typical of its period, tucked out of the way on a side gallery with a detached console on the floor of the chapel. Despite the chorus-based Great organ, the Swell is almost the predominant manual, with sub-and super-octave couplers and containing all the reeds.

Trinity College Chapel
Smith 1708; Metzler 1976

HAUPTWERK		SCHWELLWERK		RÜCKPOSITIV		PEDAL	
*Principal	16	Viola	8	*Principal	8	*Principal	16
*Octave	8	Suavial	8	Gedackt	8	Subbass	16
Hohlflöte	8	Rohrflöte	8	Octave	4	Octavbass	8
*Octave	4	Principal	4	Rohrflöte	4	Bourdon	8
Spitzflöte	4	Gedackt Flöte	4	Octave	2	Octave	4
*Quinte	2⅔	Nasard	2⅔	Gemshorn	2	Mixtur	V
*Superoctave	2	Doublette	2	Larigot	1⅓	Posaune	16
Sesquialter	III	Terz	1⅗	Sesquialter	II	Trompete	8
Mixtur	IV-V	Mixtur	IV	Scharf	III	Trompete	4
Cornett	IV	Fagott	16	Dulcian	8		
Trompete	8	Trompete	8	*Stops incorporating Smith pipes.			
Vox Humana	8						

This was Father Smith's last work and the main organ case is arguably his grandest. Two-sided and standing upon the screen, it has four towers, the outer towers being flat on plan and capped with broken pediments. The chair case is more conventional and, if anything, more richly carved.

Smith's organ was enlarged over the years, particularly by Hill, who widened the case to six towers, and by Harrison who had to hide his additions by suspending curtains down from the ceiling to the top of the case! In the recent work it was decided to return the case to its original width, and this made necessary a completely fresh start, based on the surviving Smith pipes. The resulting three-manual tracker organ, by Metzler of Zurich, is still bigger than Smith's organ and the case is consequently two divisions deep instead of one. The constraints imposed by using an old case in this way have left the Swell organ in the bottom of the case without a clear tonal outlet. The console is Germanic rather than English but, tonally, the old pipes have integrated well into the new scheme.

The University Church of St Mary the Great

Amazingly, there are two three-manual organs in this church. One belongs to the parish, and is played for ordinary services by the parish organist. Built by Miller and rebuilt by Johnson in 1961, it has 43 stops and is placed in an elevated chamber on the south side of the chancel. The other organ belongs to the university, is played by the university organist for the weekly university service, and stands on a stone loft in the western tower.

The University Organ
Smith 1698; Hill 1870; Hill Norman & Beard 1963

GREAT		SWELL		CHOIR		PEDAL	
Spitzprincipal	16	†Open Diapason	8	*Stopped Diapason	8	Open Diapason	16
*Open Diapason	8	‡Stopped Diapason	8	Dulciana	8	Bourdon	16
*Stopped Diapason	8	Viola	8	*Principal	4	Principal	8
*Principal	4	†Principal	4	*Flute	4	Bass Flute	8
*Nason Flute	4	Fifteenth	2	*Fifteenth	2	Nachthorn	4
*Twelfth	2⅔	Mixture 15.19.22	III	Cymbal 22.26.29	III	Mixture 15.19.22	III
*Fifteenth	2	Contra Oboe	16	Cremona	8	Trombone	16
*Mixture 19.22.26	III	Cornopean	8				
Mounted Cornet	IV	Clarion	4	*Pipework by Smith (1698).			
Trumpet	8			†Pipework by Turner (1713).			
				‡Pipework by Parker (1767).			

This is one of our great historic organs. Of all the Father Smith organs left to us, no other has so high a proportion of his pipes still in use (11 stops out of the original 13). Smith built the organ as a two-manual, in the then new style of placing the Choir organ in the main case, so the instrument never had a chair case. The organ originally stood forward of the tower arch on a wooden gallery, less elevated than now. The four-tower case is a little more formal and less ornate than the Trinity College case, but contains superb carving in the cherubs' heads under the towers. The cornice joining the two towers is unusual and may perhaps be explained by the

THE UNIVERSITY CHURCH OF ST MARY THE GREAT, CAMBRIDGE

fact that originally there was a clock over the central flat, replaced by the present carved panel in 1766. As built, the front pipes were gilded and the pipe-shades left in bare oak, but when the case was restored in 1963 under the direction of George Pace, this situation was reversed. He also designed the panelling between organ and tower arch which now obscures the outline of the lower case.

A short compass Echo organ was added in the eighteenth century and later turned into a Swell. In 1819 Elliot moved the organ back into its present position, from where it does sound a little remote. In the 1860s the organ was in such poor condition that the parish installed their own instrument in the chancel but in 1870 the University organ was rebuilt by Hill.

For a Victorian, Hill was remarkably careful with historical instruments. Although the mechanism of the organ was completely new, including a most unorthodox tracker-operated sliderless soundboard for the Pedal organ, he discarded only the Cornet of the original pipes; nor did he make any obvious attempt to alter the voicing. The 1806 Avery Swell reeds which Hill discarded were wrapped up in newspaper and stored under the bellows. These pipes were returned to use in 1963 when the instrument was restored by Hill Norman & Beard, after narrowly escaping a proposed 'neo-Arthur Harrison' rebuild. Up to 1963 the organ had been hand-blown (two levers required) and, as well as an electric blower, a replacement Cornet was fitted, the Pedal upperwork and the Choir organ Cymbal and Cremona being added.

How does the instrument sound? Essentially like any other good Hill organ of the 1870s, with the few modern stops increasing the versatility of the instrument. This shows how much Hill was working in a continuing tradition, so that today we still have one instrument which Father Smith, it is hoped, would not have disowned.

ELY The Cathedral
Hill 1851, 1867; Harrison 1908, 1975

Hill's 1851 organ for Ely was one of the first cathedral instruments to be placed up in the triforium, using a 'long movement' tracker action to connect to the console behind the stalls. The organ case by Sir George Gilbert Scott was loosely based on the late fifteenth-century Gothic case in Strasbourg Cathedral. As built, the organ was quite a small instrument (the tenor C Swell had only 6 stops), but Hill enlarged it in 1867 and the organ was rebuilt by Harrison & Harrison in 1908. It was this rebuild, to a tonal design influenced by his close friend Lt Col George Dixon, which both established the Arthur Harrison style and laid the foundation of his reputation. He emphasised weight of tone, with a 32ft Sub-Bordun on the Great, a large Hope-Jones style heavy-pressure Open Diapason I and smooth high-pressure reeds. Smoothness and a gradual crescendo from the softest string to full organ were the hallmarks. The enclosed Solo organ, with its families of flutes, string and reeds was also characteristic and may prove to be his most lasting work.

The rebuild of 1975 reduced the weight of the Great organ, removed the unique Horn Quint on the Swell and replaced the Pedal upperwork removed in 1908. An 8 stop Positive division was added in the pseudo-chair lower part of Scott's case, previously empty.

PETERBOROUGH The Cathedral (see Plate 6)
Hill 1894; Hill Norman & Beard 1930; Harrison 1981

GREAT		SWELL		CHOIR (enclosed)		PEDAL	
Double Open Diapason	16	†Bourdon	16	Bourdon	16	Double Open Diapason	
*Bourdon	16	*Open Diapason No 1	8	Open Diapason	8	(wood)	32
Open Diapason No 1	8	Open Diapason No 2	8	Dulciana	8	Open Diapason (metal)	16
Open Diapason No 2	8	Rohr Flöte	8	†Stopped Diapason	8	Open Diapason (wood)	16
Open Diapason No 3	8	Salicional	8	†Principal	4	Violone	16
Spitz Flöte	8	Voix Céleste	8	†Flute	4	†Bourdon	16
Hohl Flöte	8	Principal	4	†Fifteenth	2	*Dulciana	16
Stopped Diapason	8	Salicet	4	†Flautina	2	Principal	8
Principal	4	Wald Flute	4	†Flageolet	1	Bass Flute	8
Geigen Principal	4	Fifteenth	2	†Mixture 19.22.26	III	†Violoncello	8
Harmonic Flute	4	Mixture 15.19.22	III	Bassoon	16	†Gemshorn	4
Twelfth	2⅔	Cymbal 19.22.26.29	IV	*Trumpet	8	Twelfth & Fifteenth	II
Fifteenth	2	*Contra Oboe	16			†Mixture 15.19.22	III
Full Mixture		Hautboy	8	SOLO (enclosed)		Contra Trombone	32
19.22.26.29	IV	Double Trumpet	16	Quintatön	16	*Contra Oboe	16
†Sharp Mixture		Trumpet	8	*Viole	8	*Clarinet	16
29.33.36	III	Horn	8	*Viole Céleste	8	*Contra Tuba	16
†Cornet 8.12.15.17	IV	Clarion	4	Unda Maris (II ranks)	8	Contra Posaune	16
Contra Posaune	16			*Concert Flute	8	Trombone	16
Posaune	8			†Octave Viole	4	Trumpet	8
Clarion	4			Flauto Traverso	4	Posaune	8
				†Piccolo	2	Clarion	4
				*Double Clarinet	16		
				Orchestral Oboe	8	*1930 tonal changes.	
				Clarinet	8	†1981 tonal changes.	
				Vox Humana	8		
				Contra Posaune	16		
				Posaune	8		
				Clarion	4		
				Tuba	8		

Peterborough Cathedral nearly collapsed in the 1880s. When the central tower was rebuilt, the choir screen was demolished and the choir moved west of the crossing to its present position There had been an organ on the screen since before the Commonwealth, in fact a whole succession of organs dating from 1661 (Thomas Thamar), 1735 (Kellingburgh) and 180?

(William Allen), the last being enlarged by Holdich in 1848 and rebuilt by Hill about 1870. This organ was taken from the screen to the north aisle but was soon replaced by the present instrument, though some pipes from the earlier organ were re-used.

The organ stands in the north triforium, set well back so that it is generally invisible. The eye sees only Dr Arthur Hill's very fine case of 1904 projecting from the north arcade, well in front of the instrument itself. The case is one of Dr Hill's best compositions, combining Gothic Revival tracery with a classical outline, the two 16ft outer towers contrasting with the two smaller centre towers and a prominent two-storey central flat. Hill was able to combine the triforium position for the organ with an accessible place for the organist in a loft above the north choir stalls by using tubular pneumatic action. In practice, however, this proved to be unsatisfactory for hearing the instrument, and in 1930 a handsome new console was built in the gallery behind the south choir stalls, connected by electric transmission.

The Peterborough organ provides a superb variety of accompanimental sounds and is ideal for the daily choral services. As a result of the indirect sound from the triforium, however, it is less happy for recitals and nave services. A possible move to the west end, with tracker action, was discussed in the 1970s. However, the needs of the daily services are paramount and in the recent reconstruction the aim was to retain the Hill organ as built in 1894, with new action, wind supply and console mechanism. Some of the 1930 additions to the Solo organ were retained and the enclosed Choir organ, on the floor of the north aisle, formerly very mild, was given a new chorus. The overall result is a beautifully restored liturgical organ with an astonishingly good blend between the additions and the original work.

CHESHIRE

CHESTER The Cathedral
Whiteley 1876; Hill 1910; Rushworth & Dreaper 1970

GREAT		SWELL		CHOIR		PEDAL	
Gedeckt	16	Open Diapason	8	Double Dulciana	16	Double Open Wood	32
Open Diapason I	8	Stopped Diapason	8	Open Diapason	8	Open Diapason	16
Open Diapason II	8	Salicional	8	Viola	8	Open Wood	16
Open Diapason III	8	Vox Angelica	8	Dulciana	8	Violone	16
Flute à Pavillon	8	Principal	4	Stopped Diapason	8	Bourdon	16
Stopped Diapason	8	Suabe Flute	4	Principal	4	Violoncello	8
Octave	4	Fifteenth	2	Gemshorn	4	Bass Flute	8
Principal	4	Mixture 19.22.26.29	IV	Stopped Flute	4	Principal	8
Harmonic Flute	4	Sharp Mixture		Hohlflöte	2	Fifteenth	4
Twelfth	2⅔	26.29.33.36	IV	Larigot	1⅓	Octave Flute	4
Fifteenth	2	Bassoon	16	Mixture 22.26.29	III	Mixture 19.22.26.29	IV
Splitzflöte	2	Double Trumpet	16	Clarinet	8	Contra Trombone	32
Mixture 15.19.22.26.29	V	Horn	8			Trombone	16
Sharp Mixture 29.33.36	III	Trumpet	8	SOLO		Trumpet	8
Contra Posaune	16	Oboe	8	Viola	8		
Trumpet	8	Clarion	4	Celeste	8		
Clarion	4			Bourdon	8		
				Koppelflöte	4		
				Nazard	2⅔		
				Blockflöte	2		
				Tierce	1⅗		
				Larigot	1⅓		
				Cimbel 29.33.36	III		
				Regal	8		
				Schalmei	8		
				Tuba	8		

The Chester Cathedral organ has long enjoyed a considerable reputation, lasting through two rebuilds. This is all the more remarkable since the organ was originally built by the local firm of Whiteley Brothers of Chester, their only major work, though parts of the previous organ (Gray & Davison 1844) were incorporated.

The instrument stands on a bridge across the north transept in quite the most interesting of Sir George Gilbert Scott's Gothic Revival organ cases, complete with statues of angels in amongst the pinnacles. Some of the Pedal organ is placed separately at the back of the transept. Being west of the screen, the organ speaks relatively well into the nave, but is remote from the choir. Consequently, as part of Hill's rebuild in 1910, the Choir organ was removed from the screen to the south side of the choir stalls, placed in a case designed by Dr Arthur Hill, and controlled by an early form of electropneumatic action, also used for the detached Pedal. Hill also substantially revoiced Whiteley's organ, (already modified by Gray & Davison in 1895) without altering its size.

The organ was again rebuilt in 1970 and the fine Hill console was largely retained after fitting with new mechanism. Sharp mixtures were added to the Great and Swell organs and the Choir gained a Larigot and Mixture. The Solo organ, enclosed in 1910 by Hill, almost entirely changed its character, becoming largely a flute chorus, topped by a Cimbel mixture and two baroque reeds, presumably to compensate for the absence of a Positive. The Pedal gained 4ft stops and a Mixture. Apart from the Solo organ, the essential character of the organ has remained intact, as has its reputation.

GREAT BUDWORTH St Mary and All Saints' Church
Renn 1839

GREAT		SWELL		PEDAL	
Open Diapason	8	Open Diapason	8	Bourdon	16
Stop Diapason Bass	8	Stop Diapason	8		
Stop Diapason Treble	8	Principal	4		
Dulciana	8	Hautboy	8		
Flute	4	Cornopean	8		
Principal	4				
Fifteenth	2				
Sesquialtra Bass					
Cornet Treble					
Trumpet	8				

Less celebrated than Samuel Renn's other surviving instrument at St Philip's, Salford, this modest organ has, in fact been less altered. In particular, the instrument retains its GG compass Great organ as well as the tenor C Swell. Being provincial, the organ seems older than its actual age and the manual stop-list, apart from the Dulciana, could almost be an extract from a scheme a hundred and fifty years earlier.

The case belongs to the early Gothick style rather than the more scholarly style led by Pugin; the large crocketted gable over the central flat is splendidly vulgar. The two towers are reminiscent of York Minster, having an upright between each pipe. The original console remains intact, projecting from the case with a box-like fall not dissimilar to that of square pianos of the period.

MACCLESFIELD Adlington Hall
Anon 17th century

GREAT		CHOIR	
Open Diopason	8	St Diopason Ch	8
St Diopason	8	St Flute Ch	4
Principall	4	Bassoon Ch	8
Gt twelfth	2⅔		
Fifteenth	2	The stop-names are spelt as
Bl Flute bas	2	on the surviving stop-labels.
Bl Flute trib	2	
Ters	1⅗	Compass: ostensibly four
Sm Twelfth	1⅓	octaves and a third (BBB to
2 & Twenty	1	d), but bottom BBB and
Vox Humana	8	CC♯ sound GGG and
Trumpet	8	AAA respectively.

Organs that Handel played are rather like beds that Queen Elizabeth slept in – rather too numerous to be believed. However since Handel, a family friend, certainly stayed i

Adlington Hall and since the organ has every appearance of being made before Handel was born, this would appear to be one instance where the story is justified.

That much may be relatively certain, but a great deal else remains a mystery. Noel Mander, who restored the organ in 1959, believes that much of the organ was made by Father Smith, even though one stop is borrowed 'by communication', not a device otherwise used by Smith. The instrument has a curious two-level case, of which the upper front part could be Smith's work, although it could equally well have been that of Renatus Harris. The lower part, however, is much less professional, with front pipes which were formerly speaking pipes in another organ but which are now dummy. The pipes of the Great "Principall" are older and less well made than the rest and the stop list, with a Twenty-second, would have been old fashioned by 1680. Part of the key-action is 'suspended', which is French rather than English, and there are relics of an apparently never-completed French-type pedalboard. Perhaps a local builder combined surviving parts from a pre-Commonwealth organ with a secondhand instrument, or even purchased parts from Smith or Harris. Who knows? The important fact is that this is a seventeenth-century organ, complete and unaltered in all respects with the original (noisy) action, the original keyboards with ebony naturals and ivory sharps, and the original pipes with their very light nicking or very thin reed-tongues. As such it is almost unique.

ST ALBAN'S ROMAN CATHOLIC CHURCH, MACCLESFIELD

St Alban's Roman Catholic Church
Ohrmann & Nutt 1803; Gray & Davison c.1900; Church 1983

GREAT		CHOIR		PEDAL	
*Open Diapason	8	*Stopped Diapason	8	Pedal Pipes	16
*Stopped Diapason	8	*Dulciana	8		
*Principal	4	*Principal	4	*Original pipes.	
Twelfth	2⅔	*Flute	4		
*Fifteenth	2	*Fifteenth	2		
Sesquialtera 17.19.22	III	*Stopped Diapason			
Mixture 22.26.29	III	(in Swell)	8		
Trumpet	8	*Hautboy (in Swell)	8		

Ohrmann & Nutt were John Snetzler's successors. This is probably their only surviving organ, very much in the Snetzler tradition with its elegant three-tower case with twin oval lower flats, and made originally for Macclesfield parish church as a three-manual. In St Alban's Church the organ was divided either side of the west window, the case being cut down the middle. Nigel Church's restoration has reunited the two halves, provided a new tracker action and console and replaced missing pipes. For economy, the instrument has reverted to the occasional eighteenth-century custom of combining a Swell and a Choir organ on one manual.

CLEVELAND

MIDDLESBROUGH The Town Hall
Hill 1898

GREAT		SWELL		CHOIR		PEDAL	
Double Open Diapason	16	Bourdon	16	Dulciana	8	Double Open Diapason	32
Open Diapason 2	8	Open Diapason	8	Viol d'Orchestra	8	Open Diapason	16
Open Diapason 1	8	Violoncello	8	Vox Angelica	8	Violone	16
Clarabella	8	Voix Celeste	8	Lieblick Gedackt	8	Contra Dulciana	16
Harmonic Flute	8	Hohlflute	8	Harmonic Flute	4	Principal	8
Harmonic Flute	4	Salicional	8	Harmonic Piccolo	2	Violoncello	8
Principal	4	Oboe Flute	4	Clarionet	8	Bass Flute	8
Twelfth	2⅔	Principal	4			Trumpet	8
Fifteenth	2	Mixture	IV	SOLO (enclosed)		Ophicleide	16
Mixture	IV	Fifteenth	2	Viola	8		
Contra Posaune	16	Sharp Mixture	II	Stopped Flute	8		
Posaune	8	Double Trumpet	16	Flauto Traverso	4		
Clarion	4	Horn	8	Contra Bassoon	16		
		Oboe	8	Orchestral Oboe	8		
		Clarion	4	Vox Humana	8		
				Tuba (unenclosed)	8		
				Muted Chimes			
				Chimes			

This late Hill is virtually unaltered. The original console and tubular-pneumatic manual action survive. This is a grand old instrument with a wealth of romantic stops, yet with Hill's insistence on proper choruses on the Swell and Great organs, already considered old-fashioned in 1898.

The case is a typical example of the simplified Gothic detail used by the firm of Hill when Dr Arthur Hill was not designing something consciously grand. It has the standard feature, to our eyes somewhat curious, of front pipes which project through the pipe-caps and show above them.

166

CORNWALL

TRURO The Cathedral
Willis 1888, 1963

GREAT		SWELL		CHOIR		PEDAL	
Double Diapason	16	Geigen Principal	8	Gamba	8	Double Open Diapason	32
Open Diapason 1	8	Open Diapason	8	Dulciana	8	Open Diapason	16
Open Diapason 2	8	Lieblich Gedackt	8	Lieblich Gedackt	8	Violone	16
Claribel	8	Echo Gamba	8	Hohl Flute	8	Bourdon	16
Principal	4	Vox Angelica	8	Gemshorn	4	Octave	8
Flute Harmonique	4	Geigen Principal	4	Lieblich Flöte	4	Violoncello	8
Twelfth	2⅔	Flageolet	2	Piccolo	2	Ophicleide	16
Fifteenth	2	Mixture 17.19.22	III	Corno-di-Bassetto	8		
Mixture 17.19.22	III	Hautboy	8				
Double Trumpet	16	Vox Humana and		SOLO			
Tromba	8	Tremolo	8	Harmonic Flute	8		
Clarion	4	Contra Fagotto	16	Concert Flute	4		
		Cornopean	8	Orchestral Oboe	8		
		Clarion	4	Clarinet	8		
				Tuba	8		

Father Willis built this relatively modest four-manual for J. L. Pearson's new cathedral in the elevated choir chamber which Pearson typically provided. Willis was no enthusiast for case-work and, although the instrument was designed to allow a case to be added, it remains screened by zinc basses to this day. The 1963 rebuild by Henry Willis III provided a new action and console but otherwise left the instrument a characteristic example of his grandfather's work.

CUMBRIA

APPLEBY St Lawrence's Church
Anon 17th century

The case and front pipes of this organ came to the church from Carlisle Cathedral in 1684. The organ was moved from a west gallery in 1863 and the case shortened to fit into a chapel near the chancel. It was restored and returned to the west end in 1976. The original date of construction has been suggested as before the Commonwealth. However, it is more likely to have been the case of an organ built immediately after the Restoration of the monarchy in 1660 and then displaced when the new styles of Smith and Harris became accepted.

DERBYSHIRE

SANDIACRE St Giles' Church
Church 1977

GREAT (enclosed)		RUCKPOSITIV		PEDAL	
Chimney Flute	8	Gedact	8	Sub Bass	16
Octave	4	Metal Flute	4	Principal	8
Mixture	III	Principal	2	Fagot	16
Trumpet	8				

This modest two-manual tracker instrument stands high on the west gallery in a cedar double case designed by Roger Pulham. An enclosed department was required and, it being impracticable to enclose the Ruckpositiv (in the chair case), the Great organ is enclosed in a swell-box. The shutters are concealed by using the bass of the Pedal 8ft Principal as the main display.

DEVON

EXETER The Cathedral (see Plate 2)
Loosemore 1665; Willis 1891; Harrison 1936, 1965

GREAT		SWELL		CHOIR		PEDAL	
Double Open Diapason	16	Quintadena	16	Lieblich Bourdon	16	Contra Violone	32
Open Diapason I	8	Open Diapason	8	Lieblich Gedackt	8	Open Diapason	16
Open Diapason II	8	Stopped Diapason	8	Viola	8	Violone	16
Stopped Diapason	8	Salicional	8	Open Flute	4	Bourdon	16
Dulciana	8	Voix Celestes	8	Nazard	2⅔	Quintadena	16
Principal	4	Principal	8	Lieblich Piccolo	2	Octave	8
Harmonic Flute	4	Flute	4	Tierce	1⅗	Violoncello	8
Twelfth	2⅔	Twelfth	2⅔	Twenty Second	1	Flute	8
Fifteenth	2	Fifteenth	2	Cimbel	III	Fifteenth	4
Mixture	IV	Mixture	IV			Octave Flute	4
Sharp Mixture	III	Contra Fagotto	16	SOLO		Mixture	II
Double Trumpet	16	Hautboy	8	Claribel Flute	8	Trombone	16
Trumpet	8	Cornopean	8	Viole d'Orchestre	8		
Clarion	4	Clarion	4	Viole Octaviante	4		
				Harmonic Flute	4		
				Piccolo	2		
				Corno di Bassetto	8		
				Orchestral Oboe	8		
				Vox Humana	8		
				Tuba	8		
				Trompette Militaire	8		

The great case of John Loosemore's organ of 1665, standing on the choir screen, is one of the first things that one sees on entering the west end of the Cathedral. As the only one of the immediate post-commonwealth organ cases to remain in its original position, it is of major historical importance. Loosemore was 'Curator' or Clerk-of-Works to the Cathedral and this was his only large organ. The case is very distinctive, with a surprisingly gothic feel to some of the carving and ornamental work. The outer towers on the east face are more than semi-circles and have circular caps (not unlike the eastern face of the King's College, Cambridge organ, where John Loosemore's brother Henry was organist at the time). Loosemore's embossed tin front pipes gave way to Victorian replacements at the time that his famous 21ft Double Diapason bass pipes (down to GGG 32ft) were also removed. These had stood away from the organ, against the columns north and south of the screen.

The organ itself is now basically the work of Henry Willis, who put the console on the south side of the instrument and the Swell and Great organs, sideways on, in the main case, much deepened to accommodate them. Willis added a fourth manual, the Solo, placed in a west-facing replica of the chair case, raising the main case several feet to its present height above the screen. He also took the 32ft spotted metal pipes which Henry Speechly had recast from Loosemore's discarded bass pipes and stood them in their present detached position in the south transept. This organ was conservatively rebuilt by Harrison in 1936 and remodelled by them to its present eclectic form in 1965. This work included the provision of a flute chorus on the Choir organ and the Trompette Militaire, located in a high gallery halfway down the north side of the nave.

DORSET

BLANDFORD FORUM Bryanston School Church
Church 1980

GREAT		ECHO		PEDAL	
Principal	8	Bourdon	8	Sub Bass	16
Chimney Flute	8	Chimney Flute	4	Open Flute	8
Octave	4	Recorder	2	Octave	4
Spitz Flute	4	Larigot	1⅓	Mixture	III
Nazard	2⅔	Sifflet	1	Posaune	16
Fifteenth	2	Regal	16	Trumpet	8
Tierce	1⅗	Dulcian	8		
Mixture	IV-V				
Trumpet	8				

This tracker instrument, designed in collaboration with Georges Lhôte, the Swiss organ-builder, stands prominently on the chancel steps, facing down the nave. The oak case has a strong silhouette, with a central tower in the shape of a blunt 'V' and two flat side-towers. The second manual, placed behind the fretted panel above the console, is an Echo organ designed for choir accompaniment and is in no sense a Positive. The very complete Pedal organ stands in a separate case behind.

Parish Church of St Peter and St Paul
England 1794; Hill 1876; Mander 1971

GREAT		SWELL		CHOIR		PEDAL	
Open Diapason	8	Bourdon	16	Dulciana	8	Open Diapason	16
Stopped Diapason	8	Open Diapason	8	Stopped Diapason	8		
Gamba	8	Stopped Diapason	8	Principal	4		
Principal	4	Principal	4	Flute	4		
Twelfth	2⅔	Mixture	III	Fifteenth	2		
Fifteenth	2	Trumpet	8				
Cornet	IV	Oboe	8				
Mixture	II						
Trumpet	8						

George Pike England was one of the last builders to work in the style established by Smith and Harris over a century earlier. The church is eighteenth century too, rebuilt after a disastrous fire which destroyed much of the town in 1731. England's organ received a new Swell from Hill in the nineteenth century but remained in the west gallery until 1895, when it was removed to an organ chamber on the north side of the chancel. Noel Mander restored the instrument to the west gallery but made no significant changes. Despite Victorian enlargements, the instrument retains its original case as well as nearly all the original pipes, including the extremely rare eighteenth-century Cornet stop, mounted in the original manner with the pipes conveyed to a position above the remainder of the Great organ.

DORCHESTER Baptist Church
Collins 1977

GREAT		OBERWERK		PEDAL	
Principal	8	Rohr Flute	8	Subbass	16
Stopped Diapason	8	Dulciana	8	Octave	8
Octave	4	Principal	4	Gedact	8
Flute	4	Rohr Nazard	2⅔	Spitz Octave	4
Fifteenth	2	Octave	2	Nachthorn	2
Mixture 19.22	II-IV	Gemshorn	2	Fagot	16
Trumpet	8	Tierce	1⅗		
		Cymball 26.29	II-III		
		Schalmei	8		

Like many organs by P. D. Collins, this tracker instrument is extremely shallow and compact. The basically simple case of five compartments makes use of a clever front-pipe arrangement and simple pipe-shades to produce an elegant effect. The prepared-for *Brustwerk* is unusual in being placed above the impost, the Great and Pedal organs being divided either side with the *Oberwerk* on top. In addition to the usual couplers, there is an Oberwerk octave-to-Pedal coupler which could, for example, provide a 4ft Schalmei on the Pedal keys.

LULWORTH Lulworth Castle Chapel
Seede 1785

MANUAL (compass from GG)		
Open Diapason	8	Pedals GG to C (17 notes); no pipes
Open Diapason	8	
Stopped Diapason	8	*Not original.
*Viola da Gamba	8	
Principal	4	
Flute	4	
Twelfth	2⅔	
Fifteenth	2	
Sesquialtera 15.17	II	
(enclosed)		
Dulciana	8	
Hautboy (pipes missing)	8	

Richard Seede was the son of Brice Seede, who made the magnificently carved case in Chippenham parish church, though he was not as sophisticated a cabinet-maker as his father. This curious little Spanish mahogany case has a charmingly rural aspect, with pipes displayed in compartments round the sides in addition to a conventional three-tower front with gabled flats in imitation of Harris' work. However, Seede was clearly an inventive mechanic, since the organ has the earliest detached console surviving in Britain. The idea of reversing the console so that the player could look out over it seems to have originated in south Germany at the beginning of the eighteenth century, though it never became very popular in Britain. At Lulworth, Seede had the original idea of building the console into the back of a dummy chair case, the tracker action going back under the player to the instrument. The arrangement survives to this day, together with the original compass down to GG (with, as usual, no GG♯) and nearly all the original pipes.

SHERBORNE The Abbey
Gray & Davison 1856; Walker 1954; Bishop & Son 1985

GREAT		SWELL		CHAIR		PEDAL	
Double Diapason	16	Open Diapason	8	Clarabella	8	Open Wood	16
Open Diapason	8	Clarinet Flute	8	Flute	4	Bourdon	16
Open Diapason	8	Keraulophon	8	Mixture		Quint	10⅔
Stopped Diapason	8	Vox Angelica	8	15.19.22.26	IV-VI	Principal	8
Octave	4	Principal	4	Cornet	IV	Super Octave	4
Flute	4	Gemshorn	2	Trumpet	8	Trombone	16
Twelfth	2⅔	Mixture	IV	Clarion	4		
Super Octave	2	Hautboy	16				
Sesquialtera 17.19.22	III	Cornopean	8				
Cremona	8	Clarion	4				

The organ stands high in the north transept of Sherborne's magnificent Abbey Church. As built, it was a fine example of a high point in British organ-building. The instrument was rebuilt in 1954 in an unfortunate attempt to turn it into a romantic instrument, with far too many pipes crammed into a limited space. Fortunately, over half the pipes of the original instrument are still there and are now to be incorporated into a new tracker-action organ to be built by Bishop & Son. This will be of an unusual design, with the chair case containing a type of Bombarde division, designed to reinforce the Great organ and, by coupling, the Pedal section also. The forward position of the pipes in the chair case will help the sound to travel along the building and overcome the 'round-the-corner' problem which afflicts transept organs.

170

The 1856 case, designed by R. C. Carpenter, is an interesting and original Victorian restatement of the classical double organ case, complete with Gothic tracery in the form of vestigial doors. The stencilled decoration on the front pipes is one of the finest examples we have of this essentially Victorian art form.

WIMBORNE The Minster
Hayward 1664; Seede 1764; Robson 1844, 1856; Walker 1867, 1965

GREAT		SWELL		POSITIVE		PEDAL	
Quintaton	16	†Open Diapason	8	Gedekt	8	Principal	16
Open Diapason 1	8	†Stopped Diapason	8	*Principal	4	Violone	16
*Open Diapason 2	8	Viola	8	*Chimney Flute	4	Bourdon	16
*Rohr Flute	8	Vox Angelica	8	†Quint	2⅔	Salicional	16
Dulciana	8	†Principal	4	*Blockflute	2	Octave	8
*Principal	4	†Flute	4	Tierce	1⅗	Salicet	8
Koppel Flute	4	Twelfth	2⅔	Larigot	1⅓	Bass Flute	8
*Twelfth	2⅔	Fifteenth	2	Sifflute	1	Octave Quint	5⅓
*Fifteenth	2	Mixture 22.26.29	III	Cymbal 29.33.36	III	Fifteenth	4
Sesquialtera 12.17	II	Double Trumpet	16	Crumhorn	8	Octave Flute	4
Mixture 19.22.26.29	IV	Cornopean	8	Orchestral Trumpet	8	Nachthorn	2
Trumpet	8	Hautbois	8			Mixture 19.22.26.29	IV
Clarion	4	Clarion	4			Trombone	16
						Crumhorn	16
						Posaune	8
						Clarion	4
						Schalmei	2

*Hayward pipes 1664.
†Seede pipes 1764.

Robert Hayward of Bath built a two-manual organ for the Minster in 1664, 8 stops of which still survive in what, today, is a very different instrument. One hundred years later, a Swell organ was added by Seede of Bristol; a small Pedal organ by Robson came in 1844. Then, in 1856, a disaster occurred. The organ was moved from the screen to the south choir aisle and, not surprisingly, proved almost inaudible. J. W. Walker substantially enlarged the instrument in 1867 and, although its buried position was still unsatisfactory, this rebuilding lasted almost another hundred years.

The 1965 J. W. Walker rebuild was controversial, the organ eventually remaining in much the same position; the console was detached to the north side of the choir. Despite a further enlargement which included new upperwork to turn the Choir organ into a Positive, the sound in the nave is still largely indirect. As the organ lacks a proper case, the eye of the visitor is drawn to an archway opened up in 1965 and leading from the organ to the south transept. This archway is filled with a double row of bass pipes plus, at little more than head height, a spun brass horizontal Orchestral Trumpet on 7in (175mm) wind pressure. The effect of this stop is quite shattering!

DURHAM

DURHAM The Cathedral
Smith 1683–4; Willis 1876; Harrison 1905, 1935, 1970

GREAT		SWELL		CHOIR (enclosed)		PEDAL	
Double Open Diapason	16	Double Diapason	16	Bourdon	16	Double Open Wood	32
Contra Clarabella	16	Open Diapason I	8	Viole d'Amour	8	Open Wood I	16
Open Diapason I	8	Open Diapason II	8	Gedeckt	8	Open Wood II	16
Open Diapason II	8	Salicional	8	Flauto Traverso	8	Open Diapason	16
Open Diapason III	8	Vox Angelica	8	Gemshorn	4	Violone	16
Open Diapason IV	8	Lieblich Gedeckt	8	Stopped Flute	4	Dulciana	16
Gamba	8	Principal	4	Flauto Traverso	4	Bourdon	16
Stopped Diapason	8	Harmonic Flute	4	Nazard	2⅔	Contra Viola	16
Claribel Flute	8	Fifteenth	2	Piccolo	2	Octave Wood	8
Octave	4	Mixture	V	Tierce	1⅗	Principal	8
Principal	4	Oboe	8	Dulciana Mixture	III	Violoncello	8
Harmonic Flute	4	Vox Humana	8	Clarinet	8	Dulciana	8
Octave Quint	2⅔	Double Trumpet	16			Flute	8
Super Octave	2	Trumpet	8	POSITIVE (*on Choir keys*)		Twelfth	5⅓
Mixture	IV	Clarion	4	Flûte à Cheminée	8	Super Octave Wood	4
Scharf	III			Quintade	8	Octave Cello	4
Contra Posaune	16	SOLO (enclosed)		Prestant	4	Twenty Second	2
Posaune	8	Contra Viola	16	Flûte Ouverte	4	Mixture	IV
Clarion	4	Viole d'Orchestre	8	Doublette	2	Double Ophicleide	32
		Viole Céleste	8	Sesquialtera	II	Double Trombone	32
		Viole Octaviante	4	Larigot	1⅓	Ophicleide	16
		Cornet de Violes	III	Octavin	1	Trombone	16
		Harmonic Flute	8	Octave Tierce	⅘	Cor Anglais	16
		Concert Flute	4	Cymbale	III	Tromba	8
		Harmonic Piccolo	2	Dulzian	16	Cornett	4
		Cor Anglais	16	Trompette	8		
		Corno di Bassetto	8				
		Orchestral Oboe	8				
		French Horn	8				
		Orchestral Tuba	8				
		Tuba (unenclosed)	8				
		Tuba Clarion (unenclosed)	4				

Durham Cathedral, as seen from across the river, is one of the most magnificently sited Cathedrals in Britain. Father Smith built an organ for Durham. It stood on a choir screen with a double-sided four-tower main case and a three-tower chair case. This instrument was taken down from the screen in 1847, finally making way for Father Willis' divided organ after 1872. The chair case and Choir organ pipes went to the chapel in Durham Castle, now the University. The main west front of the case survives and has been set up on the wall of the south aisle.

Willis' four-manual organ was rebuilt in 1905 by Harrison & Harrison (then newly under the command of Arthur Harrison and his brother Henry), but the major tonal changes were made in 1935 when a 32ft reed was added to the Pedal, the Great organ gained a large Open Diapason I and a 16ft Contra Clarabella and the Solo organ acquired a complete family of Violes from 16ft to mixture. In 1970 a second 32ft reed arrived, plus a second Great mixture, Choir organ mutations and the complete Positive organ. This amalgam of the work of Willis and two generations of Harrisons now runs Liverpool, St Paul's London and Norwich a close fourth in terms of cathedral organ size.

EAST SUSSEX

BRIGHTON The Royal Pavilion, The Dome Concert Hall
Hill Norman & Beard 1936

The Dome, a mock-oriental extravaganza, was once the Prince Regent's riding stables. The four-manual 40-rank organ was installed when the building was refitted as a general-purpose theatre. Although built under the Hill Norman & Beard name, the instrument was really a Christie theatre organ in its design, complete with mobile horseshoe console and percussion effects. The instrument, unaltered and unrestored, continues in regular use for popular concerts by Douglas Reeve, who has been resident organist for over thirty years.

CHAILEY Heritage School Chapel
Hill 1914

Sir Ninian Comper, a pupil of Bodley, designed the elaborate and remarkable three-tower case for this organ in his unique combination of gothic and classical styles. Projecting like a chair case from the north aisle gallery, it is a pure screen, the organ being some feet from it the other side of the arch. A detached console on the floor of the chapel was provided when electropneumatic action was fitted in the 1960s.

GLYNDEBOURNE (SEE P174)

173

GLYNDEBOURNE The Organ Room
Hill Norman & Beard 1920

Many visitors to the Opera will have seen this imposing case at the end of John Christie's extraordinary Organ Room and perhaps wondered about the instrument inside it. The Organ Room, organ and case were made in 1919–20 when John Christie first became interested in organs. He persuaded Dr C. H. Lloyd, a former teaching colleague at Eton, to retire to Sussex on the promise of building an organ for him. Alas, Dr Lloyd died before the instrument was finished, and John Christie listened to every visiting expert, with the result that the instrument was continually being enlarged. This culminated in a 32ft wood Open Diapason which could only be accommodated under the Organ Room floor!

The organ case, in limed oak, was designed by Edmond Warre, architect of the Organ Room, and cost half as much as the organ itself. It never quite knows whether to be Gothic or classical but contains an astonishingly wide range of pipe sizes from the 16ft basses in the towers to quite tiny pipes over the console. John Christie became so interested in the organ that when Dr Hill died he purchased a controlling interest in Hill Norman & Beard. Later, he turned to opera and lost interest in organs; parts of the instrument were incorporated in the Dome Concert Hall organ in Brighton. What remains now is an impressive if unscholarly case and a handsome console, originally exhibited at the Wembley Exhibition of 1924. Perhaps the console, at any rate, will one day be thought historic.

NEWICK St Mary's Parish Church
Positive Organ Co 1889; Morgan & Smith 1976

GREAT		SWELL		PEDAL	
Bourdon	16	Open Diapason	8	Open Bass	16
Open Diapason	8	Rohr Flute	8	Sub Bass	16
Viola	8	Viol di Orchestre	8	Flauto Maggiore	8
Claribel	8	Octave Viol	4	Bass Flute	8
*Gedakt	8	Cornopean	8		
*Viole Sourdine	8			*These stops form the Choir	
Principal	4			section.	
*Flauto Traverso	4				
Flautino	2				

After going bankrupt on the exhibition organ now in Tewkesbury Abbey (the Grove Organ), Carlton Michell and William Thynne became manager and voicer of the Positive Organ Co, owned by Thomas Casson, a retired banker. In this organ, reputed to have been a gift of the Baden-Powell family, they continued their pioneering exploration of the technique of voicing narrow-scale stops. The plethora of such stops in this instrument forms a unique historical link between the Tewkesbury organ and the more extreme instruments of Robert Hope-Jones which were to follow. In particular, if the Swell Viol di Orchestre is original, as reputed, it must be one of the first of these extremely narrow-scale stops with their almost 'scratchy' tone.

The oak case is by J. Oldrid Scott and, with its pseudo-chair case, is similar in outline to his twin cases at St John's College, Cambridge. Here the chair case contains the Choir section, three narrow-scale stops on a separate soundboard, suggesting that originally a three-manual instrument was planned. The console, formerly projecting from the case, was reversed when electric coupling and transmission were fitted in 1976.

ESSEX

CHELMSFORD The Cathedral
Norman & Beard 1899; Hill Norman & Beard 1933, 1970

GREAT		SWELL		POSITIVE		PEDAL	
Double Open Diapason	16	Bourdon	16	Gedeckt	8	Sub Bass	32
Open Diapason	8	Spitzflute	8	Chimney Flute	4	Open Wood	16
Geigen Diapason	8	Salicional	8	Principal	2	Open Metal	16
Stopped Diapason	8	Vox Angelica	8	Larigot	1⅓	Violone	16
Octave	4	Principal	4	Cymbel 29.33.36	III	Double Dulciana	16
Spitzprincipal	4	Recorder	4	Krummhorn	8ft	Bourdon	16
Twelfth	2⅔	Super Octave	2			Principal	8
Fifteenth	2	Sesquialtera	II	SOLO		Bass Flute	8
Blockflute	2	Mixture 15.19.22	III	Claribel Flute	8	Octave	4
Mixture 19.22.26	III	Sharp Mixture 26.29	II	Viole d'Orchestre	8	Mixture 19.22.26.29	IV
Mounted Cornet	IV	Fagotto	16	Lieblich Flute	4	Trombone	16
Posaune	8	Trumpet	8	Nazard	2⅔	Rohr Shalmey	4
		Clarion	4	Flautina	2		
				Tierce	1⅗		
				Oboe	8		
				Clarinet	8		

Built as a three-manual by Norman & Beard for what was then Chelmsford parish church, this organ was enlarged to a four-manual when the church attained cathedral status. The organ case, by Philip Selfe, is a bold and simple three-tower affair with Gothic detail and short lower flats beneath a compartment of large-scale speaking pipes. It stands in a recess beyond the outer north aisle. The Recorder stop in the Swell was voiced in collaboration with Canon Galpin, the music historian, to imitate an instrument in his collection.

The tonal design was substantially changed in 1970 when a Mounted Cornet replaced the Open Diapason I, new mixtures and reeds were added to the Swell and Pedal departments and a new Positive organ fitted in an internal tone-cabinet in the upper part of the case.

LITTLE BARDFIELD St Katherine's Church
?Harris 1689; Gray 1830

This single-manual and Pedal organ has the case of an instrument made for Jesus College, Cambridge, probably by Renatus Harris. The college gave it to All Saint's Church, Cambridge in 1790 and John Gray made 'a new inside' for it in 1830, the instrument going to Little Bardfield in the 1860s. The case has rich carving and a vestigial centre tower reminiscent of the 'perspective' effects popular with Harris' grandfather, Robert Dallam.

SAFFRON WALDEN Parish Church of St Mary the Virgin
Vincent 1824; Lewis 1898; Norman & Beard 1911; Hill Norman & Beard 1972

The Gothick case on the south side of the chancel dates from the Vincent organ of 1824, as does some of the pipework of the Great and Choir organs. The 1911 work included exhaust pneumatic action and a very compact console of a type designed in conjunction with Alfred Hollins, the blind organist, with a double row of small stop-knobs (push one for 'on', the other for 'off') under the music desk. This console was placed in an unusual position on the rood screen, as is its 1972 successor of conventional stop-knob design.

In this very large church, the organ never really spoke down the nave, and in the 1972 rebuild a new nave Great section was added, up on the screen with the console, as a quasi-Positive. There is also a Bombarde section, complete with IV–VI rank mixture and horizontal Trompeta Real, the latter speaking down the south aisle and with a horizontal 16ft octave (half-length pipes) played from the Pedal organ.

THAXTED The Parish Church of St John, St Mary the Virgin and St Lawrence
Lincoln c1826

GREAT		SWELL		CHOIR		COMPASS
Open Diapason Front	8	Open Diapason	8	Stopped Diapason	8	Great and Choir
Open Diapason	8	Stopped Diapason	8	Dulciana	8	FFF (no FFF♯) to f''' 60
Stopped Diapason	8	Principal	4	Principal	4	notes
Principal	4	Cremona	8	Flute	4	
Twelfth	2⅔	Trumpet	8	Fifteenth	2	Swell
Fifteenth	2	Hautboy	8	Bassoon (pipes missing)	8	Tenor E to f''' 38 notes
Sesquialtera (Bass)	III-IV					
Cornet (Treble)	IV			PEDAL		Pedal
Mixture (pipes missing)	I-II			Pedal (open wood pipes)	8	FFF to C 20 notes (FFF♯
Trumpet (pipes missing)	8					plays an octave above on
						both the pedal stop and the
						couplers!)

Thaxted Church has two organs. The Cedric Arnold instrument at the west end, in a reputed G. P. England case, is the one generally used, but the grand Henry Lincoln three-manual in the north transept is much the more important. One of the last large organs to be made before the Hill–Gauntlett revolution, it retains its original long compass to FFF for the Great and Choir organs. Built for St John's Chapel, Bedford Row, London, the instrument has a finely moulded and carved case with an unusual blend of classical and vaguely Gothick details.

GLOUCESTERSHIRE

GLOUCESTER The Cathedral
? Dallam 1641; Harris 1665; Willis 1847, 1888; Harrison 1920; Hill Norman & Beard 1971

GREAT		SWELL		CHOIR		PEDAL	
Gedecktpommer	16	Chimney Flute	8	Stopped Diapason	8	Flute	16
*Open Diapason (east)	8	Salicional	8	*Principal	4	*Principal	16
*Open Diapason (west)	8	Celeste	8	Chimney Flute	4	Sub Bass	16
Spitzflute (west)	8	Principal	4	Fifteenth	2	*Octave	8
*Bourdon	8	Open Flute	4	Nazard	1⅓	Stopped Flute	8
*Octave (east)	4	Nazard	2⅔	Sesquialtera	II	Choral Bass	4
*Prestant (west)	4	Gemshorn	2	Mixture 29.33.36	III	Open Flute	2
*Stopped Flute	4	Tierce	1⅗	Cremona	8	Mixture 19.22.26.29	IV
Flageolet	2	Mixture 22.26.29.33	IV			Bombarde	16
*Quartane (west) 12.15	II	Cimbel 38.40.43	III	WEST POSITIVE		Trumpet	8
*Mixture 19.22.26.29	IV-VI	Fagotto	16	(Manual IV)		Shawm	4
Cornet 8.12.15.17	IV	Trumpet	8	Gedecktpommer	8		
Posaune	16	Hautboy	8	Spitzflute	4	*Wholly or partly Harris
Trumpet	8	Vox Humana	8	Nazard	2⅔	pipes.
Clarion	4			Doublette	2	The west Great and the
				Tierce	1⅗	Great reeds can be
				Larigot	1⅓	separately coupled to
				Cimbel 29.36.40	III	Manual IV.

The Gloucester Cathedral organ, almost uniquely, combines the survival of a very large amount of historic material with an otherwise mostly new instrument strongly influenced by the *Orgelbewegung*. The very fine oak chair case with mannerist decoration is now thought likely to have been the case of the organ built in 1640–1, probably by Robert Dallam. This instrument was bought back in 1661, following the Restoration of the monarchy, and it seems probable that the case was incorporated in Thomas Harris' new organ of 1665. It is certainly a fine piece of Stuart furniture, the curved flats and tall central pipe giving it a liveliness and grace not found later in the seventeenth century.

The main case is Thomas Harris' work, less well made than the chair case – indeed, some of the 'oak' is really painted pine – but its style, with broken pediments and with columns and Roman arches framing the flats, foreshadows the work of his son Renatus Harris a decade or more later. On the other hand, the use of pillars and arches to support the side overhang of the case harks back to that of the pre-Commonwealth case now in Tewkesbury Abbey and possibly by Robert Dallam, Thomas Harris' father-in-law. The front pipes show a typically Harris variety of pipe-mouth shapes.

Although Harris built a case with two fronts, it was not originally placed on the choir screen, as now, but on a loft above the south side of the choir, the present west front facing into the south transept. Its appearance from the transept would have been relatively unimportant, accounting for the painted decoration used for the pipe-shades instead of the pierced carving seen on the east face.

The organ was moved to its present position in 1718, probably by Schwarbrick, and in 1741 William Kent added Gothick pinnacles to the towers. A Swell organ, down to tenor F, was added later, though none of it has survived. 16ft 'Pedal Pipes' were added by J. C. Bishop in 1831; these remain as the Pedal Flute 16ft and are possibly the biggest scale Pedal Pipes in Britain. The effect on the tuning length is that the 16ft pipe is actually only about 14ft 6in. The organ was rebuilt in 1847 by Henry Willis, then very young, with a CCC compass to the Great, GG to the Choir and CC to the Swell, retaining Bishop's Pedal Pipes as the entire Pedal department.

Willis rebuilt the organ again in 1888, this time much more drastically. We must count ourselves lucky that Sir George Gilbert Scott's advice to remove the organ from the screen was

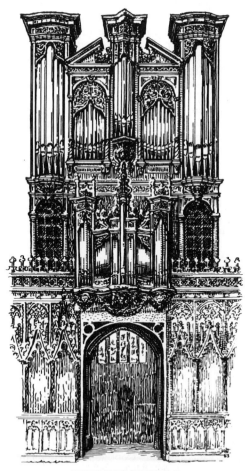

GLOUCESTER CATHEDRAL

disregarded; in the event Willis accommodated his enlarged instrument within the Harris case by deepening it so that his new soundboards could run at right-angles to the case-fronts, the console being moved to the south side of the screen. He transposed and drastically re-scaled the Harris pipes, raising the wind pressure to obtain 'the effect of a much larger organ', as he put it. Willis added a small Solo organ and some additional reeds in 1899 but by 1920 his charge-pneumatic action was in need of repair and the organ was again rebuilt, this time by Harrison & Harrison. Arthur Harrison added a huge Open Diapason I, a 32ft Open Wood in the north triforium, a new and larger Solo organ in the bowels of the screen and exhaust-pneumatic action. The resulting instrument sounded a ponderous amalgam of Father Willis and Arthur Harrison, almost totally concealing the fact that the organ still contained well over two hundred Harris pipes (including part of one of the earliest mixture stops in Britain).

Fortunately Willis' transposition of the Harris pipes had made it unnecessary for him to interfere with their mouths so that, when the time came to restore them for the 1971 organ, lengthening and re-transposition brought back the original tone. Nevertheless, the overall planning of the new instrument proved quite difficult. Willis having altered the instrument so much in 1888, the restoration of the Harris pipes implied a fresh start. The concept of a screen organ is more complex today than in the past since, with nave services and concert performances, the sound in the nave is at least as important as that in the choir and the organ must speak two ways. The Great organ was no problem, turned back to its original position parallel to the case-fronts and, with a modern manual compass, there was room for the Pedal organ at each end (save for the 16ft Flutes, concealed in the screen). The Choir was duplicated by a west-facing Positive within the lower part of the case and speaking out through a new grille, designed by Herbert Norman and replacing nineteenth-century panelling. The difficulty was, as always, the Swell organ. One scheme discussed was for a tracker instrument with the Swell above the Great. The restrictions this placed on the size of the Swell organ, and the corollary of an east console without view of the nave, proved too great an obstacle, however. The arrangement adopted, one used previously by Ralph Downes, under whose direction the organ was built, was to place the Swell in the bottom of the instrument, speaking out through grilles under the impost. The consequent slight elevation of the main case has been an unquestioned success, its previous position being more accidental than historical. This layout has, however, precluded the complete opening-up of the side arches (filled in 1888) which support the side overhang of the case, though deep recesses are now provided. Although it was not possible to reduce the case depth to its original 50in (125cm) Willis's side additions were removed and the cornices brought back into line.

Fitting an organ of this size into the old case leaves little room for bellows or mechanism and was only possible by using wind-regulators built into the soundboards and a specially developed electromagnetic key-action. This action is exceptionally rapid and also has the unique feature that the pallet opening is reduced when only a few stops are drawn, countering the excessive 'spit' found with single stops on conventional electropneumatic actions.

The tonal design of the organ was essentially that of a new instrument. The stop-list follows a basically eighteenth-century Continental model with a 16ft-based Pedal, 8ft Great, 4ft Swell and Choir and 2ft-based West Positive. Only on the Swell organ is this tempered with mild tapered string-stops and the standard English Hautboy. The reeds are mostly Willis pipes revoiced on low pressure, using new shallots and voicing styles based on eighteenth-century French practice. New flue-stops were voiced with open feet and generally without nicking. The surviving Harris pipes, mostly on the Great organ, were restored to their original scaling and speech, though they proved something of an embarrassment to Ralph Downes. This was because, even with a roofed-in case, their tonal output was very modest when heard in the nave (never a requirement of the original organ). In the event, the western Open Diapason (with its bass in the nave side of the case) was slightly increased in scale, and Ralph Downes has recently revealed that alterations were made, on his instructions, to the eastern stop also.

Overall, the organ in Gloucester Cathedral has a dual personality. Musically, it is one of our few cathedral organs with an unashamedly Continental tone quality, even if restrained in power by the surviving original material. Historically, it is our one cathedral organ which retains an original seventeenth-century double case and front pipes in something approaching their original shape and proportions, plus a not inconsiderable number of interior pipes also. The wonder is that these two personalities should be successfully combined in one instrument.

TEWKESBURY The Abbey

Tewkesbury Abbey, though a parish church nowadays, is as big as a cathedral and is fortunate in possessing two important but very different organs, one with a famous case, the other without a case at all.

The Milton Organ (see Plate 1)
? Dallam 1637; Willis 1847; Walker 1948

The case of the Milton Organ at Tewkesbury is one of the very few for which there is documentary evidence of its existence before the Commonwealth. We know that it was built for Magdalen College, Oxford, moved to Hampton Court during the Commonwealth and returned to Oxford, where it remained until displaced by a new organ by Schwarbrick in 1737. It stood on the choir screen at Tewkesbury until the 1870s but is now at floor level on the south side of the choir. The case is distinctive in having five towers and four flats, with an overhanging front with two arches either side of the console. It is now much deeper than it was when first made, but the gilded and embossed tin front pipes are a valuable and rare survival. Some writers have dated this case as early as 1580, but the quality of the cabinet-work and the similarities of some details to Robert Dallam's surviving cases in Brittany suggest that it was part of the organ he supplied to Magdalen College in 1637.

The organ itself was almost entirely replaced by Willis in 1847, and again rebuilt by J. W. Walker in 1948 when a five-manual stop-key console was provided, detached on the north choir screen, together with an additional section speaking into the south transept.

The Grove Organ
Michell & Thynne 1885

GREAT		SWELL		CHOIR		PEDAL	
Violone	16	Flauto Traverso	8	Spitzflöte	8	Harmonic Bass	32
Great Open Diapason	8	Open Diapason	8	Viole Sourdine	8	Great Bass	16
Small Open Diapason	8	Viole de Gambe	8	Gedact	8	Dolce Bass	16
Claribel	8	Voix Celeste	8	Gemshorn	4	Great Flute	8
Octave	4	Geigen	4	Zauberflöte	4	Bombarde	16
Flute Octaviante	4	Mixture 15.19.22	III	Flautina	2		
Quint Mixture 12.15	II	Contra Posaune	16	Clarionet	8		
Great Mixture		Horn	8				
19.22.26.29	IV	Oboe	8	SOLO			
Tromba	16			Harmonic Flute	8		
Trumpet	8			Violoncello	8		
				Tuba	8		
				Voix Humaine (enclosed)	8		

This instrument is very different from the Milton Organ. To start with, it has no case at all, even the mechanism being open for all to see. It was built, as a speculation, for the Inventions Exhibition of 1885 by the newly formed firm of Michell & Thynne. Remaining unsold, it was eventually purchased at a knock-down price by the Rev C. W. Grove who presented it to the Abbey, Michell & Thynne promptly going into liquidation. The organ has stood in the north transept ever since.

It is an extraordinary instrument. Open to view, the layout and action are a triumph of beautifully made improvisation. In reality, Thynne, who was a skilled voicer in pedagogic succession to Schulze, built it as an exhibition of his voicing skill. In this he certainly succeeded. Although very much a romantic organ, with its roots in the Victorian town hall, the flue and reed choruses have a drive and power which quite belie the instrument's modest size and out-of-the-way position. The Choir and Solo have beautifully voiced softer stops clearly inspired by Schulze and the pioneer narrow-scale strings employ Schulze's 'harmonic bridge' to stabilise their speech, a development that was to lead on to the very small-scale strings of Hope-Jones.

It had been proposed to move this organ to the west end, where its effect would have been truly shattering. Fortunately, it has remained *in situ* and was restored in 1981 by Bishop & Son under the direction of John Budgen. The full organ and its thrilling sound is much in demand for recitals.

GREATER LONDON

BARNES St Paul's School
Mander 1971

GREAT		SWELL		PEDAL	
Principal	8	Rohr Flute	8	Subbass	16
Gedackt	8	Salicional	8	Principal	8
Octave	4	Principal	4	Gedackt	8
Nason Flute	4	Octave	2	Gemshorn	4
Block Flute	2	Quint	1⅓	Rauschquint	IV
Sesquialtera	II	Scharff	IV	Fagot	16
Mixture	IV-VI	Regal	16		
Trumpet	8	Cremona	8		
		Clarion	4		

One of the larger British-built tracker organs of the early 1970s, the layout of this instrument is interesting because of its transitional style. The organ is not free-standing, the severe tone-cabinets, without pipe-shades, being cantilevered from the wall. The console is detached and free-standing beneath the organ, with exposed trackers rising from the top of the console.

The Swell organ provides something approaching a British 'full-Swell' reed effect in a very limited height by combining a quarter-length 16ft reed with a half-length 8ft reed and a conventional full-length Clarion.

BRENTFORD National Musical Museum
Wurlitzer 1932

The largest exhibit in the museum is a fine example of the Hope-Jones inspired Wurlitzer unit organ which had such a powerful if brief effect on popular music after 1925. With twelve ranks of pipes, controlled from a three-manual white and gold rococo-decorated horseshoe console it is, in fact, about double the size of many such instruments and includes a French Trumpet with flared brass pipes.

The organ was originally built not for a cinema but for the house of a Chicago millionaire. Subsequently brought back and modified by Wurlitzer, it was installed in the Regal Theatre, Kingston upon Thames in 1932. This was one of the later instruments, coming after the introduction of the 'talkies', though broadcast regularly in its early years. The organ was moved to the Musical Museum in 1972 under the direction of Frank Holland, founder of the museum, and subsequently restored. The instrument now incorporates a rare Wurlitzer automatic reproducing roll player from another organ and the museum has a library of music rolls of the period.

CAMBERWELL St Giles' Church
Bishop 1844, 1961

(Stop-list as built – now slightly modified)		SWELL		CHOIR		PEDAL	
GREAT		Bourdon	16	Open Diapason	8	Double Diapason	16
		Double Diapason	16	Dulciana	8	Open Diapason (metal)	8
Open Diapason	8	Open Diapason	8	Stopped Diapason	8	Double Trumpet	16
Open Diapason	8	Open Diapason	8	Clarabella	8		
Open Diapason (wood, large)	8	Stopped Diapason	8	Principal	4		
Clarabella	8	Principal	4	Flute	4		
Principal	4	Fifteenth	2	Fifteenth	2		
Principal	4	Sesquialtera 17.19.22	III	Mixture	1⅓		
Twelfth	2⅔	Mixture 26.29	II	Cremona	8		
Fifteenth	2	Doublette	II	Bassoon	8		
Sesquialtera	III	Horn	8				
Mixture	III	Trumpet	8				
Furniture	II	Hautboy	8				
Doublette	II	Clarion	4				
Trumpet	8						
Clarion	4						

This three-manual organ was one of the first instruments by Hill's rivals to copy the then new German compass from 8ft CC, instead of the old compass from 10ft GG. It was also one of the first instruments influenced by the Tractarian movement and is placed not at the west end but on the north side. George Gilbert Scott, the architect of the new church, gave the organ a curious grille-like screen, presumably because he wanted to avoid drawing attention to the instrument in this position.

The organ has two examples of the open wood Clarabella stop, which J. C. Bishop invented, often replacing the usual Stopped Diapason. Bishop also invented the mechanical composition pedals with which this organ was originally fitted, the first registration aid visibly to move the stop controls but unfortunately discarded when the organ was restored in 1961. The instrument now sounds considerably less bright and colourful than surviving Hill organs of about this period, despite all the mixtures. Whether this is original or the result of subsequent rebalancing is difficult to say.

CHELSEA Royal Hospital Chapel
Snetzler 18th century; Hill Norman & Beard 1978

GREAT		SWELL		PEDAL	
Open Diapason	8	Gedeckt	8	Sub Bass	16
Stopped Diapason	8	Salicional	8	Principal	8
Principal	4	Angelica	8	Flute	8
Chimney Flute	4	Gemshorn	4	Gemshorn	4
Twelfth	2⅔	Fifteenth	2	Twenty-Second	2
Fifteenth	2	Mixture 22.26.29.33	IV	Trombone	16
Larigot	1⅓	Bassoon	16		
Furniture 19.22.26	III	Trompette	8		
Trumpet	8	Clarion	4		

The elegant three-tower case of this organ dates back to John Snetzler and is unusual for the period in having a case waisted-in below the impost. The tall, thin flats between the towers are not original and probably replace a two-storey layout. The new organ has tracker action and follows William Hill's practice of a generous number of reeds on the Swell to maintain the intermanual balance.

St Peter's Church, Cranley Gardens
Hill 1867; Willis 1893; Walker 1908, 1922

This is the organ played by Sir Arthur Sullivan for many years. Its evolution shows the characteristic enlargement and change in musical emphasis common in fashionable churches in the Edwardian and late Victorian era. First built as a two-manual by Wm Hill with a single

Open Diapason on the Great organ, it acquired a Father Willis Choir organ, a new case and a new Large Open Diapason in 1893. In 1908 it was again enlarged, this time by Walker. The instrument then gained its present case by W. D. Caröe, a fourth manual (the Solo), a 32ft Open Wood and a new leathered-mouth Open Diapason I. This displaced the Willis Diapason to become the Open Diapason II and Hill's original stop to become number III! The organ was partially revoiced by Hill Norman & Beard in 1958. The building now belongs to the Armenian Church.

CITY OF LONDON The Dutch Church, Austin Friars
van Leeuwen 1954

Designed by the eminent Dutch organ historian Maarten Vente, this was almost the first modern two-manual tracker organ in London, only preceded by an undistinguished instrument in the Swedish Seaman's Church, Rotherhithe. The uncompromisingly classical design, without a Swell and with the second manual department a *Rugwerk* in the projecting chair case, attracted no immediate imitators, perhaps because it was so far removed from British experience at the time. The electropneumatic stop-action is unusual, two knobs being provided for each stop, one black and one white. The registration is drawn on the knobs of one colour; the next registration can then be prepared in advance on the knobs of the other colour. On touching the only piston, the organ 'changes over' and the whole process can be repeated. The only trouble is that one can never remember, at any given moment, which side one is on!

Livery Hall of the Worshipful Company of Merchant Taylors
Mander 1966

GREAT		SWELL		PEDAL	
*Open Diapason	8	*Stopped Diapason	8	Subbass	16
*Chimney Flute	8	*Principal	4	Principal	8
*Principal	4	Flute	4	Gemshorn	4
Nason Flute	4	*Fifteenth	2	Fagott	16
*Twelfth	2⅔	*Larigot	1⅓		
*Fifteenth	2	Sharp Mixture 22.26.29 III		*Incorporating Harris	
*Tierce	1⅗	Trumpet	8	pipes.	
Fourniture 19.22.26	III				

Renatus Harris' last organ was for the church of St Dionis Backchurch in the City of London, built in 1724. The church was pulled down in 1879. The organ then underwent various removals, 10 stops of original pipes eventually coming into the hands of Noel Mander. He returned them to the City by using them as the basis of a new instrument for the Merchant Taylor's Hall. The seventeenth-century hall had been destroyed in 1940 and rebuilt to the design of Sir Albert Richardson.

The organ stands on the gallery in a sumptuous mahogany case with gilded decorations and front pipes of polished tin metal, designed by Stephen Dykes Bower. The case is very architectural, with Corinthian pilasters and a pediment top above an arched flat containing the 8ft bass. The handsome console with black natural keys and solid ivory sharps is set deeply under the corbelled-out case.

The organ has tracker action to the manuals (electric to the pedals) but is not a *werk* principle organ, the layout being horizontal with the Swell behind the Great. It is essentially a recreated Harris with the Swell organ, despite the addition of a mixture and a small Trumpet, having more the character of an enclosed Choir organ.

Church of St Andrew Undershaft
Harris 1696; Hill 1875

GREAT		SWELL		CHOIR		PEDAL	
Double Diapason	16	Double Diapason	16	Stop Diapason	8	Open Diapason	16
Open Diapason	8	Open Diapason	8	Dulciana	8	Bourdon	16
Stopped Diapason	8	Stop Diapason	8	Octave	4		
Gamba	8	Gamba	8	Stop Flute	4		
Octave	4	Voix Celeste	8	Spitz Flote	4		
Wald Flute	4	Octave	4	Cromorne	8		
Twelfth	2⅔	Harmonic Piccolo	2				
Fifteenth	2	Trumpet	8				
Full Mixture 17.19.22	III	Oboe	8				
Sharp Mixture 26.29	II	Vox Humana	8				
Trumpet	8	Clarion	4				
Clarion	4						

St Andrew's is a lofty medieval church with an almost East Anglian spaciousness. The organ was built by Harris as a two-manual with one of his typical 'round-shouldered' cases.

In 1875 Hill moved the case from the west gallery to its present position at the east end of the south aisle and built a new tracker organ inside it. Hill incorporated many of Harris' pipes, including the front pipes with their characteristic varied mouth-shapes. Apart from the addition of two string-tone stops, prepared for in 1875, the organ remains unaltered since that date.

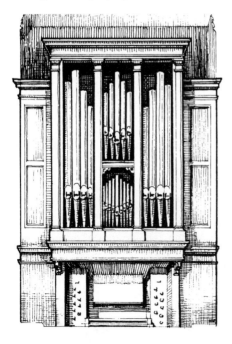

ST BENET'S CHURCH,
PAUL'S WHARF, LONDON

St Benet's Church, Paul's Wharf (The Welsh Church)
Bishop 1833, 1898; Hill Norman & Beard 1973

GREAT		SWELL		PEDAL	
Open Diapason	8	Gedeckt	8	Bourdon	16
Stopped Diapason	8	Spitzflute	4		
Principal	4	Principal	2		
Gemshorn	2	Larigot	1⅓		
Mixture 19.22	II-III	Trompette	8		

St Benet's is one of Wren's more elegant smaller churches, and one of the least spoiled. J. C. Bishop built a one-manual organ for the small west gallery. Originally there was a barrel mechanism so that it could be played automatically. The pipes of this instrument were incorporated in a new two-manual organ which Bishop supplied in 1897 and which stood at the east end of the north gallery. This organ was seriously damaged by a fire in the church and was reconstructed to make the present instrument on the west gallery in 1973. The Pedal Bourdon and about half the Swell pipes are from the Bishop instrument, the Great organ being nearly all new. The Great Mixture has a third rank at the breaks, which are thus less obvious. The Swell organ combines a 2ft-based enclosed Positive with a very narrow-scale full-length reed. The Italianate case, white-painted with polished tin pipes down to FF♯, was designed by Herbert Norman from an idea by Michael Gillingham.

St Botolph's Church, Aldgate
Harris pre-1676; Byfield 1745; Hill 1867; Bishop 1898; Mander 1966

GREAT (Upper Manual)		CHOIR (Lower Manual)		PEDAL	
*Open Diapason	8	*Stopt Diapason	8	Bourdon	16
*Stopt Diapason	8	Dulciana	8	Dulciana	16
*Principal	4	*Principal	4	Flute	8
Nason Flute	4	*Flute	4	Dulciana	8
*Fifteenth	2	Nazard	2⅔	Flute	4
*Sesquialtera	III-IV	Fifteenth	2	Fifteenth	4
Fourniture	III	Tierce	1⅗	Trombone	16
Cornet	V	Larigot	1⅓	Trumpet	8
*Trumpet	8	Twenty Second	1	Clarion	4
		*Bassoon	8		*17th or 18th century pipes.

This instrument is a prime example of an organ which has grown gradually over the years, eventually bursting out of its case before being rebuilt to a size which has returned it to within the case again.

The origins of the organ go back to a 9 stop one-manual chamber instrument reputedly by Thomas and Renatus Harris, which was given to the church in 1676 on the death of the wife of its owner. In the next century the instrument was enlarged to a small three-manual and also gained its present three-tower oak case. This is of the type with gabled cornices to the flats which Renatus Harris used in a number of his later instruments and which was copied by Jordan, Schwarbrick, Bridge and Byfield at various times between 1710 and 1750. Hill rebuilt the organ with pedals and the modern compass in 1867 and the instrument was further enlarged by Bishop, who left it with a tall swell-box projecting over the case almost to the ceiling. Happily, though, the organ remained in the gallery.

Noel Mander's rebuild in 1966 reduced the organ to two unenclosed manuals, readily accommodated in the case, plus a three-rank extended Pedal organ. New tracker action was fitted to the manuals and a new console mounted on the face of the old case. The Great organ is close to the original design and the Choir organ an amplification of the eighteenth-century department with added mutations and upperwork. The case now looks very splendid with its gilded front pipes and exuberant cherubs above the gables.

St Botolph's Church, Aldersgate
Green 1778; Speechly 1867

This two-manual instrument is the only Samuel Green organ in the City of London, and was built at the same time as the church. The church is plain outside (apart from the charming bell-turret) but richly decorated inside. The organ remains in its original position on the west gallery in Green's rather curious five-tower mahogany case. This is in the classical style, somewhat decadent by the 1770s, with carved swags as pipe-shades and other carving which is applied rather than integral with the panelling. The shape is similar to that of a three-tower case, but with small additional three-pipe towers adjacent to the seven-pipe semi-circular central tower.

Tonally the Great organ retains its typical Green gentleness despite a fairly major rebuild in the nineteenth century when the compass was changed, the Swell organ much enlarged and a Pedal organ added.

St Bride's Church, Fleet Street
Compton 1958

In 1694 Renatus Harris built an organ for St Bride's, the church with the 'wedding-cake' steeple. It stood on the west gallery but was burned in 1940, along with all the other furnishings. When the church was restored, it was, curiously, furnished with collegiate seating, all the galleries being discarded. The acoustics of the church are excellent, but the organ is placed in three chambers in the tower, speaking out through apertures in the west wall of the church. Only high up in the 'minstrels' gallery' are there any pipes placed within the church itself. Logically, virtually all the organ is enclosed in swell-boxes, even the Great. Only Compton's could have made anything at all of such a situation. The organ is large (four manuals and 98 stops, though some are by extension) and one cannot help thinking that an instrument of 20 stops, such as Renatus Harris originally provided would, if placed in a proper position, have been much more musical.

Church of St Clement, Eastcheap
Harris 1695; Gray & Davison, 1872; Wedlake 1889; Hill Norman & Beard 1936

Eastcheap has changed since the Church of St Clement was built and ends well short of Wren's church in St Clement's Lane, now a turning off King William Street. The organ was originally built as a two-manual by Renatus Harris. St Clement's was one of the churches where his famous awkwardness was displayed; the churchwardens had to call in one of the Smith family to remove the 'cheat' by which Harris had disabled the organ. Later a short-compass Swell was added but in 1872, as part of a general rearrangement of the church by William Butterfield, the west gallery was removed and the organ enlarged and moved to the south aisle by Gray & Davison.

In 1936 the organ was moved back to the west end, built directly over the porch in the absence of a gallery. The detached console was placed right at the east end of the church, adjacent to the priest's stall so that Canon Lees, the then incumbent, could leap from one to the other and be his own organist. More recently, Hill Norman & Beard revoiced the by-now very Victorian Choir organ as a 2ft-based Positive. The Great organ is reputed to be still largely made up of Harris pipes.

Renatus Harris' case at St Clement's is almost a self-parody of his style, containing no less than three oval compartments of pipes with their curved mouth-lines set in a permanent smile. With one large oval below and two smaller ones above, the resemblance to a human face is uncanny!

St Giles' Church, Cripplegate
Jordan & Bridge 1733; Willis 1863; Mander 1970

GREAT		SWELL		CHOIR		PEDAL	
Double Open	16	*Open Diapason	8	Dulciana	8	Open Diapason	16
Open Diapason	8	*Stopt Diapason	8	Stopt Diapason	8	Bourdon	16
Stopt Diapason	8	Viola	8	Principal	4	Octave	8
*Principal	4	*Principal	4	Nason Flute	4	Flute	8
*Flute	4	*Fifteenth	2	Nazard	2⅔	Gemshorn	4
*Twelfth	2⅔	Mixture 22.26.29	III	Spitz Flute	2	Mixture 22.26.29	III
Fifteenth	2	†Contra Hautboy	16	Tierce	1⅗	Trombone	16
Larigot	1⅓	Cornopean	8	Cymbel 29.33.36	III	Trumpet	8
Mixture 19.22.26	III	†Clarion	4	†Cremona	8		
Fourniture				Mounted Cornet	V		
19.22.26.29	IV-VI	*Bridge pipes.		Trumpet	8		
Mounted Cornet	V	†Willis pipes.		Clarion	4		
†Trumpet	8						
†Clarion	4						

The Fire of London destroyed most of the medieval City churches, but St Giles' stood just outside the city wall and escaped. Fate caught up with it in 1940, though, when the church was gutted by fire bombs and the organ destroyed. The present organ is based upon the Jordan & Bridge instrument from St Luke's Church, Old Street.

The glory of this organ, which stands upon a new west gallery, is the fine Jordan & Bridge three-towered case. More formal than Bridge's later cases, it follows one of Renatus Harris' designs with gable-shaped cornices over the upper flats. The case has new and quite deep sides, together with a back case, facing into the tower, made from the surviving parts of the 1700 Renatus Harris case from St Andrew's, Holborn. This is of another favourite Harris type with 'round-shouldered' cornices. The tin metal front pipes were new in 1970 as was the projecting chair case designed by Cecil Brown, betraying by its slight 'woodiness' the fact that it was designed by an architect.

The most controversial feature of the instrument was the retention of the high-pressure Father Willis reeds on the Great organ in conjunction with a tonal design which harks back to Bridge, plus some north German influence on the Choir organ. The high-pressure reeds and the Cornet are played by electropneumatic action and are also available from the Choir manual. The remainder of the key-action is tracker. The end result is an eclectic organ with a ringing, bold chorus, yet without the aggressiveness found in some neo-classical instruments.

St Helen's Church, Bishopsgate
?Bridge 1744; Bishop 1923; Hill Norman & Beard 1957

This instrument was the product of an eighteenth-century hire-purchase arrangement. It was supplied to the church by Thomas Griffin for £250, half its cost, plus £25 per annum for which, in addition, Griffin would either be organist himself or supply a substitute. The organ was probably actually made by Richard Bridge, the surviving mahogany case being a typical creation of his with 'flats' between the towers which are ogee-shaped both on plan and in elevation. Furthermore, the Great and Choir organ soundboard is probably the only remaining eighteenth-century example of the 'borrowing by communication' which enables three stops to draw on both the Choir and the Great organs and which Bridge copied from Renatus Harris.

The instrument now stands in a chapel on the south side of the chancel, having been removed from the west gallery in 1865. The case is deeper than when it was built, to accommodate the Swell and Pedal departments. Bishop made substantial tonal alterations and fitted pneumatic action in 1923; the present detached console and electric action date from 1957.

St James' Church, Garlickhythe
Knopple 1719; Gray & Davison 1866; Hill 1888

This fine instrument, with its four-towered case, has always been reputed to be the work of Father Smith. In many ways the case is very similar to the Smith in the University Church of St Mary the Great, Cambridge, save for the two-storey side flats. Furthermore, there is a circular opening in the centre of the case in the same position that a clock was placed in the Cambridge organ when new. However, this is now filled with coarse-scaled wooden dummy pipes that cannot be Smith's work; church records show that the organ was installed by a Mr Knopple in 1719, eleven years after Smith's death. The massive curved pediment which sits on the two central towers, and the plinths supporting delicate trumpet-playing angels above the side-towers, also look like afterthoughts and are similar in feeling to some of the work of Nicholas Hawksmoor, the architect. Further investigation has shown that, although some pipes on the Swell organ look like Smith's work, the Great pipes do not.

It seems likely that the otherwise unknown Mr Knopple bought a secondhand Smith case and other parts, we know not where from, and assembled them into his instrument. Despite this inauspicious beginning, the organ survived a hundred and fifty years without change, not being rebuilt until 1866.

Church of St Katherine Cree
Smith 1686; Willis 1866

This is an odd church, the City's pre-Great Fire attempt at Renaissance architecture. Father Smith built a one-manual organ for the west gallery which by 1800 had become a modest two-manual with a short-compass Swell played from the Choir keys. Smith's case still survives on the front of an 1866 three-manual Willis with later alterations.

The Cree church case is unusual in that the two flats are framed like windows with curved pediments on top, surmounted by pairs of *putti* with trumpets. This sort of architectural treatment was generally more characteristic of Harris than of Smith. The present front pipes are nineteenth century and are of plain organ metal, giving a somewhat sombre appearance. Nevertheless, in many ways this is one of the most satisfying and elegant of all the Father Smith organ cases that remain to us.

Church of St Lawrence, Jewry
Mander 1957

GREAT		SWELL		CHOIR		PEDAL	
Double Open Diapason	16	Contra Gamba	16	(in Commonwealth Chapel)		Open Wood	16
Large Open Diapason	8	Open Diapason	8	Pedal Bourdon	16	Bourdon	16
Small Open Diapason	8	Rohr Flute	8	Open Diapason	8	Contra Dulciana	16
Dulciana	8	Salicional	8	Stopped Diapason	8	Flute	8
Hohl Flute	8	Celeste	8	Dulciana	8	Octave	8
Principal	4	Principal	4	Gamba	8	Flute	4
Wald Flute	4	Fifteenth	2	Flute	4	Fifteenth	4
Twelfth	2⅔	Mixture	III	Principal	4	Octavin	2
Fifteenth	2	Double Trumpet	16	Nazard	2⅔	Mixture	III
Mixture	II	Trumpet	8	Fifteenth	2	Trombone	16
Tuba	8	Oboe	8	Tierce	1⅗	Trumpet	8
Posaune	8	Clarion	4	Larigot	1⅓	Clarion	4
				Musette (synthesised)	8		
				Clarinet (synthesised)	8		
				Tuba (in main case)	8		

Renatus Harris built an organ for this church in 1684, with a double case and carving by Grinling Gibbons. This instrument was replaced by a new organ by Gray & Davison in 1875, re-using the old case. There were later alterations and enlargements but everything was destroyed by fire in 1940.

The present organ was built in 1957, when the church was restored. The main case, on the west gallery, was designed by Cecil Brown and the front follows the general outline of Harris' case, retaining a replica of the 'sunburst' of Trumpet pipes either side of the central tower which were added by Gray & Davison to the original case. The sides, however, have pipe-fronts and the chair case is omitted, being replaced by an outsize coat of arms. The Choir organ is some 40ft (12m) away, projecting from the west wall of the north aisle chapel in its own Cecil Brown case, complete, this time, with its own little chair case and looking, on the face of it, like an independent instrument.

The organ itself was one of Noel Mander's earliest large instruments and still shows signs of pre-war influences, such as the heavy-pressure Swell reeds and Tuba. Great ingenuity was shown in fitting this sizeable instrument into the case; the Pedal Open Wood lies horizontally under the floor of the gallery!

Church of St Magnus the Martyr, London Bridge
Jordan 1712

This is the organ for which Abraham Jordan made his first swell-box, so rapidly to be copied by every other builder. The case remains, surprisingly unaltered, though the contents are now entirely late Victorian. The case is very architectural, treating the projecting but flat towers as pilasters, with semi-circular arches over the flats. An upper case, all dummy, sits between the two halves of the broken pediment.

St Margaret's Church, Lothbury
England 1801; Bishop 1983

GREAT		SWELL		PEDAL	
*Open Diapason	8	Gedact	8	Sub Bass	16
*Stopped Diapason	8	Salicional	8	Principal	8
*Principal	4	Principal	4	Flute	4
*Flute	4	Flute	4	Mixture 19.22	II
*Twelfth	2⅔	Gemshorn	2	Bassoon	16
*Fifteenth	2	Quint	1⅓		
Mixture 19.22.26	III	Mixture 22.26.29	III	*Surviving G. P. England	
Cornet 12.15.17	III	Cromorne	8	stops.	
Trumpet	8				

This instrument is an example of the recent trend to clear away later accretions from a fine organ and to build a new instrument based upon the original case and surviving original pipes. G. P. England's organ was built as a two-manual, subsequently being enlarged to three manuals. In 1879 Bryceson converted it from GG compass to CC, moving the instrument to the south aisle. The organ returned to the west gallery eleven years later, though the player moved east again when a detached console and electropneumatic action were provided in 1938. The case had been widened in the course of the various additions to the instrument; the present reduction in size has enabled it to be returned to its original proportions. The console, too, has returned to the front of the organ, and the instrument is now fitted with tracker action.

The new organ clearly draws inspiration from the surviving G. P. England pipes and, without being either soft or dull, has a gentle sound which manages to be clear yet without any noticeable starting transient. The reeds, on the other hand, have a nervous energy which can be quite startling.

Church of St Margaret Pattens
Griffin/Bridge c1750; Forster & Andrews 1886

Like the organ in St Helen's Bishopsgate, this instrument was supplied by Thomas Griffin, and the identical case, with ogee-shaped 'flats' between the towers suggests that perhaps Richard Bridge was the real maker. The organ is now essentially a Forster & Andrews of 1886. The front pipes are modern zinc copies, painted not gilded, which is a pity.

Church of St Mary, Aldermanbury
Holdich 1876; Norman & Beard 1906

GREAT		SWELL		CHOIR (enclosed)		PEDAL	
Double Open Diapason	16	Double Diapason	16	Stopped Diapason	8	Open Diapason	16
Open Diapason I	8	Open Diapason	8	Gamba	8	Bourdon	16
Open Diapason II	8	Stopped Diapason	8	Dulciana	8	Octave	8
Clarabella	8	Gamba	8	Principal	4	Bass Flute	8
Principal	4	Voix Celeste	8	Flute	4	Trombone	16
Harmonic Flute	4	Principal	4	Piccolo	2		
Twelfth	2⅔	Twelfth	2⅔	Cremona	8	Tubular-Pneumatic Action.	
Fifteenth	2	Fifteenth	2	Orchestral Oboe	8		
Mixture	III	Mixture	III				
Trumpet	8	Vox Humana	8				
		Oboe	8				
		Horn	8				

St Mary's is at the foot of Bow Lane, the last surviving City alley of shops. Damaged in the Great Fire, Wren rebuilt it in a somewhat eccentric Perpendicular style. There was once a western gallery with ante-chapel beyond and a George England organ of 1781 upon it. All this was swept away in 1876 and the present instrument is by G. M. Holdich, rebuilt by Norman & Beard and unaltered since 1906, an example of one of the better turn-of-the-century instruments.

The case is a simple Victorian post-and-rail screen, enriched with some Gothic angels and with front pipes elaborately decorated in the 'rolls of linoleum' manner.

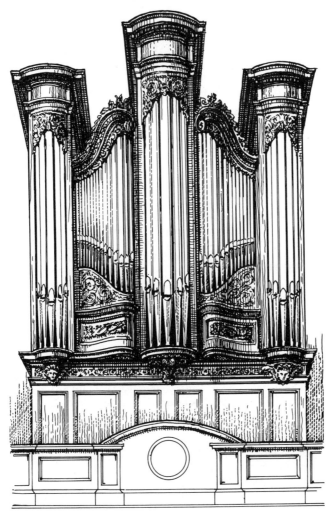

CHURCH OF ST MARGARET PATTENS, LONDON

Church of St Mary-le-Bow, Cheapside
Rushworth & Dreaper 1964

Sir Christopher Wren's imposing tower and steeple dominate busy Cheapside. The church was gutted during World War II and all the new furnishings, including the famous twin pulpits and the organ case in the west end, were designed by Laurence King. Although the front pipes are bare zinc (and of too small a scale in relation to the towers), the oak case is particularly richly carved and cleverly shaped with return cornices at the back to conceal the depth of the instrument. The front has three semi-circular towers with two smaller V-shaped towers which break up the wide flats and serve as a counterpoint to the strongly horizontal cornice, reminiscent of some of the Dallam family's work in Brittany in the seventeenth century. Quite a number of neo-classical cases have been made for the City of London since the war, not all of them entirely happy. Bow Church has the best one.

189

St Mary-at-Hill Church
Hill 1848, 1879; Hill Norman & Beard 1971

GREAT		SWELL		CHOIR		PEDAL	
*Open Diapason	16	*Open Diapason	16	Chimney Flute	8	Contra Bourdon	32
*Open Diapason	8	*Open Diapason	8	Principal	4	*Open Diapason	16
*Gamba (Gemshorn)	8	*Stopped Diapason	8	Nason Flute	4	Bourdon	16
*Stopped Diapason	8	Hohl Flute		Nazard	2⅔	*Octave	8
*Quint	5⅓	(Keraulophon)	8	Octave	2	Super Octave	4
*Octave	4	*Octave	4	Recorder	2	Mixture 19.22.26.29	IV
*Wald Flute	4	*Suabe Flute	4	Tierce	1⅗	*Trombone	16
*Octave Quint	2⅔	*Octave Quint	2⅔	Quint	1⅓	Shalmey	4
*Super Octave	2	*Super Octave	2	Cymbel 29.33.36	III		
*Flageolet	2	*Sesquialtera 17.19.22	III				
*Sesquialtera 17.19.22	III	Contra Trombone	16				
*Mixture 24.26.29	III	*Cornopean	8				
Cornet	IV	*Oboe	8				
*Krum Horn	8	*Clarion	4				
*Posaune	8						
*Clarion	4	*1848 pipes.					

The importance of this organ is that, since the loss of the Great George Street Chapel instrument in Liverpool, it is the least altered of the pre-1850 William Hill organs which represented such a new direction in British organ-building. St Mary-at-Hill Church was rebuilt after the Fire of London to the designs of Sir Christopher Wren, Father Smith supplying an 11 stop one-manual organ in 1693. This was replaced in 1788 by a 14 stop two-manual by Samuel Green which, it is believed, was damaged by a fire in the 1840s. The church was refurnished by James Savage with carving by W. E. Gibbs-Rogers and this work probably included the case of the then-new Wm Hill organ. The case is clearly the work of an architect (an organ-builder would have made the front less 'woody') and is a not unscholarly pastiche of a four-tower Father Smith case. The antiquarianism also extended to providing a console with black natural keys and solid ivory sharps.

This organ was very much a new direction. Not only did it have the German compass as used today but also a Swell organ which had grown from a short-compass accompanimental department to almost the equal of the Great. The layout suggested German influence, with the Swell over the Great and the Pedal divided either side. Furthermore, probably inspired by the hymn accompaniment ideas of Dr Gauntlett, it was potentially a very powerful organ – 15 stops on the Great organ alone – for what is not a particularly large church. The sound, in fact, is not over-powerful and has a sweet brilliance characteristic of Hill's work, achieved in this case by a combination of low-cut mouths with fairly generous pipe-scales. The organ was enlarged by Hill in 1879 when the Swell Contra Trombone was added, the Pedal augmented with 16ft and 32ft Bourdons and a 10 stop Choir organ installed. The console was adapted without changing its style and it remains today as almost the only survivor of the early German compass consoles.

The 1879 work kept remarkably close to the original style of the instrument. Only the Choir organ, outside the case at the north end of the gallery, was foreign to the original concept. In the 1971 restoration this was replaced by a new department in the north side of the lower part of the case and showing some German influence in its stop-list, just as the original instrument had, a hundred and twenty years earlier. Matching the Choir on the south side of the case are 3 stops of Pedal upperwork. The other item changed in 1971 was the design of the soundboards. It is well documented that the tracker actions of the large Hill organs were very heavy to play, and this instrument was no exception. This heaviness was largely due to the design of the soundboard pallet valves, a fault now corrected.

Although restored twice, this is probably the least-altered large pre-1850 organ which we now have, and one with present-day musical relevance as well as antiquarian interest.

Church of St Mary Woolnoth
Gray & Davison 1868; Hill 1913

GREAT		SWELL		CHOIR		PEDAL	
Double Diapason	16	Geigen Principal	8	Lieblich Gedeckt	8	Open Diapason	16
Open Diapason	8	Rohr Flute	8	Dulciana	8	Bourdon	16
Hohl Flute	8	Echo Gamba	8	Suabe Flute	4	Bass Flute	8
Principal	4	Voix Celestes	8	Clarinet	8		
Fifteenth	2	Gemshorn	4	(West end)			
Mixture		Super Octave	2	Viole d'Orchestre	8		
Trumpet	8	Mixture	III	Vox Humana	8		
		Contra Oboe	16				
		Cornopean	8				

This weighty-looking church, the work of Nicholas Hawksmoor, actually has part of Bank station in its crypt. The first organ is reputed to have been a one-manual by Father Smith. A short-compass Swell was added by G. P. England in 1805 and various others made additions before Gray & Davison rebuilt the organ in 1868. The organ was moved to its present position in the north-east corner when Butterfield stripped out the galleries in 1875. The present arrangement, with the seventeenth-century case at the west end covering 2 stops of the Choir organ operated by an early electric action, dates from 1913.

The mystery of this organ is the west-end case. The longest pipe is 6ft, so that it looks like the chair case of a much bigger organ. Furthermore, it has 'round-shouldered' cornices to the flats, giving it more the appearance of Harris' work than Smith's. Perhaps it came from James II's 'Popish Chapel' in Whitehall when the main case went to St James', Piccadilly?

St Michael's Church, Paternoster Royal
Mander 1968

MANUAL			
Open Diapason	8		Compass down to GG.
Stopt Diapason	8	Treble & Bass	No pedals.
Principal	4	Treble & Bass	
Flute	4	Treble & Bass	
Fifteenth	2	Treble & Bass	
Tierce	1⅗	Treble	
Mixture	II	Treble & Bass	

The case of this organ was made by Jordan in 1749 for All Hallows the Great Church and came to Paternoster Royal in 1893. Severely damaged during wartime bombing, what remained of the case was reconstructed around a new tracker instrument built by Noel Mander as a reproduction eighteenth-century organ.

St Paul's Cathedral
Smith 1697; Willis 1872; Mander 1977

Chancel Section

GREAT	
Double Open Diapason	16
Open Diapason I	8
Open Diapason II	8
Stopt Diapason	8
Quint	5⅓
Principal I	4
Principal II	4
Flute	4
Twelfth	2⅔
Fifteenth	2
Mixture 17.19.22	III
Mixture 24.26.29	III
Fourniture 19.22.26.29	IV
Trombone	16
Trumpet	8
Clarion	4

SWELL	
Contra Gamba	16
Open Diapason	8
Lieblich Gedact	8
Salicional	8
Vox Angelica	8
Principal	4
Fifteenth	2
Cornet 17.19.22	III
Contra Posaune	16
Cornopean	8
Hautboy	8
Vox Humana	8
Clarion	4

SOLO (Enclosed)	
Open Diapason	8
Viola	8
Viola Celeste	8
Flute Harmonique	8
Concert Flute	4
Piccolo	2
Corno di Bassetto	8
Cor Anglais	8
French Horn	8
(Unenclosed)	
Tuba	8
Tuba Clarion	4

SOUTH CHOIR	
Contra Viola	16
Open Diapason	8
Violoncello	8
Dulciana	8
Claribel Flute	8
Gemshorn	4
Lieblich Gedact	4
Flageolet	2
Sesquialtera 12.17	II

NORTH CHOIR	
Chimney Flute	8
Principal	4
Nason Flute	4
Nazard	2⅔
Fifteenth	2
Blockflute	2
Tierce	1⅗
Larigot	1⅓
Sharp Mixture 26.29.33.36	IV
Trumpet	8

PEDAL	
Open Metal	16
Open Diapason	16
Viola	16
Bourdon	16
Principal	8
Flute	8
Fifteenth	4
Sesquialtera 12.17	II
Mixture 19.22.26.29	IV
Contra Posaune	32
Ophicleide	16
Posaune	8
Clarion	4

West Section

Open Diapason	8
Octave	4
Super Octave	2
Mixture 19.22.26.29	IV
Royal Trumpet	16
Royal trumpet	8
Royal Trumpet	4

Dome Section

Vth MANUAL	
Double Open Diapason	16
Open Diapason I	8
Open Diapason II	8
Octave	4
Super Octave	2
Quartane 19.22	II
Mixture 19.22.26.29	IV
Cymbal 29.33.26	III
Contra Posaune	16
Trumpet	8
Double Tuba	16
Tuba	8
Clarion	4
Trompette Militaire	8

PEDAL	
Double Open Wood	32
Contra Violone	32
Open Wood	16
Open Diapason	16
Contra Bass	16
Principal	8
Super Octave	4
Mixture 19.22.26.29	IV
Contra Bombarde	32
Bombarde	16
Posaune	16
Clarion	8

St Paul's is a beautiful building, but an almost impossible one for which to design an organ. Most of the congregation sit under the echoing dome, still the largest church dome in Christendom, but some sit hundreds of feet away down the long nave. Bernard Smith adopted the classic cathedral arrangement, placing a double-sided organ on the screen dividing the chancel from the rest of the Cathedral. Sir Christopher Wren insisted on designing the case, leading to the famous story of a row with Father Smith (the precursor of many such between architect and organ-builder) in which Wren is said to have referred to 'that damned box of whistles'. The cause of the trouble was Smith's insistence on a 16ft CCC compass which he believed would give the organ the gravity needed in such a building. In the event, despite the concealing statuary on the top of the case, the Open Diapasons could go down only to FFF. The case which resulted is unique, having a very simple and bold structure of two towers and one single-storey flat, yet with a wealth of exuberant carving not otherwise found on organ cases in Britain.

Smith's 27 stop organ was designed to accompany the choral service in the chancel, but was less effective in the wide spaces of the nave. This was made worse when in 1860 the screen was taken down and the organ placed in the chancel. A secondhand four-manual Hill was purchased and set up in the south transept, but in 1872 Father Willis devised the present arrangement with the Smith case cut in two and placed either side of the chancel arch. This layout was

ST PAUL'S CATHEDRAL, LONDON, AS IT APPEARED UP TO 1860

made possible by Willis' invention of tubular pneumatic action. Willis provided what amounted to a new organ though he incorporated a token number of Smith's pipes. The original chair case was placed on the south side and the console placed in a replica chair case on the north side. This was a fascinating eyrie, full of little doors in the casework like an Advent calendar, through which the hidden player could spy on the progress of the service.

Willis' organ was enlarged to five manuals in 1898 and further enlargements were made in 1930, the most notable being the flared brass Trompette Militaire, voiced on 30in (750mm) wind and located in one of the arches leading to the dome. The Willis organ was notable for being very largely invisible, with less than half the instrument in the chancel cases. It relied heavily on acoustic reflection and, despite all efforts, still failed to lead singing in the nave.

193

Proposals were considered in 1973 for replacing the organ on the screen as a 60 stop tracker organ, but, in the event, Noel Mander was selected to retain most of the Willis layout and 1872 pipes in what is otherwise a new instrument. The console is now detached above the south choir stalls, east of the organ, and the chair case on the north side contains a new Positive-type department of fairly conventional 4ft-based design. The Swell organ, a much admired part of Father Willis' instrument, is almost unchanged tonally but the chancel Pedal was largely renewed and concealed behind the panelling of the north choir stalls. The enclosed Solo was also retained here with the unusual Willis III French Horn. High up in the arch off the dome the Willis pedalwork was augmented and a new Diapason Chorus provided to lead singing under the dome. To assist the congregation in the nave, for whom Renatus Harris had in 1712 proposed a six-manual at the west end, a further Diapason Chorus is placed in an arch high on the south side of the nave. At the west end itself, there is a trio of high-pressure trumpets projecting horizontally over the gallery rail, providing for a climax effect on a state occasion.

As already said, St Paul's is a glorious but impossible building for an organ. In some ways the Mander/Willis instrument, distributed in five places round the Cathedral, is an unfashionable answer to the challenge – but it does make some glorious music!

St Peter's Church, Cornhill
Smith 1681; Hill 1840, 1891–2; Rushworth & Dreaper 1959

GREAT		SWELL		CHOIR		PEDAL	
Double Diapason	16	Dulciana	16	Dulciana	8	Sub Bass	32
Open Diapason	8	*Open Diapason	8	Lieblich Gedeckt	8	Open Diapason	16
Claribel Flute	8	Dulciana	8	Viol da Gamba	8	Bourdon	16
*Stopped Diapason	8	Stopped Diapason	8	*Stopped Flute	4	Lieblich Bourdon	16
Dulciana	8	Viola	8	Octave Viol	4	'Cello	8
Principal	4	Voix Celestes	8	Flageolet	2	Lieblich Flute	8
Wald Flute	4	Principal	4	Orchestral Oboe	8	Octave Flute	4
Oboe Flute	4	Suabe Flute	4	Cremona	8	Trombone	16
Twelfth	2⅔	*Twelfth	2⅔				
Fifteenth	2	*Fifteenth	2			*Stops reputed to contain	
Tierce	1⅗	Piccolo	2			Smith pipes.	
Sesquialtra	III	Mixture	II				
Corno Tromba	8	Sesquialtra	III				
Corno Clarion	4	Double Trumpet	16				
		Cornopean	8				
		Clarion	4				
		Oboe	8				

Mendelssohn played this organ – or so claims the notice on the console of William Hill's organ of 1840, preserved in a glass case in the vestry. The reason why he played it, more than once, was because it was only the second instrument in Britain to have full compass pedals and the German compass manuals from CC to which Mendelssohn was accustomed, the other being in Christ Church, Newgate Street, rebuilt by Hill two years earlier. In order to fit it all in, Hill had widened the three-tower Father Smith case which still stands on the west gallery. The organ also incorporated a few of Smith's pipes but was otherwise new and was built to the design of the hymn-tune writer, Dr Henry Gauntlett.

Gauntlett's journeys on the Continent had impressed him with the congregational singing of the Lutheran chorales and he wanted an organ powerful enough to accompany such singing. Consequently, the Great organ had no less than 18 stops in what is a very modest-sized city church. In order to provide 16ft manual stops within a limited height, Hill used, for the first time in England, the French Bourdon stop, a stop which was to catch on very rapidly and which, later, was to become the 'universal aunt' of the Pedal organ.

Hill's console was quite a grand affair, the sharp keys being inlaid with tortoiseshell and the stop-knobs with mother-of-pearl. It was preserved in the vestry when the Hill firm rebuilt the organ with a new console and pneumatic action in 1891–2. At this time, the small choir organ was added standing outside the case on the north side of the gallery, screened by panelling. Electropneumatic action was fitted when the organ was rebuilt by Rushworth & Dreaper in 1959.

Plate 1 Tewkesbury Abbey, the 'Milton' organ: pre-Commonwealth case, possibly by Robert Dallam, originally in Magdalen College Chapel, Oxford. The five-tower form is unusual but the 'Mannerist' detail is characteristic of the period. The original tin-metal front pipes survive with their variegated mouth shapes and splendid embossing. The side overhang of the case was supported by arches, a feature later used by Thomas Harris at Gloucester Cathedral *(B. B. Edmonds)*

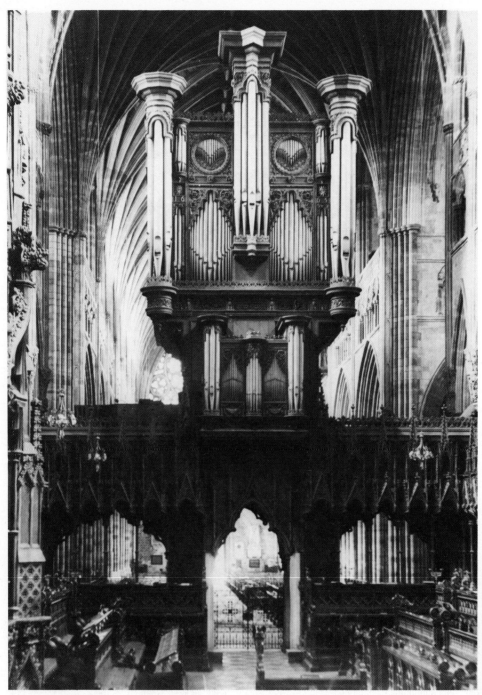

Plate 2 Exeter Cathedral: double-fronted case by John Loosemore, 1665, with original chair case. Although basically Renaissance in design, the carved cornice and impost crestings have a vaguely Gothic feeling. The elevated central tower with projecting centre pipe is unusual and the little compartments either side of the upper flats unique, the latter perhaps the result of a change of mind during construction. The use of varied mouth-pipes and foot-lengths is particularly effective; the original front-pipes were embossed as well *(Andrew Freeman)*

Plate 3 St James's Church, Piccadilly, London: Renaissance main case by Renatus Harris, 1686, built for the Queen's 'Popish' Chapel in Whitehall with carving by Grinling Gibbons. The chair case is a mid-nineteenth-century pastiche. The three-tower form with the 'round-shouldered' cornice to the upper flats was characteristic of Harris's work and the overhang at the sides of the case was general seventeenth-century practice. The putti on the top of the case and the finely carved impost rail are also typical Renatus Harris features. The unsightly wooden swell-box projecting above the case houses the full-compass Swell organ added in the nineteenth century *(Nick Turvey)*

Plate 4 Birmingham Town Hall (photographed before restoration): Renaissance survival case by William Hill, 1834. The 32ft front made it much bigger than any predecessor in Britain, but Hill's case still followed the same basic form of towers and two-storey flats as used 170 years earlier. Fundamentally a three-tower case, additional flats and towers were angled on the ends to hide the depth required for the Pedal organ, not previously provided in Britain. Despite the formal structure, details had become debased with obvious false-length pipes, the use of wreaths for pipe-shades and the short feet of the 32ft pipes – though these were shown longer in the original design sketch *(Ian Bell)*

Plate 5 Eton College Chapel: Gothic Revival case by J. L. Pearson, 1882, double-fronted, with a back-case facing the ante-chapel. Pearson was of the school of architects who made an academic study of Gothic and Renaissance forms, adapting them to the Victorian British organ. Pearson here made bold use of circular towers without intervening flats to obtain great variety of scale in this massive 32ft case

Plate 6 (left) Peterborough Cathedral: Gothic Revival case by Dr Arthur Hill, 1904. Although it lacks depth, being but a screen, this case-front contains a remarkable variety of pipe-sizes and particularly fine carved tracery on the tops of the towers. There are really four towers but the complex and original form of the case has such a prominent two-storey centre flat that, in overall silhouette, there appears to be only three

Plate 7 (right) Norwich Cathedral: Renaissance-style case by S. E. Dykes Bower, 1950, double-fronted, having a west face also. The chair case has Mannerist detail reminiscent of the east face of the case in King's College Chapel, Cambridge, and the unusual central tower of the main case has a complex shape not unlike those of the post-Commonwealth cases at Exeter and Gloucester Cathedrals. The front pipes are largely dummy and have longer feet than is usual

Plate 8 Royal Festival Hall, London: caseless organ, 1954. Although apparently neo-Holtkamp in its naked display of pipes, large and small, the appearance of this organ is largely accidental, the planned grille having been omitted. The surreal 'motif' of dummy pipes was designed by Sir Leslie Martin

Plate 9 Carrs Lane Church Centre, Birmingham: Scandinavian-style 'werk-prinzip' case by Herbert Norman, 1970. The tone-cabinet for each department is separately expressed and is devoid of applied decoration. In this example the sloping roofs follow the natural lines of the pipe-tops. For a more distant view, see the drawing on page 302 *(Author)*

Plate 10 All Saint's Church, Friern Barnet, London: case by Roger Pulham, 1984. The use of mouldings and of curved side-brackets is typical of the present-day reaction to the severe 'Scandinavian' style. The unusually wide five-tower layout is the result of the limited height available below the west windows, the departments being arranged side-by-side. The Swell organ is in the centre, the Great and Pedal organs being divided with alternate notes on either side. Note the horizontal reed in the centre, playable from the Swell manual *(Roger Pulham)*

St Sepulchre without Newgate
Harris 1676; Harrison 1932

GREAT		SWELL		PEDAL	
Lieblich Bourdon	16	Open Diapason	8	Double Open Diapason	32
Open Diapason	8	Lieblich Gedeckt	8	Open Diapason	16
Claribel Flute	8	Gemshorn	4	Sub Bass	16
Salicional	8	Fifteenth	2		
Octave	4	Cornopean	8		

St Sepulchre's (properly the Church of The Holy Sepulchre), in what is now Holborn Viaduct, calls itself 'The Musician's Church' and an annual St Cecilia Day service is held there. Architecturally speaking, the largest parish church in the City is something of a mixture since its fifteenth-century Gothic structure was gutted in the Fire of London and rebuilt in Renaissance style.

The organ is a mixture of styles too. Renatus Harris built a one-manual organ for the west gallery when the church was restored after the fire. A Swell was added in 1739 and Gray, and later Gray & Davison, made various additions including, in 1849, a very complete 10 stop Pedal organ. In 1876 the organ was moved to the north chapel, and in 1892 further enlarged to 46 stops by J. W. Walker. Finally, in 1932, the case was moved again and a much smaller organ inserted.

The result is, frankly, odd. The splendid and exuberant Harris case is cut off at the impost, perched on a screen facing west, and every conceivable piece of ornament is plastered with gilding. This includes two enormous angels which hover over the central tower, attached to and not quite concealing the end of the swell-box which faces sideways across to the chancel. The organ itself shows clearly the emphasis on foundation tone which persisted from the Hope-Jones era forty years earlier. The provision of a 16ft stop in only a 5 stop Great organ and a full-length 32ft Open Diapason in a 3 stop Pedal is surely something of a record!

Church of St Stephen, Walbrook
England 1765; Hill 1888, 1907

St Stephen's is one of Wren's most attractive City churches and its domed interior has been described as a prototype for St Paul's Cathedral. George England built a three-manual organ in 1765, and his three-tower case still stands on its gallery over the west door, embellished by some extremely good rococo carving. The organ itself was replaced by a new three-manual Hill in 1888; the Pedal organ was enlarged and new tubular pneumatic action fitted in 1907. After the war the Hill console was detached and electro-pneumatic action fitted. The organ is very cramped internally; a special long reed-knife is kept in the instrument to tune some of the more inaccessible pipes in the Swell!

St Vedast's Church, Foster Lane
Harris & Byfield 1731; Mander 1962

GREAT		SWELL		CHOIR		PEDAL	
Contra Dulciana	16	*Salicional	8	Dulciana	8	Bourdon	16
*Open Diapason	8	*Chimney Flute	8	*Stopt Diapason	8	Dulciana	16
*Stopt Diapason	8	*Principal	4	*Principal	4	Dulciana	8
Dulciana	8	*Fifteenth	2	*Flute	4	Flute	8
*Principal	4	Mixture 19.22	II	Dulciana	4	Flute	4
Nason Flute	4	Trumpet	8	Twelfth	2⅔	Flute	2
Dulciana	4			*Fifteenth	2	Trombone	16
Twelfth	2⅔			Larigot	1⅓	Trumpet	8
*Fifteenth	2			Twenty-second	1	Clarion	4
Tierce	1⅗			Trumpet	8		
Mixture	III					*Harris pipes.	
Cornet	V						
Trumpet	8						
Clarion	4						

When Wren's St Vedast's Church came to be restored after wartime fire damage, a search was made for period furnishings which had left the City of London when their churches had been demolished in the nineteenth century. The organ which Harris & Byfield had built for St Batholomew-by-the-Exchange had ended up, in an advanced state of decay, in St Alban's Church, Fulham. The instrument now stands in a splendid open position on the west gallery of St Vedast's, its distinctive three-tower oak case with ogee 'flats' beautifully restored and complete with a crown and two mitres on the tops of the towers. Noel Mander fitted a new console and tracker action to the manuals, though the Pedal and certain additional manual stops, which are extended, use electropneumatic action. Despite these additions, this organ is still an important eighteenth-century instrument.

The Temple Church
Harrison 1927, 1954

GREAT		SWELL		CHOIR (enclosed)		PEDAL	
Double Geigen	16	Quintatön	16	Contra Dulciana	16	Double Open Wood	32
Bourdon	16	Open Diapason	8	Sub Bourdon	8	Sub Bourdon	32
Large Open Diapason	8	Stop'd Diapason	8	Lieblich Gedeckt	8	Open Wood	16
Small Open Diapason	8	Echo Salicional	8	Dulciana	8	Open Diapason	16
Geigen	8	Vox Angelica	8	Salicet	4	Geigen	16
Hohl Flute	8	Principal	4	Flauto Traverso	4	Bourdon	16
Stop'd Diapason	8	Fifteenth	2	Harmonic Piccolo	2	Violone	16
Octave	4	Mixture 12.19.22.26.29	V	Dulciana Mixture		Dulciana	16
Wald Flute	4	Oboe	8	15.19.22	III	Octave Wood	8
Octave Quint	2⅔	Double Trumpet	16	Cor Anglais	16	Flute	8
Super Octave	2	Trumpet	8	Clarinet	8	Octave Flute	4
Harmonics 19.21.22.23	IV	Clarion	4			Double Ophicleide	32
Tromba	8			SOLO (enclosed)		Ophicleide	16
Octave Tromba	4			Contra Viola	16	Orchestral Trumpet	16
				Viole d'Orchestre	8	Bassoon	16
				Viole Céleste	8	Posaune	8
				Harmonic Flute	8		
				Concert Flute	4		
				Double Orchestral			
				Trumpet	16		
				Orchestral Hautboy	8		
				Horn	8		
				Tuba	8		

The Temple Church has a unique foundation, being maintained by the Benchers of the Inner and Middle Temples as a condition of their freehold of the Temple land. Its place in the history of the organ is secured by the famous 'Battle of the Organs' between Renatus Harris and Father Smith (see chapter 3). Smith's victorious organ has, alas, disappeared. Rebuilt and enlarged beyond recognition, it was destroyed by incendiary bombs in 1941. The present instrument was originally built by Arthur Harrison for the ballroom of Glentanar castle in Scotland. It was installed in the Temple Church in 1954, the only alterations being the addition of the 32ft reed and those necessary to match the livelier acoustics of the church instead of the upholstered deadness of Lord Glentanar's ballroom. The case is a modern pastiche, inspired by extant drawings of Smith's organ. George Thalben-Ball was in charge of the organ loft of the Temple Church for over sixty years making, with his predecessors Hopkins and Walford Davies, only three organists in about a hundred and fifty years.

Tower of London, Chapel of St Peter ad Vincula
Smith 1699; Elliot 1814; Hill 1844, 1877, 1890; Hill Norman & Beard 1953, 1977

GREAT		SWELL		CHOIR		PEDAL	
Double Diapason	16	Open Diapason	8	Open Diapason	8	Bourdon	16
Open Diapason	8	Stopped Diapason	8	Stopped Diapason	8	Principal	8
Stopped Diapason	8	Viola da Gamba	8	Principal	4	Flute	8
Principal	4	Voix Celestes	8	Stopped Flute	4	Flute	4
Nason Flute	4	Principal	4	Gemshorn	2	Quartane	II
Twelfth	2⅔	Fifteenth	2	Larigot	1⅓	Trombone	16
Fifteenth	2	Mixture	III	Bassoon	16		
Mixture	III	Contra Oboe	16	Clarinet	8		
Mounted Cornet	V	Cornopean	8				
Posaune	8	Clarion	4				

Father Smith built a two-manual for the gallery of Inigo Jones' famous Banqueting Hall in Whitehall in 1699 and the carving on the four-tower case has been attributed to Grinling Gibbons. Thomas Elliot rebuilt the instrument in 1814, adding a short-compass Swell organ; Hill provided a bigger Swell and a Solo in 1844 and rebuilt it again with new action and a proper Pedal organ in 1877. In 1890 the instrument was removed from Whitehall to the Tower, where it stands on the floor of the chapel, still in Smith's main case but minus a chair case. Although the fourth manual was removed at this time, the interior layout of the instrument was particularly cramped and the sound very boxed in. In 1977 the organ was completely reconstructed internally with new soundboards and tracker action to the manuals.

As early as 1855 Hopkins recorded that, apart from the case, only some wood pipes remained from Smith's organ. Basically, the instrument is now a good mid-nineteenth-century Hill, one which must have sounded very fine in the superior acoustics of Inigo Jones' Banqueting Hall.

CLERKENWELL St James' Church
England 1792; Gray & Davison 1877; Mander 1978

GREAT		SWELL		PEDAL	
*Open Diapason	8	*Open Diapason	8	Open Diapason	16
*Stopped Diapason	8	*Chimney Flute	8	Bourdon	16
*Principal	4	*Principal	4	*Principal	8
*Flute	4	*Fifteenth	2	Trombone	16
*Twelfth	2⅔	Twenty-second	1		
*Fifteenth	2	Cornet	II	*England pipes.	
Larigot	1⅓	Mixture 26.29.33	III		
Fourniture		Bassoon	8		
19.22.26.29	IV-VI				
Cornet	V				
Trumpet	8				

The Clerkenwell organ is an excellent example of an instrument growing over the years, being stripped back to its surviving original parts, with a new organ being built in the spirit of the original. The work was guided by Michael Gillingham and the fine original case of Spanish mahogany, with its carved swags and palm fronds, has been restored most carefully. The surviving G. P. England pipework forms the nucleus of the manual divisions, and the Pedal organ retains some pipes from the nineteenth-century Gray & Davison rebuild (when a Pedal organ was first provided). No trace remains of the 1929 reconstruction, when the soundboards were turned sideways and pneumatic action provided to a detached console. In the recent work the entire mechanism, soundboards and wind supply were replaced and the organ provided with a handsome console in late eighteenth-century style and a very responsive tracker action.

Tonally, the organ shows its origins in the eighteenth century, though it has a vigour which sets it apart from the work of Green and his followers. The Swell retains the 8ft Open Diapason characteristic of the British Swell but the sharper upperwork and half-length reeds differentiate the chorus from that of the Great organ. The powerful Trombone on the Pedal shows its Gray & Davison origins but nevertheless enables a small Pedal organ to balance the manual choruses.

ST JAMES' CHURCH, CLERKENWELL

EALING The Abbey
Rushworth & Dreaper 1974

GREAT		SWELL		PEDAL	
Principal	8	Stopped Flute	8	Principal	16
Chimney Flute	8	Salicional	8	Bourdon	16
Octave	4	Principal	4	Octave	8
Wald Flute	4	Koppel Flute	4	Flute	8
Twelfth	2⅔	Sesquialtera	II	Choral Bass	4
Octave	2	Block Flute	2	Nachthorn	2
Mixture 19.22.26.29.33	VI	Larigot	1⅓	Mixture 19.22.26.29	IV
Trumpet	8	Mixture 22.26.29.33	IV	Fagot	16
		Krummhorn	8	Schalmei	4

Ealing Abbey is a large Roman Catholic church, Gothic Revival in design, and with a lofty and splendidly decorated roof. The 1935 John Compton unit organ was destroyed by bombing in 1941. The present organ is Rushworth's largest essay at tracker instruments to date and stands in an elevated position on the south side of the nave. The case is a simple expression of the tone-cabinets, with the Great above the Swell and the Pedal 16ft copper front pipes divided either side. The Pedal tone-cabinets are somewhat muffled by the structure but the Great organ rings out splendidly in this large and resonant building.

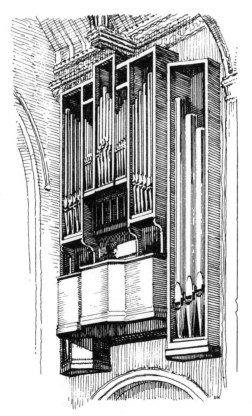

EALING ABBEY

ENFIELD St Andrew's Parish Church
Bridge 1753; Gray & Davison 1885; Hill 1908; Kingsgate Davidson 1952

There is a large board on the north wall recording benefactors to Enfield Church, one of which was a Mrs Mary Nickells who paid for Richard Bridge's organ of 1753. Of this instrument, only the case remains, but it is a very glorious survival with the original front pipes recently regilded, and the characteristic Bridge ogee-shaped 'flats' between the towers with richly carved curved panels below the pipes.

The present organ was built by Gray & Davison for the south aisle and moved, with a revised and enlarged reed chorus, to the north aisle by Hill; it was moved again to the west gallery in 1952 and placed behind the Bridge case. The instrument occupies the full depth of the gallery and the console is adjacent to the chancel. The problems so caused for choir and continuo accompaniment were relieved when, in 1972, a 3 stop chancel organ was built, standing on the parclose screen on the south side of the choir. It has a gable-topped Gothic tone-cabinet case, with doors, designed by Herbert Norman.

FRIERN BARNET All Saints' Church (see Plate 10)
Church 1984

GREAT		SWELL		PEDAL	
Open Diapason	8	Stopped Diapason	8	Subbass	16
Chimney Flute	8	Salicional	8	Gemshorn	8
Principal	4	Celeste	8	Stopped Flute	8
Tapered Flute	4	Conical Flute	4	Octave	4
Nazard	2⅔	Principal	4	Double Bassoon	16
Fifteenth	2	Octave	2	Posaune	8
Tierce	1⅗	Nineteenth	1⅓		
Mixture 15.19.22	III	Sharp Mixture 22.29.33	III	*Tracker key-action*	
		Cremona	16	Nightingale	
		Hautboy	8	Cymbal Star	
		Heraldic Trumpet	8		

This is Nigel Church's largest organ to date, and has several unusual features. The limited height below the west window precludes a vertical arrangement so the organ has the Swell in the centre with the divided Great and Pedal organs either side at the same level. This layout places the projecting Heraldic Trumpet on the Swell organ and gives the divisions a very different sound. The tight, bright sound of the Swell chorus contrasts with the broader, almost stereophonic sound of the Great Organ. The tracker action, which is of the French suspended type, is particularly responsive. The Cedar of Lebanon case was designed by Roger Pulham.

GREENWICH Royal Naval College Chapel
Green 1789; Hill 1862; Hill Norman & Beard 1952, 1966

GREAT		SWELL		CHOIR		PEDAL	
Open Diapason	8	Quintaten	16	Stopped Diapason	8	Open Diapason	16
Open Diapason	8	Open Diapason	8	Dulciana	8	Bourdon	16
Stopped Diapason	8	Stopped Diapason	8	Principal	4	Violone	16
Principal	4	Dulciana	8	Flute	4	Principal	8
Flute	4	Principal	4	Fifteenth	2	Fifteenth	4
Twelfth	2⅔	Dulciana	4	Bassoon	8	Spitz Flute	4
Fifteenth	2	Cornet	III	Festal Trumpet	8	Rauschquint	II
Furniture	III	Oboe	16			Trombone	16
Sesquialtera	III	Trumpet	8				
Cornet	IV	Clarion	4				
Trumpet	8						
Clarion	4						
Festal Trumpet	8						

The magnificent Chapel of Greenwich Hospital, now the Royal Naval College, is matched by the companion Dining Hall with its opulent painted ceiling. The first organ was built by Abraham Jordan but destroyed by fire in 1779. The present instrument is probably the larges by Samuel Green which remains in its original home. The mahogany case, with its four towers and oval compartments, shows some slight rococo influence, and is flamboyant if a little debased.

In 1789 Samuel Green was very interested in swell-boxes (the following year he was to build the entire organ in St George's Chapel, Windsor in one large swell-box) and the Swell of the Greenwich instrument was the first to have the compass below tenor C, though to FF, not CC.

Some time before 1855, the organ gained a 17 note pedalboard and a stop of Pedal pipes, as well as losing its original Cornet, but in 1862 Hill rebuilt the organ, conservatively, converting the instrument to CC compass, enlarging the Swell organ and adding a 4 stop Pedal organ at the back. Ninety years later, Hill's console was replaced by the present one. The Pedal organ acquired its present upperwork in 1966 and the Great organ Cornet was reinstated to a scale based on the surviving Green stop at Armitage.

The favourable acoustics of the Chapel probably make the instrument less soft than some of Green's other instruments had been, but, in order to add drama to the organ without altering the old work, the Festal Trumpet was added in 1966. Although not visible, this stop has horizontal pipes and produces considerable power on a low wind pressure.

Overall, this is a most important instrument. The Hill rebuild and the more recent additions have not substantially altered the character of the instrument which retains the mild and 'sweet' tone for which Green was well known.

HAMPSTEAD University College School
Walker 1980

GREAT		SWELL		PEDAL	
Open Diapason	8	Stopped Diapason	8	Bourdon	16
Chimney Flute	8	Quintaten	8	Principal	8
Principal	4	Gemshorn	4	Gedackt	8
Flageolet	2	Clear Flute	4	Wide Octave	4
Larigot	1⅓	Nazard	2⅔	Trombone	16
Piccolo	1	Principal	2		
Mixture 15.19.22.26	IV	Tierce	1⅗		
Cremona	8	Sharp Mixture 22.26.29	III		
		Cor Anglais	16		
		Trumpet	8		

An excellent oak case, designed by David Graebe, is the highlight of this J. W. Walker tracker-action instrument which replaced a 1962 electric-action extension organ destroyed by fire in 1978. With bold impost and cornice mouldings and with fielded panels matching the sumptuous furnishing of the rest of the School Hall, it shows up some of the plainer modern cases as very stark. Unusually, the pipe-shades are of beaten copper and are wittily made in the shape of oak leaves, the school emblem. The layout is clearly expressed in the case with the Swell over the Great and the Pedal in two almost detached towers either side.

The space available dictated a small Pedal organ, but not the unusual relationship between the manual divisions. Despite a 2ft Principal and Sharp Mixture, making the Swell a higher pitched department than the Great organ, it is no mere enclosed Positive. The chorus Trumpet is on the Swell, with a 16ft reed also, whilst the Great organ has a half-length Cremona and high-pitched flutes. This partial reversal of roles is unconventional; experience will show if it is successful.

HAYES Church of the Immaculate Heart of Mary
Walker 1981

GREAT		SWELL		PEDAL	
Open Diapason	8	Gedact	8	Bourdon	16
Stopped Diapason	8	Gemshorn	4	Principal	8
Principal	4	Wald Flute	4	Wide Octave	4
Blockflute	2	Principal	2		
Mixture 15.19.22	III	Mixture 22.26.29	III		
Sesquialtera	II	Trumpet	8		

Standing in front of a huge west window in this modern church, the marked silhouette of the organ case is enhanced by the coved overhang at the sides. The tonal design places the Sesquialtera on the Great organ and the Trumpet on the Swell, a relationship which takes the Swell organ out of the enclosed Positive category. Unusually for a tracker-action organ, the Swell is fitted with a sub-octave coupler.

HIGHBURY PARK Roman Catholic Church of St Joan of Arc

Walker 1963

GREAT		POSITIVE		PEDAL	
Contra Salicional	16	Spitzflute	8	Sub Bass	16
Principal	8	Rohrflute	8	Principal	8
Stopped Diapason	8	Salicional	8	Gedeckt Flute	8
Octave	4	Gemshorn	4	Fifteenth	4
Stopped Flute	4	Octave Flute	4	Gedeckt Pommer	4
Twelfth	2⅔	Nazard	2⅔	Super Octave	2
Fifteenth	2	Super Octave	2	Krummhorn	16
Piccolo	2	Larigot	1⅓	Krummhorn	8
Tierce	1⅗	Fourniture 15.19.22	III	Krummhorn	4
Nineteenth	1⅓	Krummhorn	16		
		Krummhorn	8		

This is an early example of a neo-Baroque two-manual without a Swell. Apart from the Krummhorn and the Pedal Sub Bass ranks, the whole instrument is divided over two tone cabinets, both located in the chair position at either end of the west gallery. Within the tone cabinets the pipework is placed on open display, treble pipes at the front.

HIGHGATE St Joseph's Roman Catholic Church

Hill 1899

The green dome of St Joseph's, halfway up Highgate Hill, is a prominent north London landmark. When, after the war, the 36 stop four-manual Hill was taken out of the hall of the Northern Polytechnic, Holloway, it was moved up the road to St Joseph's, where it stands on the west gallery. The instrument retains its original tubular-pneumatic action.

HOLBORN Holy Trinity Church, Kingsway

Hill 1859; Hill Norman & Beard 1970

GREAT		SWELL		PEDAL	
Stopped Diapason	8	Spitz Flute	8	Bourdon	16
Principal	4	Chimney Flute	4	Principal	8
Suabe Flute	4	Principal	2	Fagotto	16
Gemshorn	2	Sesquialtera	II	Shalmey	4
Furniture	IV	Septieme	1⅐		
		None	8/9		
		Sharp Mixture	III		
		Trompette	8		

The organ-case is based on the fire-damaged remains of the 1831 organ which stood in a former church and which was transferred to the present monumental but incomplete building in the early years of this century. It features an 1830s curiosity in the form of cast-iron Gothic ornament.

The organ itself has completely different origins from the case, if a similarly chequered history. Built by Hill in 1859 for Buckingham Palace Chapel, it incorporated pipes from an earlier instrument by Samuel Green, which remain as parts of the Stopped Diapason and Great and Pedal Principals. This instrument was seriously damaged by high explosive in World War II, losing its case completely.

The combined instrument was created in 1970 by Hill, Norman & Beard, with a new tracker

HOLY TRINITY CHURCH, KINGSWAY, LONDON

action and some two-thirds new pipes. The church is reverberant and the organ, on the rear gallery, sounds considerably larger than it really is. Its most striking feature is the unusual mutation stops on the Swell, almost unique in this country. The Septieme and the None are the seventh and the ninth harmonics of the fundamental. Used separately, together, or with the Sesquialtera (combining the third and fifth harmonics) they can produce the most astonishing and unusual tone colours to illuminate a melodic line.

St Alban's Church
Compton 1961

This is a cautionary tale. The lofty Victorian Gothic church by Butterfield has four seconds of reverberation and excellent acoustics for choral and organ music. A large four-manual by Father Willis was destroyed in World War II and replaced by the present 59 stop three-manual Compton. Under the guidance of John Compton and Jimmy Taylor, the Compton firm had developed voicing techniques which used high wind pressures to overcome the constraints of all-enclosing swell-boxes and organ chambers. When, after their retirement, this organ was

211

built in a splendid open position on the west gallery, these techniques could not be rapidly unlearned. The consequence was that, despite walls of hardboard all round the Great organ, this is probably the loudest church instrument in London.

HORNSEY St David and St Catherine's School Hall
Hill Norman & Beard 1976

GREAT		BRUSTPOSITIVE		PEDAL	
Stopped Diapason	8	Gedackt	8	Sub Bass	16
Principal	4	Koppel Flute	4	Gemshorn	4
Spitzflute	2	Principal	2	Fagot	16
Sesquialtera	II	Quinte	1⅓		
Mixture 19.22.26	III				

This straightforward tracker tone-cabinet organ stands in a corner of the hall of a modern comprehensive school. The *Brustpositive* is immediately above the music desk and has folding doors. The 4ft-based Great has the Principal in the centre portion of the case. The side-towers, containing the Pedal organ, have copper front pipes which, in fact, are stopped pipes of the Sub Bass. In such a dry acoustic, generous scales and a low cut-up on the pipe-mouths successfully avoided an over-hard tone. The case was designed by Herbert Norman.

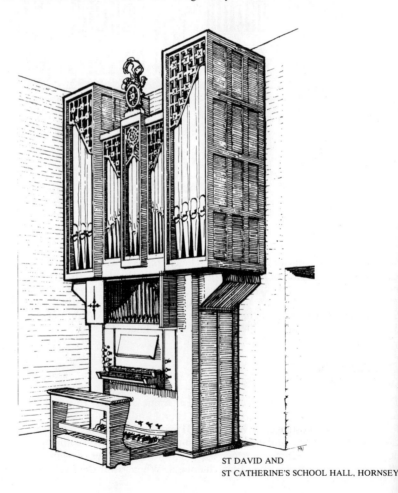

ST DAVID AND
ST CATHERINE'S SCHOOL HALL, HORNSEY

ISLINGTON Church of St John the Evangelist (RC)
Walker 1963

GREAT		SWELL		POSITIVE		PEDAL	
Quintaton	16	Open Diapason	8	Stopped Diapason	8	Open Wood	16
Principal	8	Lieblich Gedeckt	8	Principal	4	Sub Bass	16
Spitzflute	8	Viola da Gamba	8	Wald Flute	4	Quintaton	16
Octave	4	Voix Celeste	8	Quint	2⅔	Octave	8
Nason Flute	4	Principal	4	Blockflute	2	Bass Flute	8
Twelfth	2⅔	Rohr Flute	4	Tierce	1⅗	Fifteenth	4
Fifteenth	2	Octave	2	Scharf 29.33.36	III	Nachthorn	4
Tertian 19.24	II	Mixture 22.26.29.33	IV	Crumhorn	8	Mixture 22.26.29	III
Furniture 19.22.26.29	IV	Bassoon	16			Bombarde	16
Trumpet	8	Trumpet	8			Bassoon	16
		Zink	4			Posaune	8
						Schalmei	4

Some pipes from the original Bishop, Starr & Richardson instrument of 1852 were incorporated into this J. W. Walker organ, which was otherwise new in 1963. Placed on the west gallery, it has a bold, almost aggressive double case whose otherwise stark silhouette is relieved by ogee-shaped pipe-blocks and cornices between the rectangular towers. The waisted and coved main case, which is relatively shallow, houses the Great, Swell and Pedal departments, vertically disposed with the lowest speaking out through a grille in the cove below the front pipes. Despite the *werk* principle layout, the action is not tracker but electro-pneumatic. The Positive organ, in the chair case, has more Diapason tone than the flutey Positives of the previous decade and an 8ft English Swell is incorporated, yet the instrument retains more of a unity than some others of its period.

Church of St Mary Magdalene, Holloway Road
England 1814; Willis 1867

The last major organ of G. P. England, this instrument was also probably the last to be built, as a matter of course, with a traditional Renaissance four-tower case. Beautifully made in Spanish mahogany, it has, however, less carving than eighteenth-century cases, the pipe-shades being just a series of pendants between the pipes – a G. P. England trademark.

The rebuild by Father Willis in 1867 was, for him, remarkably conservative, perhaps because he was himself organist there, a position he filled for nearly thirty years. England's voicing is characterised by the smaller scales which he used for the upperwork of the Diapason Chorus. A century later this practice was to be taken to extremes, but in England's hands the upperwork had a silvery effect complementing the slightly more powerful unison.

KENSINGTON Hyde Park Chapel
Hill Norman & Beard 1961

GREAT		SWELL		POSITIVE		PEDAL	
Quintaten	16	Chimney Flute	8	Rohr Flute	8	Principal	16
Open Diapason	8	Viola Pomposa	8	Principal	4	Sub Bass	16
Gedeckt Pommer	8	Viola Celeste	8	Koppel Flute	4	Quintaten	16
Octave	4	Spitz Flute	8	Nazard	2⅔	Octave	8
Chimney Flute	4	Spitz Flute Celeste	8	Principal	2	Bass Flute	8
Super Octave	2	Octave Geigen	4	Tierce	1⅗	Spitz Flute	4
Mixture 19.22.26.29	IV	Lieblich Flute	4	Sifflöte	1	Rauschquint 19.22	II
Trumpet	8	Fifteenth	2	Cymbal	III	Trombone	16
		Quint Mixture 15.19.22	III	*Rankett	16	Fagotto	16
		Scharf 26.29	II	*Krummhorn	8	Clarion	8
		Contra Fagotto	16	*Schalmei	4	Dulzian	4
		Trumpet	8				
		Clarion	4	*enclosed			

The brief for the organ in this modest-sized Mormon church was that it should be suitable for daily concert performances. American influence is discernible in the console (with couplers controlled by rocking tablets under the music desk), in the generous Swell organ with two

Celestes, and in the Holtkamp-like display layout (which nevertheless contains five dummy pipes). The Pedal organ is to the right, with the Great organ in the centre. The Swell is at the back on two shallow soundboards side-by-side, the shutters being partially concealed by the Pedal Trombone with its 'belled' resonators.

The carpeted chapel has very 'dead' acoustics. The voicing method adopted was to use pipe-scales appropriate to a larger building, but to keep the cut-up low to generate a "sweet" sound agreeable at close quarters. A number of changes were made by N. P. Mander in 1976, mostly to the Positive.

Royal Albert Hall
Willis 1871; Harrison 1926

GREAT (first division)		SWELL		CHOIR AND		PEDAL	
Contra Violone	32	Double Open Diapason	16	ORCHESTRAL		Acoustic Bass	64
Contra Gamba	16	Bourdon	16	(first division: Choir)		Double Open Wood	32
Double Claribel Flute	16	Open Diapason	8	Open Diapason	8	Double Open Diapason	32
Open Diapason I	8	Viola da Gamba	8	Lieblich Gedeckt	8	Contra Violone	32
Open Diapason III	8	Salicional	8	Dulciana	8	Double Quint	21⅓
Open Diapason IV	8	Vox Angelica	8	Gemshorn	4	Open Wood I	16
Viola da Gamba	8	Flûte à Cheminée	8	Lieblich Flute	4	Open Wood II	16
Rohr Flute	8	Claribel Flute	8	Nazard	2⅔	Open Diapason I	16
Quint	5⅓	Principal	4	Flageolet	2	Open Diapason II	16
Principal	4	Viola	4	Tierce	1⅗	Violone	16
Viola	4	Harmonic Flute	4	Mixture 15.19.22	III	Sub Bass	16
Harmonic Flute	4	Octave Quint	2⅔	Trumpet	8	Salicional	16
Octave Quint	2⅔	Super Octave	2	Clarion	4	Viole (in Choir Box)	16
Super Octave	2	Harmonic Piccolo	2			Quint	10⅔
Harmonics		Mixture 8.12.15.19.22	V	(second division:		Octave Wood	8
10.15.17.19.21.22	VI	Furniture 15.19.22.26.29	V	Orchestral)		Principal	8
Contra Tromba	16	Contra Oboe	16	Contra Viole	16	Violoncello	8
Tromba	8	Oboe	8	Violoncello	8	Flute	8
Octave Tromba	4	Baryton	16	Viole d'Orchestre I	8	Octave Quint	5⅓
Posaune	8	Vox Humana	8	Viole d'Orchestre II	8	Super Octave	4
Harmonic Trumpet	8	Double Trumpet	16	Viole Sourdine	8	Harmonics	
Harmonic Clarion	4	Trumpet	8	Violes Celestes (2 rks)	8	10.12.15.17.19.21.22	VII
		Clarion	4	Viole Octaviante	4	Mixture (in Solo box)	
(second division)		Tuba	8	Cornet de Violes		15.19.22.26.29	V
Double Open Diapason	16	Tuba Clarion	4	12.15.17.19.22	V	Double Ophicleide	32
Bourdon	16			Quintaton	16	Double Trombone	
Open Diapason II	8	SOLO AND BOMBARD		Harmonic Flute	8	(in Swell box)	32
Open Diapason V	8	(first division: Solo)		Concert Flute	4	Ophicleide	16
Geigen	8	Contra Bass	16	Harmonic Piccolo	2	Bombard	16
Hohl Flute	8	Flûte à Pavillon	8	Double Clarinet	16	Trombone (in Swell box)	16
Octave	4	Viole d'Amour	8	Clarinet	8	Fagotto	16
Fifteenth	2	Doppel Flute	8	Orchestral Hautboy	8	Trumpet (in Swell box)	16
Mixture 8.12.15.19.22	V	Harmonic Claribel Flute	8	Cor Anglais	8	Clarinet (in Choir box)	16
Cymbale		Unda Maris (2 rks)	8			Bassoon (in Solo box)	16
19.22.26.29.31.33.36	VII	Wald Flute	4	SOLO AND BOMBARD		Quint Trombone	10⅔
		Flauto Traverso	4	(second division: Bombard)		Posaune	8
		Piccolo Traverso	2	Bombardon	16	Clarion	8
		Double Bassoon	16	Tuba	8	Octave Posaune	4
		Corno di Bassetto	8	Orchestral Trumpet	8	Bass Drum	
		Hautboy	8	Cornopean	8		
		Bassoon	8	Quint Trumpet	5⅓		
		Double Horn	16	Orchestral Clarion	4		
		French Horn	8	Sesquialtera			
		Cariollons		12.15.17.19.22	V		
		Tubular Bells		Contra Tuba	16		
				Tuba Mirabilis	8		
				Tuba Clarion	4		

The Albert Hall was an heroic cultural venture and, with its capacity of 6,000 people, demanded an organ on an equally heroic scale, duly supplied by Father Willis with five manuals and 111 stops. The four towers of the pipe-screen contain the only tin-metal 32ft front pipes in Britain, other 32ft fronts being mostly made of zinc. The arrangement of the Great organ, in display between the two largest towers, pre-dates Holtkamp's displayed organ in America by over sixty years.

Alterations to the hall which have improved the acoustics for orchestral performances have not been kind to the organ, and the instrument never had the reputation accorded to its 1875 sister instrument in the Alexandra Palace, Muswell Hill. This instrument, now dismantled, was slightly smaller but had the benefit of a long hall with a seven-second reverberation.

In 1926 the Albert Hall organ was rebuilt by Harrison & Harrison who increased the number of stops whilst reducing the number of manuals to four in conjunction with a new action. More importantly, the instrument was revoiced and the result was an organ of enormous power, based on heavy-pressure reeds, and quite capable of overwhelming a symphony orchestra at full bore. Tonal alterations in 1973 restored some of the upperwork subtracted in 1926 but the instrument still inspires one more by its power than by its charm.

Royal College of Music
Walker 1982

GREAT		POSITIVE		PEDAL	
Stopped Diapason	8	Gedackt	8	Bourdon	16
Principal	4	Chimney Flute	4	Gemshorn	8
Flageolet	2	Nazard	2⅔	Octave	4
Nineteenth	1⅓	Principal	2		
Twenty second	1	Tierce	1⅗		

Placed in a relatively small studio, this 13 stop tracker organ could easily have been over-whelmingly loud. In fact, however, J. W. Walker have succeeded in creating a relatively gentle sound aided, in the case of the 2ft-based Positive, by the use of wood for all the pipework, including two tapered ranks. The three-tower case with 4ft front is in late seventeenth-century style with excellent carved pipe-shades and carved and fretted panels between the towers.

The Royal College of Organists, Concert Hall
Hill Norman & Beard 1967

GREAT		SWELL		CHOIR (enclosed)		PEDAL	
Bourdon	16	Flûte à Cheminée	8	Salicional	8	Principal	16
Open Diapason	8	Viole de Gambe	8	Singendgedackt	8	Sub Bass	16
Stopped Diapason	8	Viole Céleste	8	Spitz Flute	4	Contra Gamba	16
Octave	4	Principal	4	Principal	2	Octave	8
Chimney Flute	4	Flûte Ouverte	4	Larigot	1⅓	Gedackt	8
Wald Flute	2	Nazard	2⅔	Sesquialtera	II	Choralbass	4
Mixture 19.22.26.29	IV	Quarte de Nazard	2	Scharf 26.29.33.36	IV	Mixture 15.19.22	III
Trumpet	8	Tierce	1⅗	Krummhorn	8	Posaune	16
		Mixture 22.26.29	III			Rohrschalmei	4
		Basson	16				
		Hautbois	8				
		Trompette	8				

Although parts of the 1903 Norman & Beard were incorporated, this organ was virtually a new instrument in 1967. It is a large instrument for such an intimate room and the display layout really makes one feel almost inside the organ. To cope with the enormous variation in acoustics between a full room and an empty one, adjustable grilles can be slid in front of the instrument.

Musically, the organ attempts a fusion between the north German style and the British tradition, with more than a nod in the direction of the French classical organ. I was closely involved with Peter Hurford in the creation of this instrument and therefore find it difficult to comment objectively. However, despite the diverse influences in its creation I believe that a surprising unity was achieved in this organ.

Royal College of Organists, Examination Hall
Walker 1965

GREAT		POSITIVE		PEDAL	
Stopped Diapason	8	Rohrflöte	8	Bourdon	16
Principal	4	Quintadena	4	Spitzflöte	8
		Fifteenth	2	Octave Spitzflöte	4

The Chaplin organ, designed as a practice instrument, combines a caseless asymmetric display layout with tracker action to the two unenclosed manuals. The Pedal organ stands to one side and has electric action.

KILBURN St Augustine's Church
Willis 1872; Harrison 1915

GREAT		SWELL		CHOIR		PEDAL	
Double Open Diapason	16	Contra Gamba	16	Viole d'Amour	8	Open Wood	16
Large Open Diapason	8	Open Diapason	8	Rohr Flöte	8	Violone	16
Small Open Diapason	8	Lieblich Gedeckt	8	Dulciana	8	Sub Bass	16
Viola	8	Echo Gamba	8	Gemshorn	4	Violoncello	8
Claribel	8	Voix Celeste	8	Flauto Traverso	4	Ophicleide	16
Octave	4	Principal	4	Harmonic Piccolo	2		
Octave Quint	2⅔	Lieblich Flöte	4	Clarinet	8		
Super Octave	2	Flageolet	2				
Mixture	III	Mixture	III				
Tromba	8	Double Trumpet	16				
Octave Tromba	4	Trumpet	8				
		Oboe	8				
		Vox Humana	8				
		Clarion	4				

This monumental church was designed by J. L. Pearson and the inside is richly decorated. The money, however, ran out before Pearson could provide a case for Father Willis' organ and the instrument is actually quite modest in size for such a church. Harrison & Harrison rebuilt the organ in 1915, providing a tubular-pneumatic action and a four-manual console, though the Solo organ never arrived. Arthur Harrison's tonal changes were restricted to adding a stopped 16ft on the Pedal (not infrequently omitted by Willis), a 16ft Swell reed, fitting smaller-scale string-stops and increasing the wind pressure of the Great reeds. The resulting instrument is basically Father Willis with Harrison touches, and is one of the most successful late Victorian organs in London.

KINGSLAND Catholic Church of Our Lady and St Joseph
Walker 1963

GREAT		POSITIVE		PEDAL	
Holzflöte	8	Spitzflöte	8	Subbass	16
Prinzipal	4	Salicional	8	Quintaton	8
Koppelflöte	4	Rohrflöte	4	Gemshorn	4
Quarte 12.15	II	Prinzipal	2	Nachthorn	2
Nasat	1⅓	Mixtur 19.22	II	Schalmei	4
		Dulzian	8		

New tracker organs were relatively rare in 1963 so this forthright J. W. Walker organ on the west gallery made more impact than one would imagine today. The effective if simple case gives the impression of tone-cabinets and includes tapered pipes from the Pedal Gemshorn on display. Unusually the Positive organ, though unenclosed, has a mild string and the electric-action Pedal organ has, as its only reed, a strong and colourful 4ft Schalmei.

KNIGHTSBRIDGE Brompton Oratory
Walker 1954

GREAT		SWELL		CHOIR (unenclosed)		PEDAL	
Quintadena	16	Baarpijp	8	Gedackt	8	Principal	16
Principal	8	Quintadena	8	Principal	4	Sub Bass	16
Rohrflöte	8	Viola	8	Rohrflöte	4	Quintflöte	10⅔
Octave	4	Céleste	8	Octave	2	Octave	8
Gemshorn	4	Principal	4	Waldflöte	2	Gedackt	8
Quint	2⅔	Gedacktflöte	4	Larigot	1⅓	Rohrquint	5⅓
Superoctave	2	Nazard	2⅔	Sesquialtera	II	Octave	4
Tertian	II	Octave	2	Scharf 26.29.33.36	IV	Nachthorn	2
Mixture 19.22.26.29	IV-V	Gemshorn (cylindrical!)	2	Cromorne	8	Mixture 19.22.26.29	IV
Trumpet	8	Tierce	1⅗			Bombarde	16
		Mixture 22.26.29.33	IV			Trumpet	8
		Cymbel 38.40.43	III			Trumpet	2
		Echo Trumpet	8				
		Vox humana	8				

The original organ was an 1858 Bishop & Starr which had been enlarged to four manuals when moved to the then new Italian baroque-style Oratory in 1884 and altered many times since, latterly by Kingsgate Davidson under the direction of Ralph Downes. This instrument was destroyed by fire in 1950 and replaced by the present J. W. Walker organ, constructed to Ralph Downes' instructions. For its time it was remarkable in the number of neo-classical features incorporated, especially the use of un-nicked flue-pipes voiced with wide-open feet and of low-pressure reeds without loads on the tongues of the bass pipes. The Choir and Great organs stand side-by-side behind the centre of the case and have internal tone-cabinets.

The overall result, as heard at the slightly detached console in front of the instrument, is uneven but has a rude vigour which had been singularly lacking in the British organ of the first half of the century. Sadly, the organ is tucked away somewhat against the roof of a side aisle so this vigour is less obvious to a listener in the nave. The boldly shaped but simple organ screen was designed by Peter Goodridge.

LIMEHOUSE St Anne's Church
Gray & Davison 1851

GREAT		SWELL		CHOIR		PEDAL	
Double Open Diapason	16	Bourdon	16	Dulciana	8	Grand Open Diapason	16
Open Diapason	8	Open Diapason	8	Keraulophon	8	Grand Bourdon	16
Open Diapason	8	Stopped Diapason	8	Clarinet Flute	8	Grand Octave	8
Stopped Diapason	8	Octave	4	Stopped Diapason Bass	8	Grand Bombarde	16
Octave	4	Fifteenth	2	Octave	4		
Stopped Flute	4	Sesquialtera	III	Flute (open)	4		
Twelfth	2⅔	Cornopean	8	Fifteenth	2		
Fifteenth	2	Oboe	8	Clarinet	8		
Flageolet (open)	2	Clarion	4				
Sesquialtera 17.19.22	III						
Mixture 26.29	II						
Posaune	8						
Clarion	4						

Of all the organs made for the Great Exhibition of 1851, this is the only one which survives virtually without change. The instrument came to Hawksmoor's majestic church when the interior was restored by Hardwick after a fire in 1850 and stands, in a case by Albert Howell, on the west gallery. Save for the addition of the bottom octave of the Swell (originally to tenor C), the instrument is as originally built.

In 1851 Davison's organs were less advanced than Hill's. As well as the short-compass Swell, the Pedal organ is less complete, although every Pedal stop is prefixed 'Grand', a frequent Gray & Davison speciality. The sound of this organ reminds one of an earlier period: the reeds have a restricted ferocity characteristic of light-pressure voicing; the sweet and gentle tone of the flue stops is reminiscent of Samuel Green; and the 9 stop Swell was still conceived by Davison as a subsidiary division to the 13 stop Great.

NORTHWOOD Merchant Taylors' School, Great Hall
Harrison 1981

GREAT		SWELL		PEDAL	
Open Diapason	8	Spitzflute	8	Subbass	16
Stopped Diapason	8	Céleste	8	Open Flute	8
Principal	4	Octave	4	Gemshorn	4
Quint	2⅔	Chimney Flute	4	Trombone	16
Gemshorn	2	Fifteenth	2		
Tierce	1⅗	Mixture 19.22.26.29	IV		
Fourniture		Cremona	8		
15.19.22.26	IV-V	Clarion	4		
Trumpet	8				

The case of this two-manual tracker matches the architecture of the hall, but its four compart-ments and single row of bass pipes does not convey the layout of the organ with Swell over Great and the Pedal divided on either side. Cecil Clutton advised the school and wanted some-thing approaching the English reed-based full Swell effect despite the very restricted height available in the swell-box. The combination of a half-length 8ft Cremona and a full-length 4ft Clarion is the result. The other unusual feature of the Swell organ is the use of a Spitzflute as the foundation of the flue chorus.

PADDINGTON Church of St Mary Magdalene
Compton 1932

GREAT		SWELL		CHOIR		PEDAL	
Double Diapason	16	Salicional	16	Salicional	16	Sub Bass	32
Bourdon	16	Diapason	8	Rohr Bordun	16	Open Wood	16
First Diapason	8	Rohr Gedeckt	8	Diapason	8	Contra Basso	16
Second Diapason	8	Salicional	8	Melodic Diapason	8	Bourdon	16
Third Diapason	8	Voix Celestes	8	Stopped Diapason	8	Salicional	16
Stopped Diapason	8	Octave	4	Rohr Gedeckt	8	Octave	8
Flauto Traverso	8	Rohr Flöte	4	Viola de Gamba	8	Flute	8
Quint	5⅓	Salicet	4	Viole Celeste	8	Salicional	8
Octave	4	Fifteenth	2	Salicional	8	Flute Octave	4
Principal	4	Cymbale	IV	Dulciana	8	Harmonics	VI
Flute	4	Fagottone	16	Vox Angelica	8	Trombone	16
Twelfth	2⅔	Trumpet	8	Principal	4	Fagottone	16
Super Octave	2	Fagotto	8	Flute	4	Tromba	8
Fifteenth	2	Hautboy	8	Rohr Flöte	4	Fagotto	8
Plein Jeu	VI	Clarion	4	Salicet	4		
Contra Posaune	16			Nasard	2⅔		
Tromba	8			Fifteenth	2		
Posaune	8			Flauto Piccolo	2		
Clarion	4			Kleine Flöte	2		
				Tierce	1⅗		
				Acuta	III		
				Trombone	16		
				Fagottone	16		
				Tromba	8		
				Fagotto	8		
				Clarinet	8		
				Clarion	4		

This is one of G. E. Street's most striking churches, completed in 1872, with a prominent thin spire, and standing adjacent to the Grand Union Canal. The organ is one of John Compton's more successful large unit instruments, although uncharacteristic in that it incorporates, without extension, pipes from the former Hedgeland/Garrard instrument. John Compton used high wind pressures to counteract the position of the organ in two enclosed chambers in the tower. The instrument retains its luminous push-stop console and is now one of the few unaltered examples of its period. The church crypt has a Casson Positive with a pretty painted case.

St Mary's Church, Paddington Green
Collins 1978

GREAT		CHOIR		PEDAL	
Open Diapason	8	Chimney Flute	8	Bourdon	16
Stopt Diapason	8	Principal	4	Principal	8
Principal	4	Twelfth	2⅔	Gemshorn	4
Flute	4	Fifteenth	2	Bassoon	16
Fifteenth	2	Tierce	1⅗		
Mixture	II-IV	Two and Twenty	1		
Trumpet	8	Hautboy	8		

The restoration of this late eighteenth-century church has shorn it of Gothic accretions. It is now a most handsome building, enhanced by Peter Collins' organ on the west gallery. The case, designed by Quinlan Terry, uses characteristic eighteenth-century forms and ornaments. The construction of the instrument is notably compact, fitting a two-manual and Pedal tracker-action instrument into a commendably shallow case. The second manual, though with the mutations essential for French music, owes as much to the eighteenth-century English Choir organ as to the German Positive. The overall tone, in this small church, has a pronounced "sweetness" which, one suspects, would not have been foreign to Thomas Elliot.

ST MARY'S CHURCH, PADDINGTON GREEN

ROTHERHITHE St Mary's Church
Byfield 1765; Gray & Davison 1882

GREAT		SWELL		CHOIR		PEDAL	
*Open Diapason	8	*Double Diapason	16	*Stopd Diapason	8	Grand Bourdon	16
†Open Diapason	8	†Open Diapason	8	*Principal	4		
*Stopd Diapason	8	*Stopd Diapason	8	*Flute	4	*Byfield 1765.	
*Principal	4	*Principal	4	*Fifteenth	2	†Russell 1816 or 1829.	
*Twelfth	3	Fifteenth	2	†Cremona	8		
*Fifteenth	2	*Oboe	8				
*Sesquialtera 15.19.22	III	*Trumpet	8				
Cornet	V						
*Trumpet	8						
Clarion	4						

This is one of the great survivors of the eighteenth-century British organ. Byfield's original stop-list is given in chapter 3 (see p 77) and almost two-thirds of his original pipes remain, plus the splendid three-tower case with its intricate carved and pierced panels and trumpet-playing angels atop the outer towers. Hugh Russell, a pupil of England, made a few tonal alterations in the early nineteenth century, also adding a small pedalboard, without pipes.

The only major changes came in 1882 when the compass of the Great and Choir organs was reduced from GG to CC, the Swell extended from fiddle G down to CC, and the lone Pedal stop provided. Fortunately, the organ was left in the west gallery, against the fashion of the time, and Gray & Davison took a very conservative line, retaining the original Great and Choir organ soundboards and making only minor changes to the pipework. The organ was restored in 1959 by Noel Mander, who changed the Great and Choir organs back almost to their 1765 specifications.

There remains an enigma, however. Inspection of the organ case shows it to have been extended rearwards in rough pine wainscot-work, the mahogany case only being deep enough for the present Great organ. Furthermore, the console has clearly been enlarged from two manuals to three. Yet parish records show that the organ was always its present size! The answer may be hidden in the fact that the organ was relatively cheap. Perhaps Byfield made it up from a cancelled order for a two-manual instrument, adding the newly fashionable Swell organ to secure a sale?

SHOREDITCH St Leonard's Church
Bridge 1754

Although outside the City, George Dance's church, built after the collapse of the medieval building, is very much in the mould of the City of London churches. Like them, it retains a fine eighteenth-century organ case on the west gallery. This has three towers with two-storey flats and gabled cornices, a design which Bridge (and others) copied from the later instruments of Renatus Harris. It is a particularly fine specimen, in mahogany, retaining the bishop's mitres on top of the side-towers and the crown on the centre tower which were symbolic of the Restoration of the monarchy after the Commonwealth.

SOUTHALL St George's Church
? Jordan 1723; Speechly 1884

One receives something of a shock on entering this Edwardian suburban church and finding the superb front of an eighteenth-century organ case on the wall. It was built for the now-destroyed church of St George, Botolph Lane in the City of London, reputedly by Abraham Jordan, and has the ogee-shaped flats and rich carving later associated with Richard Bridge.

Not all the organ is old, however. Hill had added a Swell in 1862 but the present Swell organ is Henry Speechly's work, and the organ lost its lower casework when the organ was moved to Southall in 1908. Many of the Great organ pipes are eighteenth century and may be even older. The Botolph Lane church had an organ before 1708 and the Great organ pipes are much like Father Smith's, so they could be survivors from the seventeenth century, re-used in 1723.

ST LEONARD'S CHURCH, SHOREDITCH

SOUTH BANK Royal Festival Hall (see Plate 8)
Harrison 1954

The success of the Royal Festival Hall organ occurred against all the odds. Everything was against it from the start. The acoustics were a fundamental factor. Hope Bagenal, the acoustician, wanted clarity above all else; he had a horror of bass reverberation. His theories combined with errors of construction to produce a most unforgiving hall in which a dozen double-bass players could saw away without apparent audible effect. More recently, the bass has been enhanced with electronic reverberation, to everyone's benefit, not least the organ, but 'dryness' is still the main characteristic of the hall.

Then there was the position of the instrument. The original plan was for an organ hidden in the roof space; the present arrangement with the instrument spread wide behind the orchestra only came about because Ralph Downes, the consultant, threatened to resign otherwise and was supported in his attitude by the late Sir Thomas Beecham. Even then, the appearance of

221

GREAT

Principal	16
Gedacktpommer	16
Principal	8
Diapason	8
Harmonic Flute	8
Rohrgedackt	8
Quintflute	5⅓
Octave I-II	4
Gemshorn	4
Quintadena	4
Quint	2⅔
Superoctave	2
Blockflute	2
Tierce	1⅗
Mixture 15.19.22.26.29	V
Sharp Mixture 26.29.33.36	IV
Cornet	V
Bombarde	16
Trumpet	8
Clarion	4

SWELL

Quintadena	16
Diapason	8
Gemshorn	8
Quintadena	8
Viola	8
Celeste	8
Principal	4
Koppelflute	4
Nazard	2⅔
Octave	2
Openflute	2
Tierce	1⅗
Flageolet	1
Mixture 22.26.29.33	IV-VI
Cymbel 38.40.43	III
Bombarde	16
Trumpet	8
Hautboy	8
Vox Humana	8
Clarion	4

CHOIR (enclosed)

Salicional	16
Open Wood	8
Stopped Wood	8
Salicional	8
Unda Maris	8
Spitzoctave	4
Openflute	4
Principal	2
Quint	1⅓
Octave	1
Sesquialtera	II
Mixture 29.33.36.40	IV
Cromorne	8
Schalmei	4

POSITIVE

Principal	8
Gedackt	8
Quintadena	8
Octave	4
Rohrflute	4
Rohrnazard	2⅔
Spitzflute	2
Tierce	1⅗
Larigot	1⅓
Mixture 15.19.22.26.29	V
Sharp Mixture 22.26.29.33.36	V
Carillon 29.38	II-III
Trumpet (enclosed with Choir)	8
Dulzian (enclosed with Choir)	8

SOLO (enclosed)

Diapason	8
Rohrflute	8
Octave	4
Waldflute	2
Rauschquint 12.15	II
Tertian	II
Mixture 19.22.22.26.29.33	VI
Basset Horn	16
Harmonic Trumpet	8
Harmonic Clarion	4

PEDAL

Principal	32
Majorbass	16
Principal	16
Sub Bass	16
Salicional	16
Quintadena	16
Quintflute	10⅔
Octavebass	8
Gedackt	8
Quintadena	8
Nazard	5⅓
Superoctave	4
Spitzflute	4
Openflute	2
Septerz 17.21	II
Rauschquint 12.15	II
Mixture 19.22.26.29.33	V
Bombarde	32
Bombarde	16
Dulzian	16
Trumpet	8
Cromorne	8
Clarion	4
Schalmei	4
Cornett	2

the organ caused many battles; the initial designs showed dull screens of bass pipes which, fortunately, never quite satisfied all parties. Despairing of agreement, Cuthbert Harrison laid out the instrument as if hidden behind a grille but, at the last moment, the Leader of the London County Council demanded to be able to see his 'expensive pipes'. Thus the grille was omitted and the present neo-Holtkamp open display came about, almost by accident. The somewhat curious 'motif' of dummy pipes was designed by the architect, Sir Leslie Martin, to hide Harrison's double-rise bellows. The wooden pipes in this display, by an odd irony, are so grossly overscaled as to be reminiscent of Hope-Jones' Tibias, the complete antithesis of everything which, musically, this organ stands for.

The Royal Festival Hall organ was, in fact, very much the precursor in Britain of the neo-classical instrument which had found favour on the Continent as a result of the *Orgelbewegung* (Organ Reform Movement). It could easily have been another instrument in the Hope-Jones/Arthur Harrison tradition, but the appointment of Ralph Downes ensured fresh thought and he undertook prodigious research in the course of the design. Downes had been greatly influenced by the French organ and his initial specification was largely inspired by Cavaillé-Coll with a dash of Clicquot. This gradually changed to a more eclectic scheme and, influenced by a journey to Holland, a Dutch Positive was combined with an almost American Solo organ. In the end, however, the latter was sacrificed for the provision of another Diapason Chorus on the fifth manual division, as Downes was concerned that in the unfavourable acoustics the organ might lack the power to lead massed singing. Thus the instrument today has a 32ft-based Pedal organ chorus, a 16ft-based Great, an 8ft-based Positive and 8ft-based enclosed Swell, Solo and Choir divisions. This arrangement has been criticised for an element of repetition though, in practice, it undoubtedly clinches the artistic unity of the instrument. The five manual divisions are controlled from a four-manual electropneumatic console. The technology to control an organ of this size with tracker action was not available at the time, and is questionable even now.

222

If the stop-list caused a stir on publication, the pipe-scales and voicing methods ensured continued debate. Ralph Downes had learned in Holland of the style of flue-pipe voicing without nicks and with open pipe-feet which had been espoused by the *Orgelbewegung*. Although completely outside the tradition of the Harrison firm, virtually the entire fluework was voiced on this principle under Downes' detailed practical guidance. Other than Lady Jeans' 1936 house organ, this was the first complete organ in Britain to which the technique had been applied. In the hands of subsequent imitators these methods led to a somewhat rough and aggressive effect but, at the Royal Festival Hall, Harrison's tradition of careful regulation helped Downes to minimise this tendency. It is usual in Britain for the organ-builder to choose the pipe-scales but, as the musical design was so new to the builders, all the pipe-scales were determined by Ralph Downes, based on scales given by the eighteenth-century French writer Dom Bedos de Celles. These scales were modified by reference to those used by Arp Schnitger, the eighteenth-century north German builder, and by advice from a number of Continental builders. At the time and in such strange acoustics these methods seemed to be adventurous, even foolhardy, but Downes' empiricism and attention to detail made them work surprisingly well. The reed-stops caused still more argument, having been voiced by the French voicer Louis-Eugène Rochesson, who worked entirely without loads on the tongues of the reeds even down to 32ft CCCC, a practice that, at the time, was unheard of in Britain.

The result is a unique instrument with basically Dutch-type fluework combined with Clicquot-like French reeds. The opening recitals were a sensation; one lady musician is alleged to have said to her husband, when the full-organ piston was pressed, "Darling, it's boiling". Nevertheless, the instrument had been eminently successful, attracting consistent audiences for regular solo recitals. Although it spawned no direct successors, the Royal Festival Hall organ undoubtedly legitimised the neo-classical organ in the minds of the musical public and, as such, has had a marked general effect on the design of the British organ.

Queen Elizabeth Hall
Flentrop 1967

GREAT		SWELL		PEDAL	
Chimney Flute	8	Stopped Diapason	8	Sub Bass	16
Principal	4	Koppel Flute	4	Principal	8
Stopped Flute	4	Octave	2	Stopped Flute	8
Spitz Flute	2	Nazard	1⅓	Spitz Flute	4
Sesquialtera	II	Cremona	8		
Mixture	III				

Designed by Ralph Downes, this Dutch-built organ is seldom seen by visitors, since it is stored below stage and brought up by lift when required. To suit the lift, it is notably compact, with the Swell organ behind the Great and on the same level, the shutters opening into the back of the Great tone-cabinet. The tone-cabinets are starkly expressed, without pipe-shades or decoration. The instrument is very competent but, in an auditorium of 1,100 seats, it is rather small for solo performance whilst being more than generous for continuo.

SPITALFIELDS Christchurch
Bridge 1730; Gray & Davison 1852, 1884

Hawksmoor's immense church houses an historic organ, almost contemporary with the church and still in its original position high at the west end. When built, it was the largest organ in England and has one of the richest of Richard Bridge's characteristic cases, with ogee-shaped 'flats' between the three towers and abundant carving in the curved panels beneath them. The only substantial rebuild has been by Gray & Davison, and the instrument still retains its original console and GG compass for the Great and Choir organs. Even in 1877 Hopkins recorded that it was 'one of the best in the metropolis'. Unfortunately, the organ is now silent, awaiting the time when the church restoration can be completed.

STEPNEY St Paul's Church, Shadwell
Jordan 1712; Elliot 1820; Hill 1847; Hunter c1910

GREAT		SWELL		PEDAL	
Open Diapason	8	Double	16	Bourdon	16
Stopped Diapason	8	Open Diapason	8		
Gamba	8	Stopped Diapason	8		
Principal	4	Principal	4		
Flute	4	Fifteenth	2		
Fifteenth	2	Cornopean	8		
Sesquialtera	II	Oboe	8		
Trumpet	8				

This is an instrument which has been 'discovered' only recently, being fundamentally much older than appears at first sight. As originally built by Jordan, the second manual was a combined Choir and short-compass Echo. It seems not to have been a GG-compass instrument; the case pipes go down only to 6ft F. The cherubs over the case flats are presumed to be Jordan's work but the rest of the case was gothicised by Elliot in 1820 when the organ was moved to the present church, then new. The instrument was placed in a curious position in an eastern gallery, and the Great organ compass extended down to GG. In 1847 the interior of the church was re-ordered by Butterfield, the eastern gallery demolished and the organ moved to its present position at the west end. William Hill undertook this work, adding a tenor C Swell organ made from the old pipes, and a 25 note Pedal, still remaining. The Great Gamba arrived in the 1880s, and Hunter finally extended the Swell compass down to CC around 1910.

Even though twice moved, this organ still retains a large amount of original work, largely because there has never been enough money for wholesale changes. Even retuning to equal temperament has been incomplete. The exact amount of Jordan pipework surviving remains to be determined but if, as claimed, the Great Trumpet is Jordan's work this, on its own, would be a remarkable survival.

STREATHAM St Leonard's Church
Walker 1979

GREAT		SWELL		PEDAL	
Principal	8	Chimney Flute	8	Bourdon	16
Stopped Diapason	8	Viola da Gamba	8	Octave Bass	8
Octave	4	Voix Celeste	8	Bass Flute	8
Nazard	2⅔	Venetian Flute	4	Nachthorn	4
Block Flute	2	Principal	2	Gemshorn	2
Mixture 19.22.26	III	Sharp Mixture 22.26.29	III	Bombarde	16
Trompette	8	Contra Cromorne	16		
		Trumpet	8		

The organ stands on the west gallery of this Gothic Revival church which was refurnished following a fire. The organ has a simple three-tower case with copper front pipes plus modest side-towers with wooden Pedal pipes. Despite appearances, this J. W. Walker tracker-action instrument is not really a *werk* principle organ, the Swell being behind the Great. In practice, however, this arrangement works very well and, since the Venetian Flute is really a wide-scaled Principal, this is a real Swell, not an enclosed Positive.

SYDENHAM Church of Our Lady and St Philip Neri (Roman Catholic)
Mander 1977

GREAT		POSITIVE		PEDAL	
Chimney Flute	8	Gedact	8	Subbass	16
Principal	4	Koppel Flute	4	Quintaton	8
Recorder	2	Principal	2		
Mixture 19.22.26	III-IV				

This very small two-manual tracker-action instrument is remarkable for its curious layout. The Great organ is in a chair case on the edge of the gallery, behind the player. This leaves the

Positive (with folding shutters) on its own above the console, flanked by the divided Pedal. The tone-cabinet case is plain and without pipe-shades.

TWICKENHAM All Hallows Church
Harris 1695; Gray & Davison 1870

GREAT		SWELL		CHOIR		PEDAL	
Bourdon	16	Open Diapason	8	Stopped Flute	8	Major Bass	16
*Open Diapason	8	Stopped Diapason	8	Dulciana	8	Bourdon	16
*Stopped Diapason	8	Principal	4	Dulciana Celeste	8	Octave Bass	8
*Principal	4	Fifteenth	2	Wood Flute	4	Bourdon	8
Nason Flute	4	Sesquialtera	II	Block Flute	2	Bourdon	4
*Twelfth	2⅔	Mixture	II			Posaune	16
*Fifteenth	2	Krummhorn	16			Krummhorn	16
Furniture	III	Cornopean	8				
Trumpet	8						
		*Harris pipes.					

This organ, despite several rebuildings, is one of our best survivals of the work of Renatus Harris. Built by him as a 9 stop one-manual, five of the original stops remain, together with the interesting case. The case is unusual, even by Harris' standards, having a wide circular compartment in the lower storey with a short central tower, flanked by conventional side flats, above. The front pipes, instead of being gilded, are of burnished tin metal.

The instrument is effectively now a Gray & Davison three-manual, built within the original case, which was made deeper to cover it, but retaining the Harris chorus on the Great organ. The organ had a narrow escape when the church for which the instrument had been built, All Hallows, Lombard Street, in the City of London, became unsafe and the instrument was transferred, in 1940, to the new church at Twickenham, along with the other furnishings. In a pioneer work of conservation under the guidance of Cecil Clutton, the instrument was placed on the west gallery, tracker action largely being retained.

WEST END All Saints Church, Margaret Street
Hill 1858; Harrison 1910, 1957

GREAT		SWELL		CHOIR (enclosed)		PEDAL	
Double Open Diapason	16	Bourdun	16	Contra Dulciana	16	Double Open Wood	32
Large Open Diapason	8	Open Diapason	8	Open Diapason	8	Open Wood	16
Small Open Diapason	8	Flauto Traverso	8	Lieblich Gedeckt	8	Large Open Diapason	16
Stopped Diapason	8	Echo Gamba	8	Echo Clarabella	8	Small Open Diapason	16
Harmonic Flute	8	Voix Célestes	8	Salicional	8	Sub Bass	16
Octave	4	Principal	4	Vox Angelica	8	Dulciana	16
Principal	4	Suabe Flöte	4	Spitzflöte	4	Octave Wood	8
Octave Quint	2⅔	Fifteenth	2	Lieblich Flöte	4	Principal	8
Super Octave	2	Mixture 19.22.26	III	Lieblich Piccolo	2	Flute	8
Mixture 19.22.26.29	IV	Oboe	8	Sesquialtera 12.17	II	Violoncello	8
Double Trumpet		Contra Fagotto	16	Mixture 15.19.22	III	Fifteenth	4
(enclosed)	16	Trumpet	8	Cornopean	8	Ophicleide	16
Trumpet (enclosed)	8	Clarion	4			Trumpet	16
Clarion (enclosed)	4			SOLO (enclosed)		Cor Anglais	16
				Cor Anglais	16	Posaune	8
				Clarinet	8	Clarion	8
				Violoncello	8	Octave Clarion	4
				Hohl Flöte	8		
				Orchestral Flute	4		
				Orchestral Trumpet	8		
				Tuba (unenclosed)	8		

All Saints, Margaret Street maintained its own choir school until relatively recently and has a reputation for the best High Church music in London. Architecturally, it is William Butterfield's best-known work, the patterned brickwork and internal polychrome producing an archetypal High Victorian church. Although the nave has only three bays, the lofty construction has produced a good acoustic.

Arthur Harrison rebuilt and enlarged William Hill's relatively modest three-manual and created one of the smoothest of all the Harrison instruments. It is, of course, very large for the building, but the size is used, not to create a big sound, but rather to provide a very wide range of romantic effects, each more refined than the last. The rebuild in 1957 under Cuthbert Harrison provided electropneumatic action in place of tubular pneumatic. Minor tonal changes included revoicing the 8ft Diapasons without Arthur Harrison's leathered lips. Nevertheless, this organ remains a typical Arthur Harrison instrument, a characteristic not altered by the addition in 1972 of the smooth Tuba which Harrison had revoiced for Gloucester Cathedral in 1920.

Church of the Annunciation, Bryanston Street, Marble Arch
Rothwell 1914

This narrow church has an exotic and highly decorated organ case by Sir Walter Tapper, once a pupil of Bodley. The organ itself is undistinguished but has one of the Rothwell brothers' characteristic and intricately made consoles with stop-keys placed between the manuals.

St George's Church, Hanover Square
Gerard Smith 1724; Hope-Jones 1894; Harrison 1972

GREAT		SWELL		POSITIVE		PEDAL	
Quintadena	16	Viola	8	Gedackt	8	Sub Bass	32
Open Diapason	8	Rohrflöte	8	Principal	4	Open Metal	16
Viole	8	Gamba	8	Spitzflute	4	Quintadena	16
Stopped Diapason	8	Voix Celeste	8	Nazard	2⅔	Bourdon	16
Octave	4	Principal	4	Octave	2	Octave	8
Stopped Flute	4	Open Flute	4	Tierce	1⅗	Stopped Flute	8
Fifteenth	2	Gemshorn	2	Cimbal	III	Fifteenth	4
Sesquialtera	II	Mixture	III	Trumpet	8	Choral Bass	4
Mixture	IV	Contra Fagotto	16			Mixture	II
Trumpet	8	Trumpet	8	CHOIR		Trombone	16
		Oboe	8	Open Diapason	8	Fagotto	16
		Clarion	4	Lieblich Gedackt	8	Trumpet	8
				Flauto Traverso	4	Schalmei	4
				Flageolet	2		
				Larigot	1⅓		
				Corno di Bassetto	8		
				Tuba	8		

The three-tower case of Gerard Smith's eighteenth-century case was widened by Blomfield to no less than five towers and six flats to accommodate Hope-Jones' organ, even though it also overflowed into the tower. The current Harrison instrument is also a big organ and, apart from some pipes, was new in 1972. The Positive organ is outside the old case and stands in a pastiche case in front of the organ in the position where, normally, the console would be found. The three-manual console is detached on the north gallery. The compact Hope-Jones console also remains in its original position on the floor at the east end, though now without the semicircular sweep of stop-tablets which made it important as the ancestor of the theatre organ horseshoe console.

St James' Church, Piccadilly (see Plate 3)
Harris 1686; Bishop 1852

Renatus Harris built an organ for the Royal 'Popish Chapel' in Whitehall. On the death of James II it was given by Queen Mary to St James' Church where it was re-erected in 1691. The case of this instrument, with its typically Harris 'round-shouldered' flats, still survives complete with *putti* and angels blowing trumpets on top of the tower cornices. Harris' front pipes also remain, with a characteristic variety of pipe-mouth shapes.

The Harris case acquired a new inside in 1852 when J. C. Bishop built what was otherwise a new instrument, retaining only a few of Harris' pipes. Bishop's Choir organ was placed in a relatively scholarly pastiche of a seventeenth-century chair case. In this century the instrument received an unfortunate rebuilding by Rothwell, with a massive swell-box projecting over the top of the case and the chair case left empty.

The Jesuit Church, Farm Street, Mayfair
Anneesens 1887; Willis 1926; Bishop 1979

GREAT		SWELL		CHOIR		PEDAL	
Quintaton	16	Geigen Diapason	8	Flûte Harmonique	8	Resultant Bass	32
Open Diapason	8	Rohrflöte	8	Viola	8	Open Bass	16
Stopped Diapason	8	Aeoline	8	Voix Célestes	8	Subbass	16
Gemshorn	8	Vox Angelica	8	Prestant	4	Quintaton	16
Principal	4	Echo Viole	8	Flauto Traverso	4	Principal	8
Flûte Octaviante	4	Octave Geigen	4	Nazard	2⅔	Flute	8
Twelfth	2⅔	Flûte à Echo	4	Piccolo	2	Quint	5⅓
Fifteenth	2	Piccolo	1	Tierce	1⅗	Superoctave	4
Mixture 17.19.22	III	Plein Jeu 15.19.22	III	Clarinet	8	Octave flute	4
Sharp Mixture 22.24.26	III	Waldhorn	16	Tuba Minor	8	Trombone	16
Trompette Harmonique	8	Oboe	8			Trumpet	8
Clarion	4	Trumpet	8				
		Clarion	4				

Standing divided in the west gallery and originally built by Anneesens of Belgium, this organ was substantially reconstructed by Henry Willis III in 1926. The importance of the instrument rests not so much on what it is now but on the milestone which it represented in British organ design in 1926. Encouraged by Guy Weitz, Willis achieved in this organ the first step away from the romantic tide which had culminated in the work of Robert Hope-Jones. Seen from a perspective of over fifty years later, one is perhaps distracted from the Choir organ mutations and from the Great organ chorus-work – remarkable at the time but which today we take for granted – by such 1920s features as reeds on heavy pressure.

St John's Church, Hyde Park Crescent
Hill 1865; Rushworth & Dreaper 1924

GREAT		SWELL		CHOIR		PEDAL	
Double Open Diapason	16	Bourdon	16	Dulciana	8	Open Diapason	16
Open Diapason	8	Open Diapason	8	Stopped Diapason	8	Violone	16
Cone Gamba	8	Stopped Diapason	8	Corno Flute	8	Bourdon	16
Stopped Diapason	8	Echo Gamba	8	Suabe Flute	4	Principal	8
Principal	4	Voix Celeste	8	Flautina	2	Flute	8
Wald Flute	4	Principal	4	Clarinet	8	Trombone	16
Twelfth	2⅔	Fifteenth	2				
Fifteenth	2	Mixture	II				
Mixture	IV	Cornopean	8				
Posaune	8	Oboe	8				

A superb example of the later work of William Hill, this organ originally stood on the west gallery and was moved by Hill to its present position at the east end of the north aisle in 1880. The stop-list includes Hill's favourite Cone Gamba on the Great and a very early wooden Violone on the Pedal. The reeds were revoiced in 1924 when tubular-pneumatic action was fitted but the organ remains essentially Hill, powerful without being over-assertive and a fine example of Victorian organ-building.

Church of St Martin's-in-the-Fields, Trafalgar Square
Hill 1912; Rutt 1937

The classical layout of the double case of this west-end organ is an unusual example of Victorian historical consciousness, even though the details are ponderous and wholly mid-Victorian. It contained an 1854 Bevington three-manual of 54 stops, replaced in 1912 by a slightly smaller instrument by Hill. This organ was much enlarged by Rutt, gaining an east-end division and a console at the east end of the north gallery featuring his patent luminous stop-tablets which, when on, glow in various colours according to their function.

Odeon Cinema, Leicester Square
Compton 1937

This five-manual instrument of 16 units was the last large Compton theatre organ to be made and is certainly the only five-manual ever to be installed in a British cinema. Its effect is unfortunately muffled by the unusual position of the pipework under the stage, but it remains almost the only cinema instrument to stay in regular use in its original home.

WESTMINSTER Westminster Abbey
Shrider & Jordan 1727; Hill 1848, 1884; Harrison 1937, 1983

GREAT		CHOIR		SOLO (enclosed)		PEDAL	
Double Geigen	16	Upper Division (enclosed)		Contra Viole	16	*On the Screen*	
Bourdon	16	Claribel Flute	8	Viole d'Orchestre	8	Open Diapason	16
Open Diapason I	8	*Stopped Flute		Viole Céleste	8	Geigen	16
Open Diapason II	8	(tuned sharp)	8	Viole Octaviante	4	Bourdon	16
Geigen	8	Viola da Gamba	8	Cornet de Violes	III	Principal	8
Hohl Flute	8	Gemshorn	4	Harmonic Flute	8	Bass Flute	8
Stopped Diapason	8	Flauto Traverso	4	Concert Flute	4	Fifteenth	4
Octave	4	*Nason (tuned sharp)	4	Harmonic Piccolo	2	Rohr Flute	4
Geigen Principal	4	Gemshorn Fifteenth	2	Double Clarinet	16	Open Flute	2
Wald Flute	4	Mixture	II	Clarinet	8	Mixture	IV
Octave Quint	2⅔	Cornopean	8	Cor Anglais	8	Contra Posaune	16
Super Octave	2			Orchestral Hautboy	8	Posaune	8
Mixture	V	Lower Division		Contra Tuba	16	Octave Posaune	4
Sharp Mixture	III	(unenclosed)		Tuba	8		
Harmonics	IV	Open Diapason	8	Orchestral Trumpet	8	*In the Triforium*	
Contra Posaune	16	Rohr Flute	8	French Horn	8	Double Open Wood	32
Posaune	8	Principal	4	Tuba Mirabilis	8	Open Wood I	16
Octave Posaune	4	Open Flute	4	(unenclosed)	8	Open Wood II	16
		Nazard	2⅔			Viole	16
SWELL		Fifteenth	2	BOMBARDE		Double Ophicleide	32
Quintaton	16	Blockflute	2	Contra Posaune		Ophicleide	16
Open Diapason	8	Tierce	1⅗	(from Great organ)	16	Tuba	16
Lieblich Gedeckt	8	Mixture	IV	Posaune		Clarinet	16
Salicional	8	Cremona	8	(from Great organ)	8		
Vox Angelica	8			Octave Posaune		*Reputed Jordan or even	
Principal	4			(from Great organ)	4	Smith pipes.	
Lieblich Flute	4			Tuba Mirabilis			
Twelfth	2⅔			(from Solo)	8		
Fifteenth	2						
Seventeenth	1⅗						
Mixture	V						
Contra Oboe	16						
Oboe	8						
Double Trumpet	16						
Trumpet	8						
Clarion	4						

The Westminster Abbey organ was the first cathedral instrument to be removed from a central place on the choir screen by the Victorian Oxford Movement reformers. It was built as a three-manual by Shrider & Jordan; Avery added pedals and 10⅔ft Pedal pipes, and Elliot added 21ft Pedal pipes. The instrument was completely reconstructed by Hill in 1848, when the organ was divided either end of the screen, though the Choir department remained in the chair case. In other respects this scheme was archaic, with a Great organ compass to 16ft CCC and only two Pedal stops – 16ft and 32ft Open Diapasons, the latter being laid horizontally across the screen. The Hill firm rebuilt the organ again in 1884, this time with the conventional CC compass and heavy wind for the reeds. They also placed some of the instrument up in the south triforium and, in 1895, added a remote Celestial organ, controlled by electric action and placed in the triforium of the south transept.

The instrument received its present character in 1937 at the hands of Arthur Harrison, when it reverted back from five manuals to four, the Celestial organ being disconnected (though it still exists). In 1982–3 Harrisons substantially revoiced the instrument to the present stop-list. The unenclosed section of the Choir organ is now effectively a Positive in all but name. The console has been rebuilt with five manuals, not to reconnect the Celestial organ but for a 'prepared-for' Bombarde organ in the north triforium to help lead singing in the nave, always a weak point in divided organs, where the two halves of the instrument shout at each other rather than down the length of the building.

J. L. Pearson's organ cases at Westminster Abbey are not so very old, having been made in 1899, yet their blend of classical form with exuberant Gothic detail is not only surprisingly scholarly but of a richness appropriate to a national monument. Each case not only includes a mock chair-front but is also double-sided, there being almost equally rich back-cases facing the aisles. These are in plain oak, lacking the spectacular gilding, colour and pattern which Stephen Dykes Bower applied to the nave fronts when they were re-erected in 1959.

Westminster Cathedral (Roman Catholic)
Willis 1922–32; Harrison 1984

GRAND ORGAN

GREAT

Stop	Pitch
Double Open Diapason	16
Bourdon	16
Open Diapason 1	8
Open Diapason 2	8
Open Diapason 3	8
Flûte Harmonique	8
Quint	5⅓
Octave	4
Principal	4
Flûte Couverte	4
Tenth	3⅕
Octave Quint	2⅔
Twelfth	2⅔
Super Octave	2
Fifteenth	2
Grand Chorus 15.19.22.26.29	V
Double Trumpet	16
Trumpet	8
Clarion	4

CHOIR (enclosed)

Stop	Pitch
Contra Dulciana	16
Open Diapason	8
Viola	8
Cor-de-Nuit	8
Cor-de-nuit Célestes	8
Sylvestrina	8
Gemshorn	4
Nason Flute	4
(unenclosed)	
Nazard } stopped	2⅔
Octavin } pipes	2
Tierce }	1⅗
Trumpet	8

SWELL

Stop	Pitch
Violon	16
Geigen Diapason	8
Rohr Flute	8
Echo Viole	8
Violes Célestes	8
Octave Geigen	4
Suabe Flute (triangular)	4
Twelfth	2⅔
Fifteenth	2
Harmonics 17.19.22	III
Vox Humana	8
Oboe	8
Waldhorn	16
Trompette	8
Clarion	4

SOLO (enclosed)

Stop	Pitch
Quintaten	16
Violoncello	8
'Cello Célestes	8
Tibia	8
Salicional	8
Unda Maris	8
Concert Flute	4
Piccolo Harmonique	2
Cor Anglais	16
Corno-di-Bassetto	8
Orchestral Oboe	8
French Horn	8
Orchestral Trumpet	8
Tuba Magna (unenclosed)	8

PEDAL

Stop	Pitch
Double Open Bass	32
Open Bass	16
Open Diapason	16
Contra Bass	16
Sub Bass	16
Violon	16
Dulciana	16
Octave	8
Principal	8
Flute	8
Super Octave	4
Seventeenth	3⅕
Nineteenth	2⅔
Twenty-second	2
Contra Trombone	32
Trombone (heavy wind)	16
Octave Trombone	8
Bombarde (very heavy wind)	16

APSE SECTION

GREAT

Stop	Pitch
Open Diapason	8
Stopped Diapason	8
Principal	4
Open Flute	4
Fifteenth	2
Mixture	III
Trumpet	8

SWELL

Stop	Pitch
Gedeckt	8
Salicional	8
Unda Maris	8
Gemshorn	4
Spitzflute	2
Mixture	III
Contra Hautboy	16
Cornopean	8

PEDAL

Stop	Pitch
Acoustic Bass	32
Open Diapason	16
Bourdon	16
Principal	8
Flute	8
Fifteenth	4

Henry Willis III built two heroic organs: Liverpool Cathedral (Anglican) and Westminster Cathedral (Roman Catholic). The Westminster Cathedral instrument is still an almost unaltered example of his work.

The origins of the instrument lie in the Apse organ, built by T. C. Lewis before World War I, which stands divided either side of the apse at the east end of the cathedral in two fretted and carved wardrobe-like cases. Henry Willis III, who had taken over the Lewis firm in 1918, built thé 78 stop Grand organ on the gallery at the west end in stages over the ten years between 1922 and 1932. It is controlled from a four-manual console placed behind a little tribune projecting from the centre of the marble and oak screen which covers the organ, no pipes being visible. The west-end console had tubular-pneumatic action, but in 1926 Willis provided a second four-manual console, in the east-end apse with the retro-choir, using electro-pneumatic action to control both Apse and west-end Grand organs. The distance from the Apse console to the west-end is about 100yd (90m), making it the most distantly detached console in Britain.

At a time when British organ-building was still overshadowed by the orchestral imitations characteristic of the Hope-Jones organ, Willis' instrument still included proper choruses on the Great and Swell organs and some independent upperwork on the Pedal, as well as the small-scale Choir organ mutations which were the very first signs of the return to the classical organ. It is, of course, with its heavy-pressure reeds, something of a warhorse, more suited to the music of Franck, Widor and Reubke than of Bach or Buxtehude. Nevertheless, the instrument has proved to be one of the most important organs of the first third of the twentieth century.

The recent restoration by Harrison & Harrison has been essentially conservative, the only tonal change to the west-end organ being the removal of the Tuba from the Solo swell-box. The 1922 Willis console at the west end has been refitted with new mechanism though the touch-boxes of the original pneumatic action have been kept to retain the slight 'pluck' to the key-touch characteristic of the original action. The Lewis Apse organ has been enlarged and redesigned, having had a very strong 8ft bias formerly. The 1926 Apse console has gone, replaced by a new two-manual console. Still a record-breaking distance from the west-end organ, it mainly controls the Apse organ plus selected stops from the Great and Pedal of the west-end organ and (of course!) the Tuba.

The Guard's Chapel, Wellington Barracks
Hill Norman & Beard 1920, 1971

GREAT		SWELL		CHOIR		PEDAL	
Open Diapason	8	Wald Flute	8	Gedeckt	8	Open Diapason	16
Stopped Diapason	8	Salicional	8	Clear Flute	4	Bourdon	16
Octave	4	Vox Angelica	8	Principal	2	Principal	8
Clarinet Flute	4	Principal	4	Larigot	1⅓	Gedeckt	8
Nazard	2⅔	Lieblich Flute	4	Sesquialtera	II	Fifteenth	4
Recorder	2	Fifteenth	2	Cymbel 29.33.36	III	Mixture 19.22	II
Tierce	1⅗	Plein Jeu 22.26.29	III	Trompette (Great)	8	Posaune	16
Furniture 15.19.22.26	IV	Contra Oboe	16	Trompette (Great)	4		
Trompette-en-chamade	8	Trumpet	8				

Destroyed by a bomb in 1944, only the eastern apse of the original Victorian chapel, with its elaborate mosaic decoration, survived to be incorporated into the new building. In 1971 an electronic instrument was replaced by the present organ, based on the instrument built in 1920 for John Christie's organ room at Glyndebourne, and which led to his acquisition of the Hill Norman & Beard firm. The pipe display was designed by Bruce George, architect of the Chapel. The horizontal Trompette-en-chamade is detached, opposite the rest of the instrument.

Buckingham Palace, The Private Chapel (not open to the public)
Green 1790

Open Diapason	8	Compass from GG
Stopped Diapason	8	(no GG♯)
Dulciana	8	
Principal	4	The Stopped Diapason,
Flute	4	Principal and Sesquialtera
Twelfth	2⅔	draw in halves.
Fifteenth	2	
Sesquialtera 17.19.22	III	
Furniture 19.22	II	

This large one-manual was originally built for the Earl of Scarborough, in whose country seat, Sandbeck Park, it remained for nearly a hundred and seventy years. Like all Green's work, it must have sounded very soft in the large hall for which it was built, though it suits the tiny Buckingham Palace chapel very well. The restrained and slightly formal mahogany case conceals a general swell-box which was one of the first to have louvred shutters. In this organ they are hinged on leather, not pivoted, and operated by ropes connected to a foot pedal. The 1960 restoration by Hill Norman & Beard was one of the first to return to unequal temperament.

WILLESDEN St Mary's Church
Walker 1983

GREAT		SWELL		PEDAL	
Open Diapason	8	Chimney Flute	8	Bourdon	16
Stopped Diapason	8	Salicional	8	Bass Flute	8
Principal	4	Gemshorn	4	Octave	4
Twelfth	2⅔	Flageolet	2	Trombone	16
Fifteenth	2	Mixture 22.26.29	III		
Seventeenth	1⅗	Trumpet	8		
Mixtur 19.22.26	III				

David Graebe designed the distinctive case of this very compact instrument, placed on the west gallery of this typically low Middlesex church. The roofed case has unusual curved tops to the towers and is neatly waisted below the impost. The Swell organ is placed over the Great with the Pedal at the rear, speaking through the Great organ. The tracker action of this instrument has a particularly well-balanced touch but, at first hearing, the tone seems somewhat aggressive. As is usual on current J. W. Walker organs, the Trumpet is part of the Swell organ, not the Great.

WOODFORD St Mary's Church
Grant, Degens & Bradbeer 1972

HAUPTWERK		SCHWELLWERK		BRUSTWERK		PEDAL	
Prinzipal	8	Gedackt	8	Holzgedackt	8	Subbass	16
Rohrflöte	8	Salicional	8	Spitzgedackt	4	Oktave	8
Oktave	4	Vox Angelica	8	Prinzipal	2	Grossgedackt	8
Spitzflöte	4	Prinzipal	4	Sifflöte	1⅓	Koppelflöte	4
Oktave	2	Nasat	2⅔	Sesquialtera	II	Nachthorn	2
Mixtur 19.22.26.29	IV	Gedacktflöte	2	Zimbel 29.33.36	III	Mixtur 19.22.26.29	IV
Cornet	V	Scharff 22.26.29.33	IV	Krummhorn	8	Posaune	16
Trompete	8	Fagott	16			Schalmei	4
		Hautbois	8				

The warm acoustic of this square church sets off the aggressiveness of this typical Grant, Degens & Bradbeer. The 2ft-based *Brustwerk* is placed just above the console, without doors, and the 4ft-based Swell division is on show at the top of the organ. The Pedal 8ft front pipes, divided in compartments either side of the Great, have exceptionally long feet to gain height relative to the Great organ front. In this organ the German reeds are tempered more to British taste by putting the Krummhorn on the *Brustwerk* and using an Hautbois and a Fagott for the Swell.

GREATER MANCHESTER

MANCHESTER Royal Northern College of Music, Concert Hall
Hradetzky 1973

GREAT		SWELL		POSITIVE		PEDAL	
Quintadena	16	Principal	8	Gedackt	8	Principal	16
Principal	8	Flute	8	Principal	4	Subbass	16
Rohrgedackt	8	Viola da Gamba	8	Rohrflute	4	Principal	8
Octave	4	Voix Céleste	8	Nazard	2⅔	Gemshorn	8
Hohlflute	4	Prestant	4	Octave	2	Octave	4
Octave	2	Flauto Traverso	4	Waldflute	2	Flute	4
Blockflute	2	Doublette	2	Tierce	1⅗	Nachthorn	2
Mixture VI-VIII	2	Mixture VI-VIII	1⅓	Larigot	1⅓	Rauschquint III	2⅔
Cymbale IV	⅔	Cornet V	8	Scharff IV	1	Mixture IV	2
Cornet IV-V	8	Bombarde	16	Cymbale III	½	Posaune	16
Fagotto	16	Trompette	8	Cromorne	8	Trompette	8
Trompette	8	Oboe	8			Trumpet	8
Clarion	4	Voix Humaine	8			Schalmey	4
		Clarion	4				

The most striking aspect of this organ is its frankly brutalist case, all rectangles, without a curve or a diagonal anywhere, cantilevered out from the rear wall with little apparent means of support or even obvious space for the tracker action. At a second glance, however, it is possible to appreciate the honesty of its tone-cabinet layout, with the separate identity of each division clearly visible. Clever, too, is the improvement in proportion achieved by a single white upright a quarter or a third of the way across the face of the unenclosed divisions. The Positive projects low down over the console so that in its continuo role the distance to a singer is kept to a minimum.

The fluework of the instrument is mostly very German, with no loud stops and a very even power balance between the manuals which have the usual 16ft, 8ft and 4ft pitch emphasis between Pedal, Great and Positive. The Swell, on the other hand, is more British than many recent British-made instruments, having a narrow 8ft Principal and light-toned but full-length reeds of quasi-French voicing.

SALFORD St Paul's Church, Ellor Street
Green 1787; Young 1873; Hill Norman & Beard 1969

GREAT		SWELL		PEDAL	
*Open Diapason	8	*Stopped Diapason	8	Sub Bass	16
*Stopped Diapason	8	*Dulciana	8	Principal	8
*Principal	4	*Principal	4	Fifteenth	4
*Twelfth	2⅔	*Flute	4	Twenty-second	2
*Fifteenth	2	*Cornet 12.15.17	III		
*Sesquialtera 17.19.22	III	*Hautboy	8	*Green pipes.	
Mounted Cornet					
8.12.15.17	IV				
*Trumpet	8				

Despite two moves, this Samuel Green is in remarkably original condition, retaining nearly all the original pipework plus the mahogany case and the Great organ soundboard. It was built for the west gallery of St Thomas', Ardwick, Manchester and then moved to the south-east corner of the church in 1873 by Alexander Young. He provided a new action and console as well as a Pedal stop and two short-compass stops placed on the mounted Cornet soundboard. The

ST PAUL'S CHURCH, SALFORD

instrument again received a new console and manual tracker action in 1969 when the Swell compass was extended down to CC, the Pedal organ augmented and the Cornet reinstated. Shortly afterwards, the church closed and the organ was moved to its present location. The instrument retains Green's typical soft, singing tone. It will never startle you, but then it will never tire you either.

St Philip's Church
Renn & Boston 1829; Wadsworth 1915; Mander 1963

GREAT		SWELL		PEDAL	
*Open Diapason	8	*Open Diapason	8	*Open Diapason	16
*Open Diapason	8	*Stop Diapason	8	Bourdon	16
*Stop Diapason	8	*Principal	4		
*Flute	4	*Fifteenth	2	*Renn pipes.	
*Principal	4	*Hautboy	8		
*Twelfth	2⅔	*Cornopean	8		
*Fifteenth	2				
*Sesquialtra 17.19.22	III				
*Trumpet	8				
Clarinet	8				

Samuel Renn was the main Manchester builder of the first half of the nineteenth century. The severely classical case (matching the church, with which it is contemporary) has gilded front pipes in a three-tower case with pediments over the single-storey flats. The woodwork is painted matt black, lined in gold. The console, at first sight, appears to be an adaptation, detached some 7ft (2m) in front of the organ and connected to it by a large wooden case concealing the trackers. In fact, this is original. The arrangement, known as a 'long movement', was not uncommon in the middle of the nineteenth century, though this may well be the only one to survive.

The organ was moved forward (to its advantage) in 1873 but retained its GG compass Great until 1915. Noel Mander restored the organ in 1963, fitting a new tracker action and modern pedalboard. Apart from this and the 1915 CC keys, the console appears mostly to be original and the instrument retains its tenor C Swell organ, the bottom twelve notes sounding an unenclosed Stopped Bass which is permanently on. This Swell organ adheres to the formula invented by Father Smith for his Echo organ almost a hundred and fifty years earlier in that it is a miniature Great organ, reduced almost to chamber organ proportions, a characteristic also seen in the 1818 Elliot organ at Ashridge College, Hertfordshire.

STANDISH St Wilfred's Church
Walker 1971

GREAT		SWELL		PEDAL	
Double Dulciana	16	Gemshorn	8	Violone	16
Open Diapason	8	Rohr Flute	8	Sub Bass	16
Stopped Diapason	8	Dulciana	8	Principal	8
Dulciana	8	Gemshorn	4	Bass Flute	8
Principal	4	Dulcet	4	Dulciana	8
Stopped Flute	4	Flute	4	Fifteenth	4
Twelfth	2⅔	Nazard	2⅔	Octave Flute	4
Block Flute	2	Principal	2	Piccolo	2
Larigot	1⅓	Flautino	2	Mixture 15.19.22	III
Mixture 15.19.22	III	Tierce	1⅗	Trombone	16
Trumpet	8	Mixture 22.26.29	III	Trumpet	8
		Double Trumpet	16	Clarion	4
		Trumpet	8		
		Clarion	4		

This is a fairly typical example of the instruments being made in the 1960s and early 1970s before the switch to tracker action became general. In this instance the size of the stop-list owes something to unification, resulting, on paper, in an apparently very large organ for a two-manual.

ST WILFRED'S CHURCH, STANDISH

The organ stands at the back of the church, in a truly amazing case by George Pace, with soaring diagonal towers above and inverted pyramid-shaped pendants below. Reminiscent of the New College, Oxford case, it is arguably more successful.

HAMPSHIRE

HAMBLEDON The Parish Church
Hill Norman & Beard 1969

GREAT		SWELL		PEDAL	
Open Diapason	8	Spitz Flute	8	Sub Bass	16
Stopped Diapason	8	Salicional	8	Principal	8
Principal	4	Gemshorn	4	Gedeckt	8
Chimney Flute	4	Mixture 19.22	II	Fifteenth	4
Fifteenth	2	Trumpet	8	Double Trumpet	16

Hambledon Church has an unusual double nave with a lofty arch between. The organ is on brackets high over the arch and facing east. The richly painted softwood case by Stephen Dykes Bower has two main compartments of pipes under a gabled roof, with a small circular compartment high up in the centre.

PORTSMOUTH The Guildhall
Compton 1959

CHAMBER I

Stop	PEDAL	GREAT	CHOIR
First Diapason	16	8	
Second Diapason	16 8 16	8 4 2	
Third Diapason		8 4 2⅔ 2 1⅓ 1	8 4
Subbass-Höhl Flute	32 16 8 4	16 8 4	8 4
Dulciana	16 8	8	16 8 4 2⅔ 2
Vox Angelica			8 4 1⅗
Gedeckt		8	8 4 2
Mixture (2 rks)		II	
Posaune	16 8 4	16 8 4	8

CHAMBER II

Stop	PEDAL	SWELL	SOLO
Viola	16 8	16 8 4 2	16 8
Geigen		8 4	
Rohr Flute		8 4 2	
Harmonic Flute			8 4 2
Viole Céleste		8	8
Hautboy	16	16 8	8
Trumpet		8 4	
Clarinet		8	16 8
Orchestral Oboe			8
Tuba	16 8		8 4

MIXTURES

Pedal Mixture III	8	5⅓	4	Great Mixture II	1⅓	1
Choir Acuta III	2	1⅓	1	Swell Quartane II	1⅓	1
Great Mixture IV	2⅔	2	1⅓ 1	Swell Cymbale III	2	1⅓ 1

In many ways this organ was the last of its breed. Nothing quite like it has been built since. The old Guildhall had an 1887 Gray & Davison with 32ft pipes in the case, but the building was gutted by fire in 1941. In the new hall the architects pushed the organ up into two chambers in the roof over the proscenium arch, controlled by a mobile stop-knob console on the stage. The result is a typical totally-enclosed John Compton extension organ producing 84 stops from twenty ranks of pipes. It has all the Compton features: the quick-speaking but heavy diaphone basses, the 32ft polyphone (the only unenclosed pipe in the organ), the Pedal 5 rank 'Harmonics of 32ft' and, of course, phenomenally high wind pressures, such as 8in (200mm) water gauge for the Choir Dulciana!

St Mark's Church, North End
Hill Norman & Beard 1972

GREAT		SWELL		POSITIV		PEDAL	
Open Diapason	8	Flute Conique	8	Gedeckt	8	Sub Bass	16
Stopped Diapason	8	Viola da Gamba	8	Spitzflute	4	Principal	8
Octave	4	Voix Celeste	8	Gemshorn	2	Gedeckt	8
Chimney Flute	4	Principal	4	Larigot	1⅓	Fifteenth	4
Fifteenth	2	Plein Jeu 22.26.29	III	Cymbel 29.33	II	Posaune	16
Furniture 19.22.26	III	Shalmey	16	Trumpet	8	Shalmey	4
		Trompette	8				

This compact three-manual has a remarkable case of Douglas fir, designed by Herbert Norman to complement the contemporary church. The layout is markedly assymetrical, with separate tone cabinets for the Great, Swell and Positiv organs which are respectively 8ft, 4ft and 2ft based. The bass pipes of tin, copper and spotted metal are arranged in hexagonal towers not unlike Joseph von Glatter-Götz's case for the transept organ in Freiburg Minster, Germany.

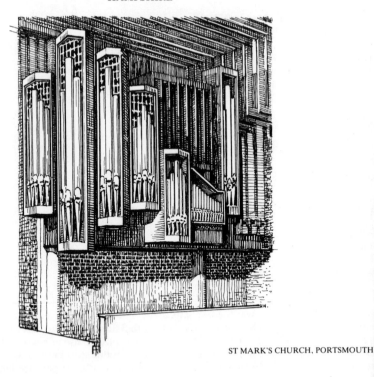

ST MARK'S CHURCH, PORTSMOUTH

St Mary's Church, Portsea
Walker 1891, 1965

GREAT		SWELL		CHOIR		PEDAL	
Double Open Diapason	16	Double Diapason	16	Violin Diapason	8	Sub Bass	32
Open Diapason 1	8	Open Diapason	8	Lieblich Gedeckt	8	Open Wood	16
Open Diapason 2	8	Dulciana	8	Dulciana Principal	4	Violone	16
Open Diapason 3	8	Echo Gamba	8	Lieblich Flute	4	Bourdon	16
Wald Flute	8	Vox Angelica	8	Harmonic Piccolo	2	Trombone	16
Principal	4	Principal	4	Clarinet	8		
Harmonic Flute	4	Flute	4				
Twelfth	2⅔	Mixture 15.19.22.26	IV				
Fifteenth	2	Mixture 22.26.29	III				
Mixture 15.19.22	III	Contra Fagotto	16				
Clarion Mixture		Horn	8				
22.26.29	III	Oboe	8				
Double Trumpet	16						
Trumpet	8						

Placed in an elevated chamber on the north side of the chancel of Blomfield's lofty church, this substantially built instrument typifies the late Victorian organ just before Hope-Jones' influence on tonal design finally took hold. At a time when the firm of Walker was famous for large bass-pipe scales, the Pedal organ lacks any upperwork at all, though it does have its own octave coupler and extra octave of pipes. The reed-stops are on elevated wind pressures and the Swell Fagotto 16ft has the characteristic wooden caps and 'pepper-pot' tops which Walker used to get a smooth tone out of a relatively small-scale pipe. There is nevertheless a full Diapason Chorus on both Swell and Great, including two mixtures on each manual. One of the Great mixtures is a Walker 'peculiar'; the Clarion Mixture was presumably so-called to make it more acceptable at a time when mixtures were already dropping out of fashion. The organ was built with a mixture of tracker and pneumatic lever action. Electropneumatic action, controlled from a new console, was fitted in 1965, though tonally the organ remains unchanged.

ROMSEY The Abbey
Walker 1848, 1888; Mander 1982

This three-manual instrument is probably the finest nineteenth-century J. W. Walker to remain to us. Originally built for the north transept, the organ was enlarged and moved into the north choir triforium in 1888. The tone is clear and ringing, less 'sweet' than a Hill would have been and less dependent on the reeds than a Willis.

The instrument retains its original (noisy) pneumatic lever action to the Great organ and also has tracker (Choir organ) and tubular pneumatic action (Swell and Pedal). Indeed, the action to the Pedal Open Diapason 32ft changes from tracker to pneumatic, back to tracker again, back to pneumatic and finally to tracker on its way from console to soundboard.

The instrument was restored in 1982 by N. P. Mander, who supplied a new Tuba to the Choir (on a fourth type of action – electropneumatic!).

SOUTHAMPTON Turner Sims Concert Hall, Southampton University
Collins 1977

GREAT		OBERWERK		BRUSTWERK		PEDAL	
Quintadena	16	Metal Gedact	8	Wood Gedact	8	Subbass	16
Principal	8	Gamba	8	Koppel Flute	4	Principal	8
Rohr Flute	8	Principal	4	Principal	2	Pommer	8
Octave	4	Quint	2⅔	Spitz Quint	1⅓	Wide Octave	4
Spitz Flute	4	Gemshorn	2	Sesquialtera	II	Mixture 22.26.29	III
Octave	2	Tierce	1⅗	Vox Humana	8	Fagot	16
Mixture 19.22.26	III-V	Scharff 22.26.29.33	IV				
Trumpet	8	Shalmey	8				

This wide but shallow tracker-action organ has a rectangular case to match the architecture of the modern hall, but one which, because of the varied sizes and layout of the front pipes and the attractive shades behind them, is considerably more interesting than the instruments in similar situations at York University (Bradbeer) and the Royal Northern College of Music (Hradetzky).

The stop-list follows a very logical *werk* principle structure, the *Oberwerk*, with a Shalmey as its reed-stop, being intermediate in pitch between the 8ft-based Great and the little *Brustwerk*. The latter has folding doors and is placed over the Continental-style console with flat jambs and projecting keys. The knobs, like the natural keys, are black. The sound of the instrument is basically north German but without the aggressiveness sometimes encountered.

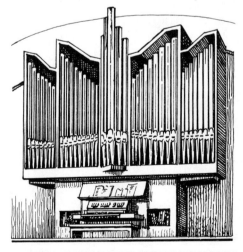

ST GEORGE'S CHURCH, WATERLOOVILLE (SEE PAGE 238)

237

WATERLOOVILLE St George's Church
Hill Norman & Beard 1970

GREAT		SWELL		PEDAL	
Open Diapason	8	Spitz Flute	8	Sub Bass	16
Stopped Diapason	8	Salicional	8	Principal	8
Principal	4	Gemshorn	4	Gedeckt	8
Chimney Flute	4	Mixture 19.22	II	Fifteenth	4
Fifteenth	2	Trumpet	8	Double Trumpet	16

The stop-list is not the only factor which determines the sound of an organ. The acoustics of the building and the pipe-scales also play an important part. It was requested that this organ should be 'just like Hambledon', seven miles up the road. The stop-list is the same but the church acoustics, west gallery position and shallow layout makes this the more successful organ. The mahogany case, with its four winged flats, central tower and tin-metal front pipes, was designed by Herbert Norman with Thomas Meakins, architect of the new church.

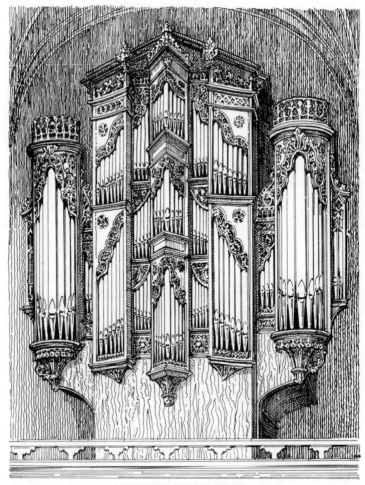

WINCHESTER COLLEGE CHAPEL

WINCHESTER Winchester College Chapel
Mander 1984

GREAT		SWELL		CHOIR (enclosed)		PEDAL	
Bourdon	16	Open Diapason	8	Stopt Diapason	8	Subbass	32
Open Diapason	8	Spitz Flute	8	Dulciana	8	Open Diapason	16
Stopt Diapason	8	Principal	4	Vox Angelica	8	Bourdon	16
Principal	4	Nason Flute	4	Clear Flute	4	Principal	8
Chimney Flute	4	Fifteenth	2	Flageolet	2	Stopt Flute	8
Nazard	2⅔	Sesquialtera	II	Larigot	1⅓	Fifteenth	4
Fifteenth	2	Mixture 19.22.26	III-IV	Cremona	8	Mixture 19.22.26.29	IV
Recorder	2	Fagotto	16			Trombone	16
Tierce	1⅗	Trumpet	8				
Fourniture 19.22.26.29	IV	Hautboy	8				
Trumpet	8						
Clarion	4						

The very flamboyant organ case on the west gallery of Winchester College Chapel was designed by W. D. Caröe for the Norman & Beard instrument of 1908. It has some strange details, including a three-storey central tower, but, for its date, is surprisingly classical in overall outline.

The new organ by N. P. Mander, presently under construction, takes advantage of the case proportions to produce a truly vertical layout, with the manual divisions disposed on three levels. This helps tonal projection and assists in the design of a good, direct, tracker key-action. The stop-list is unusual in some respects. In particular, the Swell organ, with an 8ft Open Diapason, follows the British rather than the Continental model in having the same basic pitch as the Great organ. The string stops, since the 1860s more usually found on the Swell, are here put in the enclosed Choir organ which thereby assumes a character very different from a Continental Positive.

The Chancel organ at the east end of the chapel was built in 1950 by Hill Norman & Beard in a case by Stephen Dykes Bower. Two ranks of seventeenth-century pipes from the west-end organ have now been incorporated into this instrument.

HEREFORD AND WORCESTER

BROMSGROVE All Saint's Church
Tamburini 1981

MANUAL I		MANUAL II		PEDALE	
Principale	8	Bordone	8	Bordone	16
Flauto a Camino	8	Flauto a cuspide	4	Fagotto	16
Ottava	4	Principale	2		
Decimaquinta	2	Quinta	1⅓		
Ripieno	IV	Sesquialtera	II		
Tromba	8				

This modern Italian instrument is remarkable for its finely embossed tin front pipes in a slightly heavy case free-standing at the rear of the church. The 2ft-based enclosed Manual II is placed under the Manual I with exposed shutters and, although the side-towers look like Pedal towers, they actually contain the bass of the Manual I Principale, the Pedal organ being at the back. In true Italian tradition Manual I is mainly a Diapason Chorus, though not the reticent and flutey chorus conventionally associated with Italian instruments. The action is very light, as the wind pressures are only 1½–2in (40–50mm), though this is somewhat to the detriment of the reed tone.

KIDDERMINSTER The Town Hall
Hill 1854

GREAT		SWELL		CHOIR		PEDAL	
Double Open Diapason		Double Diapason	16	Stopped Diapason	8	Open Diapason	16
and Bourdon	16	Open Diapason	8	Dulciana	8	Violone	16
Open Diapason	8	Gamba	8	Gemshorn	4	Principal	8
Cone Gamba	8	Stopped Diapason	8	Flute	4	Posaune	16
Stopped Diapason	8	Principal	4	Piccolo	2		
Principal	4	Fifteenth	2	Cromorne	8		
Wald Flute	4	Cornopean	8				
Twelfth	2⅔	Oboe	8				
Fifteenth	2						
Sesquialtera	III						
Posaune	8						

This is one of the lesser known town hall organs. It is not on the grand scale of Birmingham, Leeds or St George's Hall, Liverpool. It is a good, modest three-manual instrument which has survived unchanged from William Hill's heyday and, as such, is worth more attention and study than it has so far received.

The Swell organ is remarkably complete, looking back to its origins as an Echo Great by having a Double Diapason yet looking forward to the romantic organ with a Gamba. The conical stops are interesting too, in that although common enough on the Continent, they were almost unknown in Britain until Hill introduced them.

Hill's early large organs had rather a heavy key-touch. The Kidderminster organ retains its original tracker key-action, and at the restoration by Hill Norman & Beard in 1981 it was found necessary to put in an electropneumatic coupling action to relieve the touch with the manuals coupled.

HERTFORDSHIRE

ASHRIDGE Ashridge Management College Chapel
Elliot 1818

GREAT (from GG)		SWELL (from Tenor F)		PEDAL	
Open Diapason	8	Open Diapason	8	(18 notes from GG)	
Open Diapason	8	Stopped Diapason	8	Diapason	8
Stopped Diapason	8	Principal	4		
Principal	4	Oboe (was Hautboy)	8		
Flute	4				
Twelfth	2⅔				
Fifteenth	2				
Sesquialtera 17.19	II				
Mixture 19.22	II				
Trumpet	8				

There was a monastery at Ashridge which, when dissolved by Henry VIII, was appropriated as a royal residence. The present buildings all date from the first two decades of the nineteenth century, designed by James Wyatt in Gothick style for the Earl of Bridgewater. The chapel is tall, with a fan vault, and has excellent acoustics.

The organ is one of our most important historical instruments. It is almost unaltered from its original construction and William Hill, as Elliot's future partner, is reputed to have been very much involved with its construction. Apart from the compass and the early unison Pedal organ, discussed in chapter 3, the first thing one notices about this instrument is its softness. Its position is partly responsible, it being perhaps the first organ to be built in a chamber behind an arch, a practice later to become regrettably common. The arch is concealed by an oak screen in the Gothick style, an early example of an architect's case, designed here by Sir Jeffrey Wyatville (Wyatt's nephew). Another reason for the softness is undoubtedly the 'sweet' voicing which had begun with Snetzler's chamber organs and had been such a feature of Green's instruments. Hill later rebelled against the softness, and also the almost purely accompanimental Swell organ, but a vestige of the sweet tone remained with all his instruments.

ST ALBANS The Abbey
Hill 1861; Abbott & Smith 1907; Willis 1929; Harrison 1962

GREAT		SWELL		CHOIR		PEDAL	
Principal	16	Open Diapason	8	Quintaton	16	Sub Bass	32
Bourdon	16	Rohr Flute	8	Open Diapason	8	Principal	16
Principal	8	Viola	8	Gedacktpommer	8	Major Bass	16
Diapason	8	Celeste	8	Flauto Traverso	8	Bourdon	16
Spitzflute	8	Open Flute	4	Octave	4	Quint	10⅔
Stopped Diapason	8	Principal	4	Rohr Flute	4	Octave	8
Octave	4	Nazard	2⅔	Wald Flute	2	Gedackt	8
Stopped Flute	4	Gemshorn	2	Larigot	1⅓	Nazard	5⅓
Blockflute	2	Tierce	1⅗	Sesquialtera	II	Choral Bass	4
Quartane 12.15	II	Cimbel 36.38.40	III	Mixture 26.29.33.36	IV	Open Flute	2
Mixture 19.22.26.29	IV-VI	Corno di Bassetto	16	Cromorne	8	Mixture 19.22.26.29	IV
Grand Cornet	V	Trumpet	8	Grand Cornet	V	Bombardon	16
Trumpet	16	Hautboy	8	Fanfare Trumpet	8	Trumpet	16
Fanfare Trumpet	8	Vox Humana	8			Tromba	8
		Clarion	4			Shawm	4

Before 1962 the St Albans Abbey organ had something of a chequered career. From the dissolution of the monasteries to 1820 there was no organ at all. In that year a secondhand instrument was purchased: a three-manual Byfield incorporating a one-manual Father Smith as the Great organ. This organ was replaced in 1861 by a three-manual Hill, only the Smith Open Diapason surviving to be incorporated into the new instrument. The Hill organ was moved to the top of the stone screen in 1885, when a naked array of bass pipes was supplied by Abbott to cover the west face. Complaints that the instrument spoiled the view down the length of the Abbey led to a rebuild in 1907. Abbott & Smith used tubular pneumatic action to enable the division of the instrument into two halves, clearing the centre of the screen. The new Gothic Revival cases were designed by J. Oldrid Scott (son of Sir George Gilbert Scott) who had also been responsible for the choir stalls and the bishop's throne. A further rebuild, by Henry Willis III, took place in 1929.

The organ assumed its present form in 1962, when a major rebuild was undertaken by Harrison & Harrison, working under the direction of Ralph Downes. The layout was re-planned with the Great organ in the north case, the Swell in the south case and the Choir, really a Positive, placed in a new chair case designed by Cecil Brown, on the east face of the screen. Although 14 stops of Hill pipes and 10 of Abbott & Smith's were used again, most were taken apart and fitted with new languids so that they could be voiced with open feet and minimum nicking to match the new pipes. However, 1962 was too early for the classical revival; there are no tone-cabinets and no tracker action. The layout is slightly odd since the two Scott cases face each other across the screen so that the sound does not travel well down the length of the building, despite the semi-Bombarde nature of the Grand Cornet and the Fanfare Trumpet shared by the Great and Choir organs. It is nevertheless a very good instrument of its period, and is the focus of the bi-annual St Albans International Organ Festival.

WARE The Plough, Great Munden
Compton c1935

This three-manual twelve-rank instrument, formerly in the Gaumont Cinema, Finchley, is typical of most surviving cinema organs in that it has been transplanted to a new home. It is untypical in that the former landlord of The Plough, Gerald Carrington, was a Compton-trained organ-builder. He installed the instrument in a specially built extension to this country pub.

WHEATHAMPSTEAD St Helen's Church
Hill Norman & Beard 1969

GREAT		SWELL		PEDAL	
Rohr Flute	8	Gedeckt	8	Sub Bass	16
Principal	4	Koppel Flute	4	Gemshorn	8
Gedeckt	4	Principal	2	Gemshorn	4
Mixture 19.22.26.29	IV	Quint	1⅓	Gemshorn	2

This was the first organ with which I was concerned which is totally arranged in *werk* principle tone-cabinets. It convinced me of the additional power gained by not wasting sound in the rafters and of the warmth and resonance it was possible to achieve in a building which is acoustically 'dead'. The organ stands on two columns over the west door with Great over Swell, flanked by a divided Pedal. The contra-rotating movement of the Swell-shutters is partially concealed by vertical slats.

ST HELEN'S CHURCH, WHEATHAMPSTEAD

HUMBERSIDE

BEVERLEY The Minster
Snetzler 1769; Hill 1884, 1916; Hill Norman & Beard 1962

GREAT		SWELL		CHOIR		PEDAL	
Double Open Diapason	16	Bourdon	16	*Open Diapason	8	Double Open Diapason	32
Open Diapason I	8	*Open Diapason	8	*Stopped Diapason	8	Open Diapason I	16
Open Diapason II	8	Gemshorn	8	Dulciana	8	Open Diapason	16
*Open Diapason III	8	*Stopped Diapason	8	*Octave	4	Open Diapason (Great)	16
*Open Diapason IV	8	Keraulophon	8	*Stopped Flute	4	Violone	16
*Stopped Diapason	8	Vox Angelica	8	Nazat	2⅔	Bourdon	6
Dolce	8	*Principal	4	*Fifteenth	2	Bass Flute	8
Gemshorn	4	Flute	4	Tierce	1⅗	Principal	8
*Principal	4	Twelfth	2⅔	Sifflöte	1	Violoncello	8
Flute	4	Fifteenth	2			Fifteenth	4
*Fifteenth	2	*Sesquialtera	IV	SOLO (enclosed)		Spitz Flute	4
*Furniture 19.22.26.29	IV	Scharf	II	Hohl Flute	8	Tierce	3⅕
Sesquialtera 19.22.24	III	Contra Fagotto	16	Lieblich Flute	4	Larigot	2⅔
Posaune	8	Oboe	8	Flageolet	2	Wald Flute	2
Clarion	4	Horn	8	Orchestral Oboe	8	Contra Posaune	32
		Trumpet	8	Clarinet	8	Posaune	16
		Clarion	4			Tuba	16
				(unenclosed)		Tuba	8
				Open Diapason I	8	Octave Tuba	4
				Tuba	16	Cor Anglais	4
				Tuba	8	*Snetzler pipes.	
				Tuba	4		

There is a story about a visitor to Beverley who, looking in the centre of the town for the famous Abbey, totally failed to find it. Eventually he gave up, went for a walk down some streets leading southwards, came round a corner and found himself face to face with what, for a moment, he took to be Westminster Abbey!

In addition to its architectural glories, the Abbey also has a fine and very important organ. In the first place, there are more Snetzler stops surviving in this instrument than in any other. Secondly, the two-sided screen organ case is generally considered Dr Arthur Hill's finest work. Its shape and vertical emphasis complement the Scott screen and the building exceptionally well yet, unlike so many architect's cases, it is not 'over-woody', being so lightly constructed that one scarcely dare lean a ladder against it.

As can be seen from the stop-list, the Great, Swell and Choir organs all contain substantial numbers of pipes from John Snetzler's three-manual instrument of 1769. Incidentally, Snetzler was left-handed; if one looks at the nicks in the mouths of his pipes, they are at an angle which is only possible for a left-handed person. Snetzler's organ underwent various minor changes in the nineteenth century and was then rebuilt and enlarged by Hill in 1884 and again in 1916. The layout is unusual in that only the Great organ, Choir organ and Solo Tuba are on the screen. The Swell organ speaks into the choir from the south choir aisle and the Solo organ speaks into the south transept, screened by Snetzler's original Gothick case. There were suggestions that the layout should have been altered when a new console was fitted in 1962. With hindsight, one can be pleased that relatively few changes were made, leaving this unique combination of Snetzler's and Hill's work to sound, as the organ historian Dr Sumner has put it 'one of the most musical and charming of English organs'.

HULL St Martin's Church
Grant, Degens & Rippin 1966

GREAT		POSITIV		PEDAL	
Rohrflöte	8	Gedeckt	8	Quintatön	16
Principal	4	Spitzflöte	4	Spitzprincipal	8
Blockflöte	2	Principal	2	Hohlflöte	4
Mixture 19.22.26.29	III	Cymbel 29.33.36	III	Fagott	16
Krummhorn	8	Trompete	8		

One of the earlier Grant instruments, built before the firm went over to tracker action, this organ nevertheless has the same open foot voicing as the later instruments. With no Swell division and in an unreverberant suburban church, the result is frankly virile.

Frank Bradbeer's cases, elevated on two small galleries between the chancel and the north choir aisle, have undoubted character. They consist of triple-compartmented tone-cabinets, picked out with black lining. Each manual division is planted in three sides so that adjacent pipes are a minor third apart.

ISLE OF WIGHT

CARISBROOKE CASTLE
Hoffheimer 1602

The oldest working organ in Britain, this is a purely secular instrument, combining very simple construction with elaborate ornamentation. The richly carved case has fretted doors which open to reveal equally richly carved wooden pipes. The upper notes are hollowed out of walnut, turned and fancifully carved, with stopper handles shaped to represent thistle-heads. The short wooden keys operate a simple 'pin-action' with the pallet valves directly under the keys. The stop-action is equally straightforward with turned knobs on the ends of the three slides controlling the stops. These are 4ft and 2ft stopped flutes and a soft buzzing 8ft Regal, made with turned wood resonators. The compass is EE to C, 45 notes.

The organ is believed to be of Flemish construction, though it was apparently specially made for John Graham, Earl of Montrose, whose arms figure prominently in the decoration. His monogram appears twice on the case and alternates with the outline of a human head on the key-fonts. Elizabeth, the daughter of Charles I, died in captivity in the castle and is said to have played the instrument. Consequently, it is often referred to as the Princess Elizabeth organ.

CARISBROOKE CASTLE

244

KENT

CANTERBURY The Cathedral
Willis 1886; Mander 1979–80

GREAT		SWELL		CHOIR		PEDAL	
Double Open Diapason	16	Double Diapason	16	Stopped Diapason	8	Open Diapason	16
Open Diapason I	8	Open Diapason	8	Dulciana	8	Violone	16
Open Diapason II	8	Lieblich Gedackt	8	Principal	4	Bourdon	16
Claribel Flute	8	Salicional	8	Chimney Flute	4	Octave	8
Stopped Diapason	8	Vox Angelica	8	Nazard	2⅔	Flute	8
Principal	4	Principal	4	Blockflute	2	Superoctave	4
Flute Harmonique	4	Open Flute	4	Tierce	1⅗	Open Flute	4
Twelfth	2⅔	Flageolet	2	Larigot	1⅓	Mixture 19.22.26.29	IV
Fifteenth	2	Mixture 17.19.22	III	Mixture 22.26.29.33	IV	Contra Posaune	32
Piccolo	2	Sharp Mixture		Cremona	8	Ophicleide	16
Mixture 15.17.19.22	IV	15.19.22.26.29	V	Tuba	8	Fagotto	16
Fourniture		Hautboy	8	Tuba Clarion	4	Posaune	8
19.22.26.29	IV-VI	Double Trumpet	16			Clarion	4
Trombone	16	Trumpet	8				
Trumpet	8	Clarion	4				
Clarion	4						

NAVE ORGAN (played from Great manual)	
Open Diapason	8
Stopped Diapason	8
Octave	4
Superoctave	2
Mixture 19.22.26.29	IV
Pedal Subbass	16

Until recently, the casual visitor to Canterbury Cathedral might have supposed that there was no organ. Certainly none was visible. This was not always so. Samuel Green built an organ on the stone screen at the entrance to the choir in 1784. It was taken down in 1827 and in 1842 Hill put the organ over the south aisle with a detached console and a tracker action 90ft (27m) long! This instrument was replaced by Henry Willis, though a token number of Green's pipes were said to have been re-used. Willis put his organ 40ft (12m) up in the south triforium and without casework; he always begrudged the expenditure of money on organ cases. He clearly felt that he could rely on his heavy-pressure reeds to overcome the necessarily boxed-in and indirect sound which resulted. He also put the console on the screen, making use of a very early electropneumatic action.

This organ is well suited to accompany daily services in the choir but, through two tower arches, is extremely remote in the nave. As part of his comprehensive reconstruction of the organ in 1979–80 Noel Mander added a nave division, played from the console on the screen but speaking across the north aisle, halfway down the nave. This has a handsome if slightly squat case designed by Ian Bell, placed in a window arch with an 8ft tin-metal Open Diapason in the front, one pipe nicely embossed, and set off by gilded pipe-shades and matt black panelling edged in gold.

The main organ still retains its Willis characteristics with bold, firm reeds but, in the recent rebuilding, has gained Hill-like mixtures which add lightness to the ensemble.

TONBRIDGE Tonbridge School Chapel
Binns 1909; Mander 1980

GREAT		SWELL		CHOIR (enclosed)		PEDAL	
Double Open Diapason	16	Open Diapason	8	Lieblich Gedeckt	8	Open Metal	16
Open Diapason	8	Rohr Flute	8	Viola da Gamba	8	Violone	16
Claribel Flute	8	Echo Gamba	8	Flauto Traverso	4	Subbass	16
Principal	4	Voix Celestes	8	Nazard	2⅔	Lieblich Bourdon	16
Stopped Flute	4	Gemshorn	4	Piccolo	2	Principal	8
Twelfth	2⅔	Fifteenth	2	Clarinet	8	Bass Flute	8
Fifteenth	2	Mixture 15.19.22	III	(unenclosed)		Lieblich Flute	8
Tierce	1⅗	Oboe	8	Trumpet	8	Fifteenth	4
Fourniture		Double Trumpet	16	Tuba	8	Stopped Flute	4
19.22.26.29	IV-VI	Cornopean	8			Octavin	2
Trumpet	8	Clarion	4			Mixture 19.22.26.29	IV
Clarion	4					Double Ophicleide	32
						Ophicleide	16
						Trombone	16
						Posaune	8
						Clarion	4

Probably the most impressive example of J. J. Binns' work in the south of England, the organ is free-standing on a screen near the west end of the chapel. The case looks rather heavy but has a bold silhouette with three-quarter round side-towers, a short central tower and strongly curved cornices and pipe-blocks to the flats. The instrument always had remarkably good chorus work for its period (Binns was strongly influenced by Schulze) and the recent rebuild by N. P. Mander has made no great alteration, though the 32ft Double Ophicleide is his, as are most of the mixtures.

LANCASHIRE

BLACKBURN The Cathedral
Walker 1969

GREAT		SWELL (in two boxes:		POSITIVE		PEDAL	
Quintaton	16	Chancel and Transept)		Bourdon	8	Contra Bass	32
Principal	8	Rohrflöte	8	Prestant	4	Principal	16
Stopped Diapason	8	Viola da Gamba	8	Koppelflöte	4	Sub Bass	16
Octave	4	Celeste	8	Principal	2	Quintaton	16
Rohrflöte	4	Principal	4	Sesquialtera 12.17	II	Octave	8
Nazard	2⅔	Nasonflöte	4	Larigot	1⅓	Nachthorn	8
Blockflöte	2	Nazard	2⅔	Scharf 26.29.33	III	Fifteenth	4
Tierce	1⅗	Gemshorn	2	Holzregal	16	Recorder	4
Fourniture 15.19.22	III	Octavin	1	Imperial Trumpet		Spitzflöte	2
Plein Jeu 22.26.29	III	Mixture 12.19.22	III	(en chamade)	8	Mixture 19.(22).26.29	IV
Trumpet	8	Cymbale 29.33.36	III			Serpent	32
		Fagot	16			Posaune	16
		Trompette	8			Bombarde	8
		Cromhorne	8			Schalmei	4
		Clairon	4				

The former Blackburn parish church is a Gothick building which replaced the medieval church in 1826. John Gray built a three-manual organ in 1828 in a Gothick double case on a west gallery. The Choir organ was unusual for that date in that although placed in the chair case, it was enclosed in a small swell-box. Aristide Cavaillé-Coll, the famous French builder, put a new organ in Gray's case in 1875. This instrument was altered considerably by various people before being replaced by the present organ.

The instrument is placed in the new eastern extension of the cathedral. It is divided between four projecting platforms either side of the double arch leading to the chancel and on the east wall of each transept. The detached stop-knob console is movable. The instrument is essentially a caseless organ, not on the Holtkamp plan with massed treble pipes at the front, but with exposed basses, relying on the massing of the pipes and the different colours and textures of metal and wood to give form and variety. The pipe display includes a Pedal 32ft reed, mitred into a curious shape and called, not inappropriately, Serpent!

BLACKPOOL The Tower Ballroom
Wurlitzer 1939

This fourteen-unit three-manual is one of the few theatre instruments to remain in its original home, precisely because it is not a cinema organ but is used to accompany dancing, just like the Belgian café organs. It is nevertheless a typical Wurlitzer, made famous by the radio broadcasts of Reginald Dixon, the resident organist for many years.

BOLTON The Town Hall
Walker 1984

GREAT		SWELL		POSITIVE		PEDAL	
Quintaton	16	Bourdon	8	Stopped Diapason	8	Principal	16
Principal	8	Viole de Gambe	8	Principal	4	Sub Bass	16
Open Flute	8	Voix Celeste	8	Chimney Flute	4	Octave	8
Octave	4	Octave	4	Nazard	2⅔	Gedact	8
Clear Flute	4	Flute Octaviante	4	Gemshorn	2	Choral Bass	4
Super Octave	2	Octavin	2	Tierce	1	Mixture 19.22.26.29	IV
Mixture 19.22.26.29	IV	Sesquialtera	II	Larigot	1⅓	Contra Fagot	32
Sharp Mixture 29.33.36	III	Mixture 15.19.22.26	IV-V	Scharf 22.26.29.33	IV	Fagot	16
Double Trumpet	16	Basson Hautbois	16	Cremona	8	Trumpet	8
Trumpet	8	Harmonic Trumpet	8				
		Harmonic Clarion	4	SOLO			
		Vox Humana	8	Cornet	V		
				Trompette	8		
				Octave Trompette	4		

The original organ in Bolton Town Hall was built by Gray & Davison in 1874. It was a four-manual instrument of 48 stops, built to a stop-list by W. T. Best, reputedly a robust organ constructed in the grand manner which the Victorians considered appropriate to Town Halls. Much used to accompany the massed choirs with which Lancashire abounds, it survived with only a conservative rebuild by Hill Norman & Beard in 1938, when the console and pneumatic lever action were replaced.

The organ was destroyed by fire in 1982. J.W. Walker are to build a new four-manual instrument of 44 stops with tracker key-action. The stop-list shows Cavaillé-Coll influences in the design of the Swell organ. The fourth manual, as with many recent four manual instruments, is a type of Bombarde division.

The case, designed by David Graebe, will be a notably architectural composition, with 16ft Pedal towers supported by caryatids, a Positive projecting over the console under a curved pediment and a main case surmounted by a broken pediment reminiscent of Renatus Harris.

LANCASTER The University Great Hall
Bishop 1979

GREAT		SWELL		PEDAL	
Open Diapason	8	Gedact	8	Subbass	16
Rohrflute	8	Koppelflute	4	Spitzflute	8
Principal	4	Nazard	2⅔	Octave	4
Stopped Flute	4	Principal	2	Trumpet	8
Gemshorn	2	Cimbel 33.36	II		
Sesquialtera	II	Cremona	8		
Mixture 19.22.26	III				

Ralph Downes designed this straightforward tracker-action two-manual in association with John Budgen of Bishop & Son. It has a simple three-compartment case with the 2ft-based Swell hidden above the Great organ, behind a decorative fret, with the Pedal divided either side. The bass compartments show the lowest six pipes of the tapered Spitzflute and also the lowest notes of the wooden Subbass with their mouths turned inwards.

PRESTON Church of St George the Martyr
Willis 1865

GREAT		SWELL		CHOIR		PEDAL	
Double Open Diapason	16	Contra Gamba	16	Claribel Flute	8	Open Diapason	16
Open Diapason	8	Open Diapason	8	Viola d'Amore	8	Bourdon	16
Claribel Flute	8	Lieblich Gedackt	8	Vox Angelica	8	Violoncello	8
Gamba	8	Salicional	8	Dulciana	8	Viola	4
Principal	4	Principal	4	Gemshorn	4	Fourniture	III
Flute Harmonique	4	Flute Harmonique	4	Flute Harmonique	4	Ophicleide	16
Twelfth	2⅔	Piccolo	2	Flageolet	2		
Fifteenth	2	Mixture	III	Corno di Bassetto	8		
Sesquialtera	III	Cornopean	8	Orchestral Oboe	8		
Posaune	8	Oboe	8				
Clarion	4	Clarion	4				

This unaltered Father Willis is a particularly complete example. Note the independent Pedal, which he usually reserved only for his grandest instruments. Other stops which would have been novelties when the organ was new are the Harmonic Flutes (an idea which he copied from Cavaillé-Coll) and the Lieblich Gedackt (which he, and everyone else, copied from Edmund Schulze). The Orchestral Oboe, a difficult stop to voice, was all his own. The organ retains its original tracker action on the manuals.

LEICESTERSHIRE

LEICESTER Bishop Street Methodist Church
Smith 17th century; Hill Norman & Beard c1935

Surprisingly, this Wesleyan church contains the front of a four-tower Father Smith organ case. The pipe-shades and some of the cresting are obvious Gothic Revival substitutions but it still looks very grand, even though set into wider grille-work. The organ itself is a 1930s Hill Norman & Beard with detached semi-horseshoe-style console, but the case came to the church in 1858. Its previous owners, St Margaret's Church, Leicester had bought it from Crang & Hancock in 1773. Crang & Hancock had supplied a new organ the previous year to Chelmsford parish church (now the Cathedral), so they may have taken the Smith from Chelmsford in part-exchange, but of this we have no proof.

LINCOLNSHIRE

LINCOLN The Cathedral
Willis 1898; Harrison 1960

GREAT		SWELL		CHOIR (unenclosed)		PEDAL	
Double Open Diapason	16	Double Open Diapason	16	Bourdon	16	Double Open Wood	32
Open Diapason I	8	Open Diapason I	8	*Open Diapason	8	Open Metal	16
Open Diapason II	8	Open Diapason II	8	†Dulciana	8	Open Wood	16
Open Diapason III	8	Lieblich Gedeckt	8	†Lieblich Gedeckt	8	Violone	16
Stopped Diapason	8	Salicional	8	Gamba	8	Bourdon	16
Claribel Flute	8	Vox Angelica	8	Hohl Flute	8	*Dulciana	16
Flute Harmonique	4	Principal	4	Gemshorn	4	Violoncello	8
Principal	4	Lieblich Flute	4	†Concert Flute	4	Octave Wood	8
Twelfth	2⅔	Fifteenth	2	*Nazard	2⅔	*Dulciana	8
Fifteenth	2	Mixture 12.19.22	III	†Piccolo	2	Super Octave	4
Mixture 12.19.22	III	Oboe	8	*Tierce	1⅗	Contra Posaune	32
Trombone	16	Vox Humana	8	*Mixture 22.26.29	III	Ophicleide	16
Tromba	8	Double Trumpet	16	Cor Anglais	16	Clarion	8
Clarion	4	Trumpet	8	Corno di Bassetto	8		
		Clarion	4			*1960 pipes.	
				SOLO (enclosed)		†Pipes in chair case.	
				Gamba	8		
				Voix Célestes	8		
				Claribel Flute			
				(not enclosed)	8		
				Harmonic Flute	4		
				Orchestral Oboe	8		
				Orchestral Clarinet	8		
				Tuba (not enclosed)	8		
				Tuba Clarion			
				(not enclosed)	4		

Lincoln was Father Willis' last cathedral organ (out of seventeen!). He used E. J. Willson's 1826 Gothick case on the screen though, for want of space, the Swell organ and much of the Pedal are upstairs in the north triforium. The organ is a very complete four-manual, and although there is less upperwork than in Willis' earlier instruments, the extremes of Robert Hope-Jones were avoided. Willis' pneumatic actions were not generally long-lived and the organ was fortunate not to have been rebuilt before 1960. As it was, Cuthbert Harrison took a much more conservative line than Arthur Harrison would have done. The new console occupies the classic position on the east side of the screen, and none of the original stops were removed so basically this is still a Father Willis cathedral organ, retaining its original sound.

MERSEYSIDE

LIVERPOOL Lady Chapel Organ, Liverpool Cathedral
Willis 1910; Hill Norman & Beard 1973

GREAT		SWELL		PEDAL	
Lieblich Bourdon	16	Gedackt	8	Violone	16
Open Diapason	8	Salicional	8	Lieblich Bourdon	16
Stopped Diapason	8	Voix Célestes	8	Octave	8
Octave	4	Gemshorn	4	Bass Flute	8
Chimney Flute	4	Block Flute	2	Fifteenth	4
Fifteenth	2	Mixture 22.26.29	III	Gedackt	4
Cornet 12.17	II	Bassoon	16	Super Octave	2
Furniture 19.22.26	III-IV	Cornopean	8	Fagotto	16
Trumpet	8			Rohr Shalmey	4

The Lady Chapel was the first part of the Cathedral to be completed and its architectural style is more ornate than Sir Giles Gilbert Scott was to use later on the Cathedral itself. Among the principal ornaments is the organ on the west gallery with its striking and unusual case in a free Gothic design following no historical prototypes. Where else can one see a two-tower case with the central flat taller than the towers yet still in perfect proportion with the lofty chapel?

The organ itself was an enigma. It was the first work of Henry Willis III, built when he was only twenty-one years old and good enough to win him the contract for the main Cathedral organ. It was, however, an immature work, which gained enormously from the superb acoustic of the Lady Chapel, but unrepresentative of his later style. The instrument was rebuilt in 1973 with a new console and action and a new tonal design which gave the organ not only a more complete Pedal division but also a lightness and delicacy which previously it lacked.

Main Organ, Liverpool Cathedral
Willis 1923–6, 1960–5; Harrison 1977

GREAT		SWELL		CHOIR		PEDAL	
Contra Violone	32	Contra Geigen	16	(Positive section)		Resultant Bass	64
Double Open Diapason	16	Contra Salicional	16	Nason	8	Double Open Bass	32
Contra Tibia	16	Lieblich Bordun	16	Coppel	4	Double Open Diapason	32
Bourdon	16	Open Diapason	8	Nasat	2⅔	Contra Violone	32
Double Quint	10⅔	Geigen	8	Gemshorn	2	Open Bass	16
Open Diapason 1	8	Tibia	8	Terz	1⅗	Tibia	16
Open Diapason 2	8	Wald Flöte	8	Spitzflöte	1	Open Diapason	16
Open Diapason 3	8	Lieblich Gedact	8	Cimbel	III	Contra Basso	16
Open Diapason 4	8	Echo Viola	8			Geigen (enclosed)	16
Open Diapason 5	8	Salicional	8	(Enclosed section)		Violon (enclosed)	16
Tibia	8	Vox Angelica	8	Contra Viola	16	Dolce	16
Doppel Flöte	8	Octave	4	Violin Diapason	8	Bourdon	16
Stopped Diapason	8	Octave Geigen	4	Viola	8	Sub Bass	16
Quint	5⅓	Salicet	4	Claribel Flute	8	Principal	8
Octave 1	4	Lieblich Flöte	4	Unda Maris	8	Violone	8
Octave 2	4	Nazard	2⅔	Octave Viola	4	Violoncello (enclosed)	8
Principal	4	Fifteenth	2	Suabe Flöte	4	Stopped Flute	8
Gemshorn	4	Lieblich Piccolo	2	Octavin	2	Bass Flute	8
Flûte Couverte	4	Seventeenth	1⅗	Dulciana Mixture		Open Flute (enclosed)	8
Tenth	3⅕	Sesquialtera		10.12.17.19.22	V	Fifteenth	4
Twelfth	2⅔	10.12.17.19.22	V	Bass Clarinet	16	Octave Flute	4
Super Octave	2	Mixture 15.19.22.26.29	V	Baryton	16	Gedact	4
Fifteenth	2	Contra Hautboy	16	Corno di Bassetto	8	Flûte Triangulaire	
Mixture	V	Hautboy	8	Cor Anglais	8	(enclosed)	4
Fourniture		Krummhorn	8	Vox Humana	8	Mixture 17.19.22	III
19.22.24.26.29	V	Waldhorn	16	Trompette Harmonique	8	Fourniture	
Double Trumpet	16	Cornopean	8	Clarion	4	15.19.22.26.29	V
Trompette Harmonique	8	Clarion	4			Fagotto (enclosed)	16
Trumpet	8	Double Trumpet	16	SOLO		Octave Bassoon	
Clarion	4	Trompette Harmonique	8	(Unenclosed)		(enclosed)	8
		Trumpet	8	Contra Hohl Flöte	16	Contra Trombone	
BOMBARDE		Octave Trumpet	4	Hohl Flöte	8	(enclosed)	32
Grand Chorus–8.1.5.8.12.				Octave Hohl Flöte	4	Trombone (enclosed)	16
15.19.22.26.29	X			(Enclosed)		Ophicleide	16
Contra Tuba	16			Contre Viole	16	Clarion	8
Tuba	8			Viole de Gambe	8	Contra Bombarde	32
Tuba Clarion	4			Viole d'Orchestre	8	Bombarde	16
Tuba Magna	8			Violes Célestes	8	Bombarde	8
				Flûte Harmonique	8	Bombarde	4
				Octave Viole	4		
				Concert Flute	4		
				Violette	2		
				Piccolo Harmonique	2		
				Cornet de Violes			
				10.12.15	III		
				Cor Anglais	16		
				Clarinet (Orchestral)	8		
				Oboe (Orchestral)	8		
				Bassoon (Orchestral)	8		
				French Horn	8		
				Contra Tromba	16		
				Tromba Rèal	8		
				Tromba	8		
				Tromba Clarion	4		

This huge instrument, the largest organ in Britain, was as big a jump from what went before as William Hill's organ in York Minster had been almost a century earlier. Its whole scale of construction was unique and, indeed, remains so, yet there is remarkably little duplication and the instrument is no more than is required to match Sir Giles Gilbert Scott's huge building. The organ established Henry Willis III as a major builder and reflects his individual style. This style, whilst giving full rein to romantic contrasts of tone quality and power, also provides well-developed choruses and reed-stops which, though well controlled, are never as smooth as those of the Arthur Harrison school. Indeed, it is probably the excellence and sheer variety of romantic reed-stops which set this organ apart from its contemporaries. The statistics are unbeatable, of course: forty-eight horsepower to drive the blowers, two Pedal 32ft reeds, one enclosed in a swell-box 25ft (7.5m) high, the Grand Chorus mixture of ten ranks voiced on 10in (250mm) wind, the Tuba Magna on 50in (1250mm) of wind.

The organ was planned to have a Corona section in the tower for ethereal effects, a 30 stop two-manual and Pedal west-end section on the bridge at the rear of the nave and another two-manual section to accompany the choir in the 'central space'. The Corona section was actually constructed but was destroyed when Willis' London factory was bombed in 1941. The five-manual console in the loft on the north side of the chancel was supplemented by another in the central space in 1940. This was replaced in 1965 by a mobile two-manual console controlling 35 selected stops on the Great, Swell, Bombarde and Pedal organs. On the main console the couplers are controlled by Compton-type 'luminous touches' on the music desk; the remote swell-pedal mechanisms work on the Willis patent 'infinite speed and gradation' principle, whereby the position of the swell-pedal controls not the position of the swell-shutters but their speed of movement.

Tonal changes since the organ was completed have been few; the largely Dulciana-based unenclosed Choir organ was replaced by a Positive by Henry Willis IV in 1960 and minor changes were made by Harrison & Harrison when they restored the organ in 1977.

After the exuberance of the Lady Chapel case, Scott's cases for the Main Organ are a trifle ordinary. The scale of the building is such that the 16ft pipes in the chancel cases look short and even the 32ft pipes in the transept cases appear quite modest. It is the sound of this organ that is memorable, however. Despite the massive foundation of unison and sub-unison tone, the essentially reedy sound of the major choruses makes this a very different organ from the ponderous instruments characteristic of most 1920s organ-building.

Liverpool Metropolitan Cathedral (Roman Catholic)
Walker 1967

GREAT		SWELL		SOLO (enclosed)		PEDAL	
Violone	16	Open Diapason	8	Quintaton	16	Contra Spitzflöte	32
Open Diapason	8	Rohrflöte	8	Orchestral Flute	8	Principal	16
Principal	8	Salicional	8	Viola da Gamba	8	Violone	16
Gemshorn	8	Vox Angelica	8	Voix Celeste	8	Spitzflöte	16
Stopped Diapason	8	Principal	4	Lieblich Gedeckt	8	Bourdon	16
Octave	4	Gedeckt Flute	4	Dulciana	8	Quintaton	16
Chimney Flute	4	Twelfth	2⅔	Suabe Flute	4	Octave	8
Twelfth	2⅔	Super Octave	2	Quintadena	4	Octave Spitzflöte	8
Fifteenth	2	Flageolet	2	Nazard	2⅔	Bass Flute	8
Blockflöte	2	Sesquialtera 12.17	II	Piccolo	2	Twelfth	5⅓
Mixture 15.19.22	III	Scharf 22.26.29.33	IV	Quartane 12.15	II	Fifteenth	4
Plein Jeu 19.22.26.29	IV	Double Trumpet	16	Clarinet	8	Nachthorn	4
Contra Posaune	16	Bassoon	16	Tuba	8	Octave Flute	4
Trumpet	8	Trumpet	8	Orchestral Trumpet		Sifflöte	2
Clarion	4	Oboe da Caccia	8	(horizontal)	8	Mixture 19.22.26.29	IV
		Shawm	4	Octave Tuba	8	Contra Posaune	32
POSITIVE						Bombarde	16
Gedeckt	8			ACCOMPANIMENTAL		Posaune	16
Spitzflöte	4			(duplexed from Solo organ)		Bassoon	16
Koppelflöte	4			Quintaton	16	Tromba	8
Nazard	2⅔			Lieblich Gedeckt	8	Rohr Schalmei	4
Principal	2			Dulciana	8		
Blockflöte	2			Dulcet	4		
Tierce	1⅗			Quintadena	4		
Larigot	1⅓			Nazard	2⅔		
Sifflöte	1			Quartane 12.15	II		
Cymbale 29.33.36	III						
Krummhorn	8						
Contra Posaune	16						
Trumpet	8						
Clarion	4						

Sir Frederick Gibberd's round Cathedral poses unusual liturgical and acoustic problems. The organ is placed in a shallow chamber over the entrance to a chapel, but the building is still big enough to accept 32ft front pipes down to DDDD. Indeed the 32ft pipes are one of the unusual features of this instrument, since they are tapered, which add definition to the notes. The organ has no case in the accepted sense of the word, being screened by a symmetric array of bass pipes designed by Sir Frederick Gibberd. The best feature is the horizontal Orchestral Trumpet, whose flared brass tubes punctuate the display.

The tonal design is in the conventional style of the 1960s, with well-developed mixture-work and only slightly elevated wind pressures for the chorus reeds. The Solo organ is unusual in that it combines elements of the romantic Solo organ of an earlier era with a mild accompanimental chorus which can be played from the Positive keys like an enclosed choir. When regulating the organ, Dennis Thurlow, then Walker's voicer, had great trouble in obtaining sufficient power on the floor of the Cathedral because all the sound was disappearing up the 'funnel' at the top of the building, and the general impression of the instrument is that it is agreeable enough but lacks aggression.

St George's Hall
Willis 1854–5, 1897, 1931

GREAT		SWELL (enclosed)		CHOIR (enclosed)		PEDAL	
Double Open Diapason	16	Double Diapason	16	Contra Viola	16	Resultant Bass	64
Bourdon	16	Open Diapason	8	Open Diapason	8	Double Open Bass	32
Open Diapason 1	8	Geigen Diapason	8	Viola da Gamba	8	Double Open Diapason	32
Open Diapason 2	8	Rohr Flute	8	Hohl Flute	8	Open Bass	16
Open Diapason 3	8	Aeoline	8	Stopped Diapason	8	Contra Bass	16
Tibia	8	Salicional	8	Dulciana	8	Open Diapason	16
Viola	8	Voix Celestes	8	Vox Angelica	8	Violon	16
Stopped Diapason	8	Principal	4	Principal	4	Bourdon	16
Quint	5⅓	Octave Geigen	4	Octave Viola	4	Salicional	16
Octave	4	Wald Flute	4	Harmonic Flute	4	Quintaten	16
Principal	4	Twelfth	2⅔	Nazard	2⅔	Octave	8
Octave Viola	4	Fifteenth	2	Fifteenth	2	Principal	8
Flute	4	Piccolo	2	Flageolet	2	Violoncello	8
Tenth	3⅕	Seventeenth	1⅗	Tierce	1⅗	Flute	8
Twelfth	2⅔	Doublette 15.22	II	Larigot	1⅓	Octave Quint	5⅓
Fifteenth	2	Fourniture 15.17.19.22	IV	Septieme	1⅟7	Fifteenth	4
Seventeenth	1⅗	Contra Oboe	16	Piccolo	1	Viole	4
Doublette 15.22	II	Clarinet	8	Sesquialtera 17.19.22	III	Octave Flute	4
Sesquialtera		Oboe	8	Bass Clarinet	16	Fourniture	
12.15.17.19.22	V	Clarion	4	Orchestral Oboe	8	12.15.17.19.22	V
Mixture 15.17.19.22	IV	Trombone	16	Trumpet	8	Mixture 10.12.15	III
Contra Trombone	16	Ophicleide	8	Clarion	4	Clarinet	16
Trombone	8	Trumpet	8	Harmonic Gongs	8	Bombarde	32
Ophicleide	8	Horn	8			Posaune	16
Trumpet	8	Clarion	4	SOLO (enclosed)		Ophicleide	16
Clarion 1	4			Quintaten	16	Clarion	8
Clarion 2	4			Tibia	8	Octave Clarion	4
				Violoncello	8	Pedal Sostenuto	
				'Cello Celestes	8		
				Tibia Clausa	8		
				Violin (2 ranks)	4		
				Orchestral Flute	4		
				Piccolo	2		
				Cor Anglais	16		
				Bassoon	8		
				Corno-di-Bassetto	8		
				Vox Humana	8		
				Cathedral Chimes			
				French Horn	8		
				Double Tuba	16		
				Tuba	8		
				Tuba Clarion	4		
				(unenclosed)			
				Solo Diapason	8		
				Grand Chorus			
				8.12.15.19.22.26.29	VII		
				Tuba Mirabilis	8		

This instrument played an important part in the history of the British organ as it established Henry Willis, then barely thirty years old, as one of the three major builders of his day. As built, it had 100 stops, then a record size, and included a large number of mechanical innovations which were to be widely copied. It was the first organ to have a radiating and concave pedalboard, an innovation credited to Dr S. S. Wesley, but not outside the bounds of argument even today. Furthermore, it was the first important organ to have stop-jambs inclined in toward the player and, apart from the Willis 1851 Great Exhibition organ, the first to have thumb pistons. In other ways the organ looked backwards; it was the last major instrument to be built with the old GG manual compass and also the last to be initially tuned to an unequal temperament, both at Dr Wesley's specific insistence. Wesley's stop-list had numerous duplications; for example, three Principals, two Twelfths and two Fifteenths on the Great organ. He believed, wrongly, that these would increase the power of the organ. Some of these duplications were eliminated by Willis whilst the organ was under construction, but the power Wesley sought was achieved in another way, by Willis' excellent reeds.

The organ stands on a gallery at one end of Elmes' Victorian baroque hall in a 'case' by C. R. Cockerill which is an early example of an organ case which is not really a case at all but a screen of bass pipes. Cockerill finished off the tops of some of the pipes with crowns to stop them looking naked and the pipes themselves and their supports are richly decorated. Later imitators of this style produced boring and ugly instruments; it is the theatrical exuberance of this case that is the secret of its success.

The organ was re-tuned to equal temperament in 1867, when the Solo chorus reeds received a drastic increase in wind pressure, and in 1897 Willis rebuilt his own instrument, replacing the pneumatic lever action with tubular and altering the manual compass to the standard CC. The mixture-work was reduced and Willis enclosed part of the Solo organ. There was a further rebuild in 1931 under Henry Willis III who supplied electropneumatic action and a new console. The Choir organ was redesigned and enclosed and the Pedal reeds revoiced on 20in (500mm) wind. The Solo organ gained a new Diapason, Grand Chorus mixture and Tuba Mirabilis (on 30in/750mm wind), not unlike the Bombarde organ at the Cathedral.

Despite changes, the Swell and Great organs are still much as they were originally and one can still appreciate that in 1855 (as eighty years later at the Cathedral), it was the Willis firm's prowess at reed voicing that was the essential factor in their success.

NORFOLK

GREAT YARMOUTH St Nicholas' Parish Church
Hill 1909; Compton 1960

GREAT		SWELL		CHOIR (enclosed)		PEDAL	
Double Open Diapason	16	Lieblich Bourdon	16	Quintaton	16	Subbass	32
Open Diapason I	8	Open Diapason	8	Gemshorn	8	Open Wood	16
Open Diapason II	8	Salicional	8	Viole d'Orchestre	8	Open Metal	16
Hohlflöte	8	Voix Celeste	8	Dulciana	8	Violone	16
Spitz	8	Lieblich Gedeckt	8	Vox Angelica	8	Bourdon	16
Stopped Diapason	8	Principal	4	Flauto Traverso	8	Echo Bourdon	16
Octave	4	Nason Flute	4	Viol d'Amour	4	Octave	8
Principal	4	Fifteenth	2	Vienna Flute	4	Violoncello	8
Twelfth	2⅔	Mixture 15.19.22	III	Nazard	2⅔	Bass Flute	8
Fifteenth	2	Double Trumpet	16	Flageolet	2	Fifteenth	4
Mixture 17.19.22	III	Cornopean	8	Contra Bassoon	16	Flute	4
Cymbel 22.26.29	III	Oboe	8	Orchestral Oboe	8	Larigot	2⅔
Trombone	16	Clarion	4	Clarinet	8	Twenty-second	2
Tromba	8			Tuba	8	Posaune	16
Octave Tromba	4					Posaune	8
Tuba	8					Clarion	4

Abraham Jordan built an organ for Yarmouth in 1733 and its case was later joined by that of the Renatus Harris organ from St Peter Mancroft, Norwich. Latterly, they housed a large organ by Binns but all was bombed in the war, after which this very large church was rebuilt from a roofless shell. The present organ came from St Mary the Boltons, South Kensington, London. It was a good three-manual Hill of 1909, installed in Yarmouth by Compton in 1960. It is now chiefly remarkable for the new case in the north transept designed for it by Stephen Dykes Bower and executed in brightly coloured painted softwood. The case is bogus in the sense that it is all sham and bears no relation to the actual layout of the organ. It is nevertheless a brilliant visual *tour de force*.

KING'S LYNN St Margaret's Parish Church
Snetzler 1754; Rushworth & Dreaper 1962

This was said to have been Snetzler's largest organ, with two chorus mixtures on the Great as well as a Cornet. The Choir Dulciana is reputed to have been Snetzler's first in England. Ten stops of Snetzler's pipes survive as does his splendid case with the characteristic curved pipe-block for the flats between the three towers. The use of a 'waisted' case with carved brackets at the sides must have been a conscious archaism in 1754.

NORWICH The Cathedral (see Plate 7)
Hill Norman & Beard 1940–1

GREAT		SWELL		SOLO		PEDAL	
Primary		(main case facing west)		(main case facing west		(north and south triforia)	
(north triforium)		Contra Geigen	16	enclosed)		Double Open Wood	32
Double Gedeckt	32	Bourdon	16	Contra Viole	16	Open Wood	16
Double Open Diapason	16	Open Diapason	8	Viole d'Orchestre	8	Open Wood (minor)	16
Open Diapason (large)	8	Rohr Gedackt	8	Octave Viole	4	Open Diapason	16
Open Diapason (medium)	8	Salicional	8	Viole Celeste II rks	8	Open Diapason (minor)	16
Quint	5⅓	Voix Celeste II rks	8	Harmonic Claribel	8	Violone	16
Octave	4	Principal	4	Flauto Traverso	4	Contra Viole	16
Twelfth	2⅔	Stopped Flute	4	Cor Anglais	16	Bourdon	16
Fifteenth	2	Fifteenth	2	Orchestral Oboe	8	Lieblich Bourdon	16
Mixture 15.19.22.26	IV	Larigot	1⅓	Corno di Bassetto	8	Dulciana	16
Trombone	16	Sesquialtera	II	Vox Humana	8	Quint	10⅔
Trumpet	8	Mixture 15.19.22.26.29	V	Orchestral Horn	8	Octave Wood	8
Clarion	4	Sharp Mixture		Orchestral Trumpet	16	Principal	8
		22.26.29.33	IV	Orchestral Trumpet	8	Bass Flute	8
Secondary		Contra Fagotto	16	Orchestral Trumpet	4	Cello	8
(main case facing west)		Horn	8	(unenclosed)		Dolce	8
Gedeckt	16	Trumpet	8	Tuba Mirabilis	8	Twelfth	5⅓
Principal	8	Clarion	4			Superoctave	4
Stopped Diapason	8			CHOIR POSITIF		Fifteenth	4
Octave	4	CHOIR SWELL		(unenclosed facing east)		Octave Flute	4
Spitzflute	4	(enclosed)		Quintaten	16	Harmonics 19.22	II
Waldflute	2	Violoncello	8	Open Diapason	8	Bass Trombone	32
Quartane 12.15	II	Dolce	8	Chimney Flute	8	Ophicleide	16
Furniture		Cor de Nuit	8	Principal	4	Trombone	16
22.26.29.33.36	V-VI	Unda Maris	8	Nason Flute	4	Contra Fagotto	16
Mounted Cornet	V	Gemshorn	4	Nazard	2⅔	Schalmei	16
		Flageolet	2	Superoctave	2	Clarion	8
		Octavin	1	Blockflute	2	Octave Clarion	4
		Schalmei	16	Tierce	1⅗		
		Trumpet	8	Cymbal 33.36.40	III	Cymbelstern: 6 bells with	
						rotating star	

As with any of our major cathedrals, Norwich has a long history in terms of organs. Of the George Dallam instrument of 1664, only part of the case remains, much 'Gothicised' and now in the chapel of the adjacent grammar school. Renatus Harris enlarged the organ in 1689 and Byfield made a major reconstruction in 1760. Bishop added a 21ft GGG Pedal Open Diapason in 1834. In 1899 Norman & Beard made a new five-manual organ retaining only a few stops and some of the old casework. The fifth manual was an Echo division, not installed until 1911 but fitted with an early electric action and a hydraulically operated swell-box. It was placed at the far east end of the triforium, where it had its own Hope-Jones-style console for the benefit of the organ tuner. The 1899 instrument was seriously damaged by fire in 1938 and replaced by the present instrument. Mechanically, this was entirely new, but some old pipes survived, including seventeenth-century pipes in the Choir Open Diapason and the Bishop Pedal pipes. After the bombing of Hill's works in 1941, the Cathedral triforium was pressed into service as an organ factory, even to casting pipe metal.

The organ case, with two fronts and a chair case, was designed by Stephen Dykes Bower and installed in 1950. It shows how well a neo-classical case can succeed in a Romanesque Gothic building. There was much debate at the time as to whether the instrument should remain on the screen, and the case is relatively narrow to allow a glimpse of the eastern apse from the west end.

The organ itself was really the first major instrument to begin to break away from the Hope-Jones/Arthur Harrison mould of emphasis on solo voices, though a characteristic romantic Solo organ was provided plus a bold Tuba on 20in (500mm) wind pressure. The Pedal organ speaks both east and west from the triforia either side of the instrument but, as with all cathedral organs on the screen, the instrument has two different characters, heard from choir or nave. The Choir Positif and Choir Swell, placed in and behind the chair case, act as a two-manual instrument for daily choral services, whilst the Great, Swell and Solo organs speak westwards. There is an additional 'primary' Great organ for leading large congregations, out of sight in the north triforium. The choruses of the Swell, Secondary Great and Choir organs were revoiced in 1968–70 in collaboration with the late Brian Runnett.

King Edward VI School Chapel

This medieval building was originally a chantry chapel of the Cathedral. After the Reformation, it became a school, only becoming a place of worship again in relatively modern times. The organ on the west gallery is by Rayner of Ipswich, recently installed by Bishop in place of an odd Hope-Jones, but the case is the west chair case from the Cathedral, acquired largely undamaged after the fire in 1939. Made by George Dallam in 1664, it has the implied receding perspective of which the Dallams were so fond, though the case is hardly as he left it, having been 'Gothicised' by Salvin in 1834.

The Old Meeting House, Colegate
? Dallam 17th century

GREAT		SWELL		PEDAL	
Open Diapason	8	Stopped Diapason Bass	8	Bourdon	16
Stopped Diapason	8	Open Diapason	8		
Dulciana	8	Stopped Diapason	8	Tenor C up	
Principal	4	Viol di Gamba	8		
Flute	4	Gemshorn	4		
Twelfth	2⅔				
Fifteenth	2				

There is a tradition that the organ came originally from Norwich Cathedral. On the face of it, this is unlikely, since we know the case of George Dallam's 1664 organ was of quite different design. Fairly obviously, the case was originally the chair part of a double case and is known to have been in the Meeting House since before 1760. Details of the design and construction suggest that the case is possibly the work of Robert Dallam. Perhaps it is the case of the temporary organ which Norwich Cathedral bought secondhand at the Restoration in 1660 from a 'Rich. Plumm of Bury', Lancelot Pease supplying 'a new sett of pipes'? This would make it a pre-Commonwealth case of some importance. In any event, its original home remains a mystery. The mermaids and dolphins in the carving perhaps suggest a nautical connection?

The front pipes, with their varied mouths, are contemporary with the case otherwise the pipework appears to be less old, though much of the Great organ is still very ancient. The tenor C Swell and the one-stop Pedal organ are nineteenth-century work by Bishop.

St George's Church, Colegate
England 1802

GREAT		SWELL		PEDAL	
Open Diapason	8	Open Diapason	8	Bourdon	16
Stopped Diapason	8	Gedact	8		
Clarabella	8	Gemshorn	4		
Dulciana	8	Hautboy	8		
Principal	4				
Twelfth	2⅔				
Fifteenth	2				

The splendid medieval church retains many of its Georgian fittings, including this important G. P. England organ. The fundamentals of the organ remain largely unchanged and the instrument was restored to the west gallery in 1947 by Boggis, who added the pedalboard and Bourdon. The original small stop-knobs remain as does the 'long compass' of the Great organ down to GG.

ST PETER MANCROFT CHURCH, NORWICH

St Peter Mancroft Church
Collins 1984

GREAT		SWELL (below Great)		POSITIVE (in chair case)		PEDAL (divided)	
Bourdon	16	Stopt Diapason	8	Gedact	8	Principal	16
Principal	8	Salicional	8	Quintadena	8	Subbass	16
Spitz Flute	8	Celeste	8	Principal	4	Octave	8
Octave	4	Koppel Flute	4	Rohr Flute	4	Open Flute	8
Hohl Flute	4	Principal	2	Gemshorn	2	Bass Octave	4
Quint	2⅔	Octave	1	Tapered Quint	1⅓	Mixture	IV
Octave	2	Tertian	II	Sesquialtera	II	Posaune	16
Block Flute	2	Vox Humana	8	Scharf	IV-V	Trumpet	8
Tierce	1⅗			Holzdulzian	16		
Mixture	IV-V			Krummhorn	8		
Cymbal	II						
Trumpet	8						

The church of St Peter Mancroft is the grandest of the numerous medieval city churches in Norwich and had a fine 1707 Renatus Harris organ on a west-end gallery up to 1875. The 1875 Hele organ, rebuilt by Rushworth & Dreaper, stood in an organ chamber on the south side of the chancel. The new organ, now under construction, will again be placed on a west gallery. In order to fit closely against the tower arch, the divided Pedal soundboards will be diagonal!

SOUTH PICKENHAM The Parish Church
Bishop 1857

A medieval Gothic case in rural Norfolk! Well, not really medieval, but the next best thing, a Victorian Gothic case designed by A. W. N. Pugin. Given by Sir John Sutton, the organ is a small two-manual, the shallow roofed case having a simple silhouette with basses in the centre balanced by the contrary shape of the shutters with elaborate painted decoration. There is a tiny *Brustwerk* Swell in the extravagantly corbelled lower part of the case. The organ was built for West Tofts church, where it stood on a tribune high on the wall.

LITTLE WALSINGHAM St Mary's Parish Church
Arnold, Williamson & Hyatt 1964

GREAT		SWELL		PEDAL	
Open Diapason	8	Viola	8	Open Metal	16
Chimney Flute	8	Stopped Metal	8	Subbass	16
Principal	4	Gemshorn	4	Principal	8
Conical Flute	4	Fifteenth	2	Basss Flute	8
Nazard	2⅔	Nineteenth	1⅓	Fifteenth	4
Block Flute	2	Twenty-second	1	Conical Flute	2
Tierce	1⅗	Basset Horn	16	Mixture 19.22	
Mixture 19.22.26.29	IV			Basset Horn ⎫	16
				Basset Horn ⎬ (in Swell)	8
				Basset Horn ⎭	4

This instrument was the product of the fairly short-lived partnership of Cedric Arnold with Williamson & Hyatt. The striking case projects from the west wall with the console on the west gallery below it. The copper front pipes in the central tower and flats, together with the strong outline and diagonal emphasis of the case, set off the absence of applied decoration.

The organ is an interesting example of the transition toward the *Orgelbewegung*-inspired *werk* principle instrument with its apparent (but not real) tone-cabinets and the use of tracker action to the manuals combined with electropneumatic action to the largely unified Pedal organ. The voicing is on light pressure and the Great organ has a Cornet Separé. The Swell is unconventional in its separate Nineteenth and Twenty-second stops and the lone 16ft half-length reed.

WYMONDHAM The Abbey (illustrated opposite the title page)
Davis 1794; Hill Norman & Beard 1954

GREAT		SWELL		CHOIR		PEDAL	
Double Diapason	16	Open Diapason	8	Chimney Flute	8	Open Wood Bass	16
Open Diapason	8	Hohl Flute	8	Viola da Gamba	8	Bourdon	16
Stopped Diapason	8	Salicional	8	Principal	4	Gamba	16
Dulciana	8	Voix Celeste	8	Stopped Flute	4	Octave	8
Principal	4	Principal	4	Flageolet	2	Gedeckt	8
Block Flute	4	Fifteenth	2	Larigot	1⅓	Gamba	8
Twelfth	2⅔	Cornet 12.15.17	III	Cymbel	III	Fifteenth	4
Fifteenth	2	Mixture 19.22	II	Trumpet	8	Mixture 19.22	II
Seventeenth	1⅗	Contra Hautboy	16	Clarion	4	Sackbut	32
Mixture	II	Trumpet	8			Ophicleide	16
Sharp Mixture	III	Basset Horn	8			Clarion	8
Trumpet	8	Clarion	4			Shawm	4
Clarion	4						

The organ actually carries not James Davis' name but that of Longman & Broderip, the musical wholesalers of their day. The case which from a distance looks like a Gothick confection, is actually an astonishing assemblage of disparate parts. The four classical mahogany towers are surmounted by Gothick pinnacles and separated by crocketted and gabled flats made of oak. The lower central flat incorporates a masonic symbol. Amazingly, the organ escaped the craze for moving instruments to the chancel, the surpliced choir having to cope with an organ and organist 120ft (35m) distant. In recent years the Abbey has acquired a chamber organ, also by James Davis, which now stands at the east end.

Apart from the addition of Pedal pipes, the instrument remained unchanged until 1954, when the organ was rebuilt. Although a new console and swell-box were provided, the scheme was exceptionally conservationist for the period, tracker action being retained for the Great and Choir organs and the old console and 'nags-head' swell mechanism being preserved. The original 2¾in (70mm) wind pressure was also kept.

Additions made when the organ was cleaned in 1973 included the Choir organ Larigot and Cymbel and the Pedal Shawm and 32ft Sackbut.

NORTHAMPTONSHIRE

FINEDON St Mary's Parish Church
Shrider 1717; Holdich 1872

GREAT		SWELL		CHOIR		PEDAL	
*Open Diapason	8	Open Diapason	8	*Stopped Diapason	8	Open Pedal Pipes	16
*Stopped Diapason	8	*Stopped Diapason	8	Dulciana	8	Bourdon Pedal Pipes	16
Gamba	8	Principal	4	*Principal	4		
*Principal	4	*Fifteenth	2	Flute	4	*Shrider pipes.	
*Twelfth	3	*Echo Mixture 19.22	II	*Fifteenth	2		
*Fifteenth	2	Horn	8				
*Sesquialtera 17.19.22	III						
Trumpet	8						

Christopher Shrider was Father Smith's son-in-law and successor. He also built an organ for Westminster Abbey, of which only a few token pipes remain. With broken pediments on top of the flat side-towers, the case is obviously a three-tower version of Father Smith's four-tower case at Trinity College, Cambridge. It stands to this day in the west gallery for which it was built and retains the original 'diapering' or painted decoration on the front pipes. In the nineteenth century, G. M. Holdich rebuilt the organ, putting his console at the side, and other additions have been made since. Most of Shrider's Great organ chorus survives, however, and is reputed to be very bold and vigorous, unlike organs built later in the eighteenth century.

NORTHAMPTON All Saints' Church
Schwarbrick 18th century; Hill c1850; Walker 1982 (chancel organ), 1984 (west-end organ)

CHANCEL ORGAN

GREAT		SWELL		PEDAL	
Open Diapason	8	Gedackt	8	Bourdon	16
Stopped Diapason	8	Salicional	8	Octave	8
Octave	4	Unda Maris	8	Stopped Flute	8
Flageolet	2	Principal	4	Fagotto	16
Mixture	III	Nason Flute	4		
Cornet	III	Fifteenth	2		
		Mixture	III		
		Hautboy	8		

WEST END ORGAN

GREAT		SWELL		CHOIR		PEDAL	
Quintaton	16	Tapered Flute	8	Stopped Diapason	8	Violone	16
Open Diapason	8	Viola da Gamba	8	Prestant	4	Bourdon	16
Chimney Flute	8	Voix Celeste	8	Spindle Flute	4	Quint	10⅔
Octave	4	Principal	4	Octave	2	Octave	8
Fifteenth	2	Wald Flute	4	Larigot	1⅓	Gedackt	8
Mixture	IV	Nazard	2⅔	Mixture	IV	Nachthorn	4
Cornet	V	Octavin	2	Cremona	8	Mixture	IV
Trumpet	8	Tierce	1⅗	Orchestral Trumpet	8	Trombone	16
Clarion	4	Sharp Mixture	IV			Trumpet	8
		Bassoon	16				
		Cornopean	8				

The medieval church was largely destroyed in a fire in 1675 and the rebuilt interior is a provincial version of Wren's St Mary-at-Hill church in the City of London. Thomas Schwarbrick provided an organ in the eighteenth century and the somewhat altered case of his organ still survives on the west gallery. Hill built a fine 44 stop three-manual around 1850 which Brindley enlarged to four manuals and placed on the north side of the choir.

The usual Anglican debate over the position of the instrument (at the east end to be with a surpliced choir or at the west end for the best musical effect) has been resolved in All Saints' by the provision of two organs. The new two-manual tracker chancel organ incorporates Hill casework and some of the Hill pipes to produce an instrument which is designed for choir accompaniment even though hampered by its chamber position. The all-new three-manual tracker instrument at the west end is ideally placed, with the manual divisions in tone cabinets within the remaining parts of the Schwarbrick case together with a new chair case, and has proved to be a very musical and successful instrument, even if the horizontal (but hidden) Orchestral Trumpet is too fierce to be in character. The Great and Pedal divisions may be played from the console of the chancel organ, using an electric action.

Church of St Mary the Virgin, Far Cotton
ten Bruggencate 1978

HOOFDWERK		POSITIEF		PEDAL	
Prestant	8	Houtgedekt	8	Subbas	16
Octaaf	4	Roerfluit	4	Quintadeen	4
Mixtuur IV	1⅓	Prestant	2		
		Larigot	1⅓		
		Kromhoorn	8		

The interest of this organ lies not only in its Continental layout, with a 2ft-based *Brustpositief* behind pedal-operated doors below the waisted main case, but also in the sixteenth-century Dutch ideas incorporated in the stop-list. The three-stop *Hoofdwerk* is all Diapason tone, effectively a divided *Blockwerk*, with the flutes, the mutation and the reed all on the second manual.

OUNDLE Oundle School Chapel
Frobenius 1984

GREAT		SWELL		POSITIVE		PEDAL	
Bourdon	16	Flute	8	Gedackt	8	Principal	16
Principal	8	Salicional	8	Principal	4	Subbass	16
Flute	8	Celeste	8	Flute	4	Octave	8
Octave	4	Spitzflute	4	Gemshorn	2	Flute	8
Rohrflute	4	Nazard	2⅔	Larigot	1⅓	Principal	4
Quint	2⅔	Principal	2	Mixture	III	Mixture	III
Principal	2	Tierce	1⅗	Cromorne	8	Posaune	16
Terz	1⅗	Mixture	IV			Schalmei	4
Mixture	IV	Bassoon	16				
Trumpet	8	Oboe	8				

Frobenius of Copenhagen are building the new organ for Oundle School Chapel. The organ will have a *werk* principle layout with a chair case for the Positive and Pedal towers either side. It will stand on the west gallery. The casework will be of oak and the instrument will have tracker action and a non-radiating pedalboard.

STANFORD-ON-AVON St Nicholas' Church
Anon early 17th century

The organ case on the west gallery is reputed to have come from the Chapel Royal, Whitehall to Stanford in the late seventeenth century. Similarity to an existing oak cabinet designed by Inigo Jones suggests a date of around 1625. The front pipes alternate between elaborate embossing and decoration with gilded patterns, and there are three different shapes of pipe-mouth. The dummy chair case on the gallery edge is clearly an addition, perhaps when the main case came to Stanford.

The organ itself has been in ruins for at least ninety years. It was an 8 stop one-manual with a late seventeenth-century stop-list.

NORTHUMBERLAND

BRINKBURN Brinkburn Priory
Hill 1868

GREAT		SWELL		PEDAL	
Bourdon	16	Open Diapason	8	Open Diapason	16
Open Diapason	8	Stopped Diapason	8	Bourdon	16
Stopped Diapason	8	Principal	4		
Dulciana	8	Trumpet	8		
Principal	4	Oboe	8		
Wald Flute	4				
Twelfth	2⅔				
Fifteenth	2				
Mixture	II				

This must be one of the least-altered Hill organs in existence. The Department of the Environment, which is responsible for the Priory, commissioned the restoration of the organ in 1969, retaining hand-blowing as well as cone-tuning.

The Swell organ must have been old-fashioned even when new, since the chorus is un-developed and the department retains the subsidiary role seen in organs some thirty years earlier.

HEXHAM Hexham Abbey
Phelps 1974

GREAT		SWELL		PEDAL	
Bourdon	16	Bourdon	8	Principal	16
Principal	8	Salicional	8	Soubasse	16
Flûte à Cheminée	8	Voix Celeste	8	Octave Basse	8
Octave	4	Principal	4	Bourdon	8
Flûte Conique	4	Flûte	4	Octave	4
Superoctave	2	Nasard	2⅔	Fourniture 22.26.29.33	IV
Cornet	V	Doublette	2	Bombarde	16
Fourniture		Flûte à Bec	2	Bassoon	16
19.22.26.29.33	V	Tierce	1⅗	Trompette	8
Trompette	8	Larigot	1⅓	Chalmeau	4
Clairon	4	Cymbale 26.29.33.36	IV		
		Basson	16		
		Oboe	8		
		Cromorne	8		

Hexham Abbey, despite its name, is now a parish church and is one of the few to retain a choir screen position for the organ. The 1974 tracker-action instrument is the only organ in this country by Lawrence Phelps, the noted American designer. Unlike most screen organs, the instrument speaks one way only, to the nave, showing only a timber back to the chancel. Its classic *werk* principle layout of Great over Swell with divided Pedal takes up almost the full width of the arch, effectively shutting off the chancel. The design cleverly uses the Pedal 16ft front to integrate the 4ft-based Swell into the main case, avoiding the up-in-the-air appearance of the Great seen, for example, at Christ Church, Oxford. Lawrence Phelps worked in French Canada for many years, which explains, no doubt, the French stop-names in what has proved to be a very successful fusion of the north German tradition with a not wholly un-English Swell.

NORTH YORKSHIRE

SELBY The Abbey
Hill 1909; Hill Norman & Beard 1950

GREAT		SWELL		CHOIR (enclosed)		PEDAL	
Double Open Diapason	16	Open Diapason	8	Lieblich Gedeckt	16	Double Open Diapason	32
Bourdon	16	Rohr Flute	8	Geigen Principal	8	Open Diapason (metal)	16
Open Diapason I	8	Echo Dulciana	8	Lieblich Gedeckt	8	Open Diapason (wood)	16
Open Diapason II	8	Voix Celestes	8	Dulciana	8	Great Bass	16
Open Diapason III	8	Principal	4	Principal	4	Violone	16
Claribel Flute	8	Chimney Flute	4	Dulcet	4	Contra Viola	16
Principal	4	Fifteenth	2	Stopped Flute	4	Sub Bass	16
Octave	4	Larigot	1⅓	Flautina	2	Echo Bass	16
Harmonic Flute	4	Mixture 15.19.22.26.29	V	Dulcet Fifteenth	2	Octave	8
Twelfth	2⅔	Scharff 33.36	II	Dulcet Cornet	III	Violoncello	8
Fifteenth	2	Contra Fagotto	16	Great Posaune	8	Bass Flute	8
Mixture 19.22.26.29	IV	Horn	8	Echo Trumpet	8	Fifteenth	4
Sharp Mixture 29.33.36	III	Oboe	8	Cremona	8	Octave Flute	4
Contra Posaune	16	Clarion	4			Twenty-second	2
Posaune	8			SOLO (enclosed)		Mixture 26.29.33.36	IV
Clarion	4			Doppel Flute	8	Contra Trombone	32
				Viole d'Orchestre	8	Trombone	16
				Spitzprincipal	4	Trumpet	8
				Nazard	2⅔	Trompette	4
				Blockflute	2		
				Tierce	1⅗		
				Cymbel 33.36	II		
				Clarinet	8		
				Trompette	8		
				Tuba	8		

In 1825 Renn & Boston of Stockport built a 13 stop organ for the Abbey with two manuals but no Pedals. This instrument was moved twice and enlarged four times, ending up in 1906 as a 53 stop four-manual with a detached console and a pioneer electric action by John Compton. We do not know how successful this last rebuild was as it lasted only twenty-two days! The instrument was destroyed in a fire which gutted the Abbey. Interestingly, Compton was not invited to tender for the new organ which was supplied by Hill in 1909.

The two large three-tower Gothic cases either side of the choir were designed by J. Oldrid Scott and have typically rich carving, differing slightly in detail on the two sides. Built under the direction of Dr A. G. Hill, William Hill's grandson, the organ is one of the last large instruments of the long-lived Hill tradition. It was much used for recording by Fernando Germani after being rebuilt in 1950 by Hill Norman & Beard. The imposing detached console dates from this time, the big 'towers' either side of the manuals being designed to hinge open to reveal cupboards and piston switches. In recent years some tonal changes have been made by John Jackson of Leeds. For 1909, in the heyday of the romantic organ, the instrument is surprisingly well provided with good chorus-work, though some of the mixtures and virtually all the mutation stops are modern.

YORK Church of St Martin le Grand
Walker 1968

MANUAL	
Stopped Diapason	8
Spitz Flute	4
Block Flute	2

The tiny medieval church of St Martin le Grand was gutted by fire during World War II and refurnished after it. The appearance of the organ can best be described as 'high-tech', since the pipes stand on display in a glass-sided rectangular tone-cabinet, the whole being supported on a rectangular metal frame with exposed trackers running down to the diminutive console below.

York Minster
Elliot & Hill 1829; Harrison 1930; Walker 1903, 1960

GREAT		SWELL		CHOIR		PEDAL	
Double Open Diapason	16	Bourdon	16	Lieblich Bourdon	16	Double Open Wood	32
Gedeckt	16	Open Diapason	8	Open Diapason	8	Double Open Diapason	32
Open Diapason 1	8	Violin Diapason	8	Lieblich Gedeckt	8	Open Wood	16
Open Diapason 2	8	Stopped Diapason	8	Gamba	8	Open Diapason	16
Open Diapason 3	8	Echo Gamba	8	Gemshorn	4	Violone	16
Salicional	8	Voix Céleste	8	Claribel Flute	4	Gamba	16
Wald Flute	8	Principal	4	Twelfth	2⅔	Sub Bass	16
Stopped Diapason	8	Open Flute	4	Flageolet	2	Principal	8
Octave	4	Fifteenth	2	Tierce	1⅗	Flute	8
Principal	4	Full Mixture 15.19.22	III	Cymbal 29.33.36	III	Fifteenth	4
Harmonic Flute	4	Sharp Mixture 19.22.26	III	Contra Posaune	16	Choral Flute	4
Octave Quint	2⅔	Oboe	8	Posaune	8	Mixture 19.22.26.29	IV
Super Octave	2	Contra Fagotto	16			Sackbut	32
Block Flute	2	Cornopean	8	SOLO (enclosed)		Ophicleide	16
Larigot	1⅓	Horn	8	Viol d'Orchestre	8	Trombone	16
Tertian 26.31	II	Shalmey	4	Chimney Flute	8	Bombarde	8
Mixture 15.19.22	III			Echo Dulciana	8	Shawm	4
Furniture 19.22.26.29	IV			Concert Flute	4		
Contra Posaune	16			Bassoon	16		
Posaune	8			Crumhorn	8		
Trumpet	8			Orchestral Oboe	8		
Clarion	4			Vox Humana	8		
				Contra Tuba	16		
				Tuba	8		
				Tuba Mirabilis			
				(unenclosed)	8		

Robert Dallam made a two-manual organ for York in 1632 which survived the Commonwealth, but the present instrument dates from 1829, following destruction of the previous organ by arson. It was the first very large organ in Britain. Hill, in an attempt to obtain gravity, adopted the 16ft CCC compass used by Smith at St Paul's Cathedral, also supplying a four stop

Pedal organ with the first 32ft stops, a wood Open Diapason and a Sackbut, both of huge scale. These stops still exist, as does Sir Robert Smirke's 'prickly Gothic' case on the choir screen, with its curious alternation of single pipes and vertical posts.

As first built, the Elliot & Hill organ was quite extraordinary, with two separate 20 stop Great organs. An early high-pressure Tuba was added in 1846, a gift of George Hudson, the 'Railway King', and there were other alterations, culminating in a rebuild in 1859. At a further rebuild in 1903 by J. W. Walker & Sons, the console was moved from the east side of the instrument to the south. In 1930 Harrison & Harrison rebuilt the instrument again, giving it the Arthur Harrison treatment of increased wind pressures and smooth tone. This was reversed in 1960 when J. W. Walker & Sons revoiced the organ and moved the console back to the east side again, providing a second console on the floor of the nave. There was once a separate three-manual nave organ, built by Hill in 1863, but this was removed in 1903.

The York organ has changed its character, chameleon-like, to suit the musical needs of the day. It remains, however, a versatile instrument and one which gains immensely from its position on the choir screen.

Lyons Hall, York University
Grant, Degens & Bradbeer 1970

HAUPTWERK		SWELL (Oberwerk)		BRUSTWERK		PEDAL	
Quintadena	16	Holzgedackt	8	Gedackt	8	Subbass	16
Principal	8	Weidenpfeife	8	Spitzgedackt	4	Octave	8
Spitzflöte	8	Principal	4	Principal	2	Rohrpfeife	8
Octave	4	Rohrflöte	4	Nasat	1⅓	Gemshorn	4
Rohrquint	2⅔	Principal	2	Zimbel 29.33.36	III	Aliquot	IV
Flachflöte	2	Sesquialtera	II	Krummhorn	8	Mixtur	VI
Mixtur 15.19.22.26.29	V	Scharff 22.26.29	III-IV			Fagot	16
Trompete	8	Regal	16			Rohrschalmey	8
		Schalmey	8				

This tracker organ by Grant, Degens & Bradbeer was completed shortly after their New College, Oxford instrument, but is less unconventional. Frank Bradbeer's case is starkly rectangular, matching the style of the hall. The manual departments are disposed vertically and the front pipes are arranged in compartments, without pipe-shades. The divided Pedal is arranged at the sides on two levels.

The instrument was designed uncompromisingly for the non-romantic repertoire. In practice, however, it proved to be too austere, and in 1983 the tonal design was modified by J. W. Walker to provide an enclosed division, the *Oberwerk* having been formerly designated a Positive. The unusual 16ft Regal was originally in the *Brustwerk* and the original grave Pedal Aliquot mixture, designed to reinforce the harmonics of the 16ft fundamental, has now been joined by a more conventional Pedal mixture.

NOTTINGHAMSHIRE

HUCKNALL The Parish Church
Church 1976

GREAT		SWELL		PEDAL	
Open Diapason	8	Stopped Diapason	8	Sub Bass	16
Chimney Flute	8	Gamba	8	Principal	8
Octave	4	Principal	4	Flute	8
Gemshorn	2	Nason Flute	4	Octave	4
Mixture	IV-V	Octave	2	Mixture	III
Trumpet	8	Quint	1⅓	Trombone	16
		Sharp Mixture	III		
		Dulcian	16		
		Shawm	8		

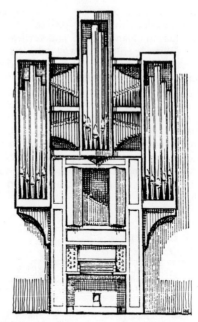

THE PARISH CHURCH, HUCKNALL

Placed in the north transept arch, adjacent to the burial place of Lord Byron, this tracker-action instrument manages to accommodate something approaching an English Swell in the *Brustwerk* position, with folding doors connected to a balanced swell-pedal. The Great organ is pushed up quite high, creating a silhouette which neatly complements the Gothic arch in which the organ is placed. The case is unusual, for Britain, in having upside-down display pipes in the lower compartments of the two-storey flats.

NOTTINGHAM Church of St Mary the Virgin
Marcussen 1973

GREAT		SWELL		PEDAL	
Principal	8	Gedakt	8	Subbass	16
Rørfløte	8	Spidsgamba	8	Oktav	8
Oktav	4	Principal	4	Gedakt	8
Spidsfløte	4	Kobbelfløte	4	Oktav	4
Nasat	2⅔	Gemshorn	2	Mixtur	VI
Oktav	2	Quint	1⅓	Fagot	16
Ters	1⅗	Scharff	V-VI	Trompet	8
Mixtur	VI-VIII	Krummhorn	16		
Trompet	8	Vox Humana	8		

St Mary's is the major parish church of Nottingham and once had a three-manual Snetzler, replaced in 1871 by a new three-manual by Bishop & Starr in an elaborate Gothic case by Gilbert Scott, loosely based on Strasbourg Cathedral. This organ was rebuilt in 1915 by Walker to a four-manual and disposed of in 1973 (the 32ft Pedal reed ended up in Cape Town Cathedral!). The present instrument is a relatively modest tracker-action two-manual by Marcussen, the respected Danish pioneer of the *Orgelbewegung*. The organ is unusually placed, speaking west across the south transept from a cantilevered platform. The Swell is a 4ft-based *Brustwerk*, enclosed by folding doors. The upper case has a simple design typical of good modern Danish furniture. Its height is augmented by reversing the foot-lengths so that the longest front pipe has the longest foot. Nevertheless, it has to be said that, in this Perpendicular Gothic church, the organ case is almost as big a shock as the uncompromisingly Scandinavian sound.

SOUTHWELL The Minster
Hill Norman & Beard 1933

GREAT		SWELL		POSITIV		PEDAL	
Double Open Diapason	16	Quintaten	16	Chimney Flute	8	Double Open Diapason	32
Open Diapason	8	Violin Diapason	8	Spitz Principal	4	Open Wood	16
Rohr Flute	8	Quintade	8	Octave	2	Principal	16
Principal	4	Salicional	8	Larigot	1⅓	Bourdon	16
Koppel Flute	4	Voix Celeste	8	Cymbel 22.26.29	III	Gedeckt Pommer	16
Twelfth	2⅔	Principal	4	Krummhorn	16	Quintaten	16
Fifteenth	2	Quintade	4			Octave	8
Mixture 19.22.26.29	IV	Fifteenth	2	CHOIR (enclosed)		Spitz Principal	8
Trumpet	8	Mixture 22.26.29	III	Open Diapason	8	Bass Flute	8
*Tuba	8	Contra Oboe	16	Lieblich Gedeckt	8	Super Octave	4
		Double Trumpet	16	Fugara	4	Nachthorn	4
*The Tuba can be coupled		Oboe	8	Stopped Flute	4	Mixture 19.22.26.29	IV
to the Choir keys.		Trompette	8	Nazard	2⅔	Bombarde	16
		Clarion	4	Flageolet	2	Posaune	16
				Tierce	1⅗	Trumpet	8
				Clarinet	8	Shalmey	4

Father Smith is reputed to have built an organ for Southwell, and we know that Snetzler repaired the organ in 1765, after fire damage. None of this now remains, having been replaced by a new four-manual Bishop in 1890 which in turn was replaced by the present instrument in 1933.

The compact two-sided oak case by W. D. Caröe stands upon the screen and was improved in 1971 by a polished tin covering applied to the zinc front pipes. As designed in 1933, the enclosed Choir organ faced east, the Swell organ west and the Great was in the south triforium, west of the crossing. Two consoles were provided; the second being movable on the nave floor.

About 1961 an unenclosed Positiv was added, in Holtkamp-type open display in the base of the screen, to act as a miniature Great in the chancel and as a continuo instrument for performances in the crossing. Later, in 1971, the Great organ was revoiced and incorporated within the screen case, leaving only Pedal basses on the triforium, so that now the whole organ sounds effectively from the screen.

OXFORDSHIRE

HENLEY-ON-THAMES Sacred Heart Roman Catholic Church
Collins 1976

GREAT		RUCK POSITIVE		PEDAL	
Principal	8	Wood Gedact	8	Subbass	16
Rohr Flute	8	Principal	4	Octave	8
Octave	4	Rohr Flute	4	Fagot	16
Quint	2⅔	Octave	2		
Gemshorn	2	Spitz Quint	1⅓		
Tierce	1⅗	Dulcian	8		
Mixture 19.22	II-IV				

This tracker-action organ probably founded Peter Collins' modern reputation. Placed on the west gallery of this modest church, it manages to be bold yet not over-aggressive. Both the main case, containing the Great and Pedal organs on a common soundboard, and the chair, containing the Ruck Positive, are extremely simple yet gain their effect from well-designed contemporary fretted pipe-shades.

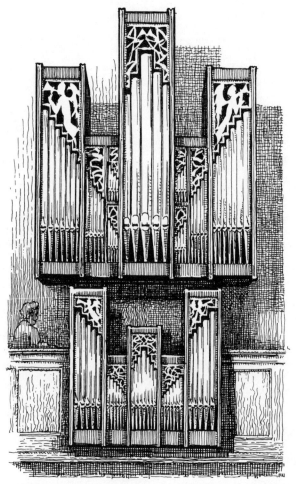

SACRED HEART ROMAN CATHOLIC CHURCH, HENLEY-ON-THAMES

OXFORD Balliol College Chapel
Harrison 1937

GREAT		SWELL		PEDAL		CHOIR	
Double Geigen	16	Lieblich Gedact	8	Sub Bass	16	Hohl Flute	8
Large Open Diapason	8	Echo Salicional	8	Open Wood	16	Viol d'Orchestre	8
Small Open Diapason	8	Vox Angelica	8	Flute	8	Wald Flute	4
Claribel Flute	8	Violin Diapason	8			Clarinet	8
Dulciana	8	Gemshorn	4				
Octave	4	Dulciana Mixture	III				
Harmonic Flute	4	Trumpet	8				
Octave Quint	2⅔	Oboe	8				
Super Octave	2						

This instrument is graced by a typically grand case by Walter Tapper. Though provided with ample overhangs at the sides, the design falls down in the unusual semi-circular-topped flats with their thin and obviously false pipes. The organ itself is a typical and, as yet, unaltered pre-war Harrison. Edward Heath, the former Prime Minister, was the Balliol organ scholar just after its completion.

266

Christchurch Cathedral
Smith 1680; Rieger 1979

GRAND ORGUE		SWELL		POSITIF		PEDALE	
Bourdon	16	Salicional	8	Montre	8	Montre	16
Montre	8	Voix Céleste	8	Bourdon	8	Soubasse	16
Flûte à Cheminée	8	Flûte Bouchée	8	Prestant	4	Flûte de Pédale	8
Prestant	4	Octave	4	Flûte à Fuseau	4	Bourdon	8
Flute Conique	4	Flûte	4	Cor de Chamois	2	Basse de Chorale	4
Doublette	2	Nazard	2⅔	Larigot	1⅓	Fourniture	
Cornet	V	Quarte de Nazard	2	Sesquialtera	II	22.26.29.33.36	V
Fourniture		Tierce	1⅗	Cymbale 22.26.29.33	IV	Basson	16
19.22.26.29.33	VI	Plein Jeu 15.19.22.26.29	V	Cromorne	8	Trompette	8
Cymbale 26.29.33.36	IV	Cor Anglais	16			Clairon	4
Trompette	8	Voix Humaine	8	BOMBARDE			
Clairon	4			Bombarde	16		
				Trompette	8		
				Clairon	4		

Christchurch Cathedral is unique in combining the functions of a cathedral and a college chapel; in size, it is nearer the latter than the former. Like New College and Magdalen College, Christchurch has a choir school and keeps up a fine musical tradition. Bernard Smith built his first two-manual organ for the Cathedral in 1680; his fine four-towered case has survived many alterations. Smith's organ was changed and enlarged by Bishop, Gray & Davison, Willis and Harrison – a roll-call of British organ-builders. What was left was eventually discarded in 1975 in favour of a new instrument planned to be built by Lawrence Phelps.

In the event the organ was built by Rieger, reputedly the last instrument to be designed by Joseph von Glatter-Götz and like all his organs, the instrument is controversial. As in many modern four-manual instruments, the fourth manual is a Bombarde division of boldly voiced reeds located with the Grand Orgue in the main case. The Pedale is placed in the rear half of the main case, which is split halfway down each side to provide outlets for the sound. The Positif is, as expected, in the chair case which, although it blends well with Smith's main case, actually dates only from 1884. The Swell organ, 4ft-based like the Positif, is placed directly above the console and speaks out through a new carved grille. It has to be said that, by pushing up the main case several feet nearer the ceiling, this layout has disturbed the balance of the Smith case, nor does the scale of the carving of the new grille sit happily with the older work.

Musically the tone of the instrument is south German, not Scandinavian like Queen's College, but the dry acoustics of Christchurch Cathedral leave it with less warmth than one would expect. There are two stop-actions, one mechanical and one electric, for control by pistons. The tracker key-action is particularly responsive, having remarkably low inertia for the size of the instrument.

Exeter College Chapel
Hill 1860; Hill Norman & Beard 1967

GREAT		SWELL		PEDAL	
Quintaton	16	Gedeckt	8	Principal	16
Open Diapason	8	Salicional	8	Bourdon	16
Rohr Flute	8	Voix Celeste	8	Octave	8
Octave	4	Principal	4	Bass Flute	8
Clear Flute	4	Nason Flute	4	Spitzflute	4
Quint	2⅔	Octave	2	Nachthorn	2
Fifteenth	2	Blockflute	2	Mixture 12.15.19	III
Tierce	1⅗	Larigot	1⅓	Trumpet	8
Mixture 19.22.26	III	Scharf 22.26.29	III-IV		
Mounted Cornet	IV	Schalmey	8		

George Gilbert Scott modelled this striking chapel after Saint Chapelle in Paris, and William Hill built a two-manual organ with a typically Scott bare front of decorated pipes topped with little gold-painted crowns. Hill enlarged the organ to three manuals in 1892, modifying the case in a replica of Scott's style and using pneumatic action to banish the console to a side arch. The console returned to the central tribune when the instrument was redesigned as a two-

EXETER COLLEGE CHAPEL, OXFORD

manual in 1967. The result is still Hill, but with neo-Baroque leanings. The case was also redesigned in 1967 and now incorporates a 16ft Principal. The ironwork behind the console was formerly part of the Scott case at New College.

Magdalen College Chapel
Gray & Davison 1855; Harrison 1936; Hill Norman & Beard 1963

GREAT		SWELL		CHOIR		PEDAL	
Bourdon	16	Violin Diapason	8	Contra Dulciana	16	Principal	16
Open Diapason I	8	Rohrflöte	8	Chimney Flute	8	Sub-bass (from Great)	16
Open Diapason II	8	Echo Salicional	8	Principal	4	Dulciana (from Choir)	16
Stopped Diapason	8	Vox Angelica	8	Spitzflöte	4	Octave	8
Octave	4	Principal	4	Octavin	2	Bass Flute (from Great)	8
Clear Flute	4	Lieblich Flote	4	Larigot	1⅓	Gemshorn	4
Octave Quint	2⅔	Mixture 15.19.22	III	Sifflote	1	Hohl Flute	2
Superoctave	2	Contra Fagotto	16	Oboe	8	Fagotto (from Swell)	16
Quint Mixture	IV	Trumpet	8	Krummhorn	8	Trombone (part Choir)	16
Harmonic Trumpet	8			Harmonic Trumpet	8		

268

There have been many organs in Magdalen. The case of Dallam's 1637 organ is now in Tewkesbury; Schwarbrick's 1737 instrument has disappeared. Gray & Davison's four-manual of 1855 has been recast three times, losing its two-stop Solo organ somewhere along the way. Rebuilt by Binns in 1905, it was converted into a smooth Harrison in 1936 and brightened up again in 1963. The organ now combines basically English choruses with a touch of its former Harrison smoothness. The 1855 Gothic double case remains, with its remarkable projecting chair case, made of stone and part of the screen. The grouping of the display pipes is reminiscent of York Minster. This instrument is scheduled to be replaced in 1985–6 by a new two-manual organ by N. P. Mander.

Merton College Chapel
Walker 1968

GREAT		SWELL		PEDAL	
Open Diapason	8	Spitzflute	8	Sub Bass	16
Stopped Diapason	8	Chimney Flute	4	Flute	8
Principal	4	Principal	2	Gemshorn	4
Koppel Flute	4	Larigot	$1\frac{1}{3}$	Mixture	III
Nazard	$2\frac{2}{3}$	Cymbel	III	Fagotto	16
Block Flute	2	Dulzian	8	Schalmei	4
Tierce	$1\frac{3}{5}$				
Fourniture	IV				
Dutch Trumpet	8				

The Merton College Chapel organ is one of the earlier British-built instruments of the tracker revival. It stands on an especially constructed gallery in front of the west window. The window was formerly covered by an extraordinary *trompe l'oeuil* painting depicting a westward extension of the chapel behind the organ, but which now has been removed. This is a pity as light from the window streams through Robert Potter's roofless organ case, destroying the silhouette of its upper part. The case is a single unit, not *werk* principle, and combines a fine three-towered classical silhouette with Gothick detail owing more to the eighteenth century than the seventeenth. The Swell organ is of the "enclosed Positive" type, based on a 2ft Principal. The Dutch Trumpet was added after the organ was finished, and is on separate electric action.

New College Chapel
Grant, Degens & Bradbeer 1969

GREAT		SWELL		POSITIV		PEDAL	
Quintade	16	Flûte-à-Cheminée	8	Holzgedackt	8	Prinzipal	16
Prinzipal	8	Salicional	8	Quintadena	8	Subbass	16
Spitzflöte	8	Celeste	8	Praestant	4	Oktave	8
Oktave	4	Prinzipal	4	Röhrflöte	4	Rohrflöte	8
Spitzgedackt	4	Flûte Conique	4	Prinzipal	2	Oktave	4
Terz	$3\frac{1}{5}$	Nazard	$2\frac{2}{3}$	Quintaton	2	Nachthorn	2
Quint	$2\frac{2}{3}$	Quarte	2	Oktave	1	Mixture IV 19.22.26.29	IV
Oktave	2	Tierce	$1\frac{3}{5}$	None	$\frac{8}{9}$	Fagot	32
Mixture 19.22.26.29	IV-VI	Larigot	$1\frac{1}{3}$	Scharfzimbel III		Fagot	16
Cornet	V	Teint $1\frac{1}{7} + \frac{16}{19}$	II	29.33.36	III	Kupfer Trompete	8
Messing Regal	16	Fourniture		Holzregal	16	Rohrschalmei	4
Trompete	8	22.26.29.33.36	V	Schalmei Krummhorn	8		
		Trompette	16				
		Hautbois	8	Cymbelstern			
		Trompeta Real	8				
		(unenclosed, horizontal)					

New College, despite its name, is of very ancient foundation. Some pipes of Robert Dallam's 1663 instrument remained in use until 1969 but the case was replaced in 1793 by a Gothick confection, effectively dividing the organ in two with an arched centre through which the west window could be seen. Willis' instrument of 1875 had yet another divided case, arranged with a lowered centre, and it retained some of Green's 1793 pipes. There was a proposal to build a new organ round the historic pipes and modify Scott's case to permit a suitable layout, but in 1968 Maurice Forsyth-Grant persuaded the college to make a completely fresh start.

The organ which resulted looks much as it sounds: bold, forthright and aggressive. The layout is unashamedly *werk* principle with separate tone-cabinets for each division clearly visible. Indeed, from the right vantage point, light can be seen between the Pedal organ cabinets and the remainder. The way in which the tall Swell integrates into the case as a whole is very clever, though the relationship between this almost brutalist metal-framed case and a medieval Gothic chapel has not been without criticism. The case was designed by George Pace, though much of the detail is due to Frank Bradbeer.

The tone of the organ is powerful and aggressive, and this records and broadcasts well. John Degens' interpretation of north German tone is essentially his own, though the instrument also includes some Maurice Grant specialities in the form of the None 8/9ft on the Positiv and the Teint 1⅓ft+16⁄19ft (the fourteenth and nineteenth harmonics of the 16ft!). The Swell is 4ft-based like the Positiv and has light full-length reeds plus the essentially solo Trompeta Real on horizontal display. The Pedal organ, even though tracker, has octave borrowings from the 16ft Principal and from the quarter-length 32ft reed. One either likes or hates this organ but, however you view it, this is an instrument with a strong and colourful character.

Pusey House Chapel
Rest Cartwright 1914

This is not the finest organ in Oxford but it may be the oddest, built to a tonal scheme best described as a cross between Hope-Jones and the Abbé Vogler. The Swell is almost pure Hope-Jones: Diapason Phonon, Tibia Clausa, (Viole) Sourdine and Horn, all at 8ft, with but a Gemshorn and Cor Anglais at 4ft. The Great, however, includes a Tuba Minor and a Cornet VIII – Dulciana, Harmonic Flute, Harmonic Stopped Twelfth, Piccolo, Tierce, Larigot, Septième and Campana – each of which can also be drawn separately!

Queen's College Chapel
Frobenius 1965

GREAT		BRUSTPOSITIVE (Swell)		PEDAL	
Gedeckt	16	Gedeckt	8	Subbass	16
Principal	8	Principal	4	Principal	8
Rohrflute	8	Rohrflute	4	Gedeckt	8
Octave	4	Gemshorn	2	Octave	4
Octave	2	Quint	1⅓	Mixture	III
Sesquialtera	II	Scharff	III	Fagot	16
Mixture	IV	Cromorne	8	Schalmei	4
Trumpet	8				

At 22 stops, this two-manual instrument is far from being the largest organ in Oxford, yet it is almost certainly the most important. The first instrument of significant size to be installed in Britain which followed the tenets of the *Orgelbewegung* in almost every particular, it has had a significant effect on the course of British organ-building. The action is wholly mechanical, to both keys and stops, and each department is housed in a roofed-in tone-cabinet clearly discernible in the organ layout, the enclosed *Brustwerk* speaking through the ornamental grille immediately above the console.

Tonally, the instrument is a straightforward example of the north German *werk* principle, with an 8ft-based Great, 4ft-based *Brustpositive* and 16ft-based Pedal, even though, for reasons of space and height, there is no 16ft Principal on the Pedal. It is indeed a model stop-list for this type of organ, with inherent balance between departments yet a clear pitch differentiation also. If one has to criticise this instrument, it can only be on the grounds that more recent instruments by Frobenius have better reeds and are, perhaps, less light-weight in the Pedal.

The well-proportioned case was designed by Finn Ditlevson, and the organ owes its existence to the efforts of James Dalton, Fellow of Queen's College.

St Hugh's College Chapel
Tamburini 1979

MANUALE		PEDALE	
Bordone (divided treble and bass)	8	Subbasso	16
Ottava	4		
Flauto	4		
XV	2		
XIX	1⅓		
XXII	1	Tracker action	
Cornamusa (treble)	8		

A one-manual organ in a double case sounds like a contradiction in terms but this Italian instrument is arranged with the manual stops in the projecting chair case, the main case behind housing only the stopped Pedal pipes. The console is reversed with the player looking between the towers of the manual case. The cases, with their striking geometrical pipe-shades, were designed by John Brennan.

St Mary the Virgin (The University Church)
Smith 1675; Walker 1950

Father Smith built a two-manual organ for the church in 1675 and the case and a few pipes still survive. The organ stands on a screen between nave and chancel, so the case has two faces. That facing the chancel is as built, with all its pipes wooden dummies carved and gilt to look like metal. The west-facing front is even odder, however. Just as the church porch is a baroque structure grafted onto a Gothic building, so the organ case has early nineteenth-century Gothick decoration grafted on to Father Smith's seventeenth-century classical case. The tonal design of the 1950 organ inside it, with a Tromba on the enclosed Choir, is best described as a pastiche of an Arthur Harrison. It is planned to be replaced by a new instrument built by Metzler of Zurich.

The Sheldonian Theatre
Harrison 1963

GREAT		SWELL		CHOIR		PEDAL	
Double Diapason	16	Viola	8	Geigen Diapason	8	Violone	16
Open Diapason I	8	Gedeckt	8	Rohr Flute	8	Bourdon	16
Open Diapason II	8	Gamba	8	Octave Geigen	4	Principal	8
Hohlflute	8	Principal	4	Nason Flute	4	Stopped Flute	4
Dulciana	8	Mixture	III	Nazard	2⅔	Open Flute	2
Octave	4	Double Trumpet	16	Octavin	2	Trombone	16
Stopped Flute	4	Trumpet	8	Tierce	1⅗		
Octave Quint	2⅔	Clarion	4	Cromorne	8		
Super Octave	2			Tuba	8		
Mixture	IV						

Father Smith built a chamber organ for the Sheldonian Theatre shortly after its opening and, later, John Harris (son of Renatus) provided a bigger one. In 1877 Father Willis built a large three-manual in a case by Thomas Jackson. Willis' organ overflowed the case, which caused much trouble, solved by putting Pedal pipes in the windows either side of the organ. The 1963 Harrison which has replaced it is more compact, allowing the whole organ to fit in the main case, with its wide two-storey central tower. The tonal scheme, although influenced by the *Orgelbewegung*, still has traces of the 1930s Harrison style.

The Town Hall
Willis 1896

GREAT		SWELL		CHOIR		PEDAL	
Double Open Diapason	16	Bourdon	16	Viola da Gamba	8	Open Diapason	16
Open Diapason (large)	8	Open Diapason	8	Dulciana	8	Bourdon	16
Open Diapason (small)	8	Stopped Diapason	8	Clarabella	8	Violoncello	8
Clarabella	8	Salicional	8	Concert Flute	4	Trombone	16
Principal	4	Voix Celeste	8	Piccolo	2		
Flute	4	Principal	4	Cremona	8		
Twelfth	2⅔	Piccolo	2				
Fifteenth	2	Contra Hautboy	16	SOLO			
Sesquialtera	III	Oboe	8	Harmonic Flute	8		
Trumpet	8	Cornopean	8	Orchestral Oboe	8		
		Vox Humana and		Tromba	8		
		Tremulant	8				
		Clarion	4				

The interior of Oxford Town Hall is a splendid confection in Victorian rococo with an unaltered late Father Willis organ in the apse behind the stage. This modest four-manual was the last flowering of the Victorian concert organ before Hope-Jones weaved his spell.

Wadham College Chapel
Willis 1862

GREAT		SWELL		PEDAL	
Open Diapason	8	Bourdon	16	Open Bass	16
Claribel Flute	8	Lieblich Gedackt	8	Sub Bass	16
Rohr Flute	8	Violin Diapason	8	Flute Bass	8
Salicional	8	Gemshorn	4		
Octave	4	Mixture	III		
Flute Harmonique	4	Oboe	8		
Spitz Flute	2	Cornopean	8		
Trumpet	8				

This early Father Willis is very different from the much later instrument in the Town Hall, although even at this early date the Pedal organ is very abbreviated. The Claribel and Harmonic Flute on the Great are typical. Note that the Salicional is on the Great, not the Swell, and there is no Celeste. This instrument has the Willis peculiarity of octave couplers from Swell to Great without octave couplers on the Swell itself.

The organ was moved to its present west-end position in 1886 when the Thomas Jackson case front was added. Less flamboyant than the Sheldonian Theatre case, it nevertheless has the same vertical emphasis with rather narrow front pipes.

RADLEY Radley College Chapel
Hill Norman & Beard 1980

GREAT		SWELL		CHOIR		PEDAL	
Bourdon	16	Open Diapason	8	Stopped Diapason	8	Double Open Diapason	32
Open Diapason	8	Gedact	8	Principal	4	Open Diapason	16
Stopped Diapason	8	Gamba	8	Chimney Flute	4	Bourdon	16
Principal	4	Voix Celeste	8	Nazard	2⅔	Sub-Bass	16
Wald Flute	4	Gemshorn	4	Gemshorn	2	Principal	8
Fifteenth	2	Piccolo	2	Tierce	1⅗	Flute	8
Sesquialtera 12.15.17	III	Larigot	1⅓	Cymbal 22.26.29.33	IV	Quint	5⅓
Furniture 19.22.26	III	Mixture 15.19.22.26	IV	Regal	16	Fifteenth	4
Posaune	8	Contra Fagotto	16	Cremona	8	Nachthorn	2
		Vox Humana	8	Trompeta Real	8	Sesquialtera 17.19.22	III
		Cornopean	8			Trombone	16
						Trumpet	8
						Clarion	4

This substantial tracker instrument stands sideways on the west gallery of the school chapel. The layout is unusual in that it is the Choir organ which occupies the *Brustwerk* position, complete with folding doors. The Swell organ, in many respects a conscious copy of a William

Hill Swell, is placed above and behind the Great. Below the Great front is a horizontal Trompeta Real which, as it is played from the Choir organ, has electric action. The large Pedal organ, also on electric action, is complete down to 32ft flue and has the bass of the 16ft Open Diapason as copper pipes in the case towers. The oak case follows a design by Herbert Norman.

WOODSTOCK Blenheim Palace
Willis 1891

GREAT		SWELL		CHOIR		PEDALE	
Double Diapason	16	Contra Gamba	16	Gamba	8	Contra Violone	32
Open Diapason	8	Geigen Principal	8	Dulciana	8	Violone	16
Open Diapason	8	Lieblich Gedact	8	Hohl Flote	8	Violoncello	8
Claribel Flute	8	Lieblich Flote	4	Flute-harmonique	4	Open Diapason	16
Quint	5⅓	Salicional	8	Piccolo	2	Octave	8
Principal	4	(Echo Viole)	8	Cor Anglais	16	Bourdon	16
Flute	4	Vox Angelica	8	Cor Anglais	8	Flute Bass	8
Quint Octaviante	2⅔	Gemshorn	4	Corno-di-Bassetto	8	Mixture	
Super Octave	2	Flageolet	2			Ophicleide	16
Piccolo	2	Mixture		SOLO (enclosed)		Clarion	8
Mixture		Contra Hautboy	16	Claribel Flute	8		
Trombone	16	Hautboy	8	Gamba	8		
Tromba	8	Vox Humana	8	Wald Flute	4		
Clarion	8	Cornopean	8	Clarionet	8		
		Clarion	4	Orchestral Oboe	8		
				Tuba	8		

This substantial late Father Willis owes its existence to a friendship between Father Willis and the then Duke of Marlborough. It stands in the Long Library, said to be the longest room in a private house in Britain, and was originally placed in an alcove halfway along one side. The 16ft display pipes are of tin metal, unusual at this period, and still retain most of their original burnished appearance, enhancing an imposing if un-architectural pipe-screen. The stop-jambs, music desk and key-cover are most elaborately inlaid, and the console is one of the few to retain early Willis thumb-pistons, the forerunners of all others. Despite the move, the organ remains in other respects as built, including tubular pneumatic action, though Henry Willis III added a Welte player mechanism so that the instrument ceased to be dependent on the services of a performer.

SHROPSHIRE

ELLESMERE Ellesmere College Chapel
Hill Norman & Beard 1969

GREAT		SWELL		POSITIV		PEDAL	
Quintaten	16	Rohr Flute	8	Bourdon	8	Sub Bass	16
Principal	8	Salicional	8	Dulciana	8	Quintaten	16
Stopped Diapason	8	Voix Celeste	8	Chimney Flute	4	Bourdon	16
Octave	4	Geigen Principal	4	Principal	2	Octave	8
Spitzflute	4	Koppelflute	4	Larigot	1⅓	Bass Flute	8
Fifteenth	2	Flageolet	2	Sesquialtera	II	Fifteenth	4
Furniture 19.22.26	III	Plein Jeu 22.26.29	IV	Cymbal 29.33.36	III	Nachthorn	4
Cornet	V	Fagotto	16	Krummhorn	8	Mixture 19.22.26	III
		Trumpet	8	Trompette (horizontal)	8	Posaune	16
						Rohr Shalmey	4

Ellesmere is perhaps best known for its situation on the Llangollen Canal, but it also has a distinguished public school of the Woodard Corporation. When the chapel was gutted by fire, the previous instrument by Kingsgate Davidson was destroyed. The present organ stands on the west gallery with the Positiv projecting forward in Holtkamp-type open display. The Pedal side wings have conventional front pipes in an unusual arrangement, polished tin pipes alternating with matt black pipes. The latter have tin mouths and polished copper bands at the top. The tonal design was an attempt to fuse the *Orgelbewegung* with the British tradition, with the belled tin-metal horizontal Trompette as an eclectic feature. However, changes after the instrument was completed moved the balance slightly back towards the romantic style.

Ellesmere College Great Hall
Schulze 1864, 1874; Norman & Beard 1906

GREAT (1864)		SWELL (1874)		CHOIR (1864–74)		PEDAL (1864–74)	
Bourdon	16	Gedact	16	Lieblich Gedact	16	Open Diapason Bass	16
Large Open Diapason	8	Geigen Principal	8	Salicional	8	Sub Bass	16
Small Open Diapason	8	Stopped Diapason	8	Flauto Traverso	8	Octave Bass	8
Hohl Flute	8	Viol da Gamba	8	Lieblich Gedact	8	Flute Bass	8
Principal	4	Voix Celeste	8	Kern Flute	8	Trombone	16
Twelfth & Fifteenth	II	Flauto Amabile	8	Lieblich Flöte	4	Trumpet	8
Mixture 19.22.26.29	IV	Principal	4	Viol d'amour	4		
Trumpet	8	Flute d'amour	4	Clarinet	8	Electropneumatic action	
		Twelfth & Fifteenth	II			(1981)	
		Horn	8				
		Oboe	8				

This important nineteenth-century instrument was built for St Mary's Church, Tyne Dock as a two-manual and completed by its original maker ten years later. Although not so large as its more famous brother at Armley, Leeds, the Tyne Dock Schulze has been altered remarkably little over the years. The instrument has all the vigour for which its maker is famous, a vigour complemented by the spacious acoustics of the hall at Ellesmere to which the instrument was transferred by Hill Norman & Beard in 1981. In some respects the musical balance is preferable to that of the Armley instrument, where the Swell is something of an also-ran compared to the dominant Great organ.

LUDLOW The Parish Church
Snetzler 1764; Gray & Davison 1860, 1883, 1891; Hill 1901; Nicholson 1982

GREAT		SWELL		CHOIR		PEDAL	
Contra Gamba	16	Bourdon	16	*Open Diapason	8	Open Diapason	16
Open Diapason 1	8	*Open Diapason	8	*Stopped Diapason	8	Violone	16
Open Diapason 2	8	*Stopped Diapason	8	Dulciana	8	Bourdon	16
*Open Diapason 3	8	Gemshorn	8	*Principal	4	Principal	8
*Stopped Diapason	8	Keraulophon	8	*Rohr Flute	4	Fifteenth	4
*Principal	4	·Voix Celeste	8	Piccolo	2	Trombone	16
Wald Flute	4	Principal	4	Corno di Bassetto	8		
*Twelfth	2⅔	Suabe Flute	4	Tuba	8	*Snetzler pipes.	
*Fifteenth	2	Fifteenth	2				
*Mixture 15.19.22	III	Mixture 19.22.26.29	IV	SOLO (disconnected)			
*Furniture 22.26.29	III	Contra Fagotto	16	Harmonic Flute	8		
Trumpet	8	Cornopean	8	Harmonic Flute	4		
Clarion	4	Oboe	8	Gedeckt	8		
		Vox Humana	8	Violin Diapason	8		
		Clarion	4	Orchestral Oboe	8		

Ludlow still has the three-tower classical case and some 13 stops of pipework of the Snetzler organ which once stood upon a gallery over the rood screen, facing west down the nave. This unusual position (recently revived at Hexham Abbey) was regarded as controversial even in the eighteenth century and was altered in 1860 when the church was refurnished under the direction of George Gilbert Scott. Gray & Davison rebuilt the organ from the old long compass to the CC compass, set it up again in its present position on a platform in the north transept and added a Solo organ. A particular feature was the Grand Tuba projecting horizontally, Spanish-style, from the upper flats of the Snetzler case, brutally cut in a line to accommodate it. Gray & Davison had fitted a similar stop (not on show) at Leeds Town Hall the previous year and clearly felt that on 5in (125mm) wind it was the answer to Hill's and Willis' high-pressure Tubas.

In 1901 Hill fitted a new tubular action and a new console detached to a position nearer the choir-stalls. The Hill action was reliable but slow and the recent restoration by Nicholson has included new electropneumatic action and the refitting of the Hill console. The tonal design

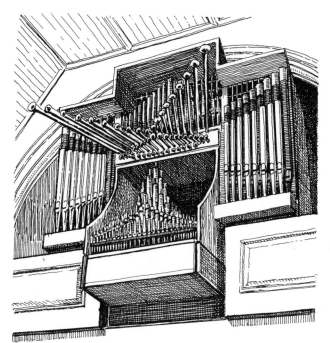

ELLESMERE COLLEGE CHAPEL

ST GEORGE'S CHURCH, DUNSTER (SEE P276)

has remained almost unaltered but the famous Tuba, though historic in its own right, has been moved back out of sight to permit its butchery of the Snetzler case to be reversed. This dichotomy of the eighteenth and nineteenth centuries runs right through the organ; a fine eighteenth-century case and fundamentally eighteenth-century Great and Choir departments combined with Victorian Swell and Pedal departments which now have an historical importance of their own.

SOMERSET

DUNSTER St George's Church
Bryceson 1868; Hill Norman & Beard 1960

GREAT		SWELL		PEDAL	
Quintaton	16	Viola de Gamba	8	Open Wood Bass	16
Open Diapason	8	Viola Celeste	8	Quintaton	16
Stopped Diapason	8	Hohl Flute	8	Sub Bass	16
Dulciana	8	Geigen Octave	4	Principal	8
Principal	4	Lieblich Flute	4	Bass Flute	8
Gemshorn	4	Twelfth	2⅔	Fifteenth	4
Dulcet	4	Fifteenth	2	Sifflöte	2
Nasat	2⅔	Tierce	1⅗	Trombone	16
Super Octave	2	Larigot	1⅓	Oboe Bass	16
Dulcetina	2	Quint Mixture	III		
Trompette	8	Contra Oboe	16		
Octave Trompette	4	Cornopean	8		
		Krumhorn	8		
		Trompette	8		

Dunster is a picture-postcard village of considerable charm and the medieval church attracts many tourists. The organ was completely reconstructed in 1960 on a bridge at the east end of the north aisle. The stop-list was considered advanced at the time but the instrument is now chiefly remarkable for the striking case which includes a horizontal Trompette with flared bells.

WELLS The Cathedral
Willis 1857; Harrison 1910, 1973

GREAT		SWELL		POSITIVE		PEDAL	
Gross Geigen	16	Lieblich Bordun	16	Rohr Flute	8	Open Diapason	16
Open Diapason I	8	Open Diapason	8	Principal	4	Geigen	16
Open Diapason II	8	Lieblich Gedeckt	8	Open Flute	4	Sub Bass	16
Stopped Diapason	8	Echo Gamba	8	Nazard	2⅔	Quint	10⅔
Principal	4	Vox Angelica	8	Gemshorn	2	Principal	8
Wald Flute	4	Principal	4	Tierce	1⅗	Flute	8
Twelfth	2⅔	Lieblich Flute	4	Larigot	1⅓	Nazard	5⅓
Fifteenth	2	Fifteenth	2	Cimbel	III	Fifteenth	4
Fourniture	IV	Mixture	III	Cromorne	8	Stopped Flute	4
Cymbale	V	Oboe	8	Solo Tuba	8	Open Flute	2
Cornet	II-V	Contra Fagotto	16			Mixture	IV
Double Trumpet	16	Trumpet	8	CHOIR (on Positive keys:		Ophicleide	16
Trumpet	8	Clarion	4	unenclosed)		Posaune	8
Clarion	4			Open Diapason	8	Schalmei	4
		SOLO (enclosed, except		Salicional	8		
		for Tuba)		Claribel Flute	8		
		Contra Viola	16	Gemshorn	4		
		Viole d'Orchestre	8	Stopped Flute	4		
		Viole Octaviante	4	Piccolo	2		
		Harmonic Flute	8	Octavin	1		
		Flauto Traverso	4	Sesquialtera	II		
		Orchestral Oboe	8	Mixture	III		
		Tuba	8				

WELLS CATHEDRAL

Wells Cathedral is best known to the public for the extraordinary inverted arch which supports the tower and separates the choir from the crossing. Immediately beyond is the choir screen with the organ on top. Robert Taunton built a double organ for the screen in 1662 and parts of his instrument were incorporated in Samuel Green's organ of 1786. Father Willis was engaged to build a new organ in 1857, but the Dean and Chapter, nervous of the more aggressive sound of Willis' organs, instructed their consultant that Green's pipework should be preserved. Willis' voicing style being quite at odds with Green's, the letter was 'lost' and the instrument was in fact all new.

Fresh from his triumph at Ely, Arthur Harrison rebuilt Willis' organ in 1910, adding a new Solo organ. Harrison & Harrison rebuilt the organ again in 1973, this time with electro-pneumatic action and a new Positive. Until 1973 the organ case was a dull screen of bass pipes, but the instrument now has a new case by Alan Rome, including a diminutive chair case for the Positive.

277

SOUTH YORKSHIRE

DONCASTER St George's Parish Church
Schulze 1862; Norman & Beard 1910; Walker 1935

GREAT		SWELL		CHOIR		PEDAL	
Sub Bass	32	Bourdon	16	Lieblich Bourdon	16	Sub Principal	32
Double Open Diapason	16	Open Diapason	8	Geigen Principal	8	Major Bass	16
Bourdon	16	Terpodian	8	Viol da Gamba	8	Principal Bass	16
Open Diapason 1	8	Echo Gamba	8	Flauto Gambe II	8	Open Bass	16
Open Diapason 2	8	Voix Celeste	8	Gemshorn	8	Violone	16
Open Diapason 3	8	Harmonic Flute	8	Salicional	8	Sub Bass	16
Stopped Diapason	8	Rohr Flute	8	Flauto Traverso	8	Major Bass	8
Hohl Flute	8	Harmonic Flute	4	Lieblich Gedeckt	8	Flute Bass	8
Stopped Flute	4	Stopped Flute	4	Flauto Traverso	4	Violoncello	8
Principal	4	Principal	4	Lieblich Flute	4	Octave Bass	8
Gemshorn	4	Viol d'Amour	4	Geigen Principal	4	Quint Bass	10⅔
Quint	5⅓	Mixture	V	Quintaten	4	Great Tierce	6⅖
Twelfth	2⅔	Scharf	III	Flautina	2	Quint	5⅓
Fifteenth	2	Cornet	IV			Fifteenth Bass	4
Mixture	V	Double Bassoon	16	ECHO (enclosed)		Tierce	3⅕
Cymbal	III-V	Trumpet	8	Tibia Major	16	Mixture	II
Cornet	IV	Horn	8	Harmonica	8	Cymbal	II
Double Trumpet	16	Hautboy	8	Vox Angelica	8	Contra Posaune	32
Posaune	8	Vox Humana	8	Flauto Amabile	8	Posaune	16
Trumpet	8	Clarion	4	Flauto Traverso	8	Bombard	16
Clarion	4			Celestina	4	Contra Fagotto	16
		SOLO (enclosed)		Flauto Dolcissimo	4	Trumpet	8
		String Gamba	8	Harmonica Aetheria	II	Horn	8
		Harmonic Claribel Flute	8			Fagotto	8
		Concert Flute	4			Clarion	4
		Clarinet	8				
		Orchestral Oboe	8				
		Tuba	8				

This great church, so visible from trains on the east-coast route, was designed by Sir George Gilbert Scott and completed in 1858. It replaced a medieval building destroyed by fire in 1852, containing an eighteenth-century organ by Harris & Byfield which had just been moved and enlarged by Hill.

Edmund Schulze was commissioned to build the organ for the new church as a result of his successful instrument for the Great Exhibition of 1851. The design was based on Schulze's 1854 organ for the Marienkirche in Lübeck, Germany, (housed in a famous sixteenth-century case but destroyed in 1942). The Doncaster organ was and is a massive instrument with a particularly complete Pedal organ. The Great and Swell have well-developed choruses and the Echo organ was an early example of romantic small-scale sounds produced by narrow-scale pipes.

Norman & Beard rebuilt the organ in 1910, adding the Solo organ and the Swell organ strings. At a further rebuild in 1935 J. W. Walker provided the present detached five-manual stop-key console.

In its day this instrument greatly influenced the development of the romantic organ in Britain, though in recent years it has attracted less attention than Schulze's later instruments at Armley, Leeds and at Tyne Dock (now at Ellesmere College).

STAFFORDSHIRE

ARMITAGE The Parish Church
Green 1790; Holdich 1861; Bird 1908

GREAT		SWELL		CHOIR		PEDAL	
*Open Diapason	8	Double Diapason	16	*Stopped Diapason	8	Open Diapason	16
*Open Diapason	8	*Open Diapason	8	*Dulciana	8	Bourdon	16
*Stopped Diapason	8	*Stopped Diapason	8	*Principal	4		
Lieblich Gedackt	8	*Dulciana	8	*Flute	4	*Probable Green pipes.	
Gamba	8	*Principal	4	Clarinet	8		
*Principal	4	Fifteenth	2				
Lieblich Flute	4	*Cornet	III				
*Twelfth	2⅔	Double Trumpet	16				
*Fifteenth	2	Cornopean	8				
*Cornet	IV	Oboe	8				
*Trumpet	8	Clarion	4				

Samuel Green's organs must have been extraordinarily soft. This instrument is not over-bold in Armitage church, yet the organ was built for Lichfield Cathedral, where it stood upon the choir screen for seventy years before being sold to Armitage. Josiah Spode, the potter, was organist at Armitage at the time and arranged the transfer, also paying for the Holdich organ at the Cathedral which replaced it.

Holdich made few changes, mainly adding a 2 stop Pedal organ down to 21ft GGG. The organ was badly rebuilt in 1908, when the instrument was belatedly given a modern compass, the chair case was disposed of and the main case altered. Some 17 stops of Green pipes survive in the instrument, including some beautifully painted front pipes and his four-rank Cornet, the oldest such stop in the country. The Pedal organ has a sub-octave coupler, the Open Diapason retaining its pipes down to 21ft GGG!

HOAR CROSS Church of the Holy Angels
Green 1779; Bishop 1876

Architecturally speaking, Hoar Cross is the summit of the Gothic Revival. Bodley's magnificent church contains a Samuel Green organ nearly a century older than itself, built for Bangor Cathedral. The instrument was given a Pedal organ and a new Swell when Bishop adapted it into Bodley's lavish case, the design of which is reputed to have been influenced by F. H. Sutton. The organ was subsequently rebuilt by Conacher Sheffield to an unsympathetic scheme. About 4 stops of Green pipes remain.

LICHFIELD The Cathedral
Hill 1884, 1908; Hill Norman & Beard 1973

As mentioned in chapter 3, Robert Dallam built a two-manual organ for the Cathedral in 1639. This was destroyed during the Commonwealth and we have no details of its successor but, in 1740, Thomas Schwarbrick built an organ for the Cathedral which was replaced in 1790 by a three-manual Samuel Green in a Gothick double case. These organs all stood upon a stone choir screen, swept away when the Cathedral was restored by Sir George Gilbert Scott. Green's organ was sold to Armitage church, where it still remains. Josiah Spode, of the pottery family, paid for a new organ which was built by G. M. Holdich in 1861. It was easily his largest work. The Green organ had no pedals and Holdich must have been disappointed when, having provided a magnificent 10 stop Pedal organ, complete from 32ft to two mixtures, Samuel Spofforth the elderly Cathedral organist declared he would never use it!

The Holdich organ was replaced in 1884 in a complicated deal whereby Hill built a new organ for the Cathedral, a four-manual this time, and sold the Holdich organ to the Royal Concert Hall, St Leonard's, Sussex. Actually, St Leonard's got a new Pedal organ and most of the Holdich Pedal remains at Lichfield. This organ was on the floor under the arches on the

GREAT		SWELL		CHOIR		PEDAL	
Double Open Diapason	16	Lieblich Bourdon	16	Spitz Principal	8	Double Open Diapason	32
Bourdon	16	Open Diapason	8	Gedeckt	8	Open Diapason (wood)	16
Open Diapason Large	8	Stopped Diapason	8	Principal	4	Open Diapason (metal)	16
Open Diapason Medium	8	Salicional	8	Chimney Flute	4	Violone	16
Open Diapason Small	8	Vox Angelica	8	Nazard	2⅔	Bourdon	16
Bell Gamba	8	Principal	4	Fifteenth	2	Echo Bourdon	16
Hohl Flute	8	Celestina Flute	4	Recorder	2	Principal	8
Stopped Diapason	8	Fifteenth	2	Tierce	1⅗	Bass Flute	8
Principal	4	Sesquialtera	II	Larigot	1⅓	Fifteenth	4
Small Principal	4	Mixture	III	Cymbel	III	Mixture	IV
Wald Flute	4	Oboe	8	Cremona	8	Contra Posaune	32
Twelfth	2⅔	Contra Fagotto	16			Trombone	16
Fifteenth	2	Trumpet	8	SOLO (enclosed)		Trumpet	8
Full Mixture	IV	Cornopean	8	Harmonic Flute	8		
Sharp Mixture	II	Clarion	4	Concert Flute	4		
Double Trumpet	16			Viole d'Orchestre	8		
Posaune	8			Orchestral Clarinet	8		
Clarion	4			Orchestral Oboe	8		
				Cor Anglais	16		
				Vox Humana	8		
				(unenclosed)			
				Tuba Mirabilis	8		
				Trompette en Chamade	8		

east side of the north transept, as Holdich's organ had been, but in 1908 the present triforium level chamber was built above the north choir aisle, the instrument speaking into the choir and transept through what formerly had been external windows. The easternmost window can still be seen, though the others are covered by J. O. Scott's finely detailed organ cases. The transept case had been made in 1884 for the north choir aisle and, when first moved, contained a horizontal Tuba projecting from below the central tower.

The 1973 restoration provided new action though the new console incorporates the carved key-cheeks, solid ivory stop-knobs and ivory tell-tale from the old one. The organ retains its 1884 tone with very little change, save for the almost total renewal of the Choir organ pipework to provide a secondary chorus and an unseen but horizontal Solo Trompette en Chamade which supplies a brighter alternative to the relatively smooth Edwardian Tuba.

The second organ in Lichfield Cathedral is a small chamber organ in the Lady Chapel with an exceptionally chequered career. It was assembled in 1764, incorporating casework from an earlier instrument reputed to have been in use in the Cathedral after the Restoration of the monarchy in 1660. It has at various times been a clothes cupboard, a village church organ and a house organ in the Bishop's Palace. There is an improbable tradition that it was built by Father Smith.

St John's Hospital Chapel
Hill Norman & Beard 1972

GREAT		SWELL		PEDAL		
Open Diapason	8	Spitzflute	8	Bourdon	16	
Stopped Diapason	8	Salicional	8	Principal	8	
Principal	4	Gemshorn	4	Bass Flute	8	
Chimney Flute	4	Nazard	2⅔	Octave Flute	4	
Fifteenth	2	Mixture	II	Double Trumpet	16 }	in Swell
		Shalmey	16	Shalmey	4 }	
		Trumpet	8			

Although free-standing, with attached console and tone-cabinet case, this organ uses electro-magnetic action, with some borrowing, mostly of basses, to achieve a very compact instrument. The Swell organ is above the Great and Pedal and the carved oak case was designed by Herbert Norman.

ST JOHN'S HOSPITAL CHAPEL, LICHFIELD

RUGELEY Hawkesyard Priory
Smith 1700; Holdich c1865; Hill 1899

When the four-tower case of the organ built by Father Smith for Eton College Chapel was displaced by 'a wretched pseudo-gothic structure' (the words of Dr A. G. Hill), it was purchased by Josiah Spode for the Roman Catholic Priory which he founded in his house at Hawkesyard Park. G. M. Holdich built a new organ inside it, later substantially rebuilt by Hill. The Smith case is best known from Dr Hill's splendid drawing of it in his book *Organ Cases and Organs of the Middle Ages and Renaissance* (second volume).

STAFFORD St Mary's Collegiate Church
Geib 1790; Hill Norman & Beard 1974

GREAT		SWELL		CHOIR		PEDAL	
Open Diapason	8	Wald Flute	8	Gedeckt	8	Sub bass	16
Stopped Diapason	8	Salicional	8	Spitz Flute	4	Principal	8
Octave	4	Principal	4	Principal	2	Gedeckt	8
Chimney Flute	4	Mixture 22.26.29	III	Larigot	1⅓	Octave	4
Fifteenth	2	Shalmey	16			Super Octave	2
Sesquialtera 12.17	II	Trumpet	8			Bass Trumpet	16
Furniture 19.22.26	III					Shalmey	4

John Geib's case, with its double-storey central tower and typical late eighteenth-century swags for pipe-shades, was for many years just bolted to the side of the 32ft Open Wood of the

ST MARY'S COLLEGIATE CHURCH, STAFFORD

1909 four-manual Harrison in the chancel. Today it stands at the back of the nave containing a new organ of 1974, the display pipes being the only musical survivors of Geib's instrument.

The organ has a classical shallowness, achieved by placing the Great and Pedal on common soundboards at impost level and the other departments vertically above, with the Choir organ behind the upper storey of the central tower. The stop-list, on paper, is fairly severely neo-classical, with an 8ft, 4ft and 2ft relationship between the manual Principals. The sound, however, inspired by the case, has a gentle sweetness somewhat reminiscent of the late eighteenth-century British organ.

SUFFOLK

FRAMLINGHAM St Michael's Parish Church
Anon early 17th century; Thamar 1674; Bishop 1969

GREAT		SWELL		PEDAL	
Open Diapason	8	Chimney Flute	8	Bourdon	16
Stopt Diapason	8	Salicional	8	Principal	8
Principal	4	Principal	4	Flute	4
Twelfth	2⅔	Open Flute	4	Fagotto	16
Fifteenth	2	Gemshorn	2		
Cornet and		Quint	1⅓		
Sesquialtera	III-IV	Mixture	III		
Trumpet	8	Cromorne	8		

The Framlingham organ is a remarkable survival, especially considering the number of times that it has been moved. It was built by Thomas Thamar for Pembroke College Chapel, Cambridge in 1674 in the busy period for organ-builders which followed the Restoration of the monarchy. The case, however, appears to be still older and is probably a survival from a pre-Commonwealth instrument. There is a definite Gothic feeling about the pipe-shades and the

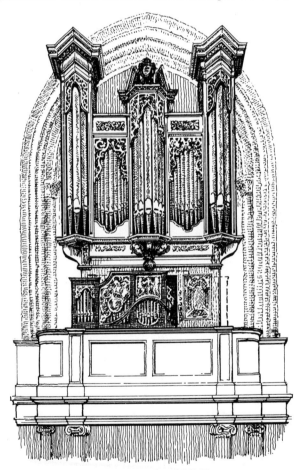

ST MICHAEL'S PARISH CHURCH, FRAMLINGHAM

intricate painted decoration on the front pipes. These have a variety of mouth shapes, even within a single tower. Either side of the console are two panels with carved perspectives of an arched and paved interior – a device which the Dallam family also used in their cases, though not quite in this form.

The organ went from Cambridge to Framlingham in 1708 when Charles Quarles provided a new instrument for Pembroke College. Over the years it acquired a Swell organ and a rudimentary Pedal and, in the nineteenth century, was moved to a chapel on the north side of the chancel. In 1969 the dismantled west gallery was re-erected in the church and the organ restored and returned to its original position on the gallery. The organist is shielded by a screen in the form of a dummy chair case; this too is old, though whether it was Thamar's work or later is uncertain. As the organ stands now, the Great organ is largely Thamar's pipework, the Swell being partly nineteenth century and partly new. There is no room in the case for the Pedal organ which is divided and out of sight in the lower part of the gallery. The restoration was directed by John Budgen for Bishop & Son. The result is a very fine organ; as the Michelin guide would say 'worth a detour', if not the journey itself.

HOLBROOK Royal Naval School Chapel
Hill Norman & Beard 1933

This often-forgotten instrument was one of the biggest new organs of the 1930s. It stands on the west gallery of this monumental chapel behind what must be the largest organ grille in Britain, with not a single pipe in sight! The four-manual console is detached at the east end of the chapel. The instrument is typical of the late romantic period, showing almost no influence of the *Orgelbewegung*. The construction of the organ is as massive as the sound, being one of the most internally spacious and solidly built organs in the country.

SURREY

DORKING Cleveland Lodge
Eule/Hill Norman & Beard 1936

HAUPTWERK		OBERWERK		PEDAL	
Gedackt	8	Quintadena	8	Subbass	16
Prinzipal	4	Rohrflöte	4	Holzflöte	4
Spillpfeife	4	Prinzipal	2	Gemshorn	4
Blockflöte	2	Oktave	1	Nachthorn	2
Quinte	1⅓	Sequialtera	II		
Mixtur	III				
Krumhorn	8				

Cleveland Lodge is the private house of Lady Susi Jeans who commissioned this pioneer instrument based on the ideas of the *Orgelbewegung*. The stop-list was thirty years ahead of its time, so far ahead that it was a long time before it attracted any imitators. Lady Jeans had the pipes imported from the German firm of Eule. Fritz Abend, their voicer, finished the organ and was also responsible for a few later alterations. The soundboards and tracker action were made by Hill Norman & Beard, who had never quite stopped making tracker organs.

GUILDFORD The Cathedral
Rushworth & Dreaper 1961

Sir Edward Maufe, the architect of Guildford Cathedral, originally planned that the organ should be divided into four portions, located in the east and west corners of each transept. Mercifully, this plan was never executed and although the Cathedral has yet to receive the west-end instrument for which its architecture seems to cry out, the organ is at least nearly all in one piece, in the north transept. The four-manual instrument incorporates an 1880 Harrison & Harrison, built by Thomas Harrison, Arthur Harrison's father. The eye, however, is drawn not to this part of the organ but to the separate Positive which stands on a tribune on the north side of the chancel. This was entirely new in 1961 and in Holtkamp-type open display.

TYNE & WEAR

FENHAM

This Newcastle suburb has recently acquired two new organs, one in the Anglican church and one in the Roman Catholic church. Both are in the west gallery and both replace electronic instruments yet are by different makers.

St Robert's Church
Harrison 1980

GREAT		SWELL		PEDAL	
Open Diapason	8	Gedackt	8	Bourdon	16
Stopped Diapason	8	Open Flute	4	Principal	8
Principal	4	Fifteenth	2	Gemshorn	4
Spitzflute	2	Mixture 19.22	II		
Mixture 19.22.26.29	IV-V	Trumpet	8		

The layout is the unusual feature of this organ, with the Swell organ under the Great and a slightly detached console with a 'long movement' tracker action. The tonal character of the Swell is mostly an enclosed Positive, though the British tradition is observed by giving it the instrument's only reed, a Trumpet.

Church of the Holy Cross
Church 1981

GREAT		CHOIR		PEDAL	
Principal	8	Gedackt	8	Sub Bass	16
Stopped Diapason	8	Chimney Flute	4		
Octave	4	Nazard	2⅔		
Fifteenth	2	Flute	2		
Nineteenth	1⅓	Tierce	1⅗		
Octave	1				

This organ too has a three-tower case, but less restraint on height has enabled Roger Pulham, the case designer, to create a more uninhibited silhouette, with sloping tops to the side-towers. Both soundboards are on the same level and the second manual is a Choir organ, a flute chorus for accompaniment, not a Positive. The tracker action is of the 'suspended' type.

NEWCASTLE UPON TYNE The Cathedral
Harris 1676; Lewis 1882; Harrison 1911; Nicholson 1981

Newcastle upon Tyne Cathedral organ was one of Renatus Harris' earlier instruments, yet the case, which is all that survives, shows all the characteristics of his mature style. In 1882, when the former St Nicholas' parish church became the Cathedral, T. C. Lewis built a new three-manual organ, adding a fourth manual in 1891. The organ and case were placed in the north transept and the case was greatly enlarged by R. J. Johnson. He added 16ft towers at each end which somewhat dwarf the chair case which he added at the same time. Harris' 'back–front' case now faces east into St George's Chapel.

GREAT		SWELL		PEDAL		CHOIR GREAT	
Subbass	32	Contre Viole	16	Double Open Bass	32	Contra Dulciana	16
Principal	16	Diapason	8	Major Bass	16	Open Diapason	8
Bourdon	16	Flûte	8	Principal Bass	16	Flute	8
Principal	8	Gambe	8	Violon	16	Geigen Principal	4
Viola da Gamba	8	Voix Céleste	8	Subbass	16	Octave Flute	4
Stopped Diapason	8	Prestant	4	Quint	10⅔	Twelfth	2⅔
Hohlflöte	8	Flûte Octaviante	4	Octave	8	Fifteenth	2
Octave	4	Doublette	2	Holz Principal	8	Seventeenth	1⅗
Gemshorn	4	Plein Jeu	IV-V	Bass Flute	8	Nineteenth	1⅓
Flûte Harmonique	4	Cymbale	III	Octave Quint	5⅓	Twenty-second	1
Grosse Tierce	3⅕	Hautbois	8	Choral Bass	4	Cornopean	8
Quint	2⅔	Voix Humaine	8	Mixture	IV		
Super Octave	2	Basson	16	Bombardon	32	CHOIR SWELL	
Cor de Nuit	2	Trompette	8	Ophicleide	16	Salicional	8
Sesquialtera	II	Clairon	4	Bombarde	16	Unda Maris	8
Fourniture	IV-V			Posaune	8	Claribel Flute	8
Bombarde	16	BOMBARDE		Tuba	4	Spitz Principal	4
Trumpet	8	Lieblich Bordun	16			Wald Flute	2
Clarin	4	Lieblich Gedeckt	8			Mixture	III
		Lieblich Flöte	4			Double Trumpet	16
CHAIRE		Quint Flöte	2⅔			Corno di Bassetto	8
Italian Principale	8	Lieblich Piccolo	2				
Stopped Flute	8	Tertia	1⅗			CHOIR PEDAL	
Spitzflöte	4	Flageolet	1⅓			Bourdon	16
Rohrflöte	4	Mounted Cornet	V			Flute	8
Nasard	2⅔	Bombarde	16			Octave Flute	4
Recorder	2	Trumpet	8				
Tierce	1⅗	Clarin	4				
Ciderne	III	Tuba en Chamade	8				
Cremona	8						

The north transept position proved to be somewhat remote for choir accompaniment so, when Harrison & Harrison rebuilt the organ in 1911, the console was detached to the choir and a new enclosed Choir organ placed with it. This was joined in 1954 by the unenclosed Choir organ from the transept to make a two-manual accompanimental department. In the 1981 work, carried out under the tonal direction of Dennis Thurlow, this section was further augmented by its own small Pedal organ. A new Chaire department has been made for the little chair case on the main organ (previously empty), and the Bombarde division replaces the former Solo. The four-manual Harrison console has been refitted and a new mobile three-manual nave console added. The Lewis organ had showed considerable Schulze and Cavaillé-Coll influence. The expressed intention of the recent work has been to return as far as possible to the Lewis style, and to add new stops in a sympathetic style (with inspiration from many countries, judging by the mixed language of the stop-names).

St Mary's Cathedral (Roman Catholic)
Church 1982

GREAT		ECHO		PEDAL	
Bourdon	16	Bourdon	8	Sub Bass	16
Principal	8	Salicional	8	Posaune	16
Chimney Flute	8	Celeste	8		
Octave	4	Chimney Flute	4		
Spitz Flute	4	Recorder	2		
Nazard	2⅔	Larigot	1⅓		
Fifteenth	2	Sifflet	1		
Tierce	1⅗	Regal	16		
Mixture	IV-V	Dulcian	8		
Trumpet	8				

Pugin designed St Mary's Cathedral and T. C. Lewis built a 35 stop three-manual, with a case by Bentley, on the west gallery. This instrument was later rebuilt in a buried position and, with the subsequent re-ordering of the Cathedral, could not be reinstated. Now, only the two Swell strings survive in the new instrument.

Nigel Church's new tracker organ stands in the north aisle, facing across the Cathedral. It is arranged in *werk* principle fashion on two levels, with the Great in the upper or main case and the Echo organ in a swell-box speaking through a grille in the narrower lower part of the case. The 10 stop Great is the same size as Lewis' original, though now there are flute mutations in place of a second Open Diapason, but the 9 stop Echo is distinctly unusual. Despite the two strings already mentioned, it is not a conventional English Swell nor, with its flute chorus, is it a north German Positive. Instead, its intentions are purely accompanimental and the result is more nearly an enclosed version of the classic British Choir organ.

The ash case was designed by the Cathedral architect, making no attempt to ape Pugin's Gothic. It is largely rectangular, with diagonal sides below the impost, a V-shaped central tower and curious vertical-slatted pipe-shades.

WALLSEND ON TYNE Church of Our Lady and St Columba (Roman Catholic)
Church 1979

GREAT		CHOIR		PEDAL	
Principal	8	Gedackt	8	Subbass	16
Octave	4	Chimney Flute	4	Open Flute	8
Fifteenth	2	Nazard	2⅔	Trumpet	8
Nineteenth	1⅓	Flute	2		
Mixture 22.26	II	Tierce	1⅗		

The splendid-looking instrument on the west gallery was designed for Nigel Church by Georges Lhôte of Geneva. The Great and Choir organs stand on the same level in the mahogany case, with the Pedal organ in a separate case behind. The instrument has a number of characteristics which have since become common in Nigel Church's work: the use of suspended tracker action, unequal temperament and, on his smaller instruments, the concentration on a Diapason Chorus on the Great and a Flute Chorus on the Choir organ.

WARWICKSHIRE

OLD BILTON St Mark's Church
Dallam 1636; Nicholson c1870

Old Bilton has one of the few fully authenticated pre-Commonwealth organ cases in existence. It was made for St John's College Chapel, Cambridge but, when the old chapel was demolished, Dallam's case was sold to Old Bilton and re-erected around a new organ. The work was supervised by the Rev F. H. Sutton who had been responsible for the discovery and restoration of the Tudor case at Old Radnor, Powys. At Old Bilton the case is used without its lower panelling to screen an organ chamber and sits on a cove designed by Sutton, who also designed the Gothic ornaments above the towers.

RUGBY Brownsover Church
?Dallam 1661

The Dallam main case in St John's College Chapel, Cambridge, acquired a companion chair case when it was re-erected after the Restoration of the monarchy in 1660. When the main case went to Old Bilton about 1870, Brownsover acquired the chair case to house a small one-manual instrument.

STRATFORD-UPON-AVON Holy Trinity Church
Hill 1841, 1889; Hill Norman & Beard 1963

GREAT		SWELL		CHOIR (unenclosed)		PEDAL	
Double Open Diapason	16	Open Diapason	8	Gedeckt	16	Open Diapason	16
Open Diapason I	8	Salicional	8	Geigen Principal	8	Violone	16
Open Diapason II	8	Hohl Flute	8	Dulciana	8	Bourdon	16
Hohl Flute	8	Voix Celestes	8	Viola da Gamba	8	Bass Flute	8
Principal	4	Principal	4	Rohr Flute	8	Principal	8
Harmonic Flute	4	Lieblich Flute	4	Gemshorn	4	Violoncello	8
Twelfth	2⅔	Fifteenth	2	Harmonic Flute	4	Fifteenth	4
Fifteenth	2	Mixture	III	Piccolo	2	Twenty-second	2
Mixture	IV	Double Trumpet	16	Clarinet	8	Trombone	16
Posaune	8	Oboe	8	Orchestral Oboe	8		
Clarion	4	Horn	8				
		Clarion	4				

William Shakespeare's tomb ensures that this is one of the most visited parish churches in the country. On entering one is struck by the unusual position of the very richly decorated three-tower double case by Bodley and Garner on a gallery over the chancel arch, facing west. Although of classical form, the style is essentially Gothic, matching the gallery. The case is surprisingly shallow and closer inspection reveals that the chair case is no more than a screen. One still does not suspect the truth, which is that the case contains only the Swell organ! The Great, Choir and Pedal hide behind an anonymous screen at the east end of the south aisle. There is a charming case by Dr Arthur Hill facing into the transept.

The organ itself is a William Hill of 1841 – one of his first German compass organs – which originally stood at the west end of the nave as a two-manual. In 1889 Hill rebuilt the organ to its present layout, adding the unenclosed Choir organ and the strings and the Double Trumpet to the Swell. The 1963 rebuild was conservative and, apart from the modern console, the instrument is in many ways a typical late Hill.

WARWICK The Collegiate Church of St Mary
Nicholson 1980

Transept Organ

GREAT		SWELL		PEDAL	
Contra Geigen	16	Flute	8	Geigen	16
Open Diapason	8	Salicional	8	Bourdon	16
Stopped Flute	8	Vox Angelica	8	Principal	8
Dulciana	8	Principal	4	Bass Flute	8
Octave	4	Nazard	2⅔	Fifteenth	4
Twelfth	2⅔	Fifteenth	2	Trombone	16
Fifteenth	2	Mixture	III-IV	Trumpet	8
Fourniture	III-IV	Contra Oboe	16		
Trumpet	8	Oboe	8		
		Cornopean	8		
		Clarion	4		

West End Organ

GREAT		SWELL		POSITIVE		PEDAL	
Bourdon	16	Gedackt	8	Stopped Diapason	8	Sub Bass	32
Principal	8	Viola	8	Nachthorn	4	Principal	16
Stopped Flute	8	Voix Celeste	8	Nazard	2⅔	Bourdon	16
Octave	4	Principal	4	Principal	2	Diapason	8
Flute	4	Octave	2	Blockflute	2	Bass Flute	8
Grosse Tierce	3⅕	Sesquialtera	II	Tierce	1⅗	Choral Bass	4
Quartane	II	Plein Jeu	IV-V	Sifflöte	1	Octave Flute	4
Larigot	1⅓	Fagott	16	Cymbel	III	Mixture	III
Fourniture	III-IV	Posaune	8	Regal	16	Contra Bombarde	32
Trompette	8			Voix Humaine	8	Bombarde	16
Trompeta Real	8			Trompeta Real	8	Fagott	16
				Trompeta Octava	4	Octave Bombarde	8

St Mary's Church stands on a hill at the top of the town and can be seen for miles. From a distance it appears to be a relatively conventional medieval building but, on approaching more closely, one is confronted by what is, architecturally, a very odd structure. The chancel and chapels are indeed medieval but the tower, nave and transepts were destroyed by fire in 1694 and rebuilt to the designs of a local architect. Their construction and outline are Gothic but the details are all classical. This juxtaposition of the two styles is always peculiar and occasionally hilarious.

The organ arrangements at Warwick have occasionally verged on the hilarious as well. Thomas Schwarbrick constructed an organ for the rebuilt church in 1717, and an Edwardian enlargement and general elaboration of the case of his instrument can be seen over the west door. In 1897 Robert Hope-Jones created a most extraordinary four-manual organ in four separate organ cases, using his electric action to control them from one console. Two rather spiky Gothic cases were placed on the east wall of the transepts, facing down the aisles, plus a third in the chancel. The chancel case has some of the narrowest display pipes ever; those in the other cases are distinguished by unusually narrow mouths.

Various attempts were made to sort out the Hope-Jones instrument but it has now been replaced. The new Nicholson is really two instruments; a 45 stop three manual in the 'Schwarbrick' case at the west end and a 25 stop two-manual in the north transept case. The other two cases are now empty. Such an arrangement necessitates electric action. The detached console on the floor of the north aisle is very much in the tradition of cathedral consoles, save only for the use of a dark-coloured wood for the stops and pistons in place of the conventional ivory.

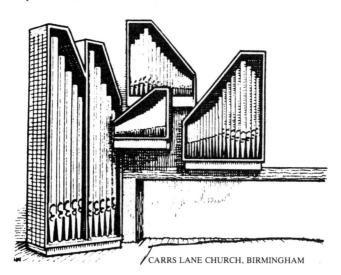

CARRS LANE CHURCH, BIRMINGHAM

WEST MIDLANDS

BIRMINGHAM Carrs Lane Church (see Plate 9)
Hill Norman & Beard 1970

GREAT		SWELL		CHOIR		PEDAL	
Open Diapason	8	Hohl Flute	8	Rohr Flute	8	Principal	16
Stopped Diapason	8	Salicional	8	Spitz Flute	4	Bourdon	16
Octave	4	Voix Celeste	8	Principal	2	Octave	8
Chimney Flute	4	Principal	4	Larigot	1⅓	Gedeckt	8
Gemshorn	2	Mixture 19.22.26	III	Cymbel 29.33	II	Superoctave	4
Sesquialtera	II	Contra Hautboy	16			Mixture 19.22	II
Furniture 15.19.22	III	Trompette	8			Trombone	16
Trumpet	8						

There was a large 1907 Norman & Beard in the old Carrs Lane Church, complete down to 32ft Open Diapason. A number of the pipes survive in what was otherwise a new organ in the new and more compact church. The instrument is laid out in an uncompromising and almost brutal array of tone-cabinets, thereby gaining in warmth of tone in an unreverberant building. The compactness of the organ is remarkable, the use of wind-regulators built into the soundboards and electromagnetic action making it appear that the organ is almost all pipes, with hardly any mechanism.

St Philip's Cathedral
Schwarbrick 1715; Nicholson 1894, 1929, 1948

Schwarbrick's organ was built for the west end, where it stood on a gallery. The case is of Schwarbrick's usual form, derived from Renatus Harris, with gabled tops to the flats. Here there is the additional embellishment that the flats are curved outwards on plan or 'breasted'. Originally it had a companion chair case which was a miniature of the main case, complete with two-storey flats and miniature gables.

The organ was enlarged by Snetzler in 1777, again by G. P. England in 1805 and moved to its present position on the north side of the chancel in 1883, losing the chair case in the process. Nicholson rebuilt the instrument in 1894 and again in 1929, when it gained a fourth manual. After the Cathedral was damaged in World War II, the organ was stored in Pershore Abbey, being reinstated in 1948. The eighteenth-century case now on the west side of the instrument, facing the north gallery, is from St Chrysostom's Church, Hockley. Despite all the changes, a considerable amount of Schwarbrick's pipework still remains on the Great organ.

The Town Hall (see Plate 4)
Hill 1834, 1843, 1890; Willis 1933; Mander 1984

GREAT		SWELL		SOLO (enclosed)		PEDAL	
*Double Open Diapason	16	Contra Gamba	16	†Viola da Gamba	8	*Double Open Diapason	32
†Bourdon	16	*Open Diapason	8	Viola Celeste	8	*†Open Diapason Wood	16
*Open Diapason I	8	**†Keraulophon	8	†Rohr Flute	8	*Open Diapason Metal	16
*Open Diapason II	8	†Salicional	8	Unda Maris	8	†Violone	16
*Open Diapason III	8	†Vox Angelica	8	†Flauto Traverso	8	†Bourdon	16
Stopped Diapason	8	†Claribel Flute	8	†Harmonic Flute	4	*Principal	8
Quint	5⅓	*Principal	4	†Piccolo	2	†Violoncello	8
*Octave	4	*Suabe Flute	4	Flageolet	1	Bass Flute	8
*Principal	4	*Fifteenth	2	†Cor Anglais	16	Twelfth	5⅓
†Harmonic Flute	4	Cornet 12.17	II	†Clarinet	8	*Fifteenth	4
*Twelfth	2⅔	†Full Mixture		†Vox Humana	8	*Sesquialtera 17.19.22	III
Fifteenth	2	15.19.22.26	IV	*Tuba Mirabilis		Mixture 22.26.29	III
Full Mixture		Sharp Mixture 22.26.29	III	(unenclosed)	8	Bombardon	32
15.19.22.26	IV	†Double Trumpet	16			†Contra Trombone	32
*Sesquialtera 17.19.22	III	†Cornopean	8	CHOIR		Ophicleide	16
Sharp Mixture 22.26.29	III	†Horn	8	*Open Diapason	8	†Trombone	16
†Double Trumpet	16	†Oboe	8	*Stopped Diapason	8	Bassoon	16
†Posaune	8	†Clarion	4	Cone Gamba	8	**†Trumpet	8
†Clarion	4			*Dulciana	8	Clarion	4
				Principal	4		
BOMBARDE				*Wald Flute	4		
(on fifth manual)				Fifteenth	2	*William Hill pipes 1834/	
Bourdon	8			*Flautina	2	1843.	
Flute	4			Mixture 19.22	II	†Thomas Hill pipes 1890.	
Nazard	2⅔			†Contra Fagotto	16		
Quarte	2			*Cornopean	8		
Tierce	1⅗			**†Krumhorn	8		
Larigot	1⅓						
Plein Jeu							
15.19.22.26.29	V-VI						
Bombarde	16						
Trumpet	8						
Clarion	4						
*Tuba Mirabilis	8						

The development of the large Victorian concert organ from the relatively small and mild instruments which were being built at the beginning of the nineteenth century owes much to William Hill. The Birmingham organ was virtually Hill's first after taking over the business from Thomas Elliot and was then second in size only to Elliot & Hill's 1829 instrument in York

Minster. Like York, the organ was built with a 16ft CCC manual compass, with the idea that it gave increased gravity, and was the first organ in Britain to have 32ft front pipes. It was also the first organ in the world to have a high-pressure reed, the Tuba Mirabilis (originally called Ophicleide). This stop was voiced on 12in (300mm) wind pressure and added in 1840.

The case of the organ was originally planned to have domes over the towers, like the Cl.rist's Hospital organ, but the length of the iron 32ft front pipes pushed the pipe-caps to the ceiling, the pipes only being squeezed in by making the feet inelegantly short. However the case is rather fine in other respects, being an elaboration of the classic English three-tower case, a design going back to Smith and beyond, with the difference that the diagonally set-back fourth and fifth towers help to conceal the fact that, unlike most of its predecessors, the organ is too large to be only one department deep.

Various alterations were carried out in the early years. The organ was originally forward of the end wall and was moved back to the present recess in 1837. After Dr Gauntlett had convinced William Hill of the superiority of the 8ft CC manual compass, combined with manual 16ft stops, the instrument was remodelled in 1843 and the space saved used to enlarge the Pedal organ from 4 stops (two 32fts and two 16fts) to 15 stops (including eight ranks of mixtures). At this time the organ was retuned to equal temperament, one of the first instruments in the country to be changed. Another pioneering advance came in 1849 with the first major use of the pneumatic lever action in order to relieve a very heavy key-touch of which even Mendelssohn had complained. In its turn this action was replaced when William Hill's son Thomas rebuilt the organ in 1890, fitting tubular pneumatic action, a new console and a largely new Solo organ. This was partially enclosed, the latest fashion at the time.

During the nineteenth century, the instruments of the orchestra gradually evolved to their present form, substantially louder than at the beginning of the century. It was found that this change had left behind the rather gentle Hill voicing when it came to using the organ with full choir and orchestra. Thus in 1933, when the organ again received a new console and action, Henry Willis III increased all the wind pressures, driving the organ harder to produce a big enough sound to support a twentieth-century full chorus and orchestra. However, Willis' style was too different from Hill's for the blend to be successful.

The instrument is now being rebuilt again, this time by Mander. The guiding principle of the work is stated to be a return to the Hill style. Thus, rather than attempt to reinforce Hill's voicing, the wind pressures will be lowered to their original values and a new Bombarde organ provided, to be controlled from the fifth manual of the new electropneumatic console. This division will provide the power needed on special occasions without compromising Hill's work. It will be based on the Willis III 16ft, 8ft and 4ft heavy-pressure Great organ reeds of 1933 plus a big mixture, a split Cornet and the famous 1840 Tuba Mirabilis. The new division will be matched by a new Bombardon 32ft/Ophicleide 16ft on the Pedal organ.

Birmingham University Great Hall
Norman & Beard 1906; Hill Norman & Beard 1967

GREAT		SWELL		CHOIR		PEDAL	
Double Diapason	16	Contra Gamba	16	Gedeckt	8	Contra Violone	32
Open Diapason	8	Open Diapason	8	Rohrflöte	4	Open Diapason	16
Principal	8	Hohlflote	8	Principal	4	Violone	16
Rohr Flöte	8	Salicional	8	Quint	2⅔	Bourdon	16
Octave	4	Voix Celeste	8	Waldflote	2	Principal	8
Spitzprinzipal	4	Principal	4	Tierce	1⅗	Violoncello	8
Stopped Flute	4	Fifteenth	2	Larigot	1⅓	Bass Flute	8
Twelfth	2⅔	Mixture 19.22.26	III-IV	Zimbel 29.33.36	III	Fifteenth	4
Fifteenth	2	Double Trumpet	16			Spitzflöte	4
Mixture 19.22.26.29	IV	Cornopean	8	SOLO (enclosed)		Mixture 19.22.26	III
Trumpet	8	Oboe	8	Viole d'Orchestre	8	Trombone	16
		Clarion	4	Harmonic Flute	8	Trumpet (Gt)	8
				Krummhorn	8	Clarion (Gt)	4
				Schalmei	4		
				Tuba	8		
				Trumpet	8		

The Norman & Beard organ, divided either side of the window and controlled by a central console, originally had a somewhat curious case by Aston Webb. This was replaced by the present array of 32ft basses when the hall was refurnished. The Choir organ is now a Positive in all but name, being provided with an internal tone-cabinet and placed low down and close to the stage. Pedal upperwork was also added, but the Solo was largely left alone so that the organ is eclectic in general design.

In 1967 the instrument was voiced to a dummy audience consisting of sacks of wastepaper placed on chairs! This scientifically calculated idea was devised by Dr K. A. MacFadyen of the University Physics Department, and was later used for the organ in the Concert Hall of the Royal College of Organists.

COVENTRY The Cathedral
Harrison 1962

GREAT		SWELL		CHOIR		PEDAL	
Double Diapason	16	Quintadena	16	Claribel Flute	16	Sub Bourdon	32
Bourdon	16	Hohl Flute	8	Diapason	8	Open Wood	16
Open Diapason I	8	Viola	8	Harmonic Flute	8	Open Metal	16
Open Diapason II	8	Céleste	8	Gedackt	8	Diapason	16
Spitzflute	8	Principal	4	Dulciana	8	Sub Bass	16
Stopped Diapason	8	Spitzflute	4	Principal	4	Dulciana	16
Octave	4	Fifteenth	2	Rohr Flute	4	Principal	8
Gemshorn	4	Sesquialtera 12.17	II	Nazard	2⅔	Spitzflute	8
Octave Quint	2⅔	Mixture 22.26.29.33	IV	Fifteenth	2	Twelfth	5⅓
Super Octave	2	Oboe	8	Blockflute	2	Fifteenth	4
Cornet 12.17	II-V	Contra Fagotto	16	Tierce	1⅗	Rohr Flute	4
Mixture 19.22.26.29	IV	Trumpet	8	Mixture 22.26.29.33.36	V	Open Flute	2
Double Trumpet	16	Clarion	8	Cromorne	8	Mixture 19.22.26.29	IV
Trumpet	8					Bombardon	32
Clarion	4	SOLO (enclosed)				Ophicleide	16
		Diapason	8			Fagotto	16
		Rohr Flute	8			Posaune	8
		Viole	8			Bassoon	8
		Viole Céleste	8			Schalmei	4
		Octave	4			Kornett	2
		Open Flute	4				
		Wald Flute	2				
		Sifflöte	1				
		Mixture 12.15.19.22	IV				
		Corno di Bassetto	8				
		Orchestral Trumpet					
		(unenclosed)	8				
		Orchestral Clarion					
		(unenclosed)	4				

The medieval St Michael's Church, which became the Cathedral in 1918, possessed organs by Schwarbrick (built 1733, rebuilt by J. C. Bishop 1836) and then by Father Willis (1887). The Cathedral was destroyed in 1940 and only the shell of the old church remains, at right angles to the new Cathedral.

Sir Basil Spence's design for the new Cathedral called for the organ to be divided either side of the high altar. Each 'half' is narrow and high, standing on four 'shelves' projecting from the east wall of the north and south aisles. There is no case as such, the treble pipes being screened by varied rows of speaking bass pipes, supported from behind. The Swell, Solo, and Choir flutework is on the liturgical north side, plus about half the Pedal flues. The Great, the Choir Diapason Chorus and the rest of the Pedal, including the Pedal reeds, are on the south side. Cuthbert Harrison's tonal specification is interesting in that whilst obviously influenced by his experience at the Royal Festival Hall, there is nevertheless a continuity with Arthur Harrison's style. This can be seen in the array of 16ft stops on the Pedal (and two on the Great) but most noticeably in the contrast between the Swell organ, dominated by an almost brassy reed chorus, and the Great organ with its relatively smoother reeds.

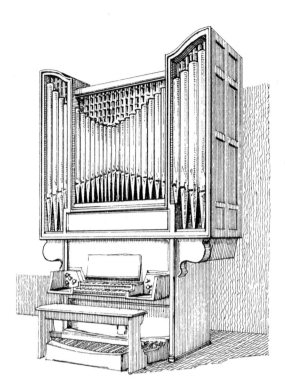

ST BARTHOLOMEW'S CHURCH,
WEDNESBURY

WEDNESBURY St Bartholomew's Church
Hill Norman & Beard 1967

GREAT		SWELL		PEDAL	
Stopped Diapason	8	Gemshorn	8	Sub Bass	16
Principal	4	Chimney Flute	4	Choral Bass	4
Mixture 19.22.26	III	Principal	2		
		Larigot	1⅓		

This two-manual tracker, with its waisted mahogany case designed by Herbert Norman, was originally built for exhibition at the St Alban's Organ Festival. It now stands on a gallery on the north side of the church, where it replaced a three-manual Brindley & Foster in 1970.

WOLVERHAMPTON St John's Church
Harris 1684; Nicholson & Lord 1881; Walker 1973

GREAT		SWELL		CHOIR		PEDAL	
Open Diapason	8	Open Diapason	8	Stop Diapason Bass	8	Open Diapason	16
Open Diapason	8	Stop Diapason	8	Stop Diapason Treble	8	Bourdon	16
Stop Diapason	8	Keraulophon	8	Principal	4	Bass Flute	8
Dulciana	8	Principal	4	Flute	4		
Principal	4	Fifteenth	2	Nazard	2⅔		
Twelfth	2⅔	Mixture	II	Recorder	2		
Fifteenth	2	Cornopean	8	Cremona	8		
Furniture	IV	Oboe	8				
Trumpet	8	Clarion	4				

Smith's victorious instrument in the famous 'Battle of the Organs' in Temple Church, London was enlarged out of recognition and finally bombed in 1941, but Renatus Harris' loser, two transplants later, is still with us. Harris sold the organ to Christ Church Cathedral, Dublin, who, in their turn, sold it to the then new St John's Church in 1762. The case is typical Harris with three towers, 'round-shouldered' upper storeys to the flats and with oval lower flats. The carving along the whole length of the impost is of particularly fine quality.

293

Byfield added a Swell organ. This was enlarged and Pedal stops added by various nineteenth-century builders, deepening the case as necessary. The organ was given a new console when converted to CC compass; this projected several feet from the instrument via a panelled tunnel concealing the trackers. The conservative restoration by J. W. Walker included a new tracker console, set nearer the organ, though still not '*en fenêtre*'. Despite the enlargements, a fair number of Harris pipes remain and this is therefore one of our more important historic instruments.

WEST SUSSEX

ARUNDEL Roman Catholic Cathedral of St Philip Neri
Hill 1873, 1890

This Gothic Revival building stands in a commanding position on top of the hill in Arundel. The Roman Catholic church did not follow the nineteenth-century Anglican tradition of east-end choirs and organs so this fine three-manual Hill stands on the west gallery under the rose window. It is not much to look at – there is a pipe-screen rather than a case – but minor modifications in 1931 and 1968 have left its essential character unaltered.

CHICHESTER The Cathedral
Harris 1678; Byfield 1725; England 1806; Hill 1851, 1859, 1888; Hele 1904; Mander 1985

GREAT		SWELL		CHOIR		PEDAL	
Double Open Diapason	16	Double Diapason	16	Stopped Diapason	8	Open Diapason	16
Open Diapason I	8	Open Diapason	8	Dulciana	8	Bourdon	16
Open Diapason II	8	Stopped Diapason	8	Principal	4	Violone	16
Stopped Diapason	8	Salicional	8	Flute	4	Quint	10⅔
Principal	4	Vox Angelica	8	Fifteenth	2	Principal	8
Suabe Flute	4	Principal	4	Nineteenth	1⅓	Fifteenth	4
Twelfth	2⅔	Flute	4	Mixture 22.26	II	Mixture 19.22.26.29	IV
Fifteenth	2	Fifteenth	2			Contra Bassoon	32
Flageolet	2	Mixture 17.19.22	III	SOLO		Trombone	16
Tierce	1⅗	Fagotto	16	Wald Flute	8		
Full Mixture 15.19.22	III	Cornopean	8	Flauto Traverso	4	NAVE	
Sharp Mixture 26.29	II	Hautboy	8	Cornet	V	Open Diapason	8
Trumpet	8	Clarion	4	Posaune	8	Stopped Diapason	8
				Cremona		Principal	4
						Flute	4
						Fifteenth	2
						Mixture 19.22.26.29	IV
						Pedal Sub Bass	16

It is a characteristic of English cathedral organs that they are altered and enlarged to take account of liturgical and musical change but are seldom completely replaced. The Chichester organ falls firmly into this category, containing some pipes which date back to Renatus Harris' organ of 1678, an 8 stop one-manual which was to be enlarged and altered ten times in the following two hundred and thirty years. This process began when John Byfield added the Choir organ in 1725, a short-compass Swell also being added later in the century. G. P. England rebuilt the organ and added a pedalboard in 1806. Unison Pedal pipes arrived in 1829, and sub-unison Pedal pipes by Gray & Davison in 1844. In 1851 William Hill supplied a new Swell organ, moving the instrument from the screen to the north transept in 1859.

In 1861 the central tower of the Cathedral collapsed into the building and the Renatus Harris case was destroyed. Dr Arthur Hill designed the present Gothic Revival three-tower main case with a simple five-compartment chair case in 1888. The main case incorporates the lower parts of some of Harris' decorated front pipes and the centre portion of the chair case includes a surviving pipe-shade from Byfield's Choir organ. The Chichester case is simpler than Dr Hill's other large cases in Beverley Minster, Peterborough Cathedral and Sydney Town Hall, Australia, but is the only one to include a chair case.

The organ was further enlarged by Hele in 1904 though, even then, it had only 34 stops, a very modest size for a cathedral organ. The instrument is now to be rebuilt by N. P. Mander. Mechanically, it will be a completely new four-manual organ of about 45 stops with tracker key-action. The very compact layout will have the Great organ in front of the Pedal at impost level with the unenclosed Solo organ in front of the Swell at a higher level. The existing Hill and older pipes will be restored but the Choir organ, in the chair case, will have new upper-work and the Pedal organ will gain a new 32ft reed. The design of the new Solo organ (Flutes 8ft and 4ft, Cornet V, Cremona 8ft, Posaune 8ft) is such that it can be used to augment the relatively small Pedal organ, especially since a Solo octave-to-Pedal coupler is included.

To accompany singing in the nave, a new nave organ is to be built in the north triforium. This will have electropneumatic action to enable it to be played from a separate one-manual and Pedal console as well as from the main organ.

HORSHAM Christ's Hospital, Big School
Elliot & Hill 1829–30; Hill 1859, 1902

GREAT		SWELL		CHOIR		PEDAL	
Double Open Diapason	16	Bourdon	16	Open Diapason	8	Open Diapason	16
Open Diapason I	8	Open Diapason	8	Stopped Diapason	8	Bourdon	16
Open Diapason II	8	Stopped Diapason	8	Dulciana	8	Violone	16
Stopped Diapason	8	Salicional	8	Octave	4	Octave	8
Octave	4	Voix Celeste	8	Stopped Flute	4	Violone	8
Twelfth	2⅔	Octave	4	Fifteenth	2	Fifteenth	4
Fifteenth	2	Fifteenth	2	Clarinet	8	Trombone	16
Mixture 17.19.22	III	Mixture 17.19.22	III				
Posaune	8	Oboe	8				
Clarion	4	Double Trumpet	16				
		Horn	8				
		Clarion	4				

The Hall of Christ's Hospital has had an organ since before 1672 when Ralph Dallam built a single-manual instrument to which Renatus Harris later added a Chair organ, replaced in 1753 by another by John Byfield. When a new hall was built in 1829 Elliot & Hill supplied a new instrument, taking the old organ in part exchange. At this time Hill was trying to create a new and grander sound. Taking his cue from Father Smith's organ at St Paul's Cathedral, he gave the new Christ's Hospital instrument a compass down to 16ft CCC, an octave lower than today. The organ also had a pedalboard of two octaves which, when coupled to the manuals, played effectively one octave lower than today. The Pedal organ itself was just one stop, a 16ft Wood Diapason, in unison with the manuals. The three-tower oak case was to the traditional eighteenth-century formula, but John Shaw's design has totally Gothick details, including extraordinary domed pipe-caps to the towers.

The organ was modified to the conventional CC compass and received a 7 stop Pedal organ from Hill in 1859. It was moved to the 'Big School' hall of the new school at Horsham in 1902 by Hill, at which time tubular pneumatic action and a new console were provided. Apart from the manual reeds and Swell organ strings, the organ appears to be much as Hill left it in 1859. With much pipework dating back to 1829, it is a valuable historical instrument. Despite the dead acoustics of the present hall, the organ possesses the singing tone-quality which is the hallmark of William Hill's work.

Christ's Hospital School Chapel
Rushworth & Dreaper 1931, 1981

This is one of the largest of the between-the-wars romantic organs. Replacing a disastrously unreliable small four-manual by Kirkland, Rushworth's placed their 70 stop five-manual in the original 1903 Aston Webb cases, divided either side of the east end of the chapel. The fundamental power and smoothness of the instrument can be judged not only from the duplication of 8ft stops but also from the wind pressures: 4½–8in (115–200mm) for the fluework and 10–20in (250–500mm) for the high-pressure reeds. Such instruments thrive on contrasts of

GREAT		SWELL		SOLO (enclosed)		PEDAL	
Double Diapason	16	Contra Viola	16	Harmonic Flute	8	Double Open Diapason	32
Open Diapason 1	8	Open Diapason	8	Viole	8	Open Diapason 1	16
Open Diapason 2	8	Stopped Diapason	8	Viole Céleste	8	Open Diapason 2	16
Open Diapason 3	8	Salicional	8	Cor de Nuit	8	Open Metal	16
Hohl Flöte	8	Vox Angelica	8	Stopped Flute	4	Viola	16
Octave	4	Gemshorn	4	Concert Flute	4	Bourdon	16
Principal	4	Lieblich Flöte	4	Orchestral Bassoon	16	Dulciana	16
Wald Flöte	4	Nazard	2⅔	Orchestral Bassoon	8	Principal	8
Twelfth	2⅔	Fifteenth	2	Closed Horn	8	Bass Flute	8
Fifteenth	2	Mixture	IV	French Horn	16	Fifteenth	4
Mixture	IV	Oboe	8	French Horn	8	Mixture	IV
Contra Tromba	16	Double Trumpet	16	Tuba	8	French Horn	16
Tromba	8	Trumpet	8			Trumpet	16
Octave Tromba	4	Clarion	4	WEST END		Trombone	16
				Open Diapason	8	Contra Tromba	16
CHOIR (enclosed)				Octave Diapason	4	Posaune	8
Double Dulciana	16			Tuba Magna	8		
Open Diapason	8						
Orchestral Flute	8						
Viola da Gamba	8						
Dulciana	8						
Echo Dulciana (Céleste)	8						
Gemshorn	4						
Flûte Harmonique	4						
Nazard	2⅔						
Piccolo	2						
Tierce	1⅗						
Larigot	1⅓						
Clarinet	8						

power and the enclosed Choir organ is much more delicate, influenced by Henry Willis III's pioneer mutations at Farm Street even to including an unhistorical Septième (since removed).

The instrument was restored by Rushworth in 1981 with new soundboards and with minor tonal changes.

SHOREHAM Lancing College Chapel
(West-end organ) Walker, 1911, 1985; (Choir organ) Frobenius 1986

WEST-END ORGAN

GREAT		SWELL		CHOIR		PEDAL	
Double Open Diapason	16	Lieblich Bourdon	16	Contra Gamba	16	Double Diapason	32
Open Diapason Large	8	Open Diapason	8	Gamba	8	Open Diapason Wood	16
Open Diapason Medium	8	Stopped Diapason	8	Salicional	8	Open Diapason Metal	16
Open Diapason Small	8	Echo Gamba	8	Dulciana	8	Principal	16
Wald Flute	8	Voix Celeste	8	Vox Angelica	8	Subbass	16
Dulciana	8	Principal	4	Lieblich Gedact	8	Bourdon	16
Principal	4	Flute	4	Harmonic Flute	4	Octave	8
Harmonic Flute	4	Fifteenth	2	Harmonic Piccolo	2	Octave Wood	8
Fifteenth	2	Mixture 15.19.22.26.29	V	Clarinet	8	Flute	8
Cornet	V	Contra Fagotto	16			Choral Bass	4
Furniture 15.19.22	III	Horn	8	BOMBARDE		Mixture 19.22.26.29	IV
Sharp Mixture 26.29.33	III	Oboe	8	Bombarde (Horizontal)	8	Contra Bombarde	32
Double Trumpet	16	Vox Humana	8	Clarion (Horizontal)	4	Bombarde	16
Trumpet	8	Clarion	4			Trumpet	8
Clarion	4						

CHOIR ORGAN

GREAT		POSITIVE (enclosed)		PEDAL	
Principal	8	Gedackt	8	Subbass	16
Flute	8	Principal	4	Principal	8
Octave	4	Flute	4	Flute	8
Rohrflute	4	Gemshorn	2	Octave	4
Octave	2	Quint	1⅓	Fagot	16
Sesquialtera	II	Scharf	II		
Mixture	IV	Krumhorn	8		
Trumpet	8				

The tall French Gothic building which can be seen from the coast road, towering over the Adur valley just behind Shoreham, is Lancing College Chapel. Begun in 1868, the chapel was substantially complete by 1911 when a typically romantic three-manual Walker was built in front of the temporary west-end.

Now that the permanent west front has been built, the organ is to be reinstated on the west gallery. It will be augmented with an enlarged Pedal organ with a 32ft reed, new Great organ reeds and a new Bombarde division with 8ft & 4ft horizontal trumpets. At 54 stops this instrument seems likely to be a major restatement of the English romantic organ.

A second instrument, in complete contrast tonally, will be placed in the choir. It is to be built by the Danish firm of Frobenius and will be a two-manual of 20 stops. It will thus be possible to play music of different periods on an appropriate instrument, without compromise. In addition the Frobenius organ will be able to provide local accompaniment for the choir, yet also lead singing in the nave with the assistance of the Walker organ, parts of which will be playable from the Frobenius console. The Gothic Revival cases of both organs are to be designed by David Graebe and Alan Rome.

WEST YORKSHIRE

BRADFORD The Cathedral
Hill 1904; Hill Norman & Beard 1961

GREAT		SWELL		PEDAL		NAVE	
Open Diapason	8	Geigen Diapason	8	Sub Bass	32	Principal	8
Principal	8	Hohl Flute	8	Open Wood	16	Octave	4
Rohr Flute	8	Spitz Flute	8	Violone	16	Wald Flute	2
Octave	4	Spitz Flute Celeste	8	Bourdon	16	Mixture	III-IV
Spitz Principal	4	Geigen Octave	4	Quintaton	16	Purcell Trumpet	
Clear Flute	4	Stopped Flute	4	Octave	8	(horizontal)	8
Fifteenth	2	Super Octave	2	Violoncello	8	(enclosed)	
Quartane	II	Quint Mixture	III	Bass Flute	8	Dolce Bass	16
Mixture	III	Sharp Mixture	II	Fifteenth	4	Salicional	8
Tromba	8	Contra Fagotto	16	Block Flute	2	Voix Celeste	8
Clarion	4	Cornopean	8	Mixture	III	Lieblich Gedeckt	8
Trumpet Major	8	Oboe	8	Trombone	16	Spitz Flute	4
Octave Trumpet	4	Clarion	4	Trumpet	8		
				Octave Trumpet	4		
CHANCEL		SOLO (enclosed)		Octave Clarion	2	NAVE PEDAL	
(lowest manual)		Viola da Gamba	8			Dolce Bass	16
Quintaton	16	Gedeckt	8			Gedeckt	16
Flûte à Cheminée	8	Orchestral Viole	8			Flute Bass	8
Principal	4	Holz Flote	4				
Koppelflöte	4	Nazard	2⅔				
Nasat	2⅔	Italian Principal	2				
Octav	2	Clarinet	8				
Tierce	1⅗	Trumpet Major	8				
Larigot	1⅓	Purcell Trumpet	8				
Sifflöte	1						

Hill built a 39 stop three-manual for what was then Bradford parish church in 1904. With the coming of cathedral status, the chancel was rebuilt on a much larger scale and the organ was enlarged to four manuals with a new 'Chancel organ' (really a Positive). A new and separate nave organ was provided with an 8ft Principal-based chorus, accompaniment stops in a swell-box and a displayed horizontal Trumpet. The unconventional case stands on four pillars and was designed by Sir Edward Maufe. The mixtures and the chancel case were modified by J. W. Walker when the instrument was overhauled in 1977.

HEPTONSTALL Church of St Thomas the Apostle
Hill Norman & Beard 1964

GREAT		SWELL		PEDAL	
Open Diapason	8	Spitz Flute	8	Bourdon	16
Stopped Diapason	8	Salicional	8	Principal	8
Principal	4	Gemshorn	4	Nachthorn	4
Chimney Flute	4	Piccolo	2		
Fifteenth	2	Quartane 19.22	II		
Krummhorn	8				

The picturesque hilltop village is dominated by this spacious church. Dividing the nave in two, a modern pulpitum supports the organ. The layout of the instrument is an unusual example of neo-Holtkamp exposed pipework combined with sound-projecting tone-cabinets. The Krummhorn and Pedal upperwork were added in 1969.

HUDDERSFIELD St Paul's Hall, Huddersfield Polytechnic
Wood of Huddersfield 1977

HAUPTWERK		SCHWELLWERK		OBERWERK		PEDAL	
Gedacktpommer	16	Holzgedackt	8	Gedackt	8	Principal	16
Principal	8	Spitzgamba	8	Praestant	4	Subbass	16
Rohrflöte	8	Celeste	8	Rohrflote	4	Octave	8
Octave	4	Principal	4	Principal	2	Rohr Gedackt	8
Spitzflöte	4	Koppelflöte	4	Quinte	1⅓	Octave	4
Gemshorn	2	Nazard	2⅔	Octave	1	Nachthorn	2
Mixture IV-VI	2	Waldflöte	2	Sesquialtera II	2⅔	Mixture VI	2⅔
Scharff IV	1	Tierce	1⅗	Cymbel III	½	Posaune	16
Trompete	16	Scharff IV	1	Cromorne	8	Trompete	8
Trompete	8	Basson	16			Schalmei	4
		Trompette	8	Cymbelstern			

David Graebe designed the case of this very fine three-manual tracker which stands at the east end of what was once St Paul's Church. The 16ft overhanging Pedal towers flank a straight-forward layout with a 4ft-based *Oberwerk* above the 8ft-based *Hauptwerk* and the 4ft-based Swell below the *Hauptwerk*. The *Oberwerk* has the tonal character of a Positive and, although the Swell has romantic leanings, the instrument is distinctly north German in flavour.

The Town Hall
Willis 1881; Harrison 1981

GREAT		SWELL		CHOIR		PEDAL	
Double Open Diapason	16	Lieblich Bourdon	16	Gedackt	8	Grand Contra Bourdon	32
Open Diapason 1	8	Open Diapason	8	Dulciana	8	Grand Open Bass	
Open Diapason 2	8	Lieblich Gedackt	8	Octave	4	(wood)	16
Open Diapason 3	8	Salicional	8	Stopped Flute	4	Open Diapason	16
Claribel Flute	8	Vox Angelica	8	Nasard	2⅔	Violone	16
Stopped Diapason	8	Gemshorn	4	Spitzflute	2	Bourdon	16
Principal	4	Flauto Traverso	4	Super Octave	2	Great Quint	10⅔
Open Flute	4	Fifteenth	2	Tierce	1⅗	Principal (wood)	8
Twelfth	2⅔	Mixture 17.19.22	III	Larigot	1⅓	Octave	8
Fifteenth	2	Mixture 19.22	II	Mixture 22.26.29.33	IV	Flute	8
Mixture 17.19.22	III	Hautboy	8	Cremona	8	Violoncello	8
Mixture 19.22.26.29	IV	Vox Humana	8	Trumpet	8	Choral Bass	4
Tromba	8	Contra Posaune	16			Mixture 15.19.22	III
Clarion	4	Cornopean	8	SOLO		Contra Bombarde	32
		Clarion	4	(Enclosed)		Grand Ophicleide	16
				Flute Harmonique	8	Trumpet	8
				Violoncello	8	Shawm	4
				Viole Celeste	8		
				Concert Flute	4		
				Piccolo	2		
				Corno di Bassetto	8		
				Orchestral Oboe	8		
				(Unenclosed)			
				Celeste (percussion)	4		
				Grand Tuba	8		

Although it came to Huddersfield in 1881, the Father Willis organ had its origins in the 1860s when he built it for the Albert Hall, Newport. There have been subsequent changes too, principally rebuilding in 1902 and 1981. The most recent work has equipped the organ with a new console and electropneumatic action, quint mixtures on Swell and Great and a new mildly classical Choir organ in an *Oberwerk* position, the original Willis Choir having been discarded in 1956. The instrument now represents a modern interpretation of the British tradition, in contrast to the more Germanic organ in Huddersfield Polytechnic.

KEIGHLEY St Joseph's Roman Catholic Church, Ingrow
Laycock and Bannister 1974

GREAT		POSITIVE		PEDAL	
Principal	8	Gedeckt	8	Bourdon	16
Rohrflute	8	Koppelflute	4	Fagott	16
Octave	4	Principal	2		
Mixture	III-IV	Quint	1⅓		
Sesqualtera	II				

This uncompromisingly neo-classical organ was one of the first instruments that Dennis Thurlow designed after he joined Laycock & Bannister. It shows that, if required, British builders *can* build *Orgelbewegung* instruments. The 2ft-based *Brustwerk* (with hand-operated doors) is below the Great but relates well in scale to the 8ft copper Principal pipes in the main case. The only reed is on the Pedal, giving a choice of foundation rare in an organ of this size.

LEEDS Holy Trinity Church, Cookridge
Hill Norman & Beard 1964

GREAT		SWELL		PEDAL	
Stopped Diapason	8	Quintadena	8	Bourdon	16
Principal	4	Salicional	8	Spitz Flute	8
Quint	2⅔	Spitz Flute	4	Nachthorn	4
Fifteenth	2	Principal	2		
		Larigot	1⅓		
		Crumhorn	8		

This relatively early modern tracker organ is unusual for a tracker in having a caseless display layout for the projecting Great organ. The church was built with an elevated organ chamber intended for an instrument with electric action, now containing the Swell and Pedal organs, behind a mesh grille. The console is below the organ and connected to it by a panelled duct containing the trackers. The instrument was one of the first in Britain to use floating levers to maintain a constant tension in the action. Although voiced largely without nicking, the organ is less aggressive than some other neo-baroque instruments of the period.

St Bartholomew's Church, Armley
Schulze 1869; Binns 1905

GREAT		SWELL		CHOIR		PEDAL	
Sub Principal	16	Bordun	16	Lieblich Bordun	16	Sub Bass	32
Bordun	16	Geigen Principal	8	Minor Principal	8	Open Metal	16
Major Principal	8	Gamba	8	Cello-und-Violine	8	Principal Bass – Wood	16
Gemshorn	8	Salicional	8	Harmonica	8	Violon	16
Hohl Flöte	8	Celeste	8	Orchester Flöte	8	Sub Bass	16
Gedact	8	Flauto Traverso	8	Lieblich Gedact	8	Quinte	10⅔
Hohl Flöte	4	Octave	4	Lieblich Flöte	4	Octave	8
Octave	4	Flauto Traverso	4	Octave	4	Violoncello	8
Rausch Quinte	II	Cymbel	IV	Piccolo	4	Flöten Bass	8
Mixtur	V	Horn	8	Cornett	II-V	Octave	4
Tuba	16	Oboe	8	Clarinette	8	Posaune	16
Trompete	8	Clarinet	4			Trompete	8
				ECHO			
		(The *Celeste* stop knob		Tibia Major	16		
		remains engraved *Rohr*		Zart Flöte	8		
		Flöte)		Still Gedact	8		
				Dolcan	8		
				Vox Angelica	8		
				Dolcissimo	4		
				Echo Flöte	4		
				Nasard	2⅔		
				Flautino	2		
				Echo Oboe	8		

The influence of Edmund Schulze on British organ-building has already been described in chapter 3. Armley is by far the largest of his instruments to survive without major changes, though in fact Edmund died before the organ reached Armley church. The instrument was built for a large wooden organ-room in the grounds of a private house. Less than ten years later it was presented as a gift to the then-new St Bartholomew's Church. The Pedal Open Metal and Sub Bass were added at this time and the organ installed under the supervision of Edmund Schulze's younger brother. The Gothic Revival case of three towers and four flats is by Walker and Athron, architects of the church. A conservative rebuild by Binns provided the organ with tubular-pneumatic action plus an extremely handsome console. Some changes were made to Schulze's reeds, but the fluework remains almost unaltered to this day.

The instrument is a fascinating and unique example of German romantic organ-building. In sound, as indeed in internal layout, the Great organ takes precedence over everything else. Schulze used wide mouths to get a big sound on low pressure and the effect of the Great chorus, capped by a famous and powerful five-rank mixture, is quite shattering. The other manuals play a subsidiary role and offer a very wide range of flute and mild string tones at several different dynamic levels, a feature of the romantic organ then relatively rare in Britain. However, it may be significant that this organ had no particular reputation before arriving at Armley church; it is the interaction between the Schulze style and this reverberant and lofty church which creates the magic.

The Town Hall
Gray & Davison 1859, 1865; Abbott & Smith 1898; Wood Wordsworth 1971

Gray & Davison had been disappointed to see the St George's Hall, Liverpool contract go to Willis after it had originally been awarded to them, so they must have been indeed pleased to receive the Leeds contract. With four manuals and 93 stops (including the 1865 Echo organ), it was nearly as big as Liverpool, and there is a story to the effect that the swell-box was so large that, when erected in Gray & Davison's factory, the builders entertained the consultants to a dinner served inside it!

The Great organ was huge (26 stops yet with remarkably little duplication), the Solo organ included an unseen horizontal Ophicleide and the Pedal had a 16ft Bombarde with iron pipes as well as a soft 32ft Contra Bombarde with half-length pipes and free reeds like a harmonium. The 32ft front pipes were also made of iron and the imposing if unscholarly case was designed by Cuthbert Broderick. The organ was famous in its day but was spoiled when the pitch was altered by Abbott & Smith. They replaced nearly all the flue-pipes with turn-of-the-century pipework of indifferent quality. More recently, Wood Wordsworth of Leeds fitted electric action and a new Positive organ, reducing the size of the instrument in other directions to a total of 81 stops, now controlled from a three-manual console.

WILTSHIRE

CHIPPENHAM St Andrew's Parish Church
Seede 1752; Gray & Davison 1879; Daniel 1965

Brice Seede built organs in the Bristol area in the eighteenth century; this is the earliest of his work of which we know. How he came to design and make the magnificent oak case which still survives is uncertain, though it is very similar to the case which graced the 1726 John Harris and Byfield organ then in St Mary Redcliffe Church, Bristol. Reminiscent of the grand houses which were being built in Bath at the time, the large central tower is capped by a heavy pediment; the front pipes in all three towers are treated as if they were Greek columns, the pipe-shades being carved in the form of Corinthian capitals!

MARLBOROUGH Marlborough College Chapel
Forster & Andrews 1876, 1914; Hill Norman & Beard 1955

GREAT		SWELL		CHOIR		PEDAL	
Double Open Diapason	16	Geigen Diapason	8	Quintaten	16	Acoustic Bass	32
Open Diapason I	8	Open Flute	8	Open Diapason	8	Open Wood	16
Open Diapason II	8	Salicional	8	Stopped Diapason	8	Open Metal	16
Geigen	8	Voix Celestes	8	Gemshorn	4	Bourdon	16
Gedeckt	8	Principal	4	Nazard	2⅔	Quintaten	16
Principal	4	Lieblich Flute	4	Blockflute	2	Gamba	16
Wald Flute	4	Fifteenth	2	Tertian 17.19	II	Principal	8
Twelfth	2⅔	Quint Mixture 15.19.22	III	Sifflöte	1	Violoncello	8
Fifteenth	2	Sharp Mixture 26.29	II			Bass Flute	8
Mixture 15.19.22	III	Double Trumpet	16	(Enclosed)		Fifteenth	4
Mixture 26.29.33.36	IV	Trumpet	8	Contra Gamba	16	Choral Bass	4
Tromba (enclosed)	8	Oboe	8	Gamba	8	Larigot	2⅔
		Clarion	4	Octave Gamba	4	Mixture 12.15.19.22	IV
				Tromba	8	Trombone	16
		SOLO (enclosed)		Tromba Clarion	4	Tromba	8
		Contra Gamba	16				
		Rohr Gedeckt	8				
		Gamba	8				
		Viole D'Orchestre	8				
		Viole Celestes	8				
		Dulciana	8				
		Concert Flute	4				
		Octave Gamba	4				
		Lieblich Nazard	2⅔				
		Flageolet	2				
		Tierce	1⅗				
		Clarinet	8				
		(unenclosed)					
		Tuba	8				

The origins of this organ go back to a Vowles instrument of 1853, enlarged and moved into the present chapel by Forster & Andrews. When they fitted pneumatic action in 1914, the firm was under the direction of Philip Selfe, and the label incorporated his name in brackets after that of the company. In the 1955 rebuild, the organ gained a fourth manual in the shape of an early light-pressure Positive, masquerading as a Choir organ. The power required to lead the singing of nine hundred public schoolboys is quite considerable, and I remember Peter Godfrey, then Director of Music, insisting that the Tuba had to be loud enough to be clearly heard over the unison singing. The four-rank mixture on the Great was added in 1977, and the Choir Sifflöte in 1979.

The elegant 16ft three-tower case is by Bodley, the architect of the chapel. The centre pipe has embossed fleur-de-lys, and is the only instance I know of embossing on zinc.

SALISBURY The Cathedral
Willis 1876, 1934

GREAT		SWELL		CHOIR		PEDAL	
Double Open Diapason	16	Contra Gamba	16	Lieblich Gedackt	16	Double Open Diapason	32
Open Diapason 1	8	Open Diapason	8	Open Diapason	8	Open Bass	16
Open Diapason 2	8	Lieblich Gedackt	8	Flûte Harmonique	8	Open Diapason 1	16
Claribel Flute	8	Viola da Gamba	8	Lieblich Gedackt	8	Open Diapason 2	16
Stopped Diapason	8	Vox Angelica	8	Salicional	8	Violone	16
Principal 1	4	Octave	4	Gemshorn	4	Bourdon	16
Principal 2	4	Flûte Harmonique	4	Flûte Harmonique	4	Lieblich Gedackt	16
Flûte Couverte	4	Super Octave	2	Lieblich Gedackt	4	Octave	8
Twelfth	2⅔	Mixture 17.19.22	III	Nazard	2⅔	Viola	8
Fifteenth	2	Vox Humana	8	Flageolet	2	Flute	8
Mixture 15.17.19.22	IV	Hautboy	8	Tierce	1⅗	Octave Viola	4
Trombone	16	Contra Fagotto	16	Trumpet	8	Octave Flute	4
Trumpet	8	Trompette	8			Mixture 12.15.19.22	IV
Clarion	4	Clarion	4	SOLO (enclosed)		Contra Posaune	32
				Violoncello	8	Ophicleide	16
				'Cello Célestes	8	Clarion	8
				Flûte Harmonique	8		
				Flûte Harmonique	4		
				Cor Anglais	16		
				Clarinet	8		
				Orchestral Oboe	8		
				Tuba (unenclosed)	8		
				Tuba Clarion			
				(unenclosed)	4		

Renatus Harris built an organ for Salisbury Cathedral in 1710, the first four-manual in Britain. The case had gabled cornices and tall superstructures on the towers (copies of a very dramatic print of this case still exist). It was replaced in 1792 by a new organ by Samuel Green in a Gothick case and presented by George III in his capacity 'as a Berkshire country gentleman'. This stood on James Wyatt's choir screen of the same date and when, some eighty years later, Sir George Gilbert Scott removed it Father Willis built the present organ, divided either side of the choir.

As rebuilt in 1934, the Father Willis organ was thought at the time to be the perfect cathedral organ. The taste that had swung away to the neo-orchestral excesses of Hope-Jones now swung back to appreciate Willis' virile reeds, complemented in the 1934 rebuild by some modest additions to the Solo organ and the Pedal. Henry Willis III's changes had actually been fairly small, so that, minor additions apart, we hear this instrument largely as Father Willis conceived it. Today's opinions are perhaps not so uncritical, particularly of the appearance of naked zinc pipes amidst the Early English glories of the Cathedral. The Henry Willis III electric action and console were rebuilt by Harrison & Harrison in 1978.

St Thomas' Church
Green 1792; Hill 1872

There is a pub in the centre of Salisbury which has a back door opening straight into the churchyard of St Thomas' Church with a path direct to the choir vestry door! In the eighteenth century, there was an organ in the west end by Schwarbrick, but when the Cathedral discarded its Samuel Green organ it went to St Thomas', where it stands today in the north chancel aisle, complete with Gothick case. The instrument matches St Thomas' quite well, so it must have sounded very delicate in the Cathedral. The organ was restored by Hill Norman & Beard in 1969, at which time turn-of-the-century additions were removed and the case returned to its original appearance. Although the Swell basses, Pedal organ, console and action are nineteenth century, the instrument is tonally very much a Green, and exhibits the restful, sweet tone for which he was renowned.

WALES

CLWYD

MOLD St Mary's Parish Church
Rushworth & Dreaper 1973

GREAT		SWELL		PEDAL	
Principal	8	Stopped Flute	8	Subbass	16
Chimney Flute	8	Principal	4	Octave	8
Octave	4	Gemshorn	2	Choral Bass	4
Wald Flute	4	Larigot	1⅓	Nachthorn	2
Tapered Flute	2	Mixture 26.29.33	III	Fagot	16
Mixture 19.22.26.29	IV	Krummhorn	8		
Trumpet	8				

Mold was Rushworth's first modern two-manual tracker organ, the fruit of Alastair Rushworth's training with Dirk Flentrop in Holland and Lawrence Phelps in Canada. It replaced a 1923 three-manual by the same firm and incorporates the Thomas Jackson case made for the Choir division of that organ. Although the Swell is a 4ft-based division, it is placed in the *Brustwerk* position immediately above the console and behind folding doors connected to a Swell pedal. The use of a flute for the Great organ 2ft stop was a characteristic of the late 1960s and early 1970s. The church is not over-reverberant and the voicing is 'sweet' rather than aggressive.

ST MARY'S CHURCH, MOLD

ST ASAPH The Cathedral
Hill 1834, 1869, 1897; Hill Norman & Beard 1966

GREAT		SWELL		CHOIR (unenclosed)		PEDAL	
Quintaten	16	Geigen Diapason	8	Stopped Diapason	8	Acoustic Bass	32
Open Diapason I	8	Hohl Flute	8	Principal	4	Open Wood	16
Open Diapason II	8	Echo Salicional	8	Nason Flute	4	Principal	16
Stopped Diapason	8	Vox Angelica	8	Octave	2	Bourdon	16
Principal	4	Stopped Flute	4	Larigot	1⅓	Octave	8
Wald Flute	4	Salicet	4	Rauschquinte 26.29	II	Bass Flute	8
Nazard	2⅔	Geigen Octave	4			Super Octave	4
Twelfth	2⅔	Fifteenth	2	SOLO (enclosed)		Mixture 19.22	II
Fifteenth	2	Quint Mixture 15.19.22	III	Keraulophon	8	Trombone	16
Block Flute	2	Sharp Mixture 26.29.33	III	Orchestral Flute	8	Trumpet	8
Tierce	1⅗	Double Trumpet	16	Krummhorn	8	Clarion	4
Mixture 19.22.26	III	Cornopean	8	Schalmey	4		
Trumpet	8	Oboe	8	Tuba (unenclosed)	8		

Robert Dallam is recorded as building an organ for St Asaph in 1635, and Abraham Jordan in 1740, but no trace of these instruments now remains. The present organ has its origins in the one-manual which William Hill built to stand upon the screen in 1834. The screen was removed in 1867 and the organ enlarged and placed in its present position in the north transept. The instrument was enlarged again by Hill in 1897, this time to four manuals.

The organ was fitted with a new action in 1966 by Hill Norman & Beard, and a detached three-manual console was provided on the opposite side of the choir. This console has the American system, where the couplers are controlled by stop-tabs, in order to reduce its height. At this time the Choir organ was remodelled as a small chorus, mutation stops provided and the mixturework generally revised. The instrument has, however, retained its generally mild character, especially as heard in the nave.

DYFED

ST DAVID'S The Cathedral
Willis c1880; Hill Norman & Beard 1951; Rushworth & Dreaper 1980

GREAT		SWELL		CHOIR (enclosed)		PEDAL	
Double Diapason	16	Lieblich Bourdon	16	Gedeckt	8	Open Diapason	32
Open Diapason I	8	Open Diapason	8	Principal	4	Open Diapason	16
Open Diapason II	8	Lieblich Gedeckt	8	Koppel Flute	4	Violone	16
Claribel Flute	8	Salicional	8	Nazard	2⅔	Bourdon	16
Principal	4	Vox Angelica	8	Octave	2	Octave	8
Twelfth	2⅔	Gemshorn	4	Tierce	1⅗	Bass Flute	8
Fifteenth	2	Flageolet	2	Larigot	1⅓	Choral Bass	4
Sesquialtera 17.19.22	III	Cornopean	8	Mixture	III	Ophicleide	32
Tromba	8	Hautbois	8	Corno di Bassetto	8	Trombone	16
Clarion	4						

Situated in 'Little England beyond Wales', St David's must be the smallest place in Britain to have a cathedral. Father Smith once built an organ for it but the present organ was built by Father Willis and stands upon the choir screen. After World War II the instrument received a conservative rebuild together with a new case by Alban Caröe. A minor problem at the time was that the shutters of the Willis swell-boxes were unbalanced, a difficulty cured by putting lever balances on top of the swell-boxes. These were normally invisible, but could be seen from the high altar, giving rise to a query from the Dean about 'the two pigeons on top of the organ which appear to bow to each other during the service'! In 1980 Rushworth & Dreaper restored the organ, recasting the enclosed Choir organ with a Positive-type chorus.

GWYNEDD

BANGOR Prichard-Jones Hall, Bangor University
Hill Norman & Beard 1973

GREAT		SWELL		PEDAL		
Principal	8	Bourdon	16	Principal	16	Cymbelstern
Rohr Flute	8	Viole de Gambe	8	Sub Bass	16	
Octave	4	Flûte à Fuseau	4	Octave	8	
Koppel Flute	4	Prestant	2	Bass Flute	8	
Spitz Flute	2	Larigot	1⅓	Choral Bass	4	
Sesquialtera	II	Cymbale 22.26.29.33.36	V	Mixture 22.26.29	III	
Furniture 19.22.26.29	IV	Bassoon	16	Posaune	16	
Trompete Real	8	Trompette	8	Zink	4	

The case of this striking-looking organ, with its detached Pedal towers, was designed by
Herbert Norman. The instrument incorporates some pipes, soundboards and lower casework
from the Lewis organ in the Tabernacle Chapel, Bangor. The stop-list is unusually complete
for a two-manual instrument. William Mathias composed a special fanfare for the horizontal
Trompete Real for the inaugural recital.

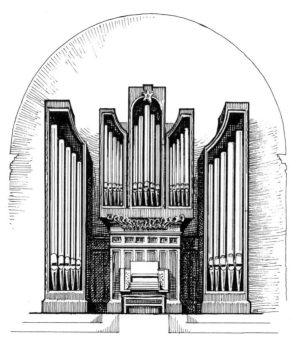

PRICHARD-JONES HALL, BANGOR UNIVERSITY

POWYS

OLD RADNOR St Stephen's Parish Church (for case, see p29)
Anon 16th century

Here, near the border between England and Wales, is the oldest organ case in Britain,
probably the only one to survive the Protestant zealots of the middle sixteenth century. Its
origins are undocumented and its date can only be guessed at as between 1500 and 1547. At

18ft high it is large for so remote a church and may have been moved there for safety from the iconoclasts. Gothic design was slow to succumb to the 'new' Renaissance art in Britain and this case is almost entirely Gothic in feeling. The case is illustrated in chapter 2 (see p 29).

The instrument was discovered in a ruinous condition in the 1860s by the Rev F. H. Sutton, without pipes or mechanism, and was restored under his direction in 1872 by J. W. Walker, who also built a small two-manual instrument into the case.

SOUTH GLAMORGAN

CARDIFF Llandaff Cathedral
Hope-Jones 1898; Hill Norman & Beard 1938, 1958

GREAT		PRIMARY SWELL		POSITIVE		PEDAL	
Quintaton	16	Viola	8	Principal	8	Contra Salicional	32
Open Diapason	8	Lieblich Gedeckt	8	Chimney Flute	8	Open Wood Bass	16
Spitzprincipal	8	Viole de Gambe	8	Octave	4	Violone	16
Stopped Diapason	8	Viole Celeste	8	Gemshorn	4	Sub Bass	16
Octave	4	Geigen Principal	4	Nazard	2⅔	Salicional	16
Principal	4	Plein Jeu 15.19.22	III-V	Blockflute	2	Quintaton	16
Koppelflute	4	Oboe	8	Tierce	1⅗	Principal	8
Octave Quint	2⅔	Contra Fagotto	16	Cymbal 29.33.36	III	Bass Flute	8
Super Octave	2	Trompette	8	Dulzian	16	Salicet	8
Tierce	1⅗	Clarion	4			Fifteenth	4
Fourniture 19.22.26.29	IV			SOLO (enclosed)		Fourniture 19.22.26.29	IV
Double Trumpet	16			Claribel Flute	8	Contra Trombone	32
Harmonic Trumpet	8	SECONDARY SWELL		Spitzflute	8	Trombone	16
Octave Trumpet	4	(*enclosed in the main Swell*		Spitzflute Celeste	8	Fagotto	16
		box)		Clarinet	8	Posaune	8
		Open Diapason	8	Orchestral Oboe	8	Octave Trumpet	4
		Hohl Flute	8	Tuba (unenclosed)	8		
		Salicional	8	Double Trumpet	16	The Secondary Swell may	
		Harmonic Flute	4	Harmonic Trumpet	8	be transferred from the	
		Salicet	4	Octave Trumpet	4	Swell to the Choir keys.	

The most striking visual feature of Llandaff Cathedral is the concrete pulpitum, standing astride the nave on elliptical arches and looking not totally unlike a recently landed space-ship. It has two functions: first, to provide a backdrop to Jacob Epstein's 'Majestas' of Christ and, within its elliptical drum, to house the Positive organ. The idea of a detached Positive went back to 1951 (when such departments were almost unheard of) when initial plans were made for rebuilding the Cathedral and organ after wartime damage. In some ways the instrument suffered from being a pioneer, the Positive being too detached, both physically (the remainder of the organ is in the north aisle) and tonally (the main organ having been reconstructed from the bomb-damaged 1938 rebuild of a Hope-Jones).

The organ was perhaps the first cathedral instrument which set out to be an eclectic organ, in the sense of an equal priority between the performance of eighteenth-century music and of the romantic nineteenth- and early twentieth-century composers. There are some hang-overs from the 1930s, notably the Secondary Swell accompanimental chorus, but the instrument was a significant milestone at a time of transition. Minor changes were made to the Swell in 1971, and in 1980 Rushworth & Dreaper replaced the 1938 coupling and piston action.

Both the pulpitum and the main case, which houses the 32ft Contra Salicional down to 21ft GGG, were designed by George Pace.

St David's Hall
Collins 1982

GREAT		SWELL		POSITIVE		PEDAL	
Bourdon	16	Quintadena	16	Traverse Flute	8	Principal	16
Principal	8	Diapason	8	Gedact	8	Major Bass	16
Spitz Flute	8	Chimney Flute	8	Quintadena	8	Subbass	16
Bourdon	8	Viola	8	Principal	4	Quint	10⅔
Octave	4	Celeste	8	Chimney Flute	4	Octave	8
Stopped Flute	4	Octave	4	Octave	2	Gedact	8
Block Flute	2	Open Flute	4	Wald Flute	2	Choral Bass	4
Rauschquint 12.15	II	Nazard	2⅔	Nazard	1⅓	Open Flute	2
Tertian	II	Gemshorn	2	Sesquialtera	II	Mixture 19.22.26.29	IV
Mixture 19.22.26.29	IV-VI	Tierce	1⅗	Scharf 22.26.29.33	IV-V	Fagotto	32
Cornet	V	Mixture		Dulzian	16	Bombarde	16
Fagotto	16	15.19.22.22.26	V-VI	Cremona	8	Trumpet	8
Trumpet	8	Cimbel 31.33.36	III			Shawm	4
		Harmonic Trumpet	8			Cornett	2
		Hautboy	8				
		Vox Humana	8				
		Harmonic Clarion	4				

St David's Hall is the National Concert Hall of Wales so it is perhaps fitting that the organ is, in some ways, a successor to the Royal Festival Hall in London. Like that instrument, the organ was designed by Ralph Downes, though there is a gap of nearly thirty years between the two instruments and there are some interesting differences.

Firstly, the organ is free-standing within the body of the hall in a series of tone-cabinets on the right of the stage. The Swell organ is clearly visible, the fret over the shutters being to the same pattern as that behind the front pipes of the other departments. There is no chair case but the Positive has been placed nearest to the majority of the audience. The main layout is basically horizontal, vertical variety coming from the way the front of each ash-wood tone-cabinet is divided into several compartments, differing in projection and height, with the tin-metal pipes of the 16ft Principal in the Pedal case and 8ft fronts for the Great and Positive.

The other main difference between this organ and the Royal Festival Hall organ is in the use of tracker key-action. Peter Collins has specialised in mechanical action organs and the action at Cardiff is quite remarkably light, given the size of the instrument and the relatively high wind pressures. Only some degree of 'sponginess' reveals the complexities resulting from a layout which is not only horizontal but slightly concave, hardly ideal for tracker action.

The stop-list is not large for a 2000 seater hall with fairly 'dry' acoustics. It is more economical than the organ in the Royal Festival Hall, having three manual choruses instead of five. Nevertheless, the overall sound is reminiscent of the earlier instrument and it has the same explosive attack resulting from the wide scales, wide mouths and high wind pressures (up to 4in/100mm) needed to get adequate volume in this hall. The Pedal organ has the widest margin of power, with reed-stops covering the range from 32ft to 2ft. Hallmarks of a Ralph Downes stop-list include a Vox Humana on the Swell and the use of a Tierce rank in the high-pitched Cimbel mixture. Less typical is the 8ft pitch-basis of the Swell organ chorus, the same as that of the Great organ, moving away from the Continental pitch difference between manuals back more towards the William Hill concept of the Swell organ. The reed-stops are less overtly French than in the Royal Festival Hall organ and thus combine better with the fluework. This is helped by the warmth added by the tone-cabinets, but the characteristic speech of un-nicked pipes gives the overall sound of the instrument a Continental flavour.

WEST GLAMORGAN

SWANSEA Brangwyn Hall
Willis 1920, 1972 onwards

GREAT		SWELL		POSITIF		PEDAL	
Double Open Diapason	16	Contra Salicional	16	Gedackt	8	Contra Bourdon	
Open Diapason	8	Open Diapason	8	Spindle Flöte	4	(extension)	32
Stopped Diapason	8	Rohr Gedackt	8	Nazat	2⅔	Open Diapason	16
Principal	4	Aeoline	8	Blockflöte	2	Bourdon	16
Stopped Flute	4	Voix Celestes	8	Terz	1⅗	Violon (Solo)	16
Twelfth	2⅔	Octave	4	Larigot	1⅓	Salicional (Swell)	16
Fifteenth	2	Flûte Triangulaire	4	Sifflet	1	Grand Principal	8
Seventeenth	1⅗	Nazard	2⅔	Cimbel	III	Flute	8
Mixture	II/III	Flageolet	2			Super Octave	4
Quartane	II	Mixture	V	SOLO (enclosed)		Gedeckt	4
Contra Tromba	16	Oboe	8	Violon	16	Recorder	2
Tromba	8	Waldhorn	16	Concert Flute	8	Mixture	IV
Clarion	4	Trumpet	8	Viola d'Orchestre	8	Ophicleide	16
		Clarion	4	Viola Celestes	8	Clarion	8
				Violoncello	8	Rohr Schalmey	4
				Salicional	8		
				Flute Harmonique	4		
				Piccolo	2		
				Clarinet	8		
				Fagott	16		
				Jagdhorn	8		
				Tuba	8		

A Willis cinema organ! Well, not any more, but that is what this instrument was when first built for the Elite Cinema, Nottingham in 1920. One of the few survivors of the early 'straight' cinema organs (built before the invasion of the 'Mighty Wurlitzer'), this instrument was built with three Open Diapasons on the Great and an Orchestral division (now the Solo) which included a Tibia. In 1934 the organ was moved to Swansea and installed in the then-new Brangwyn Hall with relatively minor alterations, the Bass Drum, Cymbals and Side Drum being retained as well as the enclosed Echo with its 'Carillon' stop.

Since 1972 the voicing of the instrument has been changed, the Positif replacing the Echo division and the Pedal organ being enlarged substantially.

SCOTLAND

FIFE

ST ANDREWS Collegiate Church of St Salvator, University of St Andrews
Hradetzky 1974

GREAT		POSITIV		SWELL		PEDAL	
Bourdon	16	Gedackt	8	Bourdon	8	Subbass (open wood)	16
Prinzipal	8	Prinzipal	4	Viola	8	Prinzipal	8
Hohlflöte	8	Kleingedackt	4	Celeste	8	Gemshorn	8
Octave	4	Nazard	2⅔	Prestant	4	Choralbass	4
Spitzflöte	4	Waldflöte	2	Flute	4	Nachthorn	2
Superoctave	2	Tierce	1⅗	Doublette	2	Mixtur 19.22.26.29.33	V
Mixtur 15.19.22.		Larigot	1⅓	Cornet	V	Posaune	16
26.29.33	VI-VIII	Scharff 26.29.33.36	IV	Mixtur 19.22.26.		Schalmei	4
		Krummhorn	8	29.33.36	VI-VIII		
BOMBARDE				Fagott	16		
Cornet	V			Trompet	8		
Prestant	4			Oboe	8		
Trompet	8			Vox Humana	8		
Clarion	4						

Although nominally a four-manual organ, this could be said to be really a three-manual in disguise, since the Bombarde division of this Austrian-made organ consists largely of reeds and a Cornet, voiced on a higher pressure than the reedless Great. The Pedal, Great and Positive follow Hradetzky's fundamentally German style with the usual 16ft, 8ft and 4ft pitch emphasis to the respective manuals. Like the same builder's instrument at the Royal Northern College of Music, Manchester, there is a second Cornet on the Swell. Here, however, the Swell organ is 4ft-based, not 8ft, though this has not prevented the provision of two mild strings. The Pedal, unusually, has only one 16ft flue which, despite its name, is made of open pipes.

The appearance of the organ is similar to a large two-manual, with wide semi-circular 8ft Pedal towers, a tall central Great organ case and a projecting Positive. The pipe-shades have a delicate vine-like tracery which contrasts oddly with the plain treatment of the towers which have no mouldings either top or bottom. The Swell organ is placed under the Great and is set very low so that the Great is not unduly elevated. This is made possible because the console is detached and reversed in front of the whole organ. The tracker action is complicated thereby but the terraced jamb layout of the crisply styled low console is very distinctive.

GRAMPIAN

ABERDEEN Mitchell Hall, University of Aberdeen
R. H. Walker 1972

GREAT		FRONT POSITIVE		PEDAL	
Chimney Flute	8	Gedeckt	8	Subbass	16
Principal	4	Rohrflote	4	Gedecktbass	8
Twelfth	2⅔	Principal	2	Superoctave	4
Wald Flute	2	Nasat	1⅓	Mixture	II
Tierce	1⅗	Cymbel 22	I	Schalmei	4
Larigot	1⅓	Krummhorn	8		
Twenty-second	1			Tracker action.	
Trumpet-en-chamade	8				

Designed by Peter Walker, this is the major work of R. H. Walker & Son, who broke away from the old established firm of J. W. Walker. The instrument stands on a gallery flanking the proscenium arch of the Mitchell Hall and is essentially a *werk* principle organ. The second manual, the Positive, is in the lower part of the waisted case, the tone-cabinet having hand-operated doors. Above it, a horizontal Trumpet projects from the Great organ soundboard. The Great is unusual in having no mixture, although there are 1⅓ and 1ft stops. The Cymbal on the Positive has one rank only.

LOTHIAN

EDINBURGH Church of St Andrew and St George
Wells–Kennedy 1984

GREAT		SWELL		PEDAL	
Open Diapason	8	Stopped Flute	8	Subbass	16
Stopped Diapason	8	Salicional	8	Octave	8
Principal	4	Principal	4	Fifteenth	4
Gemshorn	2	Chimney Flute	4	Trombone	16
Cornet 12.17	II	Fifteenth	2		
Mixture 19.22.26.29	IV	Mixture 26.29.33	III		
		Hautboy	16		
		Trumpet	8		

This free-standing tracker-action organ, at present under construction, will be the first major instrument by this Northern Ireland firm outside the Province.

Reid School of Music, University of Edinburgh
Ahrend 1978

HAUPTWERK		RUCKPOSITIV		PEDAL	
Praestant	8	Gedackt	8	Subbass	16
Hohlflöte	8	Praestant	4	Octave	8
Octave	4	Rohrflöte	4	Octave	4
Spitzflöte	4	Waldflöte	2	Posaune	16
Nasat	3	Quinte	1⅓	Trompete	8
Octave	2	Sesquialtera	II		
Mixture	IV-V	Scharff	IV		
Trompete	8	Dulzian	8		

The small firm of Ahrend, from the Dutch–German border, made its initial reputation by the scrupulous restoration of early instruments. It now specialises in making organs without compromises to modern ideas, either in mechanism or in tonal design. At Edinburgh there is, of course, no enclosed division, the instrument being a straightforward *Hauptwerk* and *Ruckpositiv* instrument in a double case perched on a narrow projecting tribune. The main case has closeable doors, though its actual design has no historic model and features a pedimented central flat flanked by two broad towers. The chair case is similar and both cases have unusually formal patterned pipe-shades.

As expected, the manuals both have well-developed choruses, though, strangely, the Pedal does not and relies heavily on the reeds. These are essentially German in character, not the quasi-French reeds to be found in so many neo-classical organs. The instrument is tuned in unequal temperament. A less useful archaism is the need to turn round, or reach behind, to alter the registration of the Positive, the stop-knobs of which project from the chair case. The equally archaic suspended tracker action is free of inertia and very responsive.

St Mary's Episcopal Church, Dalkeith
Hamilton 1830

GREAT		SWELL		CHOIR		PEDAL	
Open Diapason	8	Gamba	16	Open Diapason	8	Bourdon	16
Stopped Diapason	8	Open Diapason	8	Gamba	8	Open Diapason	16
Diapason Flute	8	Dulciana	8	Stopped Diapason	8		
Principal	4	Principal	4	Principal	4		
Gemshorn	4	Mixture	III	Flute	4		
Twelfth	2⅔	Oboe	8	Clarionet	8		
Fifteenth	2						
Mixture	III						
Trumpet	8						

Organs were uncommon in Scotland when this instrument was built, being banned in the Presbyterian church. However, this tracker-action organ, spread across the west gallery, does not suffer by comparison with instruments south of the border. Although the case, without pipe-shades, is somewhat severe, the pipework is all of tin-metal and the organ is voiced on under 2in (50mm) of wind.

St Stephen's Church
Willis 1880

GREAT		SWELL		CHOIR		PEDAL	
Double Diapason	16	Lieblich Bourdon	16	Viola da Gamba	8	Open Diapason	16
Open Diapason	8	Open Diapason	8	Dulciana	8	Bourdon	16
Open Diapason	8	Salicional	8	Lieblich Gedact	8	Violoncello	8
Claribel Flute	8	Vox Angelica	8	Claribel Flute	8	Bass Flute	8
Flûte Harmonique	4	Lieblich Gedact	8	Lieblich Flöte	4		
Principal	4	Gemshorn	4	Flûte Harmonique	4		
Fifteenth	2	Flageolet	2	Gemshorn	4		
Mixture 17.19.22	III	Vox Humana	8	Piccolo	2		
Bombard	8	Cornopean	8	Corno di Bassetto	8		
Clarion	4	Hautboy	8				

St Stephen's Church is an imposing landmark in Edinburgh's Georgian New Town. Inside, the elegant and uncluttered building is octagonal and Willis' organ was originally built on the gallery. The organ has undergone no significant change in over a hundred years but the church floor was raised to meet the gallery in 1956. This has still left an amply tall church and the reduction in absorption has probably aided the acoustics.

As is not uncommon in Scotland, the organ and pulpit are all one piece of furniture, with the console below the minister's desk. The organ front itself includes a 16ft bass in a simple post-and-rail case which was the standard Willis provision where there was no architectural intervention. The original tracker action, with pneumatic lever assistance on the Great, remains in use. The tone of this instrument is most impressive, especially the reedwork which combines power and grandeur with the regularity and absence of coarseness which were Father Willis' trademark.

STRATHCLYDE

FASLANE HMS Neptune
Hill Norman & Beard 1970

GREAT		SWELL		PEDAL	
Stopped Diapason	8	Gemshorn	8	Bourdon	16
Principal	4	Chimney Flute	4	Gedeckt	4
Mixture 15–12.15	I-II	Spitz Flute	2		
		Sesquialtera 12.17	II		
		Cymbal 29.33	II		

An organ in a nuclear-submarine base! – well, in the Anglican chapel to be precise. The instru-

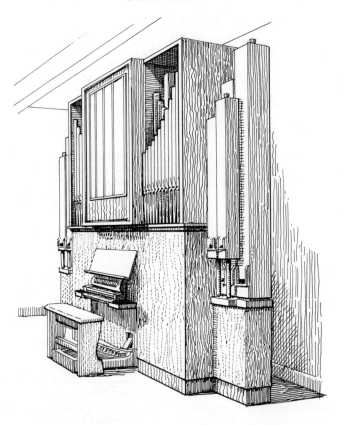

HMS NEPTUNE, FASLANE

ment had to occupy the minimum depth and height although ample width was available. The organ is arranged with the Swell in the centre, over the console, with the Great organ divided over two tone-cabinets, either side of the Swell. As a result, the organ is 17ft (5m) wide, yet little more than 2ft (0.6m) deep.

GLASGOW St Andrew's Cathedral (Roman Catholic)
Willis 1903

Henry Willis II organs are not very common; this one came to the Cathedral in 1981 from a Congregational church. As with Father Willis organs, it is the reed-stops which carry the day and although the instrument, at 31 stops, is of modest size for a cathedral and has little upper-work, it fills the Gothick building very adequately from its vantage point on the west gallery. The original 'floating-lever' pneumatic action has been retained.

The Bute Hall, Glasgow University
Lewis 1903; Hill Norman & Beard 1962

GREAT		SWELL		POSITIF		PEDAL	
Double Open Diapason	16	Geigen Principal	8	Quintaten	16	Harmonic Sub Bass	32
Open Diapason I	8	Hohl Flute	8	Chimney Flute	8	Great Bass	16
Open Diapason II	8	Echo Salicional	8	Principal	8	Sub Bass	16
Spitz Principal	8	Voix Celeste	8	Koppel Flöte	4	Contra Gamba	16
Dulciana	8	Stopped Flute	4	Octave	4	Lieblich Bourdon	16
Stopped Diapason	8	Octave	4	Wald Flöte	2	Octave	8
Clear Flute	4	Super Octave	2	Quint	1⅓	Principal	8
Octave	4	Plein Jeu 15.19.22	III	Principal	1	Violoncello	8
Gemshorn Principal	4	Scharf 26.29.33	III	Zimbel 29.33.36	III	Bass Flute'	8
Twelfth	2⅔	Contra Fagotto	16	Trumpet	8	Nachthorn	4
Fifteenth	2	Cornopean	8	Clarion	4	Fifteenth	4
Cornet 12.15.17	III	Oboe	8			Sifflöte	2
Mixture 19.22.26.29	IV	Clarion	4			Quartane 19.22	II
Trumpet	8					Contra Trombone	32
Clarion	4	**SOLO (enclosed)**				Ophicleide	16
		Quintade	8			Trumpet	8
		Viole de Gambe	8			Clarion	4
		Viole Celeste	8			Trompette en Chamade	8
		Concert Flute	4				
		Nasat	2⅔				
		Piccolo	2				
		Tierce	1⅗				
		Cor Anglais	16				
		Krummhorn	8				
		Hautbois	4				
		(unenclosed)					
		Tuba	8				
		Tuba Clarion	4				
		Trompette en Chamade	8				

This organ was one of many which were given by Andrew Carnegie to Scottish churches and institutions in the first decade of this century. The hall having been subsequently treated with acoustic tile, the organ had to be revoiced at the rebuild in 1962. The instrument also gained a new Positif department, a much revised Solo organ and largely unextended upperwork on the Pedal. A horizontal Trompette en Chamade was provided, projecting from below the two central flats of the three-tower case. Even in this large hall, it is on only 4½in (112mm) of wind.

PAISLEY The Abbey
Cavaillé-Coll 1872; Hill Norman & Beard 1928; Walker 1968

GREAT		SWELL		POSITIVE		PEDAL	
Bourdon	16	Chimney Flute	8	Salicional	8	Contrebasse	32
Montre	8	Gambe	8	Unda Maris	8	Contrebasse	16
Spitzflute	8	Voix Céleste	8	Traverse Flute	8	Principal	16
Bourdon	8	Principal	4	Bourdon	8	Sub Bass	16
Prestant	4	Flute Octave	4	Principal	4	Salicional	16
Stopped Flute	4	Nazard	2⅔	Chimney Flute	4	Octave	8
Quint	2⅔	Gemshorn	2	Nazard	2⅔	Gedackt	8
Octave	2	Tierce	1⅗	Doublette	2	Choralbass	4
Blockflute	2	Plein Jeu 15.19.22.26	IV-VI	Wald Flute	2	Open Flute	2
Cornet	IV	Cimbel 31.33.36	III	Larigot	1⅓	Mixture	
Mixture 19.22.26.29	IV-VI	Corno di Bassetto	16	Sesquialtera	II	19.22.26.29.33.36	VI
Bassoon	16	Hautboy	8	Mixture 26.29.33.36	IV	Bombarde	16
Trumpet	8	Voix Humaine	8	Cremona	8	Bassoon	16
		Trumpet	8			Trumpet 1	8
		Clarion	4	**BOMBARDE**		Trumpet 2	8
				Principal	16	Shawm	4
				Octave	8		
				Harmonic Flute	8		
				Prestant	4		
				Quartane 12.15	II		
				Plein Jeu 19.22.26.29.33	VI		
				Cornet	V		
				Bombarde	16		
				Trumpet	8		
				Clarion	4		

Aristide Cavaillé-Coll, the famous French organ-builder, made only a handful of instruments for Britain. One of these was the 24 stop two-manual which he built for Paisley Abbey. It had a fully specified Grande Orgue with 16ft, 8ft and 4ft reeds and a III–IV mixture. The enclosed Récit was, however, quite different from a British Swell organ, with only 8ft reeds and no Diapason Chorus at all. This instrument stood in the nave and, in 1928, formed the basis of the much larger organ built when the Abbey choir, previously in ruins, was restored. The 1928 instrument was a four-manual (Great, Swell, enclosed Choir and enclosed Solo) with 66 stops, including Pedal extensions, and exhaust-pneumatic action. Mechanically, it was a new organ, though it incorporated all the Cavaillé-Coll pipework. Nevertheless, with Trombas and other heavy-pressure reeds, it was a typical heavy-toned instrument of the 1920s, relieved only by the early use of narrow-scale mutations on the Choir organ.

The present instrument has resulted from a rebuilding of the 1928 organ by J. W. Walker, under the direction of Ralph Downes. By rearranging the manual departments vertically behind the Choir case (Swell, almost unseen, over Positive, over Great) and with the fourth manual controlling a 16ft-based Bombarde division speaking through the narrow arch into the transept, a bolder projection of sound has been achieved. Acoustic reflectors were put behind the Bombarde, Great and Positive soundboards for the same reason. Although the wind pressures were reduced to normal and much of the Cavaillé-Coll pipework retained, the instrument is essentially a Ralph Downes organ rather than a reconstructed Cavaillé-Coll. The reeds have regained their French sound on light wind pressure but the fluework, voiced with open feet, has more of a Dutch than a French flavour.

A naked screen of 16ft pipes covers the opening into the transept, placed there in 1968, but the Choir has a case with lace-like Gothic tracery, a hallmark of the work of Sir Robert Lorimer, made for the 1928 organ. The 1968 tin-metal front pipes set off the rich if somewhat flat-fronted case most handsomely.

TAYSIDE

DUNDEE St Paul's Cathedral
Hill 1865; Rothwell 1937; Hill Norman & Beard 1975

This 40 stop three-manual Hill was not seriously altered by Rothwell when he supplied one of his special consoles with stop-keys between the manuals. When Rothwell's action gave out, the instrument had a further conservative rebuild with a conventional stop-knob console and electropneumatic action. Tonally, the instrument retains its William Hill characteristics of good blend and good manners and the ability to give a good account of music of almost any period.

OLD SCONE Scone Palace
Elliot 1813

GREAT (from GG)		SWELL (from tenor F)		PEDAL (from GG)	
Open Diapason	8	Open Diapason	8	Pedal Pipes	8
Stop Diapason	8	Stop Diapason	8		
Dulciana	8	Principal	4		
Principal	4	Hautboy	8		
Flute	4				
Twelfth	2⅔				
Fifteenth	2				
Mixture	II				
Furniture	II				
Trumpet	8				

Like the almost identical organ at Ashridge College, Hertfordshire, this instrument is an extremely important survival from the era before Gauntlett and Hill, and one which has suffered even less alteration. In particular, the Trumpet retains its original tongues and has a distinct edge to it. The organ stands at one end of the room and the oak case is, in fact, a screen with three compartments of gilded dummy pipes and Gothick decoration. In contrast to eighteenth-century practice, when the consoles were set into the case *en fenêtre*, it here projects from the case, and with low square jambs and a folding music desk is reminiscent of pianoforte construction of the period.

NORTHERN IRELAND

COUNTY ANTRIM

BELFAST St Patrick's Pro-Cathedral
Hill Norman & Beard 1974

GREAT		SWELL		PEDAL	
Open Diapason	8	Spitzflute	8	Sub Bass	16
Stopped Diapason	8	Salicional	8	Principal	8
Octave	4	Chimney Flute	4	Fagotto	16
Gemshorn	2	Principal	2		
Furniture 19.22.26.29	IV	Larigot	1⅓		
Trumpet	8	Cymbal 29.33.36	III		

Standing on the west gallery, this tracker organ has a 'long movement' so that the console is brought forward to the gallery edge. The Swell is in the *Brustwerk* position under the Great organ but nevertheless incorporates a string stop.

The mahogany seven compartment case with copper and tin front pipes was designed by Herbert Norman.

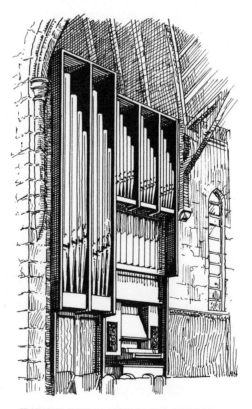

ST SIMON'S CHURCH, BELFAST (SEE OPPOSITE)

St Simon's Church
Rushworth & Dreaper 1973

GREAT		SWELL		PEDAL	
Principal	8	Chimney Flute	8	Bourdon	16
Gedeckt	8	Koppel Flute	4	Octave	8
Octave	4	Spitz Flute	2	Choral Bass	4
Block Flute	2	Larigot	1⅓		
Mixture	III	Krummhorn	8		

This tracker-action organ replaced an earlier instrument destroyed by fire. It stands in a tall chamber on the north side of the choir and has a somewhat Scandinavian appearance, with the Great front divided into three asymmetric compartments and the Pedal, on the left side, into two. The Swell occupies a *Brustwerk* position under the Great, with exposed shutters, and is basically an enclosed Positive.

The Ulster Hall
Hill 1861, 1903; Mander 1978

GREAT		SWELL		CHOIR		PEDAL	
Double Diapason	16	Double Diapason	16	Stopped Diapason	8	Double Open Diapason	32
Bourdon	16	Open Diapason	8	Principal	4	Open Diapason	16
Open Diapason I	8	Stopped Diapason	8	Rohr Flute	4	Violone	16
Open Diapason II	8	Salicional	8	Nazard	2⅔	Bourdon	16
Stopped Diapason	8	Voix Celeste	8	Flautina	2	Octave	8
Gamba	8	Saube Flute	4	Tierce	1⅗	Bass Flute	8
Quint	5⅓	Octave	4	Larigot	1⅓	Fifteenth	4
Principal	4	Fifteenth	2	Dulciana Mixture 19.22	II	Sesquialtera 12.17	II
Tenth	3⅕	Full Mixture 15.19.22.26	IV	Cymbal 22.26.29.33.36	V	Mixture 19.22.26.29	IV
Twelfth	2⅔	Double Trumpet	16	Bassoon	16	Contra Bombarde	32
Fifteenth	2	Oboe	8	Cremona	8	Contra Fagotto	16
Full Mixture 15.19.22.26	IV	Cornopean	8			Trombone	16
Sharp Mixture 22.26.29	III	Trumpet	8	SOLO		Clarion	8
Double Trumpet	16	Clarion	4	Harmonic Flute	8		
Trumpet	8			Harmonic Flute	4		
Posaune	8			Harmonic Piccolo	2		
Clarion	4			Grand Cornet			
				1.8.12.15.17	V		
				Furniture 12.15.19.22.26	V		
				Cymbal 29.33.36.40	IV-VI		
				Corno di Bassetto	16		
				Clarinet	8		
				Vox Humana	8		
				Contra Tuba	16		
				Tuba	8		
				Tuba Clarion	4		

A combination of municipal pride and William Hill at his best have made this a particularly grand instrument, and one which has survived the passage of time surprisingly well. The four-towered case is bold, if unscholarly, and features a Spanish-type horizontal Trumpet – presumably Hill's riposte to those installed elsewhere by his great rivals Gray & Davison at about the same time. The organ was conservatively rebuilt with new action and console by Hill in 1903, and again by Mander in 1978. The present horizontal reeds are new, as are the Solo organ mixtures, the Choir mutations and the Pedal organ upperwork, but the main corpus of the instrument is unchanged, leaving it, almost without question, the finest large organ in Ireland.

COUNTY DOWN

DOWNPATRICK Down Cathedral
Green late 18th century; Harrison 1914, 1965

GREAT		SWELL		CHOIR		PEDAL	
*Double Open Diapason	16	*Open Diapason	8	Rohr Flute	8	Open Diapason	16
*Open Diapason I	8	Lieblich Gedackt	8	Spitz Principal	4	Sub Bass	16
*Open Diapason II	8	Echo Gamba	8	Wald Flute	4	Octave	8
*Stopped Diapason	8	*Principal	4	Block Flute	2	Flute	8
*Octave	4	*Dulciana Sesquialtera		Quint	1⅓	Fifteenth	4
*Super Octave	2	12.15.17	III	Cimbel 29.33.36	III	Mixture 19.22.26.29	IV
*Sesquialtera 12.17.19	III	Mixture 22.26	II	Cremona	8	Trumpet	16
*Mixture 22.26.29	III	Contra Oboe	16				
Full Mixture		Trumpet	8			*Mainly pipes by Green.	
12.15.19.22	IV						

Although this organ arrived in Downpatrick in 1802, a gift of King George III, Samuel Green had been dead for several years so its original destination is a mystery. It was built as a two-manual and was modern in the sense that the second manual was a Swell not a Choir organ and that the case was in the fashionable Gothick style. Green had added Gothick arches and little

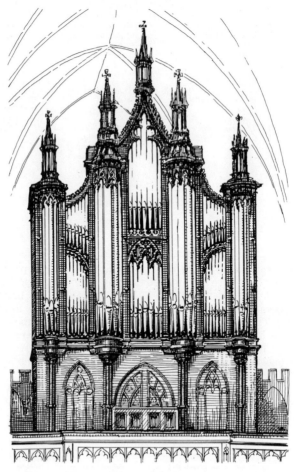

DOWN CATHEDRAL

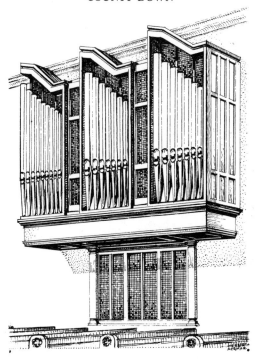

GLENDERMOTT PRESBYTERIAN CHURCH, LONDONDERRY (SEE P320)

spirelets to what is fundamentally a conventional four-tower case, double-fronted and standing on a screen. We are fortunate that the case has escaped alteration and is now one of the best of its type to remain to us.

The organ itself acquired more Swell stops and a couple of Pedal stops in the nineteenth century but was not much changed until 1914. Arthur Harrison fitted tubular-pneumatic action but was uncharacteristically self-effacing over this instrument, adding Swell strings and reeds plus a small Choir organ but leaving Green's flutes and choruses unaltered. The 1965 rebuild provided electropneumatic action and used extension to provide Pedal upperwork. The 1914 Choir organ has become a Positive in all but name and the Swell and Great have each acquired an additional mixture to give the instrument the 'bite' which is always missing from Green organs unless augmented or moved to a smaller building.

HILLSBOROUGH The Parish Church
Snetzler 1773; Coombe 1868; Evans & Barr 1924; Wells–Kennedy 1970

GREAT		SWELL		CHOIR		PEDAL	
*Open Diapason	8	Gedact	8	*Chimney Flute	8	Open Diapason	16
*Stopt Diapason	8	*Principal	4	*Flute	4	Principal	8
*Principal	4	Blockflute	2	*Fifteenth	2	Nachthorn	4
*Fifteenth	2	Sesquialtera	II	Larigot	1⅓	Quint	2⅔
*Sesquialtera		Mixture 26.29.33	III	Cimbal 29.33.36	III	*Twenty-Second	2
15.17.19.22	IV	*Contra Oboe	16			Posaune	16
Mixture 19.22.26.29	IV	*Trumpet	8			Cremona	4
Cornet	V						
*Trumpet	8					*Snetzler pipes, all or in part.	

Despite its vicissitudes, this is the least-altered large Snetzler that remains to us. Standing on the west gallery of this Gothick church and contemporary with it, Snetzler's instrument has a

Gothick case which nevertheless retains classical proportions. In 1868 the organ was converted from GG to CC compass and the console refitted. Later rebuilds left the instrument with tubular-pneumatic action and a somewhat mutilated case.

The 1970 restoration by Wells–Kennedy, under the direction of Christopher Gordon-Wells, involved new tracker key-actions, casework restoration and a new tonal design. This made use of the original pipes to create new choruses with pitches spaced according to the *werk* principle from 16ft Pedal to 2ft Choir.

England 1795

The church also possesses a very fine 1795 six stop one-manual chamber organ by G. P. England, formerly in Hillsborough Castle. Two reed-stops, in a primitive 'nags-head' swell-box, were added by Robson in 1856.

COUNTY LONDONDERRY

LONDONDERRY Glendermott Presbyterian Church
Hill Norman & Beard 1973

This 8 stop two-manual is principally remarkable for the three-compartment asymmetric case by Herbert Norman with copper and spotted-metal front pipes.

SELECTED BIBLIOGRAPHY

Andersen, P. G. *Organ Building and Design* (Allen and Unwin, London, 1969). Sets the British organ in its European context.

Audsley, G. A. *The Art of Organ-Building* (2 Volumes) (Dodd, Mead & Co, New York, 1905) (reprinted Dover, Mass., 1978). A comprehensive description of late nineteenth-century organ construction, well illustrated.

Audsley, G. A. *Organ Stops and their Artistic Registration* (Gray, New York, 1921). A glossary of organ stop-names.

Blanton, J. E. *The Organ in Church Design* (Albany, Texas, 1958). An architect's view of the instrument, by a protagonist of Holtkamp's uncased organs.

Clutton, C. and Niland, A. *The British Organ* (Batsford, London, 1963) (Methuen, London, 1982). A historical survey and a comprehensive gazetteer of organ cases.

Downes, R. *Baroque Tricks* (Positif Press, Oxford, 1983). Ralph Downes' own story of his association with organ design and voicing.

Elvin, L. *Organ Blowing, its History and Development* (Elvin, Lincoln, 1971). The history of organ blowing, surprisingly interesting.

Freeman, A. *English Organ Cases* (Musical Opinion, London, 1926) (reprinted Positif Press, Oxford, 1977). Still the standard work.

Hill, A. G. *Organ Cases and Organs of the Middle Ages and Renaissance* (London 1883, 1891: reprinted Knuf, Hilversum, 1966). Prized especially for the line drawings of old cases.

Hopkins, E. F. and Rimbault, E. F. *The Organ, its History and Construction* (Robert Cocks, London, 1855, 1870, 1877). The gazetteer, with over 200 stop-lists, is particularly valuable.

Klais, H. G. *The Organ Stop-list* (Praestant Press, Delaware, Ohio, 1975). The rationale of stop-list design, with examples.

Mahrenholz, C. *The Calculation of Organ Pipe Scales* (Positif Press, Oxford, 1975). The definitive work on this specialist subject.

Norman, H. and Norman, H. J. *The Organ Today* (Barrie & Rockliff, London, 1966) (David & Charles, Newton Abbot, 1981). A handbook of organ construction.

Pacey, R. *The Organs of Oxford* (Positif Press, Oxford, 1981). A complete guide.

Pearce, C. W. *Old London City Churches, their Organs, Organists and Musical Associations* (Vincent, London, c1909). Guide to an area with many historic instruments.

Perrot, J. *The Organ from its Invention in the Hellenistic Period to the end of the Thirteenth Century* (Oxford University Press, London, 1971). An exhaustive account of the organ's beginnings.

Plumley, N. M. *The Organs and Music Masters of Christ's Hospital* (Christ's Hospital, Horsham, 1981). Includes many details of the Hill/Gauntlett revolution.

Robertson, F. E. *A Practical Treatise on Organ-Building* (Sampson Low, Marston,

London, 1897). An engineer's view of the principles of organ construction.

Rowntree, J. P. and Brennan, J. F. *The Classical Organ in Britain* (vol 1 1955–74; vol 2 1975–78; vol 3 1979–83) (Positif Press, Oxford, 1975, 1979, 1984). Stop-lists and illustrations of modern tracker organs.

Sutton, F. H. *Church Organs: their Position and Construction* (London, 1872, 1883: reprinted, Positif Press, Oxford, 1982). Sound sense on the positioning of organs in churches.

Thistlethwaite, N. *The Organs of Cambridge* (Positif Press, Oxford, 1983). A comprehensive and scholarly guide.

Whitworth, R. *The Electric Organ* (London, 1948). Organ-building from a 1930s standpoint.

Williams, P. *A New History of the Organ from the Greeks to the Present Day* (Faber & Faber, London, 1980). Organ history, world-wide, from an author with definite opinions.

Wilson, M. *The English Chamber Organ, History and Development 1650–1850* (Oxford, 1968). The definitive work on old chamber organs, of which there are still a surprising number in existence.

Wyatt, G. *At the Mighty Organ* (Oxford Illustrated Press, Oxford, 1974). An account of theatre organs and their players.

See also the *Journal of the British Institute of Organ Studies* published by Positif Press, Oxford, annually from 1977.

INDEX

INDEX